SOLDIER 'I'

THE STORY OF AN SAS HERO

D0963790

OSPREY
PUBLISHING

During the Second World War, David Stirling, founder of the SAS, had just outlined to Field Marshal Montgomery an audacious plan for one single squadron of SAS to penetrate miles behind heavily fortified enemy lines to attack the Tripoli to Tobruk coastal road along a 400-mile front. Montgomery paused for a moment, then turned to his staff officers and said: 'Gentleman, the boy Stirling is mad. Quite, quite mad. But in war, there is a place for mad people.'

SOLDIER 'I'

THE STORY OF AN SAS HERO

PETE WINNER
MICHAEL KENNEDY

First published in Great Britain in 2010 by Osprey Publishing,
Midland House, West Way, Botley, Oxford, OX2 0PH, UK
44-02 23rd Street, Suite 205A, Long Island City, NY 11101, USA

E-mail: info@ospreypublishing.com

© 2010 Osprey Publishing Ltd.

A CIP catalogue record for this book is available from the British Library

ISBN: 978 1 84603 995 9

Michael Kennedy and Pete Winner have asserted their right under the Copyright,
Designs and Patents Act, 1988, to be identified as the Authors of
this Work.

All photographs not otherwise credited are from Pete Winner's collection.

Every attempt has been made by the Publishers to secure appropriate permissions
for materials reproduced in this book. If there has been any oversight we will be
happy to rectify the situation and a written submission should be made to the
Publishers.

Front cover image courtesy Simon Roberts

Page layout by Myriam Bell Design, France
Typeset in Adobe Garamond
Originated by PPS Grasmere Ltd, Leeds, UK
Printed in China through Worldprint

10 11 12 13 14 15   10 9 8 7 6 5 4 3 2 1

For a catalogue of all books published by Osprey please contact:

NORTH AMERICA
Osprey Direct, c/o Random House Distribution Center
400 Hahn Road, Westminster, MD 21157, USA
E-mail: uscustomerservice@ospreypublishing.com

ALL OTHER REGIONS
Osprey Direct, The Book Service Ltd., Distribution Centre, Colchester Road,
Frating Green, Colchester, Essex, CO7 7DW
E-mail: customerservice@ospreypublishing.com

Osprey Publishing is supporting the Woodland Trust, the UK's leading
woodland conservation charity, by funding the dedication of trees.

www.ospreypublishing.com

Contents

Foreword

I first met Pete (or Snapper as he was called then) in 1984. I had just joined the SAS at the age of 24, and had been sent out to join the rest of B Squadron in the jungles of South East Asia.

I'd only just been introduced to the rest of the troop and was enjoying a quick brew with them under the canopy, when Snapper and four of his mates came crashing through the jungle, looking for the new boy. It didn't take long for Snapper's torchlight to find me, and from the residual glow of the fire we were brewing our tea on, I got a vague glimpse of him: a tall, bearded guy, with a flat face and a nose broken so badly it seemed to be heading east when he was facing north. His accent was dramatic Northern, and he stretched the last word of the sentence he spat out at me, as he and his mates loomed over me in the darkness. 'You a fookin' Masonnnnnn?'

Snapper was obsessed; he was sure that the Freemasons were infiltrating the Regiment. It had become a running joke – the troop had set up a 'lodge' in the jungle, where Snapper and his mates spent their evenings conducting spoof rituals with their trouser legs rolled up. That was my first meeting with the man who'd become Soldier 'I', and fortunately, I was able to reassure him that I hadn't been sent by the Masons on any kind of secret mission. But my first impression of Snapper was that he was as mad as box of frogs, and someone I would do well to keep away from.

The next time I came across Snapper was when our squadron was back in the UK and we were in training to join the counter-terrorist team. I spent quite a lot of time with him during those months as we practised our 'room clearing' skills in the training building in Hereford known within the Regiment as 'The Killing House'. The Killing House was the only place where the Regiment's assault teams were able to fire live ammunition, and it was here where I really began to see Snapper's skills first-hand. Of course, it turned out that there was a whole lot more to Snapper than I had first thought.

Snapper was, and is, a Regimental institution. An outstanding soldier, he was one of the SAS troopers who successfully stormed the Iranian Embassy in 1980. He also played an enormous role in the Falklands War in 1982. If that isn't enough, Snapper was also one of the pioneers of undercover operations in Northern Ireland. He tells it all here in his remarkable book.

But perhaps Snapper's greatest piece of soldiering took place in the battle of Mirbat, which occurred during Operation *Storm* – the secret war fought by the British in Oman in 1972. Over 250 well-armed Communist insurgents attacked the isolated SAS base near the coastal resort of Mirbat, and Snapper (manning the machine gun) together with eight fellow SAS soldiers, chose to fight against overwhelming odds until reinforcements arrived. If the Communists had come to dominate this area, the whole of the Western world would have been held to ransom, since over half of the world's oil passes through the Straits of Hormuze, just off Oman in the Persian Gulf. But the nine men resisted fiercely, and pretty much won the war single-handedly. For this reason, Operation *Storm* remains one of the most famous actions ever carried out by the SAS, and to this day, is one of the Regiment's proudest moments.

But Snapper's skills don't stop there. Many of the undercover techniques that he helped to develop are still used by the Regiment today in their anti-terrorist operations. They certainly helped me tremendously during my two years in Northern Ireland as an undercover operator.

Snapper is a true innovator, and really pushed the boundaries of soldiering within the Regiment. It was always him who would say, 'Let's try it a different way,' or, 'Hang on a minute, what if we do it like this instead?' There's a real creativity to the art of combat, and Snapper has it in spades. Not only during training back in Hereford, but also out in the field where it really counts. Without people like Snapper, the Regiment would not be the same professional fighting force it is today.

If it's Regimental war stories you are after, Snapper's are among the very best. Sure, he might have had the occasional incident of paranoia along the way, but as one of our mates, Nish, always used to say back in the jungle, 'Just because you are paranoid doesn't mean that no-one is out to get you.'

I met up with Snapper again in Kabul, in 2006. It was great to see him, even if he did make me pay for the tea. He was still as mad as a box of frogs, and had enough weapons and radios dangling off him to take on the whole of the Taliban single-handed. Nothing much had changed. But seeing him out in Afghanistan reminded me once more of the debt the British Army owes to guys like Snapper. If you think of the soldiers running around in body armour and helmets in Afghanistan today, spare a thought too for Snapper and his fellow soldiers. Apart from their weapons, the only kit they had back then was a pair of shorts and desert boots. Remarkably, they still managed to win through, and this book shows you how.

This is a book by a true soldier, who really gets what soldiering is all about – the good, the bad, and the ugly.

Andy McNab DCM MM

1

New Territory

'You are a time bomb, trooper, a time bomb just waiting to explode.'

The Colonel's words were still beating in my head as I lay back on the bed. His face, bulging with anger as he roared out his verdict, floated before me. It did not matter whether I opened my eyes or closed them, he was still there, accusing, taunting, assailing my self-respect. 'What happened yesterday was a total disgrace, a total insult to the Regiment. We cannot and will not tolerate this behaviour. You've had your chances but this is the last straw.' A time bomb waiting to explode.

This was it then. The end of the road. On Colonel's orders for the third time. That must be some kind of record. Usually Colonel's orders meant you were finished, RTU'd, out in the cold. I was lucky. I was still serving with the SAS – at least for a little while longer, anyway. It all now hinged on the official medical reports. The Colonel seemed confident that they would provide the ammunition he needed. He had me right in the middle of his sights now. He could pull the trigger at any time.

I looked around me nervously. Ward 11 of the British Army Psychiatric Unit – the thinking man's Belsen. Was this really the end of the line? Everything in the room was white, clinical and empty. Empty walls, empty windowsill, empty tabletops, empty cupboards. My holdall lay slumped on the floor unopened. I reached down into a side-pocket and pulled out a picture of my favourite pin-up, smoothed out the creases and wedged it into a tiny gap at the top of the bedside table. It was a relief to see the splash of colour, the bright, smiling face, the beckoning body.

I glanced out of the single window. Nothing but dreary grey London rooftops. A feeling of isolation swept over me. I turned back to the room and swung wide the cupboard doors, rattled open every drawer, gazing into the emptiness, seeking clues. There wasn't a single trace of the previous detainee – not even a shirt button, a screwed-up ticket or the cellophane wrapper from a cigarette packet. Everything had been swept clinically clean. If only I could have found something, no matter how small, it would have given me some sense of reality, a feeling that others had passed this way before me.

I prowled around the room like a caged animal. This was new, unfamiliar territory. I was jetlagged from the sudden transfer from camp, heady from disorientation. I needed to establish my base, my reference point, my safety zone. At least in the jungle or in the mountains you knew the likely spots where the enemy might be waiting. Training and experience taught you where danger lurked. But here it was different. There was a feeling of threat, but I could not tell where it was coming from or how bad it was going to be. I needed to unscramble my head.

It was like being in an enemy pen, except the guards wore white coats. I'd been told there was even an escape committee – the boys in the pathology lab. They'd test my blood every day and wouldn't let me go under the wire until my LFT count was down to normal.

I came in on a Thursday. The first few days would be observation. I knew what that meant. I knew all the tricks of the interrogation trade. They'd put me under stress by making sure I was completely bored. Completely deprived of all my normal activities and pleasures. Then they'd monitor me to see if I was showing any signs of stress or unusual behaviour: apprehension, restlessness, weird tendencies, withdrawal symptoms. Then, after they'd softened me up, the advanced sentence, the brainwashing would begin.

The door opened and a white-coated nurse came in. He looked at me very closely. Not a flicker of emotion registered on his face. He said nothing. I wondered whether he was one of them, part of the system. I imagined him making mental notes, assessing the situation in detail: where I was in the room, whether I'd arranged my things, my general demeanour and my facial expression. He put a small, brown tray on the bedside table, glanced at the pin-up, then at me. I wondered if this had been my first mistake. There was a plastic beaker of water on the tray and two torpedo-shaped pills, bright green at one end, pink at the other. 'Take both of them,' was all the orderly said as he quickly retreated, locking the door behind him.

I decided to go along with the game at this stage, play it by their rules. They'd know anyway from the urine samples whether I'd taken the pills or not. I picked up one of the torpedoes, held it up to the light and rolled it between my finger and thumb. I wondered why they'd chosen these particular pills, what mind-bending drug was concealed in the thousands of tiny balls cascading around inside the coloured cases. I wondered what ragged phantoms would come springing out to haunt me from deep within my psyche after being locked away for all these years. I wondered who 'they' were, the faceless doctors I'd yet to meet. Would they be distant and calculating like the orderly, or would they be friendly and sympathetic, creep up on me and catch me with my guard down, trick me into trusting them? Was that the deadly ambush that awaited me? Sod it! Who dares wins! Here's to Queen and country... I grabbed both the pills and gulped them down. A faint smile of steely defiance curled on my lips.

Outside, the wind grew stronger and the dark clouds jostled and thickened. Scuds of rain crackled against the window with increasing frequency. Suddenly, the pregnant clouds burst their waters and spawned tiny, watery serpents which slithered down the glass panes, frantically seeking the sanctuary of some unseen pool below.

I sank onto the bed and closed my eyes. 'You're a time bomb, trooper, a time bomb just waiting to explode.' I tried to shake the Colonel out of my head. Then, from nowhere, a confusion of pictures burst into my mind. A kaleidoscope of scenes from fourteen years of remote battles and secret operations spun in front of me. It was just like the high-speed slide show of farms, villages, towns and cities that had flashed before my eyes as I'd gazed blankly out of the car window driving down the M4 from Hereford to London. Back through time my mind slid on a crazy helter-skelter ride: the Falklands War, the Embassy siege, Hong Kong, Northern Ireland, the battle of Mirbat, Operation *Jaguar*.

Before I knew it, the sharp odour of cordite was stinging my nostrils again. The hair on the back of my neck prickled as I heard again the distinctive thwack of a bullet hitting bone and flesh. I shuddered at the banshee-screams of the wounded, grown men reduced to grovelling, frightened children calling unashamedly for their mothers, amid the roar of battle – shrieks of terror whose echoes would resound forever.

Round and round I tumbled, freefalling through the whirling pictures. Then, suddenly, I was sucked through the black hole at the centre of the spinning kaleidoscope.

2

Initiation

'Good morning, gentlemen, welcome to Bradbury Lines.'

It was spring 1970. A dozen rows of hopeful recruits sat facing the Colonel, 135 of us in all. The Colonel smiled a cold half-smile. At his station in life, he had left far behind the feelings of trepidation that we were now all experiencing at the start of this new venture. He stood in front of us on the stage of the training-wing theatre, a slightly weatherbeaten figure dressed in an old camouflage windproof and a pair of faded OG trousers. Even the famous beret looked a little discoloured. He was leaning on the lecturing stand, smoking an old roll-up and flicking the ash into an empty pyrotechnic container. He had the appearance of a man who was used to roughing it, but the unruly look went only as far as his dress. His hard, chiselled features and steady unflinching gaze told a different story, the story of a man who knew his mind with clinical precision.

'You have a difficult task ahead of you. First, three weeks of rigorous selection, during which time we subject you to what we colloquially and, I might add, very appropriately refer to as Sickener 1 and Sickener 2. Then, fourteen weeks of continuation training, a parachute course, and finally combat survival training. Nearly twenty-six weeks of exhaustive scrutiny. Half a year of uncertainty. You could get your marching orders at any point along the way – usually when you least expect it. We've even been known to fail someone on their very last day!'

A ripple of unease and a hardening of resolve flickered through the assembled rows.

'The SAS is only as effective as the people in it. Think about that. It's a crucial point. A field commander might devise a perfect plan for winning a battle, but without strong, co-ordinated support from the men on the ground, all would be lost.'

The Colonel's eyes penetratingly scanned the intent faces of his audience.

'It was said of Lord Nelson that his whole fleet acted as if they were one great marine body directed by a single intelligence. What we are looking for over the next few weeks are men to join our regimental body, to become one with us. But not just any men. They've got to be the right men, special men. Men with initiative, stamina, intelligence, patience and not least a sense of humour. In Korea, the British Army had thousands fighting thousands. With the SAS it's different. We are a specialist group within the British Army. We are special because we operate in small groups and we move alone. We are not looking for team players. What we want is the individualist, the man who can survive on his own but who has the self-discipline to work as part of a team.'

I gazed abstractedly at the Colonel, taking in the details of his clothing. I noticed the winged-dagger badge sewn onto his beret. I fixed my eyes with envy and determination on that badge, and for a moment I was mesmerized as his head moved in rhythm with his speech.

The Colonel flicked the ash off his roll-up and his eyes took on a hardened look. 'There's always been war and there always will be war. Look at any decade, it's always the same: 1961 Kuwait, 1962 Brunei, '63 Borneo, '64 East Africa, '67 Aden, '68 Belfast. It's an endless litany. When the social workers run out, someone's got to wave the big stick. When society's body is ill, someone's got to take care of it. Whether it's the ice-laden mountains or the scorching deserts, the steaming jungles or the stinking souks, the windswept moorlands or the sinister streets, we'll be there. Terrorists, guerrillas, insurgents, freedom fighters, call them what you will, we'll be there.

'There will be plenty of excitement and adventure, but you won't be paraded as heroes for all to see. America suffered from fighting the Vietnam War in the full glare of the media. Public opinion handcuffed the generals to the rulebook. Here in the SAS we learn from other people's mistakes. No publicity, no media. We move in silently, do our job, and melt away into the background. You won't achieve fame and fortune with us. But what you will achieve is self-respect, deep self-respect, and a unique identity as part of a group who have found that same self-respect. The few of you who succeed will not just be joining a regiment, you'll be joining a family, a very exclusive family. If you have got the stamina, the willpower and the guts, we'll welcome you with open arms and make you one of us. And if you haven't, then it's been very nice knowing you.' The Colonel looked up and down the rows again with searching eyes, then swiftly walked off the stage.

A voice from the rear shouted, 'Be at the Quartermaster's stores in fifteen minutes!'

Outside, the sun was just clearing the top of the wooden plinth on which the four-sided clock was set. Around its base, gleaming in the sunshine, were three large bronze panels inscribed with the names of the soldiers who had died – the ones who, in Regimental parlance, had not beaten the clock. A smaller panel with a quotation worked on it was fixed to the front. I could just make out the words 'barr'd with snow' and 'that glimmering sea' on the plaque. As I looked up, a ragged crow flapped lazily along behind the clock and over the perimeter fence towards the neat rows of houses that formed the Redhill suburbs of Hereford. I thought of the people there who were going about their ordinary day-to-day routines, and then I thought of the drama in which 135 nervous recruits were about to play a leading role.

When I reached the stores, I was astonished at the sight that greeted me. It was like a Saturday-afternoon jumble sale at a church bazaar. I was amazed at the apparent disorder and lack of discipline. But the conversation was subdued. No one wanted to get earmarked as a possible troublemaker. I edged forward and found myself at the front of the queue. The corporal behind the counter glanced at me and then disappeared between long rows of large wooden pigeonholes. He reappeared with a bergen rucksack filled with all I would need for the selection phase. I took one look at the bergen and realized immediately that in bad weather the untreated canvas would just soak up rain like a sponge and get heavier and heavier. The metal fittings cracked on the counter-top as the corporal threw the bergen unceremoniously down. I checked the contents: sleeping bag, 57-pattern webbing belt, poncho for wet-weather protection, two 1½-pint water bottles with carriers, standard Army prismatic compass, heavy and cumbersome, Ordnance Survey maps of the Brecon Beacons and Elan Valley, brew kit and three twenty-four-hour ration-packs for the first major hurdle looming up: the three-day trial at the weekend, otherwise known as Sickener 1.

Then it was on to the armoury round the corner from the QM's department. There we were given the old-fashioned Lee Enfield .303 rifles. The issuing officer explained that the modern weapons were kept strictly for operational duties, and added ominously, 'They'll be in real shit order, the Lee Enfields, with what they'll have to go through in the next three weeks, no matter how much you strip and clean them.'

I made tracks from the armoury out into the sunshine again and, with a grumbling stomach, headed for the cookhouse. As I pushed through the grey swinging doors I was hit by a barrage of noise: crashing plates, hissing steam, clinking mugs, metal chair-legs rattling as they were scraped across the dull-red tiled floor, the steady roar of over 200 voices in animated conversation. The L-shaped room was filled with the warm, appetizing aroma of freshly cooked food. Through another door, in the far corner, a group of men I had not seen before were making an entrance, joking and laughing loudly. To judge from their air of confidence and deliberate step they were obviously Sabre Squadron. Two shining aluminium-and-glass serveries ran the length of each leg of the room. Behind them, men decked out in regulation kitchen whites were gliding swiftly backwards and forwards among the steaming vats and clanking ovens, going about their business in apparent chaos but no doubt following some well-rehearsed routine.

I got to the head of the queue and started to move along by the hotplate. I was in for a surprise. It looked like a tribal feast day in the jungle. There was food, mountains of food. I had never seen the likes of it in all my years of service in the Army. I picked up a tray with anticipation and pushed it along the front of the hotplate. Next to a tureen of steaming hot soup, a large wicker basket overflowed with chunks of bread. A mound of rich yellow butter, which looked as if it had been tipped straight out of the farmyard urn, had several knives carelessly protruding from it. In the middle section there was a choice: a help-yourself tray full of lamb chops, swimming in savoury juices, and a mammoth joint of beef impaled on a spiked turntable. A large cook was poised over the beef with a gleaming carving knife and a long, two-pronged fork. He looked as if he would be equally at ease wielding a machete in the jungle. I motioned towards the joint.

'How many slices?' the cook asked.

I couldn't believe my ears. I'd been so used to the routine of the regular Army cookhouse. There, some jumped-up pimply-faced cook, with a deathly pallor from never seeing daylight, feeling cocky knowing he was out of reach behind the counter, would hit you with a ladle and squeak, 'One egg, laddie,' if you so much as looked at a second. 'Two please, mate,' I ventured, still not sure quite what was happening.

The cook stabbed the fork into the joint and deftly swung it round on the turntable to get the right angle for carving. The meat compressed as the gleaming knife bit into it, and rich juices oozed from the pink centre. 'Crackling?'

'Too true!' And a huge chunk of ribbed crackling was deposited over the two thick slices of meat. I rearranged the dishes on my tray and just about found space for the sponge pudding with custard that rounded off the meal.

I looked up and spotted the other three members of the patrol I'd been assigned to, hunched over the end of a table. I crossed the room and sat down with them.

'Jesus Christ, somebody pinch me, I must be dreaming.'

'I'd heard a rumour that airborne forces get double meat rations, but this is ridiculous.'

'There's got to be a catch. It'll be tea and wads the rest of the week.'

'No, there's no catch. Don't get paranoid already. An old mate of mine gave me the whisper. It's like this every day, plenty of protein to build up the stamina. You need it here.'

'I hope you're right. I've got to have my four square meals a day. I get dizzy if I miss breakfast. I don't go for this mean and hungry look. I reckon you've got to have plenty of meat on you to stay healthy.'

There was a lull in the conversation as our attention was focused on the more serious business of eating. I looked around the other three members of my patrol. Jim, from the Black Watch, Royal Highland Regiment, and proud of it. Small, stocky with shining eyes set in a round, friendly face. Neatly parted short brown hair. A barrel-shaped body, obviously tough. Then Andy, the company joker, known to all as Geordie. He was in the Light Infantry, but whenever asked, would reply with a stiff salute, 'Sixth Queen Elizabeth's Own Gurkha Rifles!' He had a tough bony head topped by already-thinning black hair. What he lacked in the way of hair on his scalp, however, he more than made up for with a hirsute growth on his thick dangling arms and prominent chest. His most noticeable feature was an over-large mouth. It was as big as the North-West Passage, and gaped obscenely whenever he spoke, revealing his teeth and gums so that he looked like an ape challenging an intruder.

And finally, Tommo the Scouse, Royal Fusiliers. Tall, muscular in a compact sort of way, with tufts of blond hair as stiff as a yard-brush sticking straight up. Snub nose, and ears bent over slightly at the top. He looked like an overgrown leprechaun – and a malevolent one at that. The nearest he ever came to a smile was a cross between a leer and a snarl, which would slowly appear as attempts to engage him in conversation were met with a sullen 'yeah,' 'that's right,' 'dunno.' I never could guess what was going on in his mind, and for that reason never felt comfortable when he was around. In fact, I didn't trust him as far as I could throw a fully laden bergen.

After the first rush of food had hit our stomachs, I said to Jim, 'There's a lot of you lads down here. Talk of the Charge of the Jock Brigade!'

'Yeah, it is a bit like that. But when it really hits you what it's like up there – the perpetual rain, the decrepit tenement blocks stinking of urine, the empty rusting yards of Clydeside, the brawls on Buchanan Street on a Saturday night – you know you either take to the bottle or you take to the road. Me, I was down the mines for six years before I joined the Army. I looked around me one day and couldn't see a future. So I said to myself, "Jimmy, if you join the Army what would you be leaving behind?" And you know the answer that came? A living hell, a long, slow, coal-dust-coughing hell. I decided to take me chances in the Army, I knew it couldn't be any worse. If I could survive six years down the pits, I figured I could survive anything.'

'Even the SAS selection course?'

'Believe me, pal, it'll be a piece of piss in comparison. Have you ever been down a pit?'

'No.'

'I thought not.'

'But why the SAS?'

'Oh you know, the adventure, the excitement, a chance to be more involved. A chance to do the special jobs.'

'What about you, Geordie?'

'This is why I applied, the food.'

We all looked at him, slightly puzzled.

He went on, 'I wouldn't say we're poor back home, but when it comes to tea-time, the wife nails a kipper to the back of the kitchen door, and me and the kids, we all line up with a slice of bread in our hand and wipe it on the kipper as we file past.'

The eternal joker. It was a tendency no doubt triggered by the nerves of the moment. Geordie used his humour like a shield, to ward off people or situations he felt uncomfortable with. In spite of this, I was rather warming to him; I felt I could detect a real thinker beneath the surface.

We looked at Tommo, waiting for his story. He pushed his chair back suddenly and stood up. 'Anyone for a brew?' he asked in an agitated voice. He slouched across the room to two large aluminium tea-urns next to the hotplates. One of the urns was dripping tea onto the floor from the black plastic tap. No one seemed to bother. Tommo returned with three huge mugs of tea in one hand and one in the other. He was totally unconcerned that two of the three mugs were tilting and splashing scalding tea over his hand.

'Tommo, what's your story? Why did you volunteer?' I asked as he put the mugs on the table and sat down again.

'Dunno. A change of scene I suppose.'

We waited patiently for a few moments but nothing more came.

'It was the boredom of garrison duties that got to me. Standing on guard in some obscure camp in the middle of nowhere in Germany, where you knew there was no threat. I ask you, were the Russians going to march hundreds of miles through hostile territory just to take out our insignificant little camp? Two hours on, four hours off, two hours on, four hours off. So it went on and on and on. Tedious in the extreme. I'll tell you something. Did you see the grass inside the camp gates when you arrived here? A foot high if it was an inch! Hell, I thought, I've got the wrong place here! Can you believe it – an Army camp with grass a foot high! That's why I joined, to escape the bullshit. They've obviously got a sense of priorities here. They don't do things for the sake of it, I like that. Beat the boredom, beat the bullshit, beat the clock, that'll do me.'

Even as I spoke, I felt slightly uncomfortable with what I'd said. It was true as far as it went, but somehow I felt it didn't go far enough. I sensed that something deeper was driving me, something that as yet still eluded me. I decided there were too many new things happening right now; my brain was having the luxury of sorting through the debris of the old.

'I reckon selection's a real cartilage-cracker,' pronounced Geordie with the hint of a frown.

Tommo looked at him but said nothing.

'Piece of piss,' reiterated Jim, confidently waving a teaspoon in the air to emphasize his lack of concern.

'Well, I for one will be glad when it's all over and we can get stuck into the real business we're supposed to be here for,' I said firmly.

'Whatever that might be,' added Tommo out of the blue. The three of us looked at him quizzically as we drained the last of the tea from our mugs.

That afternoon was spent doing preliminary weapons training and then a four-mile run. We had a training run every day around the leafy lanes of the Herefordshire countryside bordering the camp on the opposite side to the town. The gently rolling hills in the immediate vicinity were deceptive. They often concealed small but steep-sided valleys. There also seemed to be at least two of these valleys near the end of the run, where the incline would tear viciously at already tired leg muscles. If anyone was going to fail at the weekend, it wouldn't be through lack of basic fitness.

The rest of the first week passed swiftly, each day following a similar rhythm and merging into the next. I got to know my patrol better as the week wore on, but we didn't bond together as mates. We were all still wrapped up in our own personal battles to prove ourselves. And anyway, I thought most of these men will fail the course and you don't want to get friendly with failures. As the weekend loomed ahead, I could sense all around that the nervous bravado of the first day was gradually giving way to deepening apprehension. Indeed, as more detailed rumours began to circulate about Sickener 1, the very thought of it was enough to break some men. 'Crap-hats,' we called them. They'd collected their rail warrants and were on Hereford station, Platform 4 homeward bound, before selection had even begun in earnest.

We were given the Friday evening off and advised to get an early night. The afternoon's training run had finished around five o'clock. I had just enough time to shower, change and head into town before the shops closed. If I failed selection it couldn't be through lack of preparation. From the previous candidates who'd failed the course and from the information I'd gleaned during the week, I'd worked out what I would need: two dozen Mars bars, a bottle of olive oil, a Silvas compass, squares of foam padding, two sheets of clear Fablon, curry powder, Tabasco sauce, powdered milk and waterproof walking gear.

I stepped onto the bridge crossing the River Wye and leaned over the parapet. 'Welcome to Hereford, Historic Capital of the Wye Valley,' the sign on the bridge said. The water flowed lazily by beneath me. I gazed at a much older and smaller stone bridge, which crossed the river about a hundred yards downstream from the modern road bridge where I stood. A neatly manicured lawn behind a church manse fell steeply down to the water's edge just beyond the stone bridge. Newly leafing trees clung precariously to the riverbanks and dangled long thin branches into the water. A young couple were locked in an embrace under the trees by the putting green, luxuriating in the warm evening sunshine. Very nice too, I thought, feeling slightly envious.

I quickly located the shops and bought the necessary items, loaded up and headed back for camp.

Later that evening, the atmosphere in the spider was exceptionally subdued – and sober. The thought of what was to come the following morning was enough to convert even the hardest drinkers to temporary abstinence. By 9.30pm a good number of the beds were already resonating with snoring heads. I decided it was time to join them. I threw off my shirt and slacks and hit the pillow.

It seemed as if I'd only just begun to drift down into a deep, welcome sleep when something suddenly reversed the direction of my consciousness. In a flash, I was brutally awake and confused. I strained to make sense of what was happening. Some time must have passed since I'd gone to bed. It was dark and very quiet. I lay on my back, completely motionless, my eyes wide up, staring up towards the ceiling. A moment later I heard a groan, followed by the rustle of sheets and a stifled sigh. What the hell's going on, I thought. As the vague realization began to dawn, I wondered if I was having some weird, tension-induced dream. More sounds, coarse, high-pitched nasal sounds. Then a grunt, an mistakably female grunt; panting, pained almost, gradually rising in pitch, volume and frequency until it peaked in a sharp, drawn-out squeal followed by a sigh of relief.

A wave of sexual excitement rippled up and down my spine. I tilted my head in the direction of the sounds and caught a whiff of cheap perfume. The sweet smell was unmistakable in the heavy male air of the spider. A permed blonde head and glinting earring emerged momentarily from among the tumbling sheets of the next bed. This can't be happening, I thought, Geordie in bed with a woman. I felt almost dizzy, as if I'd got up too quickly from a prone position. I turned away and onto my back again and spent a few moments deliberately composing myself, reminding myself where I was and what I was doing there.

The groans and sighs began again, more frantic and physical than before. Geordie was like a stag in a rut. I glanced at my watch. It was one o'clock in the morning, my sleep had been broken and in a few hours I had to face Sickener 1, a severe test of physical endurance lasting three days for which I would need every ounce of energy I possessed. Another groan. I turned towards Geordie, anger welling up inside me, and opened my mouth to speak. Nothing. Not a word came out. A feeling of admiration at his sheer nerve combined with a vague acknowledgement that it wasn't right to interrupt a man's sexual performance somehow dammed up the wave of anger. The torrents of abuse simply swirled and foamed around inside me.

I put my head beneath the sheets to try to shut out the disturbance, but I knew it was no good. The more I chased sleep, the more it eluded me. I kept telling myself I would drift off at any moment. I began to perspire with the frustration of not being able to sleep. I twisted my body into every position imaginable, trying to relax. I explored every corner of the bed seeking a cool patch in the sheets. Who dares wins, I thought, as Geordie finally fire-crackered into an Olympian climax.

3

Sickener 1

I heard another noise. Oh Christ, I thought, don't tell me Geordie's going for another shot. I turned over and half-opened one eye. In the first glimmer of dawn I saw that most of the men in the spider were already awake, either standing up and pulling on their OGs or sitting on their beds lacing up their boots. I sat up instantly. My heart pounded for a few seconds, priming my body to the same level of alertness as my mind. Years of training and discipline came to my rescue. I sprang out of bed, switched my mind on and put my body into automatic pilot. I glanced at my watch: 4.30am. I didn't even dare contemplate how much sleep I'd finally managed to get, or whether it would be enough to see me through the day.

Within minutes everyone was outside, piling into the six Bedford four-tonners lined up ready to take us to our torture. We set off westwards, then turned north up the A470, following the River Wye towards the Elan Valley, deep in the Cambrian Mountains of mid-Wales. The Elan Valley – that was the first con. It sounded like some mythical green and pleasant land. Well, it might have been green but it certainly wasn't pleasant, as we were very quickly to discover.

I looked around the twenty bodies being shaken about in the Bedford. There in the corner, hunched over a cigarette, was Geordie. I motioned to the man next to him to change places with me and, with one hand on the side of the swaying truck to keep my balance, made my way up to the front to sit next to him. One or two of the men looked up at me, vaguely puzzled by what was happening, then dropped back down to stare at their boots, mentally steeling themselves for the ordeal ahead.

'What the hell were you up to last night?' I asked Geordie, hardly concealing my astonishment.

'Having a good fuck,' Geordie replied bluntly.

'Any chance of having twos-up when we get back?' enquired Jim, appealing to Geordie's generosity.

'You can piss off, she's mine!' replied Geordie, in a distinctly ungenerous fashion.

'Did it ever cross your mind like it did the rest of us that an early night might be useful?' I continued.

'Early night! That's about as exciting as having your sinuses syringed.'

'How did you manage it, anyway?'

'I stayed in town last night and went on the piss. It was dead easy. Women – the hero's perk! They were all swooning around me. They saw my suntan and thought I was already in the SAS. I didn't tell them that I'd just come back from exercise abroad with the LI.'

'I don't know about hero's perk, but she certainly perked you up, Geordie, more than once from the sound of it,' muttered Jim.

'No, I meant how did you manage to get her through the gates?' I went on.

'I didn't. We went in the back way, down Web Tree Avenue, across the empty plot of land and under the fence behind B Squadron basha.'

'But aren't you knackered? I reckon you must have screwed your way through the equivalent of a half-marathon last night. You know what they say about sportsmen having a leg over the night before a big match.'

'Knackered, no. It relaxes me. Best remedy for tension I've ever found.'

'It might have relaxed you, but it kept half the bloody spider awake,' mumbled Jim in a disgruntled voice.

'What's up lads, can't you get your end away? I tell you what: you can all take turns with her when I go abroad, and don't worry about contraception – she told me her old man's had a vasectomy!'

The conversation subsided and was replaced by the rattle of the Bedford as it headed north. The drone of the engine had a hypnotic effect, and I found my mind drifting back to the Blue Room in Bradbury Lines and to the pre-exercise briefing that our instructor Tim had given us. This had been my first sight of the man I would grow to respect enormously as the years went by.

Tim was a tough, craggy Northerner who hailed from Manchester. He had a six-foot frame, muscular from years of thrashing through the Malayan jungle, a ramrod-straight back and a broad chest. His sandy-coloured hair was tousled and he had bushy eyebrows. Although he was quick to show his dissatisfaction at the first sign of incompetence, he was generally very quietly spoken. His tough exterior hid a generous soul. Over the next few days he would help me on several occasions with patient extra tuition in map-reading. At first I never quite knew how to take him. He could appear to be full of encouragement one moment and cut you to shreds the next. He had at one and the same time the benign look of a kindly uncle and yet a cool remoteness in his eyes. Above all, he was sure of himself. A veteran of many campaigns, he had the Military Medal to his credit.

His words came drifting back and I stared out of the back of the Bedford. 'As you know, lads, the first three weeks are called Initial Selection. But really, "selection" is the wrong word: it should be "rejection". No matter what the pressures are to keep the numbers up, we aim to reject not select. Let me warn you right now: no one gets in the back door. If you don't match up to the standards, you're out. Believe it or not I would like you all to pass. You won't, of course. In fact very few of you will. It wasn't all that long ago that on one selection course we failed every single trainee.'

If anyone had managed to build up any confidence, by now it was rapidly draining away.

'Don't think we are putting you through these agonies for the fun of it,' Tim continued. 'SAS doesn't stand for Savage and Sadistic. No, you see, an inferior soldier means a weak link. You might get away with that in the regular Army where you can hide among the crowd. But a weak link in a four-man patrol means a weak patrol, a dangerous liability. So if you fail on a single point, it's RTU, and down to Platform 4.'

Tim glanced around the assembled trainees. 'One more thing,' he said. 'Don't even think of cheating, and I'll tell you why. In the SAS we have a very special kind of cosmetic surgery. You've heard of the nose job. Well here we've got the red-line job.' He reached into the breast pocket of his windproof and pulled out a thick felt-tipped pen. 'If you haven't got what it takes, it'll be a red line through your face on the photograph in training wing, and that's you finished.'

My thoughts of Tim's first briefing were interrupted as the wagons turned off the main road at Rhayader and headed down the B4518 towards Caban Coch Reservoir. Halfway along the reservoir, the road, now no more than a single track with passing places, took a sharp right. Shortly afterwards the Bedford jolted to a halt, giving a rude awakening to those who had temporarily escaped back into slumber. All we could see out of the back of the wagon was a vast expanse of desolate hills rolling into one another, the ridges along the tops looking like the scarred backs of a school of stranded whales.

Tim walked briskly across and pulled down the tailgate of the Bedford. He then addressed his two patrols. 'Welcome to Sickener 1. This is what we call sorting the wheat from the chaff. This is where we nail the weekend adventurers, the day releases from Broadmoor and the eternal swanners.' He glanced over his shoulder and pointed to a hill that loomed up into the mist. The slope was so severe it looked like the side of a building. Tim said simply, 'There's only one way from here lads, and that's straight up.'

I checked my kit, checked my compass and started to sweat.

The next three days were spent in a nightmare world of physical pain and mental torture, being beasted across the hills by Tim, not just getting from point to point but, as Tim explained with relish, cross-graining the bukits. This meant going straight from trig point to trig point instead of contouring around the obstacles on some of the gentler slopes. It was demoralizing going down the other side of a hard-won piece of high ground knowing that you then had to climb back up again to the trig point, when all the time you could see a straight ridge linking the two points as inviting as Blackpool Promenade. And meanwhile the menacing figure of Tim always seemed to be hovering, staring and making mental notes. Just when you least expected it he would materialize as if from nowhere, suggesting that this was perhaps too much for you and wouldn't you really be better off calling it a day and returning quietly to your own regiment. All such exhortations had to be strenuously rejected. Even the slightest sign of hesitation could mean a red-line job.

A primal sense of self-preservation and survival of the fittest quickly began to surface in me. Seeing the misfortunes of others – seeing someone really struggling, cursing through clenched jaws, 'Shit, I feel like I've been kneecapped' – was enough in an odd sort of way to spur me on, thinking, well I may be knackered, but I'm not as done in as he is. And all the time, in rhythm with the blood pounding through my ears, the same questions beat through my brain, 'What am I doing here? Will I make it?' – and each time I got the same answer, 'I've got to. I must carry on.' It was as if my thinking process had closed down. Swept along at an ever-increasing pace by this powerful experience, my mind became clouded by the strain of constant alertness, my vision channelled to a single point. And that point was only ever the present moment. There was no spare capacity of mental energy, no space to think either side of that single point, or either forwards or back in time. Total concentration had to be in the present. Failure lurked at every second. It was as if I was wading across a fast-flowing river, seeking with each step a firm rock base to put my weight on, fearing at every moment that my foot might slip and I would be swept away by the torrent.

Towards the end of the first afternoon, a heavy squall hit us. It was vicious in its suddenness and its intensity. We were caught without our windproofs, our shirts unbuttoned to the waist. Within seconds my hair was matted against my forehead and rivulets of water ran down my neck and over my chest. I was quickly soaked through, my OGs clinging clammily to my skin. All I could do was to put my head down and keep on going up to the top of the hill. To my horror, as I stumbled wearily over the last rise I saw that the ground fell away again to be met by a near-vertical rock-strewn slope leading up to the real summit, which was already swathed in racing storm-clouds. Conditions were deteriorating. 'What do I do now?' I thought. As I hesitated, turning my back to the wind and catching my breath, two other volunteers came alongside. Their shoulders sagged visibly when they saw the size of the task ahead of them. They looked at each other and both recognized the same thought in the other.

'Sod this for a game of soldiers,' one of them muttered.

They hadn't seen Tim coming up behind them. Tim said in his gruff northern accent, 'Right, you lads, get back down to that road and wait for the transport.'

As I watched them dejectedly trudge away, I said to myself, 'I'm fucked if I'm going to jack now!' I readjusted my bergen which was getting heavier by the minute as it soaked in the rain, took a firmer grip on my .303 and headed off into the gloom, with Tim hovering menacingly in the background waiting for the slightest hint of weakness to pounce again.

The route up to the top of the hill narrowed into a ridge which became more and more exposed to the driving storm the higher I got. The rain was hitting me horizontally, stinging my face until my cheekbones went numb. The wind howled into my ears until they ached. Quite suddenly, halfway up, I became aware that far from feeling even worse I somehow felt lighter. There was a new spring in my step. My breathing was deep and rhythmical. It was as if my breath was energizing and waking up my whole body. My senses now became more acute. I relished the velvet tingle of the rain as it fell down my face. The sweet saltiness of sweat prickled the corners of my mouth, the ground smelled warm, earthy and close.

Near the summit, I covered the last few yards on all fours; the wind's ferocity had increased tenfold; and it was completely impossible to stand upright. I had never before experienced anything so powerful. I could not believe that moving air could make you feel as if you were being hit by waves of water. When the others reached the top we huddled together, shouting to make ourselves heard above the roar of the wind. One trainee, moving into the middle of the group to get some shelter, tried to steady his compass on the wildly flapping map to get a bearing for the final RV of the day. Tim loomed up, his face a mask of grim determination. 'Come on lads, on your feet and over the top before you all die of exposure.' Trying not to show our reluctance, we set off down again.

Base camp that night was set up in the lee of some woods. The storm had died away almost as quickly as it started. Already, what was left of the wind had dried most of the heavy rain from the ground. As we unsaddled our bergens, Tim greeted us with 'Well done lads, that's the easy bit over with. You can get some hot food inside of you now. You're probably ready for it. I'm sure you've been looking forward all day to tonight's feast.' Tim had every right to joke about it. It would certainly be hot – our hexamine stoves would see to that – but whether the twenty-four-hour rations would qualify as a feast was doubtful. The food was in stark contrast to what we had been used to back at the cookhouse, but still I scarcely felt it was a hardship. In my mind, I'd already written off the whole three days as a 'head down, arse up and keep going till you're told to stop' exercise.

I had some difficulty getting my boots off. The rain had swollen the para-cord and tightened the knots. After picking away at them, and breaking a fingernail in the process, I finally managed to ease off the sodden leather. My feet seemed to sigh with relief as the boots came off and I immediately felt a different person. I tugged off my wet gear and slipped into the dry kit I'd kept in a plastic bag in my bergen. I filled my one-pint mess tin with water and put it to boil on the stove, then found a packet of beef stew from my ration-pack, ripped it open and sprinkled the unappetizing contents into the simmering water. I crumbled some tack biscuits and threw them into the stew to thicken it up a bit. Then the masterstroke: in with the garlic and chilli sauce I had bought in town. A fearsome relish, my all-time favourite! It would knock a crap-hat down at fifty paces. The racing spoon moved at double-quick pace between mess tin and mouth.

After making a mug of tea from my brew kit – with the help of the real powdered milk I'd brought along instead of the poor-quality Army-issue powder which always floated to the top and looked like dandruff on the surface – I cupped my hands around my mug for warmth and glanced at the other lads. I was unsure whether or not to strike up a conversation in case it was an RTU offence. The problem was that nobody told you the rules. It was a form of psychological warfare. So I took the safest way out, stared into my tea and kept my mouth shut.

It suddenly grew darker as a large black cloud glided in from the right and obscured the setting sun, splitting its watery evening light into broad beams that fanned out over the hills in a breathtaking display.

I got up and walked away from the rest of the lads, looking for a level piece of ground to sleep on. In view of my tiredness and the failing light it was rather a quick scan of the terrain but I managed to find a reasonable spot. I brushed away the broken branches, pulled out any stones that protruded from the earth so that they wouldn't dig into my back, and laid out my sleeping bag. I then rigged up my waterproof poncho to cover my sleeping area. The secret was to keep it as tight as possible so the rain would run off. I checked the OG para-cord at each corner, ensuring that it was as taut as I could make it without tearing the material. I crawled into my sleeping bag and, utterly exhausted, stretched out my aching body. A shower of rain crackled on the canvas as the large cloud I'd seen passed directly overhead. The sound of the steady rain was strangely peaceful and soothing. I curled up, luxuriating in the soft dry touch of the Royal Engineers boiler suit I'd changed into. It had been washed a thousand times and felt like silk against my skin. As I drifted off to sleep I decided I was going to wear it for the rest of selection. Its softness would be a good defence against bergen blister.

We spent most of the second day wearily cross-graining bukits again. But worse was to come. Tim had saved up the most challenging ordeal for the end. He lined us up and introduced us to the horrors of the entrail trench: a ditch beside a hawthorn hedge, two feet deep, four feet across, filled with stagnant water and rotting sheep's innards. A real cesspit! 'It's time to go back to Mother's womb, lads, afterbirth and all!' began Tim. 'Now let us imagine we're dug into a trench in Korea under heavy fire. Up front we've got no man's land littered with blown-up bodies. It's dusk and you have to do a night patrol to gather intelligence on the enemy's position. The only way to do it is over the top with the leopard crawl, right through the bodies, the bits of brain splattered on the rocks, the guts and gore strewn over the ground. Right, who's first?'

Geordie visibly blanched. Jim swallowed hard. Tommo's sneer became even more pronounced.

'Oh, I see. Perhaps it's because you don't know what the leopard crawl is that no one's moving,' said Tim. 'You don't want to be embarrassed by your ignorance. I can't see any other reason for your reluctance. Right, who knows how to do the leopard crawl?'

A few blank faces stared back at Tim. I took the bull by the horns. 'I do.'

'Good. Then perhaps you would be so kind as to demonstrate it for the benefit of your mates here along this stretch of ground in front of us all.'

'Right, Tim.' I got down flat on my stomach and, using only knees and elbows, proceeded to crawl along while holding my rifle horizontal to the ground, pressed against my forehead. The idea was to keep the lowest possible profile to avoid being seen by the enemy.

'Very good, just like an officer on the job,' observed Tim wryly after I had struggled along for a few moments. 'Right, as you're obviously an expert you might as well continue across the trench while you're down there!'

I took a deep breath and plunged into the foul mess. It was an ugly experience. Two feet doesn't sound very deep, but when you are crawling on all fours so close to the ground it is very deep. As I felt the loathsome liquid begin to crawl through the gaps in my clothing, I really understood for the first time why they called this part of selection Sickener 1. Halfway across, weighed down by my bergen, I felt my belt snag on a rock. I couldn't use my hands to free myself as they were holding my rifle clear of the surface. I had to resort to wriggling free by shaking my hips – and as I did so I set up a turbulence in the water, and the filthy stinking sheep-gut-filled liquid splashed up around my lips. I coughed and spat out in disgust.

As each trainee made it through the ordeal we assembled on the other side of the ditch, with the noisome liquid dripping from our clothes, until we stood watching the last man struggle across. The only consolation was that this was the last exercise of the day. Smelling like old decrepit tramps in a doss house, we settled down for the night.

At first light on the final day, as I rubbed my numbed limbs back into life, Tim gave his instructions: we were to set off straight across the river in front of us. As we waded across, our rifles above our heads, up to our chests in fast-flowing water, Tim watched us comfortably from a nearby bridge. Although dripping wet, at least when we emerged on the far bank we were fresher and cleaner than we had been after the previous day's ordeal. I thought to myself, I've survived two days and nights. Only one more day to go and it's back to basha, a decent meal and a soft bed. I focused my mind on this comforting picture all that day as we sweated again over endless bukits. I locked out every urgent protest from my body, which had never been pushed to such physical extremes; and I ignored every scream from every tortured muscle.

As the afternoon of the following day drew to a painful close, we were briefed on the final exercise of the day: the stretcher race. We had to cover the last mile carrying a stretcher, upon which Tim perched – complete with loaded bergen, heavy rifle and satisfied smile. Labouring towards the final RV, just when I thought I couldn't force another step out of my weary body, I caught sight of the Bedford four-tonners lined up in the distance. Thank Christ for that, I thought.

'There you are lads,' barked Tim. 'Your ticket to easy street. Your transport out of hell!'

The pace quickened, the relief swept over me; it wouldn't be long now. When we were about a hundred yards short, I heard the engines cough into life. They're just warming them up, I thought to myself. Then, to my horror and disbelief, one by one the Bedfords pulled away and disappeared like a bad dream down the road through the woods. Shit, I thought, we've been conned.

By now the other patrols were alongside. Tim walked stiffly to the front of the shredded soldiery. 'Fresh orders from the top,' he boomed. 'The transport has been called away on a rush job. Alternative transport is to be found ten miles from here,' and he rattled off a new grid reference.

Suddenly, Tommo exploded. He lunged at Tim with clenched fists, screaming, 'You bastard!' I just managed to push him to one side and the punch whistled past Tim's ear. Two of the other lads knocked Tommo to the ground and restrained him until he was led away, muttering and snivelling, and thrown into the twat wagon.

'That's amazing,' I said. 'That's the first time I've seen him reveal any real emotion. Mind you, I can't say I'm surprised at what happened. I didn't like the look of him from the start.'

'That's what happens when you bottle it up so much,' said Tim knowingly. 'You can only hold it back for so long, then you explode.'

We set off on the compass bearing, heads bowed, a Para NCO at the front. I was determined not to end up like Tommo. The pain returned in all its throbbing sharpness. All I could see in front of me, through glazed eyes, was yet another hell. Suddenly, as we struggled over the brow of a hill, we could not believe it – salvation! There they were – the Bedfords. We looked back at Tim. He was expressionless. Nobody dared say a word. We just plodded on in stunned silence. As we got nearer we realized that the Bedfords were definitely on our compass bearing. I strained my ears for the sound of an engine starting. Surely they wouldn't do it twice, would they? A hundred yards, fifty yards, twenty yards. I was praying harder than I'd ever prayed in my life. Ten yards, five yards.

Tim moved to the front as we reached the wagons, gripped the tailgate of one of the Bedfords and said, 'Think yourselves fucking lucky they're not really ten miles away!'

I collapsed into a corner of one of the Bedfords, totally exhausted, but exhilarated at having passed my first big test. 'Only two more weeks to go,' was the last thing I remember thinking before dropping into a deep sleep that even the rattling, jolting Bedford could not disturb. A blissful interlude. A lull before the next storm.

4

Sickener 2

All too soon we were back to the familiar hard physical grind. Week Two. The future didn't look too bright to me just at that moment. We were down to ninety out of the original 135, and the worst was yet to come. I was tormented by the possibility that I might be No. 89, the next candidate for Platform 4. My desire to succeed was strong enough, but all the time I wondered whether my mind and body would carry me through. I certainly got to know myself better during the three weeks of selection. I discovered to my surprise that just when I thought my energies were totally spent and failure was beckoning with open arms, I would suddenly open up reserves of stamina that I never knew existed. It was as if an inner resolve, so deep I couldn't truly fathom its nature, lay at the very core of my being, like a steel rod refusing to bend or break.

It was on Day Three of Week Two that we were introduced to the controlled agonies of the Skirrid, a stark, barren monolith that towered ominously 500 metres above the surrounding flat green countryside near Llanfihangel. From the trig point at the top there was a commanding 360-degree view of the land for miles around, and for that reason it was ideal for map-reading exercises. The problem, of course, was that you had to get to the top first, saddled with full kit, and inevitably we were assembled not at the gently sloping side, but at the foot of the near-vertical side. So fierce was the slope that when I checked the map, all I could see was a brown blur of bunched-up contour lines floating threateningly in a sea of green.

I set the bearing on my Silvas compass and lined up the arrows. They pointed straight to the top, directly up the steep side. We set off wearily, a private in the REME up front. When we reached the summit, it was down again, change the leader, then back up. Tim kept us at it all day without respite. Beads of perspiration fell from my forehead and clouded my eyes with a salty film; sweat trickled down my spine and collected in the small of my back. The bergen pounded with each painful footfall, the straps pulling viciously at my shoulders. My calf and thigh muscles gradually tightened until they were virtually locked rigid, and the blisters on my feet grew larger and more inflamed by the hour.

The only relief came at midday, when we paused to take a visual map-reading test. When my turn came, the more I tried to concentrate and stare at the map, the more the contour lines and compass settings became first a blur, then a swimming morass of shapes, like a crowd of elvers in a fast-flowing stream. It was almost as if my mind had become disconnected from my optic nerves. I could still see the shapes and lines, but no message was getting through to my brain. I shook my head and tried to clear it, and fortunately managed just in the nick of time to remember one of Tim's survival rules: calmness and coolness at all times. I took a deep breath, determined not to be hurried beyond my own judgement. Mercifully, the features on the map gradually came back into meaningful focus, and with them Tim's magic formula for map-reading: grid to mag add; mag to grid to get rid. It worked.

I passed. My blisters didn't, though. After touching the trig point on top of the Skirrid for the last time and beginning my final descent, all I could think of during the journey to the bottom was getting my boots off and hitting the blisters with another shot of Jenson's Violet!

As we drank our final brew of the day, Geordie exclaimed, 'I'm going to get rat-arsed when this lot's over!'

Tim looked at Geordie and frowned. 'It's not the answer to everything, believe me. I remember when we were on operations in Malaya, one day we decided to march over the hill and visit one of the other troops. When we came down towards the beach we found the building the other troop had been using as a base. It was empty and no one was around. I began to feel apprehensive. My heart pounded as we reached the beach and saw what appeared to be bodies scattered around on the sand. My God, I thought, they've been ambushed! They're all dead! They were dead all right – dead drunk, lying face down, their mouths full of sand. It turned out they'd found a native still, together with several large tin cans full of *sansu* – that's rice wine. It took us ages to bring them round and they were really ill. It was days before they were fully recovered.'

Recounting this anecdote, Tim was beginning to warm to us. Stories from his days in Malaya now started to flow freely.

'As the Colonel explained to you,' he went on, draining the last of the tea from his mug, 'we are essentially a unit that keeps a low profile and jealously guards the secrecy of our operations. Even a winged-dagger badge spotted in the wrong place can blow your cover completely. I remember in the latter part of 1952, A Squadron were called up to Penang from our base in Kuala Lumpur to deal with an outburst of terrorist activity. On the move up to Penang we endeavoured to conceal our identity by sporting the blue berets and cap badges of the Manchester Regiment. But as soon as our squadron HQ was installed in Mindon Barracks, our OC, a colourful ex-Indian Army officer, quickly dispelled any notion of a low-profile operation by driving around in a scout car, flaunting his winged dagger for all to see and ostentatiously smoking cigarettes through a long cigarette-holder. Can you imagine the scene! He quickly acquired the nickname El Supremo. He managed to get away with it, but it's not to be recommended I assure you!'

Unlike the first two weeks, when we were part of a team, the third week – test week – we were strictly on our own. We were now being subjected to a finely tuned trial of motivation and navigation, and individual effort against the clock. Distances and bergen weights increased daily. To add to the pressure, we had to undergo deliberate disorientation techniques – last-minute changes of plans, sudden extra distances, later nights and earlier mornings than had been announced – all designed to break down our natural defences, to take us to the edge of exhaustion and rebellion, to the point where our true characters would come through. No acts of bravado, no fake façades could survive this scrutiny. Deep-lying personality flaws that would normally have taken years to reveal themselves stood out in stark relief. The instructors were like scientists employing accelerated-ageing techniques. All mental and physical stress fractures had to be identified and rejected before they grew large enough to cause a disaster.

Day Three of Week Three, and we were heading for the ordeal of point-to-point three times over the highest bukit in the Brecon Beacons. Compared to Pen-y-fan, the Skirrid looked like a pimple on a pig's arse! The strain was now beginning to tell. Our numbers had already been depleted by well over half since Day One of Week One; the red felt-tipped pen had been really busy.

Platform 4 was getting busier by the day. There had been a steady stream of dejected egos heading for the station over the last two weeks. Selection had brought back down to earth those who had thought it would be easy, the jokers and shirkers who'd just fancied a few weeks away from the normal routine, a chance to impress their mates and girlfriends, and all but destroyed the self-esteem of the serious candidates. They were easy to spot. They sat on the ancient-looking 'GWR'-inscribed wooden benches on Platform 4, hunched over, not saying a word, drawing deeply on their cigarettes, brooding on their failure. Excellent soldiers to a man – but not excellent enough. The train rattles in, the doors swing open, they step on board and they've already left Hereford, a town they'll probably never see again. A few seconds later, the train pulls out – and the dream has ended.

The Bedfords coughed into life at 4.00am. I eased my shattered frame – blisters, bergen rash, aching muscles and all – into the most comfortable position I could find, and we rumbled out of the camp gates. As we picked up the A438 and passed the sign for RAF Credenhill on our right, I carefully surveyed my preparations. I checked that the strips of foam were still taped in place around the frame of my bergen. This padding gave some relief from the constant thudding and the sweat-induced friction rash that resulted. After starting the week at 35lb, today my bergen had tipped the scales at 40lb as it swung on the spring balance in the early-morning mist shrouding the camp. Even though I was a young and impressionable soldier, I knew there was no sense in having the weight made up to the required level by the addition of bricks, which was the usual practice. I would rather carry 40lb of Mars bars! I checked that my socks had been thoroughly soaked in oil. I'd heard from an old sweat that olive oil reduced the friction between skin and wool. Its efficiency would certainly be put to the test today.

As the Bedford laboured up the increasingly steep inclines, temporarily held up behind an even slower tractor pulling a rusty cylinder full of evil-smelling manure, we got our first view of the Black Mountains, rising just to the east of the Brecon Beacons, as we crossed the border into Wales. All I could see were slate-grey outlines of the ridges and peaks. They were too high for any detailed features to be discernible. A few miles further on, just after joining the A470, which winds its way southwards through the town of Brecon and on to Merthyr Tydfil, we got our first sight of Pen-y-fan – all 2,906 gruelling feet of it. 'There she is, lads, there's the monster,' said Geordie cheerfully. 'Pen-y-fan! Sounds like a cheap prize from a fairground stall, doesn't it? Well, we're certainly going on a merry-go-round, but we won't be riding and it won't be fuckin' fun!'

We were passing signs to Brecon more frequently now: ten miles, eight miles, six, five, a countdown to torture. As the Welsh place-names became increasingly unpronounceable, the small towns we passed through became more and more dreary. Rows of terraced houses with stained pebbledash and faded paint stared coldly at us as we went by. We finally pulled up in a rough stone car park just beyond the Storey Arms, a small, white-walled building nestling close to a copse of newly planted conifers. In its time it had been a pub, then a café, and was now a YMCA hostel. It was 6.00am.

It was like a Le Mans start. Fifty bergens, having been weighed again to ensure no one had jettisoned any of the ballast, were lined up in a row across the road. We were assembled 100 yards back from the rucksacks and waved off by Dave, the SSM. When the arm came down, I sprinted to my bergen, hoisted it onto my back as quickly as the weight would allow, crossed the car park to a gap in the trees and pushed through the gate. I splashed through the stream that tumbled down from behind the saddle of Pen-y-fan and across the bottom of the path leading up to the summit. It was into this stream that the next two times around I would throw myself face down, seeking momentary relief in the cool water. Then it was up the pink-tinged sandstone path peppered with glistening sheep droppings that ribboned its way up to the top of Pen-y-fan. Once at the top, we had to drop down the other side beyond a long gentle ridge, sweep around the foot of the ridge, cross the plain, then continue over the road we'd travelled up, right around, behind and over the imposing peak which faced the Storey Arms, down the slope and back to the car park to begin all over again – and then again. I reckoned it would be not far short of thirty miles in all.

Many hours later, as I hovered briefly on the summit of Pen-y-fan for the last time, soaked in sweat and on the verge of exhaustion, bracing myself against the wind as it tugged furiously at my equipment and contoured the material of my boiler suit tightly around my limbs, an instructor materialized as if from nowhere and advanced on me menacingly. Then he hit me with the question, 'What's 240 multiplied by 250, divided by 12?' Oh God, I couldn't believe it, mental gymnastics in my state, when it was all I could do to put one foot in front of the other. I composed myself and worked through the question methodically, then put my brain into fast forward and gasped out an answer: 'Five thousand.' The instructor's face was expressionless as he gave me a qualifying nod. Relief swept through me and I headed for the final descent. My pace quickened when I saw the three Bedfords parked on the road far below me in the distance, shimmering through the heat haze – the final RV. I went for it.

One more day to go, but the last day was the worst. Day Five, Week Three, the endurance march. Otherwise known as Sickener 2, this was the climax to initial selection, the ultimate challenge of strength, stamina, motivation and good old-fashioned guts. Forty-six miles cross-graining the Beacons, complete with rifle, four 1½-pint water bottles slung from my belt and a 55lb bergen crucifying my back, and twenty hours to do it all in. I'd worked it out: one Mars bar per bukit. I would need the two-dozen box. When I saddled up I could hardly move. The thirty-seven of us who were left set off at first light from the disused railway station at Talybont, which lay eight miles almost due east from the Storey Arms across the mass of Pen-y-fan and the surrounding hills. By the end of that long day it would need only one Bedford to cart the weary survivors back to camp, and even then there would be some empty places in the twenty-seater.

I pushed across jagged stones, squelched through peat bogs, crushed through lime-green beds of young fern shoots and picked my way across stagnant pools of water by jumping from one clump of reeds to another. The olive oil on my socks didn't help this time; the friction in my boots felt like someone pushing a hot, razor-sharp file across the skin of my ankles. Backwards and forwards relentlessly with each step, sapping my willpower and determination, until it felt as if the file was sawing against raw bone. I kept repeating out loud over and over again as the sun rose higher and hotter, 'I've got this far, I'm fucked if I'm going to jack now!' I was overwhelmed by feelings of isolation and loneliness. I felt as though I was the only person for miles around. I must keep going. I must keep going. The sun was getting fiercely hot. It was one of those rare spring days that was a match for the best that summer could offer.

Midday. I'd been going eight hours and I reckoned I was still less than halfway round the course. The sun was extraordinarily hot for the time of year. Just our fucking luck, I thought, on the very day we could have done with some cloud cover and a cool breeze. As I paused momentarily to get my bearing, my legs began to give way under the load of the bergen. My lungs felt raw, as if someone had thrust their fist down my throat and ripped a layer of skin off them. My facial expression became set in a glazed stare. 'What the fuck am I doing this for?' I asked myself. Do I really want to suffer like this? No answer came back. I scanned my brain but could find no logic with which to talk myself into any more pain.

I mopped my brow with my sleeve. 'It's worst than the fucking desert, this,' I murmured to myself. At the mention of the desert, my breath suddenly got quicker and I felt a stirring deep within my guts. I stared into the heat haze liquefying the ridge up ahead. But it wasn't the ridge I saw. Through the shimmering haze emerged gradually the sight that had haunted me for the last two years: Silent Valley, the neat rows of white headstones gleaming reproachfully in the fierce desert sun of Aden; the final RV of mates in the Royal Engineers who'd worked alongside me to keep the machinery of the British Army in tiptop condition so that the infantry could keep up the fight against the Communists and prevent them from overrunning Aden.

I'd joined the Royal Engineers intending only to stay long enough to learn a trade that I could then take back with me to Civvy Street. I wanted it all nice and quiet, none of the *Boy's Own* heroics for me. Then Aden turned my life upside-down. I'd been there only two months when the British Army was slung out of Aden by the Commies. What use all the constant bullshit and training? I couldn't believe it. We were loading our kit, we were surrendering, jacking, sold down the river by the politicians. Men had died for this; what the hell were they giving it all away for? Could they not see the huge strategic importance of Aden, dominating the entrance to the Red Sea and the Suez Canal? What the fuck was going on? I was twenty-one and didn't have a clue. I knew nothing about politics. All I knew was that it was my first campaign and we were pulling out. In my book it was abject surrender, a personal insult.

In my naivety, I had thought that after Aden we would return to the UK. Instead we found ourselves dumped in RAF Sharjah, another shithole. We spent nine months in 1968 building roads, helipads and landing strips in the area. For me it was nine months of questioning, nine months of restless soul-searching, until finally I seized my chance the day I saw on the notice board the DCI, the monthly British Army bulletin: 'Wanted: men of exceptional morale and motivation for high-risk operations and exercises world-wide. Contact 22 SAS.' I knew absolutely nothing about 22 SAS. Nor did any of my mates. Nobody had even heard of them. I was intrigued even more; my appetite was whetted. It had to be better than building airstrips in the desert. That was thirsty work, but my thirst for action and revenge was even greater.

That was it – revenge. That's what had kept me going through the pain barriers these last three weeks. I'd heard vague rumours throughout selection of a stepping-up of Communist activity in the Middle East, and that moves were afoot to do something about it. It all suddenly made sense. Here was my chance to get my own back on the CTs after that humiliating withdrawal. My vision cleared. I took a deep breath, hoisted my bergen higher and pushed on, my body refuelled by the recollections that had drifted through my mind.

I kept a steady mechanical pace going through the rest of the afternoon and early evening, pausing only for water and the occasional Mars bar. My luck held and I got round in under twenty hours. I had cracked the greatest physical challenge of my life. Of the thirty-seven runners who had set off from Talybont at first light, only seventeen of us made it, seventeen out of the original 135 who had put themselves forward for selection. With extreme relief, I removed my 55lb bergen, eased it into the back of the four-tonner and, with rifle in hand, struggled up the tailgate, crawled into a corner and collapsed into a merciful sleep.

Back at training-wing basha, I was told to take twenty-four hours' rest and recuperation. I needed no second bidding after my extended ordeal. I'd overcome three weeks of discomfort, despair and desolation. I'd finished the course – but whether or not I'd passed was another matter. The tension grew as the hours ticked by. Hardly anyone spoke; the die was cast. The frustration at not being able to do any more, not being able to improve on my performance in any way, was enormous. It was a highly nervous trainee who was summoned to training wing the next day to see the OC. I stood before him like an exhausted gladiator looking up at Caesar's podium. Which way would the thumb point – up or down? When he spoke, only one word pierced through my battered brain.

5

From Hereford to the Jebel Massif

Badged!

The prize was mine. After passing initial selection and spending five more months doing exhaustive tests, I became the proud owner of the famous beret and SAS wings. I was now a member of the Praetorian Guard! Somehow I had come through the continuation training unscathed: weapons, explosives and first-aid training; language and initiative tests; a 1,000-yard swim in the OGs; jungle training and survival; and resistance-to-interrogation training. I was on the road back after the humiliation of Aden. As I reached the door on my way out of training-wing basha I looked up at the sign above the exit: 'For many are called but few are chosen'. A few years later, Lofty Wiseman would amend this to read, 'Death is nature's way of telling you that you've failed selection'.

I headed towards the Sabre Squadron lines. I had been posted to B Squadron along with two other trainees called, in characteristically colourful fashion, Clutch-plate and The Honk. The latter looked like a working-class Charles Bronson. Of my original patrol, Tommo had long been back in his parent regiment; Geordie had put himself out of the running by breaking both his ankles jumping from a bedroom window to escape a jealous husband; while Jim had sailed through in a seemingly effortless manner to be posted to G Squadron, having survived six months of selection as he had survived his six years down the pits. Out of the original 135, only a handful were left to be spread between the four Sabre Squadrons. As Tim had forewarned, it had been more of a rejection process than a selection process.

We entered B Squadron office and turned left into the squadron interest room. The first thing about the room that caught my attention was the sight of a huge buffalo head, complete with horns, high up on the wall at the end of the room. Some trophy, I thought. The unfortunate beast must have strayed onto the live firing range. The rest of the walls were covered with memorabilia from campaigns going right back to Malaya in the early 1950s: photographs, certificates, old ammunition belts, bits of webbing equipment – it looked like a military museum.

We heard a noise behind us and turned to be confronted by an intelligent-looking character with silver hair and piercing blue eyes. It was the squadron commander, known, as we later found out, as the Duke. 'Welcome to B Squadron, lads – come into the office.'

We followed the Duke into his office, and as he sat down behind his desk I was intrigued by the difference between the interest room and this room. Not a photo anywhere – just curtains, dark-blue curtains covering every wall from corner to corner. I wondered what secrets were concealed behind them. I was soon to find out. After a short welcoming speech, the Duke pushed back his chair with a sudden clatter, stood up and drew back the blue curtain to his immediate right. There, pinned to the wall, in full technicolour, was a map of Muscat and Oman, a little-known country at the southern tip of the Arabian peninsula. The word 'SECRET' was stamped in large red letters just above the Straits of Hormuz. I recognized the map immediately. I'd sweated in that region for nine months with the Royal Engineers back in 1968 constructing roads and helipads at places like Nizwa and Bidbid.

The Duke began his briefing. It was a broad outline of the task ahead. When he had finished, I could feel the excitement welling up inside. At last I was going back. My first operation too! I could hardly believe my luck.

A strategically vital campaign was being mounted against Communist insurgents. After the fall of Aden and success in Vietnam, Communist ambitions were high. Some said it was part of a worldwide conspiracy. There had been a deep-rooted fear of Soviet expansionism ever since the Red Army, our allies during the Second World War, suddenly shattered all semblance of co-operation by sweeping though the whole of Eastern Europe as far as Berlin – to impose their own, iron-fisted political philosophy on the countries cowering in their wake. The Communist wave was again gathering momentum in Arabia. A breakwater had to be built somewhere to smash its force.

It was hoped that the breakwater would be Dhofar, the southern province of Oman, immediately adjacent to Aden. It was a medieval region, isolated from the more prosperous and advanced northern states by a 400-mile-wide desert, which rose up at its southern tip into a huge plateau called the Jebel Massif – a natural fortress some 3,000 feet high, nine miles wide and stretching 150 miles from the east down to and across the border with Aden, newly named the People's Democratic Republic of Yemen.

Because of its wild terrain the Jebel had fallen easy prey to the Communists. For us, it was not ideal as a theatre of war owing to its remoteness and the fact that so little was known about it. Hours spent by the intelligence boys in 'the Kremlin' back in Bradbury Lines, poring over military reports, literary works and travel accounts, had done little to dispel the aura of mystery surrounding the place. However, the British government believed it was critical to halt the Communists' advance here, before they could seize the one jewel in Oman's crown: the northern coast of the country beyond Muscat called the Musandam Peninsula, dominating the Straits of Hormuz, a major political and economic flashpoint in the Arabian Gulf. It was through these straits that the bulk of Middle Eastern oil flowed daily to ensure the continued running of the free world's economy. If the Communists captured this vital terrain, they could hold the whole of the Western world to ransom by threatening to block the flow of oil and thus cause a mortal thrombosis in the heart of the Western economy. We simply could not afford to fail – the stakes were too high.

Since early 1970, small SAS groups supported by Firqats – bands of local tribesmen loyal to the Sultan of Muscat and Oman – had established a few precarious toeholds on the coastal plain immediately facing the Jebel. Operation *Jaguar*, the mission I was about to take part in, would be the first operation to attempt to establish a firm base on the Jebel to stem the relentless advance of the Communist forces. B Squadron and G Squadron 22 SAS were to support two companies of the Sultan's Armed Forces, along with a pioneer platoon of Baluch Askars – tough little fighters from Baluchistan – and five Firqats of Jebeli tribesmen; approximately 750 fighting men in all. We were to seize an old SAF airstrip called Lympne, which was situated on top of the plateau. This would give us an airhead capability in the east.

The night of 1 October 1971 was chosen. The Khareef monsoon, which covers the plateau with cloud and mist from June until September, would be finished, and that night there would be no moon to betray our presence. We were to climb to the top of the Jebel Massif in full battle order and seize the airstrip by first light on 2 October. Enemy forces in the area were unknown. They were rumoured to number over 2,000. That meant we would be outnumbered by at least three to one. Into the valley of death rode the 750, I thought – only we would be struggling in on foot. And as for the People's Front for the Liberation of the Occupied Arabian Gulf or, as we knew them, the Adoo – no wandering band of vagabonds, thieves and bandits these! They were brave and cunning fighters, ruthless in pursuing the aims of their political masters, skilled tacticians, their leaders having been trained in Communist countries abroad, and armed with the latest

Chinese and Soviet bloc weapons: Kalashnikov AK-47s, Simoney semi-automatics, RPG-7s and 82mm mortars.

The Duke finished his briefing, and the blue curtain swished smoothly back along its runners to conceal once again its veiled secrets. He glanced at the door through which the squadron sergeant major had just entered and, with a final nod of head, the meeting was terminated. We followed the SSM next door into his office, where he briefed us on a move to the army training area at Otterburn. Here we would take part in fire-and-movement exercises as part of a shake-out before going to Dhofar.

The discomfort of the parachute seat of the Hercules C-130, which had taken off from RAF Lyneham earlier in the day, produced a sudden spasm of cramp in my thigh, waking me with a jolt. After a quick shift of position to ease the pain, I checked my watch. In less than thirty minutes we would land in Cyprus for a refuelling stop before the second leg of the journey to RAF Salalah, in the heart of Dhofar.

I looked up and down the crumpled shapes sleeping around me. There was Fuzz, a wiry character from Oldham with crinkle-cut hair; Roger, a tall, slim, swarthy bloke from Bristol, so skinny you could play a tune on his ribs – but deceptively strong with it; Pete, a veteran of many contacts, a natural comedian – he was on the mortar line and called his mortar tube Winston; and then the three Fijians: Labalaba, Valdez and Sekonia. The British Army had undertaken a recruitment drive in Fiji back in 1961, when the Borneo campaign was first beginning and good jungle soldiers were at a premium. Labalaba, known as Laba, was a colossus of a man, born to be a warrior, a man who seemed to have stepped straight from the pages of myth and legend. Valdez was cast from the same rugged mould, wiry hair and all, a fighter for whom battle held no fears, for whom winning, not surviving, was the all-important goal. Sekonia, known as Tak, was solid and stocky, as sturdy as an English oak and just as dependable in a storm. He had a heart of gold and a deep, mellifluous voice which came right up from his boots. His strong Fijian accent gave the impression he was chewing and sucking the words before allowing them out in well-measured phrases. With sideburns more like wardrobes, thick black curly hair and coal-nugget eyes, he was an impressive sight walking down any street. He was to fight alongside me like a brother throughout my career – a rare phenomenon in the SAS where, as a matter of course, team members were changed on a regular basis.

I looked out of the window. We were just crossing the Cypriot coast. It wouldn't be long before we landed at RAF Akroterion. A voice crackled over the aircraft intercom system: 'Fasten your seat belts.' The bleary-eyed sleepers began to stir. An RAF loadmaster struggled over bodies, kit and equipment to take his position at the rear door ready for landing. The C-130 hit the runway with a disturbing thump that shuddered through the plane. The pilot won't be proud of that one, I thought. We got out of the plane, glad to have the chance to stretch the stiffness out of our limbs, and were taken by coach to the cookhouse while the C-130 was being refuelled.

It was a relief to enter the air-conditioned room after the heat of the runway. I made my way to the hotplate and started to pile food onto my plate. I'd got used to the lavish fare at Bradbury Lines. It was my unlucky day; I must have picked the cook going through the male menopause. As I lifted an extra sausage, he swiped my knuckles with a ladle. I couldn't believe it – the cook was trying to rip me off for a reputation. I knew the answer: grab his wrists and glue his hands to the hotplate. I wasn't quick enough and he retired to the safety of the white-tiled wall at the rear of the serving area. I was about to jump the hotplate when the master chef appeared. His face was a ghoulish mask, scarred by a thousand fry-ups.

'This hotplate is for rissoles not arseholes,' I said, pointing at the sullen cook.

The master chef launched into his plea of mitigation. 'The lad's been away from his wife for five weeks,' he spluttered.

'Poor bastard,' I sneered as I carried my scoff to the nearest table.

Leaving the tensions of the RAF cookhouse far behind, the C-130 reached cruising height. I took a sip from one of the cardboard cups of orange juice passed down the plane by the loadmaster and began to address the problems of the immediate future. The night of 1 October was going to be some night. At Otterburn I had been designated a member of the GPMG sustained-fire team. Because I was a new boy, I ended up number two. This meant I would have to carry a GPMG tripod, weighing over 30lb, plus 1,000 rounds of GPMG link ammunition – 500 wrapped around the body and 500 in the bergen. This was before the rations, water, belt kit and personal weapon, a 7.62mm SLR, were taken into consideration. And all in the heat of an Arabian night. It was going to be some sweat. It was no wonder the SAS became known as the 'donkey soldiers' by the Firqats. I thought of the other members of the gun team: Jimmy, the gun controller; Lou, the observer; and number one, Sean, a Parachute Regiment corporal, the trigger man. They had all been in action before. I was the odd man out, but it gave me confidence to think I was surrounded by such seasoned soldiers.

The thump of the Hercules landing gear hitting the tarmac at RAF Salalah brought me back to the present. I looked out of the window. The first thing that caught my attention were the Strikemaster jets, secured in their own individual sandbagged emplacements, covered by camouflage nets. It was a reassuring sight. Air support was going to be at a premium. This was a prophetic thought; I little realized that the intervention of the Strikemasters would later save my life.

As the Hercules swung round into the taxi bay I caught my first view of the Jebel.

'There she is lads, there's the monster!' Geordie's words at the first sight of Pen-y-fan in the Brecon Beacons all those months ago came echoing back as if it had been yesterday. If I hadn't realized it at the time, the rigours of selection, the painful point-to-point over Pen-y-fan and the ruthless red-lining certainly made sense now as I gazed out of the window at this new challenge that awaited us. More bergen-humping, more blister-cursing – but this time it would be for real. Tim's endeavours to forge a chain with no weak links would soon be put to the test. Our mettle was about to be put under severe stress in the pitiless furnace of the Arabian sun.

Compared to the awesome ramparts of the Jebel Massif, Pen-y-fan was like a nipple on a 42-inch bust. The sight before us was stunning. Out of the totally flat area known as the Salalah plain suddenly rose the sheer sides of this huge great plateau. It reminded me of pictures I'd seen of Ayers Rock in Australia. But it was far vaster, an Ayers Rock spreading out in all directions. Once on the summit of this high ground in a few days' time, we would be heading into the unknown – that was, if we were able to get to the top in the first place.

As the four powerful Allison turboprop engines of the C-130 shut down and the tailgate lowered with a slow mechanical whine, a shockwave of heat rolled down the inside of the plane's fuselage, passing through and hitting us before we had even eased ourselves out of our cramped sitting positions. We stumbled down the tailgate into the full glare of the sun. It felt like walking into the middle of a nuclear explosion, so fierce was the heat, so intense the glare. Christ, I thought, as my eyes began to water, I hope we don't have long to wait. We didn't. A convoy of armour-plated Bedfords suddenly swung onto the tarmac and came to a halt just short of the tailgate. 'Get those Firkins working, hey,' shouted the squadron quartermaster sergeant, a flamboyant Irishman called Paddy, flailing his arms around like an out-of-control puppet as he swung down from the cab of the first Bedford. He set to work organizing the unloading and sorting of all the squadron kit.

At long last all the gear was packed into every available bit of space on the Bedfords. We then clambered on top of our huge pile of bergens, ammunition boxes and equipment and tried to find a comfortable spot.

'Best place to sit, this,' said Fuzz, smiling serenely from the top of the biggest bergen.

'Why's that?' I asked, shifting my position uncomfortably.

'Because if we go up on a mine we've got insulation from the blast,' he answered, adjusting his hands cupped between his legs.

This was no idle joke. What few roads there were in Dhofar were all known to be mined, so uncomfortable travel over rough terrain parallel to the roads was the only option. But even this was not foolproof. The Adoo were known to seek out the regularly used diversions and lay mines on them, too. They would cunningly conceal the presence of a mine by rolling an old tyre over the area to make the existing tyre-tracks look continuous. We set off with a last flourish of 'Move your loins, hey!' from Paddy. He finished all his orders with 'hey', and when he was really excited, 'hey, hey!'

The first leg of our journey took us to the SAS base at Um al Gwarif, a sandblown dump in the middle of nowhere. Next to it stood the hutted camp of the Sultan's Armed Forces, a base camp for the resident battalion serving in the area. As the convoy of armoured Bedfords swung through the camp perimeter, the first thing that caught my eye was an old whitewashed fort complete with ramparts and slitted windows. A triangular red and green flag flew stiffly from a pole attached to the topmost turret. I felt as though I was back in the Crusades. Indeed, one of the Firqats had even taken the name of Saladin, that great Muslim warrior who clashed with Richard the Lionheart. From Saracen swords to guerrilla grenades; from Jerusalem to the Jebel Massif; from Saladin to the Salalah plain.

The lead Bedford swung round and came to a halt at midday on what looked like a volleyball court. A layer of fine sand settled on everything. I tried to dust myself down but didn't make much impact on the light-brown film which covered me. I jumped down from the Bedford and looked around. There were only two buildings – an armoury and a radio-operations room. Everything else was tented. Over to my left was a large British Army marquee, and off to the side a number of bivouac tents. There's the hotel, I thought.

'Let's get moving, hey, hey!' shouted Paddy, standing on one leg like a Masai warrior, and thrashing his arms about like a combine harvester to emphasize the urgency. We began the task of unloading the Bedfords.

It was late afternoon by the time the kit and equipment were sorted out. With the radio equipment finally stored away in the signals shack, we picked up our bergens and belt kits and headed towards the hotel. I grabbed the first empty bivouac tent and looked inside. Nothing, just the hard desert floor. I opened my bergen and removed my sleeping bag. I pushed the bergen to the far end of the bivouac and placed my belt kit in front. This would make a good pillow. Then I unrolled my sleeping bag and laid it out the full length of the tent. After a final attempt at dusting down my OGs – in shit order by this time – and already bitten by mosquitoes, I laid my head on the belt kit and fell into an exhausted sleep.

Grey metal, black tape. I stared through sleep-filled eyes at the airborne tin mug floating before me. Thick black masking tape overlapped the rim. I reached forward and took the mug – Christ, it was hot! Without the masking tape I would have needed asbestos lips.

'Stand by your boots with your beds in your hands.' It was Roger, with a feeble attempt at an early-morning joke. He was standing at the entrance to the tent, holding the flap back. The sun glinted on his ribs so that they looked even more prominent than usual.

I was in no laughing mood. The mosquitoes had been zapping into me all night and I was covered in bites. I grunted and took a swig of tea.

'Get your shit together, we've got a briefing from the green slime in the marquee in thirty minutes. Oh, and don't forget to take your Paludrin.' With that, Roger disappeared and I was left to nurse my insect bites.

Paludrin, the anti-malaria tablet. Over the next few months I would grow to hate this morning ritual. I peeled back the tin foil containing the pill and placed the white tablet on my tongue. The bitter taste made me retch. I took another swig of tea and swallowed hard, but the sour taste remained. What a breakfast, I thought.

The atmosphere inside the marquee was one of excitement mixed with anticipation. There was a low hum of conversation as we awaited the arrival of the 'green slime' to give us the big-picture brief. We had split into our teams, and each team sat around a standard British Army six-foot table, our maps of Dhofar spread out in front of us. I glanced at the personalities around my table. They were all studying their maps intently. I said nothing and did the same.

The hum of conversation died down as the Intelligence Corps officer entered. The Duke, who was sitting at the front, rose to greet him. They shook hands and the Duke launched into his introduction. 'Gentlemen, this is Captain Jackson. He will give you an update on the situation on the Jebel.'

Jackson withdrew a pointer from its container and turned to the Dhofar map, which was pinned to the briefing board with the words 'Operation *Jaguar*' emblazoned in black across its top. 'Gentlemen, we have done a feasibility study of the eastern area.' The pointer drew circles on the map. 'We have identified a start line for the operation against the airfield at Lympne. On 30 September we will leave Midway, an SAF staging post north of the Negd plain, and drive by convoy south-east until we hit the foothills of the Jebel and the entrance to this major wadi here.' The pointer traced a line on the map and came to a halt at the beginning of the Jebel.

The speech was rolling off his tongue like a lizard down a windowpane.

'From here we will follow the wadi bottom until we run out of motorable track. We will then debus and move on foot to an area known as Mahazair Pools. The monsoon has just finished, so there should be plenty of water here. This will be our rest area. It is from this location that we will mount the operation on the night of 1 October.'

His voice droned on; he wasn't telling me much I didn't already know. We had gone over the plan at Otterburn with the Duke. All that had been missing was the timeframe. Right now I was more worried about the immediate problem of humping the GPMG tripod to the top of the Jebel.

'We expect a running fight for a few months. Then we anticipate a surrender from the Adoo before the next monsoon begins in June. Nobody has yet stayed on the Jebel during the monsoon, so we don't want operations to be prolonged into this period of time. It should be all over by the next monsoon.'

He continued on about logistics, but I was thinking of this last gem – 'all over by the next monsoon'. That didn't say much for the Adoo's expected resistance. I was puzzled. The SAS's own intelligence unit in the Kremlin had drawn an altogether more complimentary picture of the Adoo's capabilities. But I pushed this thought to the back of my mind. As far as I was concerned, a short, sharp campaign would suit me fine. A few months and then back to the Sports and Social in Hereford, and with a bit of luck a go at Geordie's bird. After nine months in the desert she wouldn't know what was in store for her, lucky woman!

My thoughts of the hostel dance hall in Redhill next to the camp were suddenly interrupted. 'Any questions?' Jackson's voice barked.

'Yeah, why don't we do a parachute drop?' a voice from the Seven Troop table shouted.

Captain Jackson looked surprised, as if he'd been asked what the Adoo had eaten for breakfast that morning. 'How do you mean?' he replied.

'Well, we can't see the point of humping all that kit and equipment to the top of the Jebel, risking ambush, injury and heat exhaustion, when we could parachute straight onto Lympne and be fit enough to go into action immediately. After all, we do have air superiority.'

This caused a buzz amongst the Head Shed. Their brains, heavy with complicated tactical theory, had possibly missed the obvious.

They chewed the option around for a while, then vetoed it on the grounds that the amount of enemy activity in the area was unknown. Shame, I thought, that could have been the answer to the tripod problem.

*　　*　　*

The five-round burst hit the Figure 11 target nine inches above the four-inch-square white patch. Sean slid forward from the firing position and slipped the hinge-clip off the foresight of the GPMG barrel. He then took the foresight blade between his thumb and forefinger and screwed it up with confident precision into the error. Having replaced the hinge-clip, he once more took up his firing position, the second pad only of the index finger on the trigger and only the thumb behind the pistol grip, so as not to influence the movement of the gun by the natural side-pull of closing fingers.

We were now on the 100-metre firing point of Arzat ranges, zeroing the second spare barrel of the GPMG. As Sean rotated the elevation drum to lay the sights, I checked over in my mind the list of equipment we would have to carry into battle in a few days' time: the tripod weighing 30lb, two spare barrels weighing 6lb each, spare return spring, dial sight, marker pegs, two aiming posts, aiming lamp, recoil buffer, tripod sight bracket, spare-parts wallet and the gun itself weighing 24lb. Then there was the ammunition: 1,000 rounds of 7.62mm GPMG link weighing 60lb. The equipment would be split between the members of the team, and I calculated that I would end up carrying over 100lb of hardware – and that didn't include water, rations and personal kit.

My mental arithmetic was interrupted as the gun hammered out another five-round burst.

'Check targets,' shouted Jimmy.

Sean and I walked forwards to the butts and squinted at the Figure 11 target pasted on the screen. 'Spot on!' shouted Sean with satisfaction. The mean point of impact of the group was three inches above the white patch – the correct zero position. 'Come on,' said Sean, 'we'll fire a check group into the other Figure 11, then wrap this up.'

* * *

Midway was a disused oil-exploration camp about fifty-five miles north of the Jebel, now consisting of a number of Twynam huts scattered around an old airstrip. We had arrived by Skyvan from RAF Salalah the previous afternoon, and it was now first light on 30 September. We were on our way. The operational equipment had been packed into every spare bit of space on the armoured Bedfords, and now, with personal weapons and belt kits to hand, we sat on the mounds of kit in quiet anticipation. I looked back down the convoy. There were about 250 of us. The assault force had been split into two. The majority of B Squadron and G Squadron 22 SAS, the Firqat Al Asifat, the Firqat Salahadeen and the Baluch Askars were tasked to assault the airfield at Lympne on foot. The remainder of the force would be choppered in after a firm base had been established.

The Head Shed suddenly appeared from the makeshift operations room in one of the Twynam huts. This is it then, I thought, we're going for it. After a final check down the convoy, the Duke jumped confidently into the first truck. The Bedfords spluttered into life and a Saladin armoured car took up the lead position to offer some protection against mines. We moved off towards the camp perimeter. Once clear of the camp we immediately swung off the road and started driving cross-country, parallel to the road, so as to avoid the mines, and I settled down to what would prove to be one of the most uncomfortable journeys I had ever been on.

For fifty-odd miles, the arid moonscape terrain of the Negd leading to the Jebel was interlaced by dozens of dried-up stream beds. Each one would cause the truck to lurch wildly like a roller-coaster out of control, alternately twisting my spine with a vicious slewing motion and then smashing my coccyx on the metal equipment box I was sitting on, like a hammer on the anvil. The day wore on. The Arabian sun beat down savagely on men and equipment. My loosely flapping sleeve was worn dark from constantly mopping my brow. A thick layer of fine sand soon covered hands, face, clothing, weapons and kit. It floated everywhere, rising silently between the floorboards, sucked into the rear of the vortex of turbulence swirling behind the charging Bedford, propelled through the canvas sides in thick plumes by the sudden manoeuvres of the wildly bucking vehicle.

Speed was of the essence. No allowance could be made for personal comfort. Some of the lads held sweat-rags over their mouths and noses; others had given up bothering. The dusty sand mixed with the moisture of perspiration to produce a grimy, gritty mess that stuck uncomfortably to the skin. By mid-afternoon I was feeling dog-rough. The heat was getting to me, and the sight of a lad in one of the other trucks vomiting over the side did nothing to improve my morale. I looked longingly at the graded road over to our right; then the mental image of a mine injury to the human body jolted me back to reality. After another age, I glanced into the distance – and at last I could see the mouth of the wadi which signalled the final leg of the journey.

The sun suddenly seemed to lose its fierce, molten-metal incandescence and cool to a mellow golden glow. The desert landscape became sharper, its outlines more pronounced in the change of light. It took on the depth and perspective of an oil painting, rather than the hazy wash of a watercolour with which the noon glare had painted it. It seemed to relax and sigh out the heat of the day and await with a hush of expectancy the magnificent display of the setting sun.

By late afternoon we had hit the wadi and left the boulder-strewn, sand-filled stream beds of the Negd far behind. The going in the wadi bottom was much easier, as the floor consisted of a smooth layer of tightly packed pebbles and small boulders. Ahead of us in the distance the plateau towered formidably. I gazed upwards at the sides of the wadi, the sheer rock faces casting huge shadows across the convoy. It was an immense relief to get away from the oppressive heat of the Negd. With the sun sinking in the west it was getting cooler every minute. I was beginning to feel better. I looked around the truck. Everything was in shit order, sand everywhere. I removed the magazine from my SLR and worked the cocking handle. There was a horrible grating sound of sand on metal. I looked at the round that had been ejected; that too had a fine film of sand on it.

I had just torn off a piece of four-by-two cleaning flannelette to pull through my rifle barrel when the convoy came to a sudden halt. I looked up ahead and saw that the wadi had narrowed to such an extent that it was no longer motorable. 'That's it, lads,' said Jimmy. 'We'll have to hoof it from here.' Shit, I thought, the cleaning will have to wait. I placed the round back in the magazine, placed the magazine on the weapon and cocked the action. Then I took my rifle-oil bottle out of my map pocket and squeezed oil onto the side of the breechblock. That would have to do until we got to the night basha spot.

Word passed down the convoy that the Duke wanted all team leaders for an O group, and the remainder of us were to unload the operational kit. Jimmy grabbed his SLR and belt kit and disappeared over the side of the Bedford. By the time the O group had finished and Jimmy had returned, we had sorted the heavy loads out. Most of it was ammunition. I had 400 rounds of GPMG link ammunition wrapped around my body and getting on for 600 rounds in my bergen. Then there were four SLR magazines with twenty rounds in each on my belt, and with the three water bottles as well it must have weighed around 30lb. 'When it comes to slaughter, all you need is bullets and water.' Where had I heard that before?

I pushed the thought to the back of my mind and looked at the GPMG tripod. It's about time I got you ready for carrying, you bastard, I thought. I lifted the tripod so that the legs were vertical. I then gripped the tripod cradle between my thighs and unlocked both front leg-clamp levers. The legs swung forward into the high-mount position, and

I relocked the clamp levers. I would now be able to carry the tripod on my shoulders with the front legs resting on my chest and the rear leg training backwards over the top of my bergen.

When Jimmy returned he gave us a quick brief. There was nothing new. It was just as the green slime had said. From here it would be on foot to Mahazair Pools, our night staging post. It was time to saddle up. I was already wearing belt kit and the GPMG link. Next I dragged the heavy bergen onto my back, and finally Lou helped me locate the tripod on my shoulders. As I took the weight, the metal of the tripod cradle dug viciously into the flesh at the base of my neck. Lou said it looked as if I was being strangled by a black octopus. Christ, I inwardly groaned, I must have 130lb suspended about my person.

As I paused to gain my balance, I was suddenly aware that the ghosts of relatives long since deceased were drifting through my mind. My father had told me the stories, many, many times. There was the story of my great-grandfather, who was reputed to be the strongest man in his home town. He worked for the local brewery and often, for a bet, he would pick up a barrel of beer – weighing all of 300lb – and put it on the back of a horse-drawn cart as if it were a bag of sugar. Huge dray-horses would regularly step on his feet and he would remain completely unconcerned, going about his business as if nothing had happened. He was a hard man, who thrived on the rigours of a tough working life. Coming home one day, he slipped and fell, breaking four ribs; his wife wanted to call the doctor but he refused, telling her to get a gallon of buttermilk instead. 'Blows you out, buttermilk,' he said, 'it'll soon push them back into place.' And then there was the story of my grandfather building a new garage by hand when he was seventy-two. Forty-two or fifty-two OK, but *seventy-two*! He tore a blood vessel in his heart in the process, but still lived another ten years afterwards. I had a tradition to maintain, family pride and honour. I took a deep breath, picked up my SLR and began to march.

Leaving the convoy of Bedfords to make their way back to Midway, we strung out crocodile-fashion in teams and started to climb out of the wadi. Within seconds I was soaked in sweat. I wasn't sure the human frame could withstand such stress. There was so much pressure on all my moving joints that it felt as if my sinews and ligaments were about to snap, like rubber bands stretched too far. I feared my body would end up crumpled in a heap on the ground with the offending tripod on top of me. I staggered along like one of the Saturday-night drunks on Buchanan Street Jim had been talking about during our first meal in Hereford. My worst fears were confirmed when a signaller collapsed under the weight of his radio equipment, and one of the lads in Nine Troop suddenly doubled up, palms of hands on knees, spewing his guts out.

I had just started praying for the enemy to appear so I could be released from the pain when we moved into a flat open area, which Jimmy informed us was Mahazair Pools, the night basha spot. Thank fuck, I thought, as I carefully eased the weight off my shoulders and unsaddled my bergen. I reached for my last water bottle. It was empty. My thirst was fearsome. Rifle in one hand, empty water bottles swinging in the other, I walked across to the pools. My body felt strange and disjointed, as if someone had taken me apart and reassembled me in the wrong order. Now that we had stopped, the strain I'd locked into my body was released in a gush of heavy perspiration.

6

Isolation Ward

The beads of sweat trickled over my pulsing temples, ran down my jaw and dripped from my stubbled chin onto my already-soaking shirt. It was now virtually dark. I could hardly see anything around me, but all was reassuringly quiet. So far so good. But the worst was yet to come: I was soon going to be facing a crucial trial.

For the moment, though, my body was craving water to replace the fluids it had lost over the last few hours. I reached out, picked up the plastic beaker from the brown tray and greedily gulped the tepid liquid. It was Thursday night. I'd been here eight hours already. I had to face six days of the same monotonous routine, six days of swallowing mind-bending green-and-pink torpedo pills. BET they called it – behavioural exposure therapy. The pills were meant to soften me up, to break down the barriers and allow the memories and traumas I had supposedly suppressed for all these years to come bubbling back to the surface where I could confront them, be exposed to them and so gain some kind of miracle cure. Six days of strictly supervised food-and-drink intake so that I could lie here detoxifying from any excesses I might have been indulging in. Detoxifying! That was a joke, when I was forced to take those pills which had God only knows what powerful chemicals in them. And six days of isolation – lying here all alone. They considered me a high-risk case, so they were monitoring my behaviour scrupulously and keeping me apart from the others. Only when I had passed this test would I be allowed into the general ward.

I went over to the window and opened it. The cool November air streamed over my face, staunching the flow of perspiration. The sudden change of temperature cleared my head and shook me fully back to the present. Beyond the dark band in the immediate foreground, where I could just make out the vague shapes of occasionally rustling trees, the great metropolis spread out under a glowing halo of misty neon orange as far as the eye could see. And if you went to that distant point on the horizon, I reflected, it would spread out yet again as far as the eye could see, like a vast alien colony on some distant science-fiction planet. It was an awesome contrast to the tiny, remote native villages I was used to seeing on operations, and to my home in Hereford where, on a night like this, you could look out and see ranges of hills and mountains forming a natural backcloth to the cluster of houses under the floodlit cathedral tower.

My thoughts were interrupted by a sonorous reverberation emerging from the background roar of the city. I looked up and watched as a 747 from Heathrow banked overhead and growled up into the night sky, the flashing navigation lights gradually getting fainter and merging with the stars. I thought back to those flights at the beginning of my career, in the C-130 from RAF Lyneham to Akroterion and on to Salalah, and in the Skyvan from Salalah to Midway. Had I changed? Was I disfigured by mental scars? Was I really so different from that eager young soldier, toiling his way up the Jebel in the heat of an Arabian night to face his first conflict all those years ago?

I closed the window and sank back onto the bed. As I drifted off into a restless sleep, I was disturbed by faint sounds from a distant radio. Someone was slurring the dial through the channels, creating a weird collage of strident noises.

7

Operation *Jaguar*

'Allaaaahu akbar, Allaaaaahu akbar.' The eerie ululation of the muezzin calling the Firqats to prayer rose to a high-pitched wail and drifted through the failing light of the evening. The shamag-clad Firqats gathering at the night basha spot squatted on the ground in large circles. With their FN rifles upright, gripped between their knees, they responded in a unison of strange melodies. The holy month of Ramadan was due to begin on 20 October. During Ramadan, Muslims are not allowed to eat or drink between dawn and dusk, and obviously this could have severely hampered our movements – after all, an army marches on its stomach. But since we could not afford to wait until the end of November, the Firqats' religious leader had agreed to grant them the impunity permitted to Islamic warriors fighting a holy war. The prayers meant that the operation was about to begin.

I glanced at my watch. Thirty minutes to go. We sat around in small groups, listening to the Firqats and watching the shadows lengthen. We talked in low voices. We fell silent. We dozed. We gazed at the stars. We thought of home. We ate. We drank mug after mug of tea, filling ourselves up with liquid like camels in preparation for the trek ahead. We checked our equipment. We cleaned and oiled our weapons for the tenth time. We filled our water bottles and we filled our magazines. We thought of the task ahead and we felt the adrenaline begin to stir in our limbs. And we stared through the gloom at the great blackness of the Jebel plateau that loomed up in front of us, attempting to gauge the height we had to climb, the pain barriers we would have to surmount.

The minutes slipped by as we waited for complete darkness. I did yet another mental check on my equipment. Was the GPMG 100 per cent serviceable? Would we have stoppages? Where was the spare-parts wallet? Did I have the rear mounting pin? I glanced again at the watch suspended around my neck on a length of para-cord. Ten minutes to go. I fingered the two syrettes of morphine that were attached to the para-cord with masking tape just above the watch. Would I need to use them? Could I remember the medical drill? I recollected talking to Iain Thomson in Hereford. He told me he had taken thirteen syrettes after being ambushed in Borneo. It struck me as strange. We had been informed that more than three syrettes and you would be dead anyway. I made a mental note to get the full story from him one day.

I checked the safety-catch on my SLR. Five minutes to go. I was beginning to feel anxious. What if they were waiting for us on the way up? What if the airfield was heavily defended? How would I react? Suddenly there was a noise from the Firqats' area: the sound of equipment being moved, the clink of link ammunition against a metal water bottle, a rifle falling to the ground, a low hum of conversation. Above, the sky was completely dark – no moon. All around, men were clambering to their feet, pulling on equipment, adjusting straps and webbing belts. At long last, I thought with relief, we're off. Jimmy had gone through the plan that afternoon as we sat around the pools of Mahazair, so every man knew exactly what he had to do. We pulled on our loads and joined the ever-growing crocodile of heavily laden figures ready to depart.

The only noises now were the odd clink of a weapon, the whispers of the radio operators doing their final checks, a nervous cough. After a few minutes the radios crackled down the line. I knew this was the signal. Zero hour: time to move! Suddenly the crocodile shuffled forward as the

Firqat guides up front led off into the darkness. I shifted the tripod on my shoulders into a less painful position and began carefully picking my way through the darkness. The death march had begun.

We led off south-eastwards in single file. At first the ground sloped gently upwards, then, gradually, the gradient got steeper and the going got tougher. The weight of the tripod was digging into my breastbone and I was soon bathed in sweat. After an hour, word came down the line to 'take five' and the crocodile came to a halt. I removed the tripod and slumped to the ground with relief. Out came the water bottle and I drank greedily. We had been told by the Firqat guides that there was a well four hours' march from Mahazair where we could refill our water bottles, so I wasn't too worried about water discipline; three hours to go, three water bottles – no problem. Little did I realize that when it came to distance, speed or direction, the Firqats were notoriously unreliable in their estimates. After about five minutes the column struggled to its feet. I hoisted the tripod back onto my shoulders and plodded on.

We moved onwards and upwards, halting every hour for a water stop. The night was hot and humid, and after four and half hours I had begun to feel very weary. I was down to less than half a water bottle, and still no sign of the well. 'Take five' – the words were a blessed relief. I lowered the tripod to the ground, sat down against a large rock and looked at my watch: 0100 hours. Out came the water bottle. I took a swig and it was all gone. That was it. I'd just have to suffer.

We moved off and the pace became slower. The column was growing more and more fatigued and the going was getting even steeper. Then, after about a quarter of an hour, we suddenly came to an unscheduled stop. At last, it must be the well, I thought, and unhitched the tripod once again, sat down and eased the straps of my bergen off my shoulders.

We sat for about fifteen minutes eagerly awaiting the water resupply. When there seemed to be some confusion up ahead, people talking and moving about, it didn't really worry me.

I was enjoying this long break, feeling the strength seeping back into my weary limbs. Suddenly Jim the Jock, a trained medic, moved up the line and disappeared into the darkness. That was an ominous sign. 'What's going on?' I wondered. I was soon to find out.

The radio just ahead crackled into life and I saw Lou whispering to the team leader. He turned to look at Sean and me. There was a grim look on his face. 'Ginge's collapsed with a heart attack,' he said. 'Apparently he was carrying too much weight.'

'How much is too much?' I wondered, eyeing the tripod and my bergen with renewed suspicion.

I moved forward to see if I could help. When I saw Ginge lying on his back over a rock, I realized immediately what must have happened. When we'd stopped for a break he must have rested his bergen on top of the rock to take the weight off his shoulders – he'd been carrying three large radio sets. The bergen had obviously slipped over the back of the rock, pulling Ginge with it, then wedged itself underneath the base. Spreadeagled over the rock, Ginge, weakened by the effort of the march, was completely paralysed, pinioned by the weight of the bergen, the straps biting into his chest and severely restricting his breathing. The shock had been too much for his heart.

While two men hoisted the bergen back up, Jim the Jock gently eased Ginge out of his straps and laid him down on the ground. With the first two fingers of his right hand feathering his neck, he felt for Ginge's jugular pulse. He couldn't find anything. He felt the other side of Ginge's neck. Still no pulse. Emergency measures were required, and quick! Jim began unceremoniously thumping Ginge's chest and giving vigorous mouth-to-mouth resuscitation.

Come on, Ginge, for fuck's sake. I was silently willing Ginge back to the land of the living as much for the squadron's sake as for his own. A death or critical medical incident would seriously compromise the operation, requiring a casevac chopper to evacuate the casualty, thus giving away our position to the Adoo.

Thump. Thump. Thump. Ginge's body jerked under the blows like a comatose psychopath receiving electric-shock treatment. Three minutes had passed and still there was no sign of life. Jim the Jock was getting desperate. He put his hand on Ginge's forehead. It was extremely hot, seemingly at boiling point. As a last resort, Jim decided to try and bring his temperature down. He undid his water bottles and splashed the remains of his precious supply liberally over Ginge's head, face and chest. Five minutes had now gone by. Jim prised Ginge's mouth open and forced the last half-pint down his throat. To everyone's immense relief, Ginge suddenly spluttered back into life, raising his head in bewilderment. We split all his kit up and spread it out amongst the other team members, ready to move off again. That poor bugger Ginge, I thought, virtually dead one minute and having to resume this ordeal the next. The death march was beginning to live up to its name.

Jim would pay dearly for his generous action by nearly collapsing with heat exhaustion himself two hours later. He had started off the march already half-dehydrated, having contracted some kind of bug at Mahazair Pools that had him vomiting violently two or three times. Seeing how much the other lads were suffering from the heat, however, Jim had decided not to ask any of them for water – they seemed to be in as bad a state as he was. Strict water discipline was part of SAS training and it went against the grain to ask anyone else for any. When Jim began to fall behind the rest of the crocodile under the combined weight of the GPMG, 600 rounds of link, spare barrels, working parts and rations, Arthur Hormby – who was later to make a bid to be the first man to row the Pacific Ocean single-handed, and die in the attempt – came to encourage and remotivate him. He also helped Jim in a more direct way: he took over the GPMG, and Jim carried Arthur's SLR.

The women of Hereford would be mightily relieved to know that Jim had survived this particular ordeal. Small and stocky, he was not one of the six-foot-six Greek-god iron-pumping brigade. He was, however, not at all perturbed by his lack of height. Quite the opposite – he felt it was a positive advantage: there was less for the enemy to aim at. What he lacked in stature, he more than made up for in impish schoolboy charm. With bright eyes, ragged brown hair the colour of ten-year-old malt whisky, an engaging grin and soft Edinburgh burr, he had the local ladies lining up, curious to know him better. And, being a gentleman, of course Jim was always more than willing to satisfy their curiosity.

It was 0200 hours before we got under way again. As we tunnelled through the night, I did a time appreciation. It would be getting light around 0530 hours; that only gave us about three hours to get into position for the final assault. Looking ahead, I could just make out the dark mass of the plateau against the sky. The cold metal of the tripod cradle dug deeper into my neck, my mouth and throat felt as though I'd been chewing hot ashes, and my knee joints ached and throbbed. But the thought of the Kalashnikov assault rifles waiting up ahead kept me going.

We stumbled on, the stops becoming more frequent. We had to be on that plateau by first light. Maybe they would hit us even before it got light. The Adoo knew the terrain well, and could move over it tactically in complete darkness and in total silence. I tensed at the thought and became more alert. My imagination went into overdrive. I began to perceive outcrops of rock as crouched Adoo waiting in ambush; the rustle of a night animal as an enemy scout scampering back to the main group to report on our movements; vague shapes in the sand as fresh Adoo footprints. I could now understand the reports I'd heard of patrols firing at phantom enemies.

0400 hours. The column began to suffer the first symptoms of heat exhaustion. This was far worse than any march I'd done on selection. I realized now why the training-wing staff had tested us to destruction. This was no place for the weak. The surfaces of my lips, tongue, mouth and throat were dehydrated and cracked like the baked mud of an old stream bed. I wished, illogically, that the Khareef monsoon would return – even though this would have made our progress impossible. I thought of all the stories I'd heard or read of people suffering from extremes of thirst, and what they'd resorted to: castaways on boats drinking fish blood, or their own urine, or even, as a last resort, the seawater itself – although they must have known that this was a completely irrational thing to do and that their thirst would return with redoubled intensity. I thought of all the stories I'd heard from Korea of thirst-parched soldiers drinking water straight from the paddy-fields – even though the fields were liberally sprinkled with human faeces, the only available fertilizer – or slashing open truck radiators and drinking the filthy orange liquid – rust, antifreeze and all.

As we pressed on up the ever-steepening slope, the pace up front unexpectedly slackened. I noticed something metallic glinting on the track – it was a ration-can. Then there was another. Then a block of hexamine, complete with cooker. Gradually the whole track became littered with rations and hexamine blocks. Who could be doing this? Suddenly my foot went down on something soft. It was a large tube of condensed milk. I was puzzled. Only the Firqats were issued with this type of milk. That must be it then. I realized the Firqats were unloading their supplies, that they were on the point of jacking. Well, I though, I'm fucked if I'm jacking. I pushed on with increased determination, stirred to greater effort by signs of weakness in others – just as I had been on selection.

0500 hours. I looked ahead. I could just pick out the great crocodile lumbering up the steep incline. We can't be far now, I thought. It will be first light in thirty minutes. I watched as the heavily laden figures ahead disappeared over the skyline. This must be the top of the plateau. With great relief I struggled on to the crest. But when I looked over the top, my heart sank with a thump. It was a false crest, and the column was now descending into a wadi. I took a deep breath and pressed on. As I made my descent, the weight bore down even more cruelly on my knee and ankle joints. All I could think of were the Duke's words at the briefing – we must be on Lympne before first light. I prayed that we would be in a defensive position before the Adoo guns opened up.

0530 hours. As we hit the wadi bottom, the first light of dawn shimmered in the east. I looked around me. We were surrounded by high ground. This was turning into an almighty cock-up. So much for the plans of the green slime. The column was now strung out in the wadi bottom in all-round defence, eyes nervously scanning the high ground, weapons ready for immediate action. The minutes slipped by; the wadi grew visibly lighter. I felt the anxiety gripping my guts. Suddenly a voice mimicking John Wayne broke the silence. 'We should be on the high ground,' it drawled. It was Pete from the mortar team, stating the obvious. He carried on up the line, breaking the tension with his performance. When he got to the Firqats, they couldn't see the joke and thought he was the majnoon.

Jimmy had received a message to the effect that the Firqat guides were not sure of the track up to Lympne. So two members of the mountain troop, Mel and Cappie, had gone ahead to do a recce. We spent fifteen agonizing minutes in the wadi bottom before the breakthrough came: they'd found a small track leading up out of the wadi and onto the top. 'Saddle up,' shouted Jimmy, 'we're going for it.' The column was now mobile again, and we started the final steep climb up to Lympne.

0630 hours. At last, with daylight streaking across the landscape, we struggled cautiously onto the edge of the scrub ground that passed for the airstrip. As we proceeded to move tactically, by teams, across the open space, every last muscle was gorged with adrenaline, ready to react at a split-second's notice. I braced myself for the crack-thump of incoming rifle fire, or the dull thud of a mortar being fired and the swishing noise of the shell falling from high above. To my amazement there was nothing, not a sound.

Inexplicably, we were going to take the position unopposed. It was only later that we discovered the reason: Sean Branson had been detailed to lead a diversionary attack to the south and his decoy had been successful in drawing the Adoo away for just long enough for us to establish ourselves on Lympne. We moved quickly into all-round defence to build our sangar from the loose rocks that littered the ground.

Jimmy had just made a decision on where to build the sangar when two figures suddenly appeared on our left. It was the Duke and Colonel John. I was surprised; I hadn't seen Colonel John since he had addressed us at the beginning of selection. The two had their heads together for a moment, then the Duke turned and said to Jimmy, 'I want your team on the high ground over there.' I looked where his finger was pointing. It was way over on the left flank, possibly an hour's tab away. Extreme exhaustion and intolerable thirst swept over me once again as I dragged my heavy load back onto my shoulders.

'Why do they call Major Perry the Duke?' I whispered to Lou as we trudged off.

'Because he keeps marching us up these fucking big hills and marching us back down again!' came Lou's caustic reply.

We toiled onwards in sullen silence, with Jimmy leading us past the other members of the assault force – some of whom were well on their way to completing their sangars, which made me feel even worse.

It took us nearly an hour to reach the high ground. By the time we had completed the short steep march to the top, and thankfully lowered the bergens and equipment to the ground, it was just 0815 hours. The death march had lasted over twelve hours. Each man in his own way had come as close to expiring as Ginge had; each man's thread of life had been frayed through until all that remained were the flimsiest of fibres, held together by the extremes of endurance.

And still there was no time to rest. When we had a job to do, everything else, even bodily needs, took second priority.

We started building a sangar, wrenching the boulders out of the ground with our bare hands, stacking the rocks in a rough circle until we'd built a dry-stone wall three feet high and eight feet in diameter. Next we had to mount the gun. The tripod already formed a triangle with its legs. All I had to do was unlock the leg-clamp levers, lower the whole tripod until the cradle was just clear of the sangar top, then relock the clamp levers. The cradle was then levelled and the front mounting pin withdrawn. Sean had already serviced the gun for mounting, with the gas-regulator correctly set and the recoil buffer fitted. He now inserted the rear mounting pin into the body of the GPMG, lifted the gun into position on the cradle slot projection and pushed it fully forward, locking it with the front mounting pin. All that remained was to open the top cover, load a belt of 200 rounds, cock the action and apply the safety-catch.

As the top cover closed with a metallic click we heard the first helicopters arriving with the back-up force. It was a marvellous sight from our dominant position: lift after lift of helicopters and Skyvans bringing in more companies of SAF, artillery pieces, mortars, ammunition, rations, the remainder of the Firqat Khalid bin Waalid and – last, and most importantly – water!

Amidst all the hustle and bustle of the airlift, I didn't notice the figure approaching in the distance. Then a movement caught my eye, and I turned to see a giant shape bounding up the rear slope of our position. As it approached nearer I could see it was Laba. He must have had 500 rounds of GPMG link wrapped around his muscular frame, and in his right hand, supported by a sling, he carried a GPMG as though it was a green-slime pointer. In his left hand and on his shoulder I saw salvation: two five-gallon plastic jerrycans of water. We encouraged him over the last few hundred yards with shouts of, 'Come on, Laba, we're pissing fresh air here' and, 'Hurry up, Laba, my mouth's like the bottom of a parrot's cage.' When he finally appeared at my side, perspiring profusely, I could have hugged his sweaty bear-like frame. More of a master of understatement even than the Brits, he said only four words before disappearing again down the slope to return to his own position. 'Here's your water, lads.' It was like giving caviar to pigs. We filled our mugs again and again and greedily gulped down the tepid liquid. Iced champagne never tasted so good.

For the rest of the day we consolidated our position, improved the sangar and brewed tea. Where were the Adoo? So far not a shot had been fired. The opinion of the rest of the team was that the Adoo, angry at having been fooled by the decoy, would by now have moved back up from the south and would be lying low, playing a waiting game, before probing our defences for any sign of weakness. I looked around the sangar and saw that the gun was laid on possible Adoo approaches. It was a reassuring sight. A belt of 200 rounds hung down from the top cover and coiled in the sangar bottom. The weapon was cocked and ready to go. The team rested against the sangar walls, Sean and I in easy reach of the GPMG while Jimmy and Lou lounged at the back by the radio. Although we were all shattered out of our minds, we were still switched on. We fought back the temptation to close our eyes as the day slipped by, as the torpid dullness of mid-afternoon gave way to the changing light of late afternoon.

Suddenly, after a brief conversation on the radio, Jimmy announced that he and Lou were going to the Duke's O group. They grabbed their weapons and belt kit and disappeared down the slope of the position. Sean lit a hexamine block and placed it on a small metal cooker. He filled his mess tin from the jerrycan and placed it on the flame. Then, reaching into the side-pocket of his bergen, he withdrew his brew kit. I watched his movements and relaxed in anticipation. I could murder another brew.

Without warning the world erupted. A stream of green tracer, made more luminous in the paling light, raced out and over our position. It was like watching cat's-eyes on a motorway at night – floating gently in the distance, then cracking past at crazy speed close by. The Adoo had arrived. I grabbed my rifle and hugged the sangar wall, the adrenaline coursing through my body. The whole of the western perimeter exploded with the stuttered popping of incoming small-arms fire. I looked round at Sean. He was low-profile, but continued stirring the brew. From where we were there was little we could do. We were on the eastern flank, and all the fire was coming from several hundred yards away in the west.

'Don't worry,' said Sean, 'they're only overs. Have a mug of tea.' He knew from experience that there was no danger. This was nothing to him. He'd been with the Paras in Aden getting shot to shit every day. I reached for my mug as another stream of tracer arced over the position. Sean looked unconcerned as he poured his brew. I glanced over the lip of the sangar and could see the puffs of smoke from the return fire on the western perimeter. I could just make out the distinctive long-drawn-out bursts of fire from the other sustained-fire gun. Were they in the thick of it too? My anxiety heightened, along with my frustration. There was absolutely nothing I could do to help Fuzz and the lads. We could not abandon our own position. All we could do was sit and wait and hope. I sipped my tea, my mind in overdrive, imagining all sorts of horrors happening down below.

After about twenty minutes, the Adoo's attack slackened until only sporadic firing could be heard on the western perimeter. Gradually this died away, and silence descended again on the position. I looked down the slope and to my intense relief could just see the two figures of Jimmy and Lou running across the makeshift airstrip. They arrived at the sangar, blowing like whales and sweating copiously, jumped in, removed their belt kit and sat down.

'Make us a brew,' said Jimmy. 'I'll put you in the picture.' Over a mug of tea he then filled us in on the situation. 'As far as we can make out,' he said quietly, 'a force of between twenty and thirty Adoo hit the positions over on the west. They used AK-47 Kalashnikovs and RPD light machine guns as back-up. We took no casualties. The other SF team are claiming two hits. As anticipated, all they were doing was testing our strength, then they bugged out, possibly to their tribal stronghold at Jibjat.'

I sank back with relief, smiling to myself at my recent wild imaginings.

'As for the O group,' continued Jimmy between gulps of tea, 'the Duke and Colonel John are not happy with the airstrip. Apparently it's breaking up under the sheer weight of today's airlifts. So tomorrow we're going to move lock, stock and barrel the 7,500 yards to Jibjat to build a new one. So make sure you're ready to go at first light tomorrow morning. That's all I've got for you.'

He went quiet and put the mug of tea to his lips. As for me, I quietly mused on the choice of location for the new airstrip, coinciding as it did with the Adoo stronghold.

Now came the job of securing the position for the night routine. A guard list was drawn up, and the timings were pulled out of a hat. It was decided that because there was plenty of manpower on the eastern perimeter, each man would do a one-hour stag, the first stag starting at 1800 hours and the last stag finishing at 0600 hours. The SF sangar was cloaked in darkness as Lou sat alert by the gun, having drawn first stag. I lay back against the sangar wall, my rifle within easy reach, now feeling quite the veteran. Even though I had not fired a shot in anger myself, I'd had my first exposure to enemy fire. I closed my eyes, and for the first time in over twenty-four hours I sank into a welcome sleep.

Dawn found us busily packing our bergens and servicing the tripod and GPMG for carriage. We had a Chinese parliament before first light to discuss the move across to Jibjat in detail. Every man knew exactly what to do and where to go. Around 0700 hours we carefully destroyed the sangar we'd so painstakingly built only the night before, dragged on our heavy loads and took up our position in the formation that was preparing to advance. It was a marvellous sight. We were drawn up into dozens of extended lines, nearly 800 fighting men in all; camouflaged figures as far as the eye could see. It looked as if we'd just come up out of the trenches and were marching across no man's land. It was curious to reflect that no matter how far modern technology and weaponry had advanced, the basics of soldiering were often still the same as ever. I just hoped we were going to be luckier than those poor bastards at the Somme.

By about 1100 hours on 4 October, after a brisk firefight, we had established a defensive position on Jibjat. All that remained was to consolidate our position and clear the airstrip. By mid-afternoon the work was well underway. I sat in the SF sangar on my bergen, idly squinting through a pair of binoculars at two demolition guys from Six Troop who were putting the finishing touches to the tree-stump still blocking the airstrip.

A raucous voice suddenly drifted over the location: 'Chin in, shoulders back, thumbs in line with the seams of your trousers!' I swung the binocs to a spot of dead ground just below the Firqats' position. The owner of the voice was Laba. He was standing ramrod-straight, with a mortar aiming post tucked under his arm like a guardsman's pace-stick. In front of him, drawn up in two ranks, were about a dozen young Firks. Laba was taking them on a mock drill parade. I stared in amazement as he went through the range of drill movements, a wicked smile on his face.

'Squad shun, stand at ease, open order, march!'

He was using the textbook method, straight from the Guards drill depot at Pirbright, namely EDIP – explanation, demonstration, imitation, practice. The Firqats were perfect mimics. By the look of them they were enjoying every minute of it. Their brown faces cracked into broad grins beneath their chequered shamags. After an ambitious attempt at a general salute/present arms, Laba dismissed the squad amid wild applause from the Firqat sangars.

It had been a brief moment of relief in a tension-filled day, a crazy interlude – but not altogether unexpected from a man who, when walking over zebra crossings, would often exclaim, 'Now you see me, now you don't!' and whose party piece was eating cigarette sandwiches – literally consuming half a dozen cigarettes between two slices of bread. This impressive demonstration of a cast-iron Fijian digestive system gave rise to the rumour with which the lads used to tease Laba, namely that his great-grandfather had eaten Captain Cook! They were closer to the truth than they realized. During one particular drunken binge, when the alcohol had well and truly loosened our tongues, Laba claimed he was a blood-brother to the British missionary fraternity. When challenged on this rather startling claim, Laba revealed that his great-great-grandfather had roasted John Wesley during a hangi and then eaten him. Not satisfied with the main course, he had gone on to eat Wesley's leather boots, marinated in coconut juice, as a sweet.

Over the next seventy-two hours we continued to consolidate on the Jibjat position. Skyvans, helicopters and Caribou transport planes airlifted in defence stores, ordnance, water and rations. It was then decided that the whole force would be split into two fire groups. The first fire team, which became known as the East group, would probe deeper into the eastern area.

It didn't take long for them to attract trouble. It was a fierce, determined attack. As late afternoon slipped into early evening, from our position we could see the eerie display of gracefully arcing tracer standing out sharply in the failing light, a *son et lumière* of life and death. It was the beginning of six days of desperate fighting. The combined strength of two half-squadrons was unable to prevent the Adoo from getting to within grenade-throwing distance, and the East group suffered the consequences accordingly. Steve Moors became the first SAS man to be killed in action by direct gunfire during operations in Dhofar.

Meanwhile, back on Jibjat with the West group, we had been employed on clearing patrols round the area. On one such patrol was heard the greatest misjudgement since Chamberlain waved his piece of paper in the air and proclaimed the immortal words 'peace for our time'. We had just come under fire from an Adoo patrol and managed to get the SF into cover. I closed the top cover on a belt of 200 rounds, and as the gun hammered out a burst of fifty rounds, a movement to the left caught my eye. A figure sat cross-legged out in the open, totally unafraid, totally convinced of his own immortality.

It must be the squadron headcase, I thought. No soldier in his right mind would expose himself in such a deliberate way, with the lead flying viciously overhead.

'This is the biggest non-event of the year!' shouted the headcase.

Suddenly a round zipped by and hit him in the leg. He moved with an agility that defied description, and in such a state of panic that he burned his arm on the hot metal of the GPMG barrel, before coming to rest among the empty shell-cases that littered the ground behind Sean and me. With a pained expression on his face he pointed to the injured limb. I ripped at his OGs and exposed the wound. To my amazement, it was not the entry wound I'd expected. Luckily for him it had been a spent round, and there, just visible below the skin, I could make out the dark-brown shape of a 7.62mm short, an AK-47 round. It had hardly drawn blood. I held the leg as a shell dressing was applied. We waited for the firing to die away and then, with the help of Pete from the mortars, carried the first SAS casualty of Operation *Jaguar* to the airstrip for casevac. Some non-event, I thought!

Colonel John and the Duke now set their sights on yet another move further west for us. They particularly had their eyes on an Adoo area known as the Ain waterhole. A probing patrol on 6 October had resulted in two Adoo killed, one Firqat wounded, and Steve from call sign 21 having to control the mortars onto an Adoo Guryunov heavy machine gun to cover the withdrawal.

The advance on the Ain waterhole began on 9 October. We arrived in the area in the early morning without making contact with the Adoo. That was the first stage. The second stage wouldn't be so easy. We were on high ground dominating the area of the waterhole. To our front was a huge horseshoe of high ground which formed a natural amphitheatre. Most of the high ground was hidden by thick thorn bushes, ideal cover for a waiting enemy. The waterhole itself was about 600 metres away, at the far end of the U-shape formed by the legs of the horseshoe, which opened up towards us. The plan was straightforward. The mortars, call sign 25, and the SF team, call sign 26, would hold the high ground and give fire support if needed to the three action groups, call signs 22, 23 and 24, and the FKW, call sign 21. These four call signs would advance tactically into the bowl and secure the waterhole.

The legs of the tripod made a metallic clunk as they hit the stony ground. I made a quick adjustment to the mount position and tightened the locking levers. I levelled the cradle and locked off. Next I centralized the deflection and elevation drums, then fitted the gun, pushing the front mounting pin home until the locking stud clicked into position. Sean now flicked up the rear sight-leaf and set it on the 300-metre graduation, laying the sight onto a rocky outcrop on the tree-line by use of the deflection and elevation drums. Finally the legs were sandbagged and the sight rechecked. The master blaster, as Sean had christened the SF, was now ready. Jimmy had found us an excellent concealed firing point with panoramic views of the whole area. If a firefight developed, we would have a grandstand view.

The discussion began just before the FKW were due to begin their descent into the bowl. One party wanted to mortar the high ground and fry the tree-line with a mixed-fruit pudding before the call signs moved off. The other party insisted that time was running out and that every Adoo in the area would be homing in on the waterhole if we didn't make a rapid move to secure it. A tricky decision. So a compromise was reached. As the FKW, followed by call signs 22, 23 and 24, moved off, Derek, the boss of the mortars, silently registered the high ground, marking possible Adoo firing points on the plotter board.

I closed the top cover of the gun on a belt of 200 rounds and Sean cocked the action. The safety-catch remained at 'fire'. The atmosphere in the sangar was tense. It didn't seem right leaving the high ground when the tree-line remained uncleared. Sean sat with his index finger feathering the trigger of the gun. Lou scanned the area with a pair of binocs. Jimmy sat by the radio. The whole area was quiet and still in the early-morning sun. The only sounds were the rustle of clothing and the clink of equipment as the call signs passed close to the SF sangar heading down towards the waterhole.

I reached for the spare binocs and focused in on the FKW as they skirmished forward in an extended line. They had gone about half the distance to the waterhole when suddenly they began dropping to the ground and adopting the prone position. Several of them lifted their arms and waved the action groups forward. This wasn't in the plan. The FKW were supposed to go all the way. It was their tribal area, their waterhole. They should be taking the position to boost their morale. By now the action groups were cautiously moving through the line of Firqats.

A high-velocity round cracked overhead, shattering the still of the morning. My ears rang as it passed close by. There was a split-second pause, then the whole of the high ground erupted – AK-47s, RPD light machine guns and somewhere a heavy machine gun hammering out its deadly rhythm. A stream of green tracer floated high over the mortar position, harmlessly disappearing at 1,100 metres – the tracer burn-out point.

'There it is!' screamed Jimmy and Lou in unison. Jimmy rattled off a fire-control order. 'Range 400 metres. Go right 100 metres from the rocky outcrop. Heavy machine-gun concealed in the tree-line. Lay.'

My eyes were drawn to the area indicated. It looked like a fire in the tree-line, streams of bluish smoke rising from the top branches of the thorn bushes. It was the HMG. It must have just recently been dragged out of the arms cache, the preservation grease and oil burning as the weapon grew hotter. It was a mistake, a real giveaway. I was once more thankful for the thoroughness of our own preparations.

'Rapid fire!' screamed Jimmy. Sean squeezed the trigger and hammered out the burst of thirty rounds to ensure a close pattern of shots in the target zone.

I watched the stream of reddish-orange tracer as it overshot the target. We were all right for line, but firing high. 'Fire another long burst and

I'll turn it down on the elevation drum,' I shouted. I unlocked the elevation drum and gave it a quick tweak downwards. Sean fired a long burst, and, with another small turn on the elevation drum, I watched with satisfaction as the tracer descended into the area of the smoke.

As I locked off the elevation drum, Jimmy screamed, 'On!' I clipped a fresh belt of 200 rounds onto the old belt and began feeding the beast. Stream after stream of tracer zapped into the area of the heavy machine gun, the sound of the GPMG drumming in my ears. The mortars had now begun firing, adding to the din of battle, the phosphorus rounds exploding in cascades of white flashes among the thick thorn bushes.

The battle raged on. The Adoo HMG had stopped firing, but the crackle of small-arms fire came from all directions. The mortars kept up a steady bombardment, setting fire to the tree-line. The mixed-fruit pudding was cooking up nicely. Sean was doing a traversing shoot along the high ground above the waterhole, the tracer ricocheting skywards.

Suddenly the radio crackled into life – 'Valdez is hit'; and Jimmy relayed the ominous words, 'Ambush party, high ground to the right, watch my tracer.' He dropped the radio receiver, grabbed his SLR and fired off about a dozen tracer rounds into the high ground on the right flank, indicating the Adoo firing position. Sean swung the gun round, laid the sight on, and sent a stream of tracer hammering into the ambush area, blasting the ambush party to eternity.

At last, under the sheer weight of SAS firepower, the Adoo attack began to slacken off until only the odd round cracked over the position. It had not gone as planned. Valdez had been seriously wounded and the action groups had had first-hand experience of a reluctant Firqat. On the plus side, it appeared that the Adoo had broken contact and we had acquired a new piece of real estate. I felt strangely elated; I was still on an adrenaline high. It could have been a lot worse, we could have taken more casualties. I heard Jimmy talking over the radio. He finished the message and placed the receiver on the ground. 'The casevac chopper is on its way,' he said quickly.

I looked down into the bowl. Green smoke swirled upwards from a smoke grenade, identifying the location of the casualty-evacuation point. The chopper suddenly swooped in low and landed in the area of the smoke. All binocs were anxiously trained on the high ground, but there was no sign of the Adoo. They had melted away into the adjacent Wadi Dharbat. After a few minutes, the tempo of the helicopter blades suddenly increased as the chopper lifted off, and Valdez was away towards RAF Salalah and the field surgical theatre.

Late afternoon found us on the high ground above the waterhole. We had moved across once the FKW and the action groups had secured the area. The evidence of battle was everywhere: piles of 7.62mm short empty cases, blood trails, pieces of flesh and bits of clothing – but no bodies. They had been dragged away. They had even dragged away the Guryunov HMG that we had blasted earlier on. The distinct smell of phosphorus hung in the air, filling my nostrils as I got down to the serious business of making a brew. Water was short: I emptied my last bottle into the mess tin, then opened up the jaws of the hexamine stove and balanced the tin on them. I was down to three blocks of hexamine from the last packet of eight. I picked one out and broke it into pieces to make the flames hotter and boil the water more quickly. All in all it was much better than the old Bengazi burner.

As the flames licked around the bottom of the tin, my concentration was disturbed by a suntanned figure approaching the sangar.

'Look at that,' said Henry, a wiry Scot from Lanarkshire. In his hand he held his tin mug. It was stained with blood. 'When we lifted Valdez onto the chopper, the flap must have been open on my water-bottle carrier, and the blood from his smashed femur must have dripped through.' He stared at the blood for a moment, then asked for a brew.

'I've no spare water for cleaning,' I said, looking at my now-empty water bottle.

'We're the same, it was hot down there.'

As he looked towards the waterhole in the distance, I grasped the mess tin of hot tea and poured it onto Valdez's congealing blood.

'I suppose I'll have a change of personality at the next full moon,' Henry said mischievously as he lifted the bloodstained mug to his lips.

'You'll end up looking like a toby jug,' I said, roaring with laughter. This was a standing joke in the Regiment about the Fijians. Fit and swarthy when young, in later years they often lost their muscles to comfortable fat as a result of eating too many fish curries. 'What happened to Valdez down there?' I asked, on a more serious note.

'A classic come-on, a real shit storm,' replied Henry, with a slight tremor in his voice. 'The Adoo opened fire from the high ground to our front with AK-47s and RPDs. Valdez and the Honk made a split-second decision to swing off to the right flank and get on the high ground just below the tree-line.'

Henry paused and took a swig of his strange-coloured cocktail. 'As they got about halfway up, the Adoo hiding in the tree-line opened fire. An AK-47 round hit Valdez in the thigh, just above the knee, shattering his femur. The Honk came up and sprayed the area with his gimpy. Apparently Valdez wasn't too pleased with this, as it was attracting enemy fire and he couldn't move into cover. He was screaming, "Stop firing, for Christ's sake, stop firing." The Honk stopped firing and pumped a syrette of morphine into his left thigh, then dragged him away into dead ground.' Henry finished talking and once again put the bloodstained mug to his lips.

'How did the casevac go?' I enquired.

'Smooth as snake shit,' replied Henry. 'The chopper happened by chance to be flying over the area on its way to Jibjat. So we redirected him by sarbe onto the casualty. It did cause a problem with the Firqat, though, because the casevac was immediate. They thought we were getting preferential treatment. Apparently a Firk was seriously injured the other day and he had a wait before the casevac chopper came. I don't think pure coincidence is in the FKW book.'

We now moved into a dangerous phase of the operation. By 12 October, the FKW, B Squadron and G Squadron 22 SAS and one company of SAF had advanced approximately twenty-five kilometres into Communist-held territory. We had built a defensive position, with all arcs covered by reinforced sangars, at a location known as White City. Now we had to move out and dominate the surrounding area. With the main Adoo stronghold in the east only eight kilometres away, in the Wadi Dharbat, it was going to be no picnic.

By the middle of October we had experienced our first mortar attack. The Adoo gunner craftily fired a few rounds and then moved position before his mortar barrel got too hot to dismantle – and before we could get a fix on his position.

To keep the Adoo from closing in on the perimeters and to make our presence felt, the Duke initiated an intensive aggressive-patrol programme. Each day we would sweep out from White City and look for trouble. It was on one such aggressive patrol that I had my first brush with death. We were having a duel with a switched-on Adoo machine-gunner.

This guy was good. No wild, inaccurate bursts of fire, just well-aimed, controlled double taps. He had us pinned down behind a small hillock of broken rocks. The slightest movement would draw fire. Two or three rounds would crack savagely overhead, just high enough to let us know that if we moved position or tried to skirmish forward he would nail us.

Sean and Lou were detached from the team that day, so Jimmy had taken over as gunner. He was losing his patience. The cold calculating bastard with the machine gun was getting to him. To compound the problem, his fieldcraft had been so good that we hadn't even been able to identify his firing position. As the minutes slipped by, Jimmy grew more and more impatient. He badly wanted this cool customer, who was getting dangerously close to malleting us. Jimmy decided we would first identify the firing position. He would fire a burst on the SF, and I would scan the area to our front to see if I could spot the location of the return fire. This is shit or bust, I thought, I'll have to be fucking quick.

Crack-crack-crack. The switched-on machine gunner was quicker. As Jimmy squeezed the trigger and I began feeding the belt into the gun with my right hand, a 7.62mm short ricocheted off the ammunition belt, went through my little finger and finally embedded itself in Jimmy's trigger arm. The ploy had worked, however. One of our snipers over on the left got an indication, squeezed off a shot from his L42 and gave the machine-gunner a third eye.

I rolled into cover, a stab of pain shooting up my lower right arm. I glanced down at my hand – there was a small amount of blood around the wound. I had been lucky. The round had only penetrated the fleshy outer edge of the finger near the base, close to the knuckle, missing the bone completely. The second bit of luck was having one of the best medics on the Jebel pinned down behind the same cover. Nick Dawson was the son of a Harley Street surgeon and had been a fourth-year medical student before quitting to join the SAS, fired by a compulsive desire to become an explosives expert. He now worked quickly to apply the shell dressing to my wound, saying quietly that I probably wouldn't even need stitches, it was only a graze. As Nick crawled over to attend to Jimmy, the adrenaline began to drain from my bloodstream. My body relaxed and I lay back, my face breaking into a broad grin as I reflected on how fortunate it was that the machine-gunner had reacted so quickly. A few more seconds and my head would have been out of cover and directly in the line of his sight!

Dawn next day. I awoke from a restless sleep. The sangar was cold and silent. The steady throb in my right hand had kept me awake most of the night; I had only just managed to doze off in the last couple of hours. Now, with first light streaking in from the east, I dragged myself out of my sleeping bag and sat on an empty ammo box. My eyes felt gritty, my mouth felt dry and my hand ached uncomfortably. It was a well-known fact that there was gas gangrene in the air and wounds tended to rot very quickly. So I decided there and then that I would go down to the FST in RAF Salalah and get my hand checked out. I didn't want to miss any of the action just because of an infected flesh wound. As my eyes wandered idly over the empty ration-box in the corner, a thought suddenly occurred to me. It was resupply day. That was it then. I would cadge a lift on the resupply chopper.

Resupply day was always a relaxed day, a day we all looked forward to. The big bird in the sky brought such luxuries as mail from home, cigarettes, water, ammunition and possibly, if we were lucky, fresh rations. Jimmy was already down at the FST, having been casevac'd after the contact. So I cleared it with Lou, picked up my SLR and belt kit and headed towards the airstrip.

I had reached the area of call sign 24 when I suddenly heard the raucous shout, 'Incoming'. Shit, not now, I thought. Next moment the throaty swishing roar of an incoming mortar rang in my ears, followed by the high-explosive crump of detonation. I needed a sangar – fast! I crouched and quickly looked to my left. There was a small ridge in the ground, running north to south. Built into this ridge was a sandbagged sangar with a heavily reinforced roof for defence against mortar and rocket attack. As I heard the distant thump of the next incoming mortar, I moved rapidly towards the sangar, brushed aside the blanket door and went in.

As the sound of the second mortar bomb exploded in my ears, I don't know which had more impact: the high-explosive detonation or the interior of the sangar. I couldn't believe my eyes. I thought for a moment I must have been hit by the mortar and was halfway to heaven. Either that or I was seriously hallucinating. The sanger created the illusion that you had been transported into another world, a world of psychedelic lights, pin-ups and heavy rock music. The sound of Jimi Hendrix reverberated in my ears. Green, red and yellow lights flashed from every corner, flickering and reflecting off bandoliers of GPMG ammo, grenades, freshly oiled weapons and numerous glossy *Playboy* centrefolds. Along the wall in front of me stood the power supply for this assault on the senses. Dozens of old A41 radio batteries were stacked from floor to ceiling in great piles, linked by a myriad of coloured wires.

After a few moments I became aware of an eerie figure amidst this confusion of sound and light. The figure was reclining on an old Army camp bed and wore only a chequered shamag around his head, an olive-green towel around his waist and a battered pair of flip-flops on his feet. It was Scotty. His body, deeply suntanned, seemed sculpted in bronze – smooth, round, perfectly formed sinews and muscles linked and rippling into each other with statuesque fluidity; and his face seemed chiselled from granite – forehead solid and square, high cheekbones, and proud, aquiline, hawk-sharp nose, whose fierceness was mellowed by the soft grey-blue of his deep-set eyes. He looked like a demented DJ as he worked the switches to control this fantastic light display. The switches consisted of live .50-calibre Browning rounds, suspended from the beam running along the top of the sangar wall on wires of differing lengths. The electrical contact was completed by the .50-calibre rounds being swung like pendulums across dozens of nails driven at varying angles into the sandbagged walls. The nails were connected to the batteries by an array of wires.

I stared at amazement as Scotty expertly flicked the Browning rounds across the electrical contacts with his fingers and toes to the heavy beat of 'Purple Haze'. I was intrigued. Where had the disco lights come from, in the middle of a defensive position on a plateau in Dhofar? As I looked more closely at the flashing red light just in front of me, I had the answer. They were all Land Rover headlights. But what about the different colours? I wondered.

'Vehicle fluid,' said Scotty above the whine of Jimi Hendrix, answering the question that flickered across my bemused features. 'I filled the light lenses with brake fluid for red, hydraulic fluid for green, engine oil for yellow.' He paused and then added rather proudly, 'A combination of fluids and water gives you special effects.'

The resourcefulness of the soldier is legendary. Fantastic stories of improvised articles created from the most unexpected materials had come out of the Japanese POW camps during the Second World War. But no one would believe this.

Scotty had been famous for many things, including being the first Ansell's Bitter man on TV. That had come about when, unbeknown to him, his girlfriend had sent in an application on the back of a beer-mat, together with a photograph. He passed the preliminary stages with flying colours – an altogether different kind of selection. When it came to the audition, his good looks were matched by his drinking prowess. Unlike Scotty, some of the most macho-looking men he was up against could not drink a pint down in one before the eagle eye of the camera without giving away some sign of strain – an exaggerated gulp, moisture in the eye, a quick catching of breath. Even those who could were unable to pass the second test – ambling up to a bar in a natural and unselfconscious manner. With his success, Scotty's picture soon adorned advertising hoardings all around Hereford. To his dismay, trainee graffiti artists embellished his handsome features with moustaches, glasses and sexual organs of record-breaking dimensions. The first two additions really upset him! Yes, Scotty had been at the centre of many renowned escapades; his exploits were fabled. But this sangar took the prize.

The hallucinogenic atmosphere in the sangar had even made me forget the pain in my hand. Having not heard any mortars impacting for some time, I decided to leave Scotty and his bizarre illusion and return to reality to await the chopper. With Jimi Hendrix hitting the last bars of 'Purple Haze', I brushed aside the blanket door. As I stepped through it, my mind spun with the contrast between the scene I'd just witnessed and the ordinary world outside. I looked up and narrowed my eyes against the harsh glare of the Arabian sun.

8

Transfer

The fierce white light cut into my face and burned my eyes. My hand throbbed and ached with redoubled intensity. My mind was overloaded with sensory input. It short-circuited and for a few moments the electrical impulse messages crackled around my brain in chaotic disorder like dry leaves wildly spun around a dusty cul-de-sac by a twisting gust of wind. After a few moments the storm subsided and I gradually began to focus on the near distance. Tubular grey metal protruding from just beyond my feet against a whitewashed wall background. White sheets beneath my stretched-out-legs. A bed. A hospital bed. What had happened? I must be in FST Salalah already! Somewhere I'd lost a couple of hours. All I could think was that another incoming mortar must have blasted me into unconsciousness while I was awaiting the chopper.

'Get your kit together, we're transferring you to the general ward.' The disembodied voice pierced through the chatter of noisy thoughts inside my head. General ward – what does he mean? I looked down at my tightly clenched fist and slowly unfolded the gripped muscles. Not a mark, no flesh wound to be seen. I looked up at the white-coated figure standing by the door, a hand still on the light switch. The neon strip hummed above my head.

'What's going on?' I voiced the words indistinctly, as if I'd just been punched in the mouth and was speaking through swollen gums and dislodged teeth.

'We're transferring you to the general ward.'

I glanced outside. It was still dark. 'What time is it?'

'Six-thirty.' Seeing my confusion, he added, 'Wednesday morning.'

'Wednesday morning!' I couldn't understand it. 'But I thought I wasn't due to change over until this evening. What's all the rush?'

'An urgent case has just come in. We need the room.' He seemed reluctant to tender even this much information. I decided not to persevere.

I followed the nurse down the corridor. Our footsteps echoed in hollow rhythm over the pale-brown and yellow lino squares that covered the floors of the corridor in a monotonous symmetrical pattern. The drab walls were pockmarked as if they'd been hit by gunfire. Circular chunks of the smooth pale-green surface had fallen away to reveal grainy craters of white plaster beneath. We walked past narrow opaque windows reaching up to the high ceilings. We walked past red No Smoking signs and faded posters pinned to the wall exhorting anyone who cared to pay attention to eat the right food, to take the right amount of exercise and not to drink to excess. We walked past mysterious doors leading off in different directions marked 'Private – No Entrance'. We walked past three tubular-steel trolleys parked up flush against the left wall of the corridor, their disproportionately small black wheels protruding at different angles.

Finally we turned left into the general ward. It was a bit like the spider back at Hereford. It was split into regular sections, each one providing dormitory accommodation for eight men. A small rectangular office was strategically positioned at the end of each section, with a sliding window overlooking the beds through which the nurses could monitor what was going on in the ward.

I couldn't see a great deal. Two safety-lights glowed dimly high overhead to reveal only the general position of the beds and the vague bulk of their sleeping occupants. I was shown to my bed and the nurse departed without a word. I didn't feel comfortable in this unknown environment. A thorough reconnaissance report on any new terrain was one of the first lessons of survival. I resolved to case the geography of the place and assess its inmates as soon as an opportunity arose.

The lights went on at 7.00am, and the world around me slowly began to stir, shuffle and cough into life. What a sight met my eyes! A bunch of bleary-eyed, burnt-out misfits, dishevelled and unshaven, endeavouring with trembling hands to struggle into their clothes and make themselves ready for breakfast. They were like bit-part actors in some slow-motion silent film version of Dante's *Inferno*. A grotesque contrast to the early-morning urgency I was used to on operations. I felt completely separate from them. I felt sharp and alert. My mind was already working out how I could beat the system.

After breakfast and my reconnaissance of the ward area I barged into the office just at the end of my ward and fired impatient questions at the duty nurse.

'What am I supposed to do around here all day? How can I pass the time?'

The nurse looked up from his contemplation of a set of LFT charts and replied vaguely, his mind on other things, 'There are newspapers every day. And there's TV, radio…' and dropped his eyes back down to scrutinize the graphs.

'That's no good for me, mate,' I insisted. 'I'm an active person. I'm used to moving around, getting things done, being involved. As it is I'm stuck here floating round in a sea of flopped-out alkies. I can't hack this.'

'Well that's how it is. I can't see you've got a great deal of choice. And anyway it's no good complaining to me – I don't draw up the rules around here.'

'But my body is used to regular physical exercise. I'll lose my edge after a few days of this routine.'

'There is a three-mile morning run each day that you'll be taking part in from tomorrow onwards.'

'Oh great! Three miles! That's a stroll to the corner shop for me. I'm used to doing ten miles a day.'

There was a pause. He didn't say anything. He didn't even look up from the LFT charts.

I could see I wasn't getting anywhere. I padded off to the lounge area and slumped in a chair. I picked up a newspaper and distractedly read what was going on in the outside world.

An hour went by, then two. I dropped the last paper onto my knees in despair. I contemplated with gloom the prospect that the burning fires of my motivation and energy, fuelled by excitement, adventure and action, were about to be smothered by the blanket of routine and monotony that was descending on me. I had to do something. Suddenly, as I flipped through an old publication on the Second World War, a faded black-and-white photo of a large gun in action jumped off the page and hit me right between the eyes. I realised how close the hospital was to the Woolwich Artillery Museum. I remembered passing the road sign pointing to it on the drive in. That was it! The Mirbat gun.

I got up and walked silently towards the fire escape I'd located on my earlier recce. My inner radar was alert for any signs from the nurses that they suspected my behaviour might be unusual in any way. With a last glance at the only office that had a view of the fire escape, I slowly eased up the quick-release bar, careful to avoid making any metallic clunks, pushed the door open and stepped out onto the studded black metal platform. I took a deep breath of fresh air with relish. Then, silently easing the door to behind me, I climbed swiftly and noiselessly down the latticed iron treads, as cautiously as if I were moving through the jungle under threat of an enemy ambush. I hurried across the grassy area surrounding the hospital and strode confidently along the nearby street.

Once inside the museum, I fixed my eyes intently on the gun for so long that the rest of my surroundings began to melt into the background. The other artefacts on display, the other visitors walking around, the moustachioed security man dozing in the chair in the corner of the overheated room, arms folded, his head tilting forward and threatening to cast off his peaked cap at any moment, everything else faded away into the distance.

I scrutinized the gleaming barrel on the twenty-five-pounder. I smiled to myself as I recollected that it had certainly been in no showpiece condition when I last saw it, pumping out a continuous barrage of roaring shells. Covered in dust and oil, riddled with bullet marks, and with the cross-country tyres deflated and shredded, it had been in real shit order. It was the last artillery gun of its type to be used by British troops in action. And what action it had been! A heroic, cataclysmic struggle, the final decisive encounter with the Communist Adoo pouring down from the Jebel like lemmings all those years ago. And yet it seemed like only yesterday. As my mind drifted back, the confused, urgent jumble of battle sounds rang in my ears again, faintly at first like the sound of distant surf, and then gradually getting louder: the whoosh of mortars and the thump of artillery; the hailstone rattle of machine guns and the whip-crack of rifles; the shouts and the screams, the groans and the gasps, the clamour, the cries and the curses of the men caught up in the middle of it all.

And as I continued to stare, a picture began to take shape in my mind's eye, a painting by the artist David Shepherd. A print of it hung on my wall back home in Hereford, and I'd spent many a nostalgic moment gazing at it. It depicted three soldiers in a gun pit huddled around the breech of the twenty-five-pounder, with the Mirbat Fort under siege on the skyline. I studied the group of three men again now in my imagination and reeled off the litany I'd intoned so many times before: he's dead, he's dead, and his back is so badly scarred with gunshot wounds it looks like an OS map of the Brecon Beacons, an aerial photo of Crewe sidings. I was the lucky survivor. I could have been the fourth man. The situation was desperate. Volunteers were called for. I stood forward but I was turned down. I was needed to man the radio set. My mate went instead. He was a good mate.

They were all good mates. I owe it to you lads to win through again.

I felt reassured. I'd found a reference point. This was what was real – the adventure, the danger, the humour, the camaraderie under fire; not the alien environment of Ward 11.

I returned to the hospital hoping to slip back into the routine as if nothing had happened. It was too much to expect. I was immediately confronted by one of the nurses. He was at 50,000 feet.

'Where the hell have you been?'

'The Woolwich Museum.'

'Like hell you have.'

'What do you mean?'

'You know damn well what I mean. You've been drinking, haven't you?'

'No way! There's no pub around here anyway. I've done a recce.'

'Don't try and be clever with me. You've got some booze stashed in the boot of your car, haven't you? I know your type.'

'You're wrong, mate. I've been to see the Mirbat gun.'

'I've never heard of the Mirbat gun. I don't believe a word you're saying. Right! Into the office – I'm going to breathalyse you.'

It was a real breathalyser, just like the ones the police use. As I put the mouthpiece to my lips and exhaled deeply, I thought of all the times I'd evaded the local police back in Hereford after wild nights in the Pal-U-Drin Club. Was my luck about to run out in the ignominious surroundings of Ward 11? We both stared at the contraption in silence waiting for the result.

Negative.

'There must be something wrong with this one,' he said, squinting at the digital read-out. 'We'll have to do it again.'

Negative result once more.

'I still don't believe your story. You can explain your case to the Major.'

I was whistled in to see the Major, the top military psychiatrist. I went through my story again, but was noisily interrupted.

'What battle of Mirbat? I've never heard of it! You've made it up. You've picked up the name from a newspaper and fabricated some cock-and-bull story. You're having delusions.'

'You could easily check it out, *sir*.' I could barely disguise the latent contempt in the word.

The Major hesitated, looked me up and down, then said, 'All right, I will check it out. But if we find out you are lying...' His voice tailed off as he shot me an intimidating glare.

I wandered back to my bed. I was confident. I wasn't going to let my mates down. No way was I hallucinating. Mirbat was no figment of a fevered imagination, no creation of a bullet-crazed brain. 19 July 1972. Mirbat was real all right, as real as the roar that flowed in over the breeze – London's pulse and heartbeat. And what was it that kept the heart of the metropolis beating? What was it that flowed through its veins, vessels and arteries? Oil! Oil to fire the generating stations, oil to power the lorries, oil to light the streets, oil to heat the buildings, oil to insulate the homes and keep the inhabitants in their cocoon of cosiness and comfort. And from where did it flow, that oil, where did it spring up? Arabia, where life was harsh, food was poor, shelter was scarce; where the monsoon was a continual scourge and mosquitoes a constant enemy; where, simply, people froze when it was cold and scorched when it was hot. Arabia, where to ensure the free flow of that precious stream I and my mates had undergone rigour, hardship and danger for months on end, fighting alongside tribesmen loyal to the Sultan. Some of my best friends had fallen in that inhospitable terrain, their life-blood seeping through the sand to mingle with the black liquid that even now, as I lay on my bed, was pumping through the nation's heart.

I thought again of David Shepherd's painting of the twenty-five-pounder, and then I remembered the plaque on the wall at home next to it. The plaque was inscribed with words from *Henry V*:

> Old men forget: yet all shall be forgot,
> But he'll remember with advantages
> What feats he did that day.

I remembered all right. I remembered what feats we did that day.

9

The Battle of Mirbat

After a while I closed my eyes and started to descend into a fitful sleep. I remember thinking that I would only need to survive a few more days of this routine, the creeping listlessness that came with the drawn-out activity, the sudden threat that came with the odd unexpected attack, and then it would be back home, back to what I knew, back to get on with the rest of my life. Monotony was making a fierce assault, but strong willpower reinforced by endless hours of rigorous training was putting up determined defences. Whatever happened, I would give a good account of myself. I wasn't going to let my mates down at any cost. That was the single most important thought I held fast in my mind. Like a shipwrecked sailor clinging to driftwood, I knew that, come calm or storm, I would pull through if I could just hold onto the one thing I knew was solid.

The darkness got deeper and I slid into the realms beyond dreams.

* * *

In the dark of that night, the lingering Khareef monsoon wrapped the Jebel Massif in mournful clouds of mist and drizzle. Before first light, 300 hand-picked Adoo warriors crouched motionless behind the tumble of ragged boulders strewn at the foot of the Jebel ramparts, watching and waiting. Droplets of rain ran down their stony, weatherbeaten features as they stared out impassively over the shadowy pre-dawn scene that lay before them: the mud-walled dwellings of the garrison town of Mirbat huddled up against the shore, and the slow, leaden swell of the sea to the south.

Their commanders surveyed the town's defences: just to the north of the town, a shallow wadi ran from east to west; 500 metres beyond and parallel to it stretched the barbed-wire perimeter fence; and in the gap between the two lay their main obstacles – the Wali's fort and the British Army Training Team headquarters (the 'Batt House') down by the wadi, and to the north-east, nestling close to the perimeter wire, the Dhofar Gendarmerie fort, with the twenty-five-pounder located at the base of its walls.

The Adoo were certainly not risking anything. They were armed to the teeth with the choice of the latest Soviet weapons: AKM and AK-47 rifles; heavy, medium and light machine guns; two 75mm RCLs; 81mm, 82mm and 60mm mortars; grenades and rocket-launchers; and one 84mm Carl Gustav. And each man had been issued with a large reserve of ammunition. This was the battle they had to win. This was the one upon whose outcome the political and economic fate of the whole of Western Europe could depend. Muscat and Oman with the Straits of Hormuz were a glittering prize to capture, and Mirbat was the jewel in the crown. This was to be a day they hoped would live for ever in their folklore, a day whose exploits would be retold over and over by tribesmen elders with greying beards, sucking pensively on rough pipes as they sat cross-legged by the camp-fires, watched in awe by young boys eager to grow up to be warriors themselves. This was a day to restore morale with a resounding victory.

The Adoo were taking no chances. These were the Communists' elite shock troops, three hundred well-trained, well-armed men against a pitiful opposition: twenty-five DG in the perimeter fort, one Omani gunner manning the twenty-five-pounder, thirty Askars in the Wali's fort, a scattering of Firqats embedded with their wives in Mirbat itself and nine SAS in the Batt House.

* * *

Forty miles away, at Um al Gwarif, Lofty Wiseman stirred from a listless sleep, levered himself upright on his bare metal bed, rubbed the sticky secretions from his eyes and glanced at the luminous dial on his G10 watch. It was just before 0500 hours, the start of another day at SAS base camp. He looked outside. Beyond the barred windows and whitewashed walls of the armoury, he could just make out through the drizzle the vague shapes of the first of the lines of bivouac tents housing G Squadron, who had come to relieve B Squadron now that the latter's tour of duty on the Jebel and the coastal plain was coming to an end. It would be just another routine day for Lofty. Ammunition would be counted, checked, listed and issued to G Squadron for the pre-deployment shake-out. They would move to Arzat ranges, where weapons would be checked, double-checked and meticulously zeroed. In this way they could keep themselves in a state of constant alertness just in case anything should happen. The day's work for Lofty had been reduced significantly with the deployment of advance parties from G Squadron into strategic locations throughout the sultanate to facilitate a smooth handover. The only forces remaining in Um al Gwarif were a handful of NCOs and around forty troopers.

* * *

At a signal from their leader, the Adoo crept forward without a sound, as noiseless as fish gliding through water, to occupy their predetermined assault positions. One group established a line of 81mm and 82mm mortars 2,000 metres north of the town. Two groups went further south, fanning out on either side of the town, to attack from the seaward side. Before dawn, the still-sleeping inhabitants of Mirbat garrison were completely surrounded.

* * *

'I don't drink on ops, you know that, Fuzz.'

It was 5.00am in a top-floor room in the Batt House. The final few bars of the last song on side two of *Easy Rider* were quietly playing out on the battered cassette-player in the corner, as Fuzz made one last attempt to persuade Tak to have a swig from the illicit half-bottle of rum that had kept them company through the long night. The other Fijian, Laba, had had no such reservations. The three of them were slumped on their beds, still fully dressed, in Jesus sandals, shorts and shirts. While the other lads slept the monotony away, Laba, Tak and Fuzz – now designated an honorary Fijian – had drunk, talked and sung right through the night. What did it matter anyway? They would not be doing much the next day. They never did. They only went out now and again on patrols, and they were mostly uneventful. Just the occasional threat from a minor skirmish. The most difficult part was finding the discipline to stay alert. Nothing ever really happened at Mirbat. It was one long rest period.

Meanwhile, the Adoo sent a scouting party to probe further forward towards the first obstacle in their way – the Jebel Ali hill, which rose 1,000 metres due north of Mirbat, dominating the coast and plain. They suspected this could conceal an enemy outpost. Their suspicions were well founded; it was manned by a section of the Dhofar Gendarmerie. The Adoo lead scouts surrounded the hill and sealed off all escape routes. The unbelieving DG woke up staring death in the face. They only managed to loose off a few shots before the outpost was overwhelmed with ruthless efficiency in a matter of seconds, its occupants put to the knife and silenced forever. Fearing that the sounds of the shots must have alerted the BATT, the Adoo mortar line opened fire.

* * *

Lofty was beginning to have that end-of-tour feeling. He cheered himself up with the thought that in a few days' time, B Squadron would be all packed up and winging their way back to the UK, the married pads returning to their families, the young thrusters to a bit of sex and athletics in the Redhill Sports and Social. No more monsoon, no more heat, no more dust, no more flies. Just cool beer and hot women. He turned slowly on his back and stared up at the fan whirling in the gloom above his bed. This always enabled him to think better. The hypnotic movement and faint vibrating beat of the fan helped him to dispose of all irrelevant thoughts so that he could concentrate solely on the task in hand. He allowed the gentle breeze from the revolving blades to waft over him to clear his mind as he began to make a mental checklist of his responsibilities for the day.

* * *

Crump. Crump. Crump. Fuzz propped himself up on his bed on a crooked elbow and squinted at the bulky Fijian figure still lying down in the shadows. 'Laba, they're throwing a few in.'

'No problem, Fuzz, it's the dawn chorus. Regular as clockwork once they start. You don't need a watch round here!'

'Yeah, it's just the Adoo coughing themselves awake,' said Tak laconically. 'Another tedious day in Dhofar.'

Crump. Crump. Crump.

'That was closer. They're getting a bit brave this morning,' said Fuzz, his voice tightening slightly.

'Don't worry,' soothed Laba reassuringly, 'there's no small-arms fire. They're just stonking us.'

Crump. Crump. Crump. Fuzz was now on his feet. 'I don't like the sound of this. That was too close for comfort. We'd better go and see what they're up to.'

The first ranging rounds from the Adoo mortars were already impacting just outside the perimeter wire as I leapt out of bed, pushed past Fuzz, Laba and Tak and scrambled up the half-pyramid of ammunition boxes that served as a ladder up to the roof. When I reached the top I threw myself behind the .50-calibre Browning, my stand-to position in the command-post sangar built on the flat roof of the Batt House. One moment fast asleep, the next under attack, I drew a sharp breath and cursed softly, my left hand closing instinctively on the first incendiary round protruding from the ammunition box. I snapped open the top cover of the .50-calibre and positioned the ammunition belt on the feed tray. The belt held a mixture of incendiary and tracer rounds in a ratio of four to one, the incendiary rounds designed to explode on impact. With the links uppermost I manoeuvred the belt into position with my left hand. With my right hand I closed the hinged cover and cocked the action with a single practised twist of the wrist, feeding an incendiary round into the breech. The cold metal of the trigger felt comforting to the touch as I took up the first pressure, released the safety-catch and stared in disbelief at the scene unfolding before me.

* * *

Confident he had everything organized for the relieving squadron, Lofty swung off his bed, slipped into his well-worn shorts and desert boots and creaked open the wooden door. He screwed his face up into a grimace as the cool drizzle of the interminable monsoon washed over his early-morning pallor, making him blink away the last grains of sleep. He ambled past the radio-and-ops room and headed for the armoury. G Squadron transport, two armour-plated Bedfords, stood parked ready on the volleyball court. Several figures clad in OGs were milling around talking in low tones. One character caught Lofty's eye. Slowly and meticulously he was lacing his boots on the ammunition-store steps. Lofty brushed past him, undid the padlock and pushed open the heavy metal armoury door. He stood still for a moment peering into the store, getting his eyes used to the gloom inside, then set to work issuing the ten GPMGs and 2,000 rounds of ammunition for the day's zeroing detail on Arzat ranges. Working with quick mechanical precision he didn't take long. As the last 200-round liner of GPMG link rattled its way onto the back of the Bedford, he began securing the ammunition-store door. 'Time for breakfast and a quiet cup of tea,' he said to himself.

* * *

Two thousand metres away, in the dark foothills of the Jebel Massif, I could clearly see the vivid flashes of six mortar tubes leaping into the night, dramatically illuminating their concealed baseplate positions. Nearer, from the Jebel Ali, the muzzle flashes of incoming machine-gun and rifle fire sparked white-hot gloom. What the hell's going on, I thought, where's the DG night picket? Green tracer from an RPD light machine gun rioted furiously against the walls of the DG fort on the northern edge of the town. A frenzied salvo of mortar bombs suddenly impacted, blowing away part of the perimeter wire. The fire mission crept slowly forward until the last round exploded on the edge of the town, sending pieces of shrapnel each the size of a fist screeching over the Batt House.

Since arriving in Dhofar in 1971, during the months spent skirmishing with the Adoo on Operation *Jaguar*, I had developed a sort of sixth sense, a feel for contacts with the enemy. I had a bad feeling about this one; it looked like high drama. Over the last three months there had been several stand-off attacks on Mirbat, with the Adoo bugging out after scattering four or five mortar bombs inside the barbed-wire perimeter fence. The Adoo had just been letting us know they were there, trying to prove their virility, maintain their morale. But this time it was different. The intensity of this deployment had all the tell-tale signs of a determined attack.

With my heart beating furiously against my rib-cage, threatening to burst through at any moment, and with a sickening surge of gut fear hardening like cement in my stomach, I squinted through the dark at the defensive layout of the Batt House. It seemed totally inadequate against the firepower of the attacking Adoo, a shanty-town hut against a nuclear bomb. Over to my left, on the north-west corner of the flat-roofed building, a GPMG in the sustained-fire role had been mounted in a sandbagged sangar. Behind the gun, awaiting the order to open fire, their eyes aching intensely with concentration, crouched Roger and Geoff. From my sandbagged sangar on the north-east corner of the roof I looked down to a pit ten metres away from the house. I could just make out the wiry figure of Fuzz hunched over the illuminated dial sight of the 81mm BATT mortar. At his elbow knelt Tak, almost invisible in the gloom, cradling a high-explosive mortar bomb in his hands as though it were a rugby ball. To the rear of the mortar position, Tommy worked frantically preparing the mortar bombs for firing, unscrewing the plastic tops of the containers, withdrawing the bombs and checking that the charge cartridges were securely in position, withdrawing the safety-pins, replacing the prepared bombs in their containers – fins protruding from the openings to facilitate easy withdrawal – and stacking the containers in a tier system so there would be as many as four dozen bombs ready to hand at any one time.

I glanced over my shoulder to the far side of the command-post sangar. I looked at Bob, the CPO. Calm, cunning and totally professional, he stood balancing the mortar plotter board on the edge of the sangar wall as if he was about to conduct an orchestra. In his right hand, held close to his ear, was a Tokia walkie-talkie. He was staring intently in the direction of the Adoo mortar line. His sunburnt brow became as furrowed as a seventy-year-old Sherpa's as his mind wrestled with the problems of estimating bearing and elevation for the BATT mortar site.

That, then, was the sum total of our defences. All in all, with our Second World War twenty-five-pounder, .50-calibre Browning and 81mm mortar, compared to the firepower of the Adoo, it was as if we had brush-handle battering rams against a reinforced steel door. If we had known also that we were outnumbered by nearly thirty to one, we would have already been mentally composing a plea of mitigation for an imminent confrontation with our Creator.

My appraisal of the Batt House defences was suddenly interrupted by a noise on the pyramid of ammunition boxes that led up to the sangar. I looked round to see the grim face of Mike Kealy, the commander of our eight-man civil-aid team, appearing over the sangar wall. His morphine syrettes, watch and ID disc on the para-cord swinging around his neck rattled noisily when the cord became briefly entangled with his SLR as he pulled himself over the sangar wall. On his feet he wore only a pair of flip-flops.

He crouched and moved quickly across the floor of the sangar, carefully avoiding the open ammunition boxes, and took up a position just by my right elbow. His face spoke a thousand words. He was trying to inject some interpretation of the situation into his logical Sandhurst mind. He looked me square in the eyes and, holding my stare, said in a quiet, steady voice, 'Go down to the radio room and establish communications with Um al Gwarif.' As I applied the safety-catch to the .50-calibre, I heard the throaty swish of an artillery round. We both ducked as a blinding flash followed by the crump of detonation sent a large plume of smoke spiralling crazily skywards from the centre of the town. Christ, that was no mortar, I thought, with a shiver of trepidation.

I ran down the sangar steps, crossed the small open area leading to the radio room, pushed in through the door and seated myself at the folding six-foot table. On the table, amidst a pile of message pads, codebooks and well-thumbed *Penthouse* magazines, stood the PRC 316 patrol radio set. The set was already tuned in, so it was just a matter of turning it on, adjusting the fine tuner slightly, then hitting the morse key. With the set switched on, the mush in the earpiece of the headset sounded like hailstones on a skylight. I gripped the morse key between index finger and thumb and tapped out the net call sign: 'OA. OA. This is 82. Radio check. Over.'

A bead of sweat broke out on my brow, rolled down the side of my face and splashed a dark stain onto the dusty cover of the codebook. As I waited for the reply, my finger quivered nervously on the morse key. Suddenly the base signaller at Um al Gwarif sparked into life and keyed back the answering code: '82. 82. This is OA. QRK 5.'

I unclenched my jaw and let out a low sigh. Relief swept though me as I heard the morse signal boom through the earpiece at full strength. I was just reaching for the codebook when a sharp explosion rocked the Batt House. The building shuddered violently from wall to wall as bits of plaster fell from the ceiling, and for an instant the room was filled with choking dust. Things outside were getting extremely serious. Looking down at the cover of the codebook, I realized it was going to take too long to code messages before keying them back to base. It was at this point that I took the first major decision of the battle that was developing all around us: I would ignore the complicated coding procedure and send all messages to Um al Gwarif in plain-language morse. This was a major deviation from regulations, a serious breach of security, as all radio messages in Dhofar required coding before transmission. Fuck the rulebook, I thought, as I gripped the morse key and tapped out my message, the Adoo know we're here anyway! 'OA. OA. This is 82. Contact. Under heavy fire. Wait. Out.'

As I finished the message and placed the headset on the pile of message pads, another explosion pummelled the Batt House, the sudden intensity of the explosion rocking the building to its foundations. It felt like being at the epicentre of an eight-Richter-point earthquake. Sand ran down in fine trickles from the expanding wall cracks, and big pieces of plaster from the wall in front fell onto the signals table, covering the spare radio batteries in dust and masonry.

* * *

Lofty gave the padlock a couple of tugs. Having reassured himself that the armoury door was once more securely locked, he turned and set off

The perimeter fort at Mirbat. The coastal town's first line of defence, it was initially manned by just twenty-five Dhofar Gendarmerie and one Omani gunner. (Jason Jones Travel Photography/Getty)

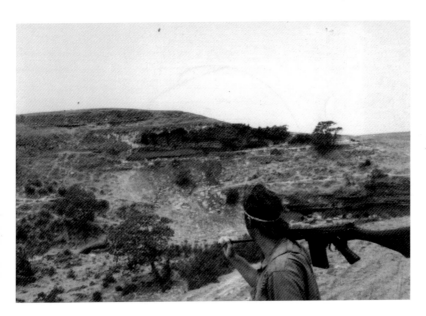

Operation Jaguar. *The first campaign for a newly badged SAS trooper.*

Changing the clutch on a Land Rover, Mirbat 1972. The battle was fought a week after this photo was taken.

On patrol in Dhofar, 1971.

Mirbat plain as it was at the time of the battle. At left is the battleground, with the perimeter fort most clearly visible. On the other side of the town the G Squadron reinforcements landed by helicopter, about 3kms inland, and advanced around the back of the town to relieve the Batt House and the Mirbat forts. This photo was taken from a Skyvan resupply aircraft in 1974. (Brian Harrington Spier)

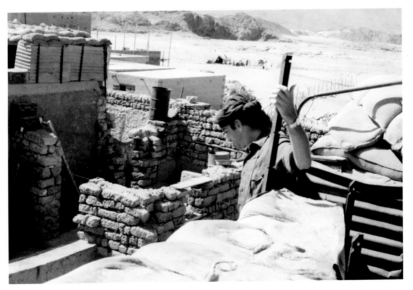

An officer in the sangar on the roof of the Batt House, in a 1974 photo taken before the British withdrawal from Oman. The .50-calibre machine gun position was on this wall in the foreground, and the Jebel Ali can be seen in the distance. (Brian Harrington Spier)

The view from the Batt House to the perimeter fort, where the twenty-five-pounder lay. This is the 500-metre run that Mike Kealy, Tak, and Tommy all made under heavy enemy fire to keep their single artillery piece firing. The gun pit was Laba's stand-to position, where he raced as soon as the first Adoo mortar shells exploded. (Brian Harrington Spier)

The front of the perimeter fort. The remains of the twenty-five-pounder gun pit can be seen in the foreground. During the battle, the heavy wooden door behind was locked, denying Tak entry. (Jason Jones)

The battleground of Mirbat. The Batt House (1), and the Wali's fort (2) surrounded a small cluster of buildings, including a school, a mosque, and a clinic run by the BATT medics. The wadis provided some cover for those dashing to relieve the fort, which lies to the north-east. (Brian Harrington Spier)

Looking over the battleground, towards the Jebel Massif. The Jebel Ali, the hill on which the Dhofar Gendarmerie picket was killed, is to the left, off the edge of this photo. (Brian Harrington Spier)

Labalaba during Operation
Jaguar, *Dhofar 1971.*

Labalaba's posthumous Mention in Despatches. Many believe he deserved the VC.

Labalaba's grave. The hero of Mirbat is buried in St Martin's Church, Hereford, under the winged dagger of the SAS and the harp and crown of the Royal Irish Rangers. Tommy's grave is in the row behind Laba's.

Left to right: General Service Medal; Falklands Medal with rosette; SAF Campaign Medal; Victory in Dhofar Medal. The Accumulated Service Medal, for 1,000 days in a combat zone, has since been awarded.

REGIMENTAL CONDUCT SHEET [Only Regimental Entries, see Q.R., 1975, paragraph 5.551 and Annex H to Chapter 5.]

Army Form B 120 (Revised 3/77)

Sheet No. _____ TWO

Record of continuation sheets

Sheet No.	Date taken into use	Initials of Officer

This sheet will not be destroyed on any account

1. Number	2. SURNAME (capital letters)	3. Christian or Forename(s)
▮▮▮▮		Peter

4. Regiment, Corps, or Service (pencil entry)	5. Date of attestation, etc.	I CERTIFY that the particulars in boxes 1–6 are in accordance with the documents in my possession and that an appropriate entry has been made in the relevant AFB 121.
RE	26.12.61	
	6. Date of submission of AFB 116/176A	R.O. 3
	070379	Records Officer / Officer Commanding — Date 8·3·79

Station	Rank	Court, etc. (C.O., D.C.M., G.C.M., A.S.A., Court of Summary, Jurisdiction, Crown Courts, etc.)	Date of Trial	Offence(s) of which accused was actually found guilty (The full statement and particulars of each offence should be given)	Name(s) of Witnesses (Summary disposals only)	Award, sentence or direction dispensing with trial	Signature of C.O. or person whose duty it is to make the record
Kowloon	Lcpl (ASgt)	Magistrates Court S Kowloon	21 Sep 78	On 12th August 1978 in Red Mill Inn, 20 Ashley Rd, Gd Floor, Kowloon, in this Colony, being a public place, had with his an offensive weapon namely a knuckle-duster without lawful authority or reasonable excuse, contrary to Sect 33 (1) of the Public Order Ordinance, Chap 245, Laws of Hong Kong.	Police	Be Caned for Six (6) Strokes	[signature] A MELLOR RO3 Records Offr
					SPENT 20 SEP 1983		1A3 Trg Regts RE

The sins of Soldier I! Pete Winner's Regimental Conduct Sheet.

down the steps. He was surprised to see the same trooper still there doing his boots up. He was just about to question the usefulness of this time-consuming exercise in perfectionism when the Duke approached. With a grim look on his face he took Lofty to one side and told him quietly that the town of Mirbat was under heavy attack and that he should prepare a step-up operation and a quick move to the SAF headquarters at RAF Salalah.

* * *

Things were getting hot. I could hear the throb and rumble of distant explosions, the murderous whistle of shrapnel. I decided it was high time to move back to the command-post sangar on the roof and get the .50-calibre Browning into action as quickly as possible. I sprinted up the sangar steps to my gun position, checked the ammunition belt once more and eased the safety-catch to 'fire'. Suddenly an enormous explosion slammed into the tower of the DG fort. It gouged away a huge chunk of masonry, leaving a gaping hole with jagged edges silhouetted against the first glimmer of dawn. The flash of detonation briefly illuminated the Second World War-vintage twenty-five-pounder artillery piece located in the defensive sangar at the base of the fort walls. The figure of Laba was clearly visible kneeling behind the gun's protective armoured shield. 'That looks like a 75mm RCL,' Bob shouted at Mike Kealy above the roar of six explosions detonating in rapid succession. My ears screamed with the roar of the noise and for a moment I was totally disorientated, until I realized with immense relief that it was the BATT mortar initiating a pattern of harassing fire.

I shook the noise and confusion out of my head and studied the landscape that rolled away into the distance. The darkness was receding, and the first flickers of light revealed the blurred and shadowy foothills of the Jebel. The battle now began to flare up, roaring into a sense-stunning and mind-numbing conflagration. The din and racket of combat reached a frenzied crescendo, all the noises running into one another to create a surreal clatter of machine guns, green tracer ricochets leaping like firecrackers around the buildings and walls of the town, the throaty swish of incoming mortar rounds followed a few seconds later by the deadly crump of detonation, and the ear-splitting explosions of the BATT mortar returning fire. I looked at my watch: it was just about 0600 hours.

The two machine guns on the roof remained silent. This could be another stand-off attack, albeit a particularly determined one, so we didn't want to risk compromising our position by giving the Adoo tell-tale gunflashes to aim at. I looked over to the left. The thirty Askars in the Wali's fort evidently had the same idea. The ramparts bristled with old bolt-actions .303s, but they remained silent. As the first rays of dawn filtered through the thick, spongy monsoon cloud hovering over the plain, the flashes of the Adoo mortars became paler. Far from diminishing as the light exposed the Adoo mortar positions, the bombardment increased in its ferocity. The racket from the Spargen heavy machine gun and the LMG fire gradually escalated. All along the wire for as far as the eye could see, plumes of sand and earth spewed as if from distant volcanoes. Winged daggers of flame leapt skywards. The air above and around me teemed with the cracks and hisses of the lethal lead zingers. I glanced nervously around the roof. The other members of the team were at their stand-to positions, poised over their guns like cobras ready to strike. We were waiting, our fingers welded to the triggers, every muscle and nerve rigid, screwed tight with the tension of facing the unknown.

* * *

Lofty, showing no sign of emotion, his face blank and expressionless, his eyes methodically searching the reopened ammunition store, worked flat out issuing all the GPMGs, semi-automatic rifles and M79 grenade-launchers he could find. A human chain was formed to hump box after box of 7.62mm link and ball ammunition from the store to the trucks. Between them the men had soon loaded 20,000 rounds. In a matter of minutes the ammunition store had been cleaned out. As dawn broke over the volleyball court, the dangerously overloaded Bedfords, sagging heavily under the weight, stood ready to go.

* * *

Forty well-armed Adoo formed into an extended line and began moving at a brisk pace across in front of me towards the DG fort, following the line of a shallow wadi that ran between the perimeter wire and the Jebel Ali. I stared at them intently. The figures broke into a run. My eyes felt like oversized pebbles pressing achingly into my sockets as I continued to stare. Beads of sweat broke out on my forehead. My breathing resumed a steady and rhythmical pattern. I took up the first pressure on the trigger of the .50-calibre.

This was it. The few fleeting moments before the battle is joined. Too late now to do any more training. Too late now to fine-tune and zero the weapons. Too late now to strip and oil the mechanism's liquid-smooth action. The same pitch of intensity in human experience as at birth and death themselves. The fear wells up and you welcome it. Without fear you cannot perform fully. Without fear you do not have that razor-edge extra of concentration that can make the difference between you and the enemy, between life and death. The few fleeting moments before battle is joined. You mentally go through every move. There's nothing else to do. You are on automatic pilot. You lapse into unconscious behaviour patterns, comforting routines: the curled finger caressing the smooth metal trigger, the moist hand rubbing against the rough trouser material, the blowing of cool air onto tightly bunched-up fingers, the anxious chewing on the bits of broken skin at the edges of fingernails. The few fleeting moments before battle is joined.

I looked around at Mike Kealy for the order to open fire. Mike had his back to me. He was looking towards the DG fort. With a sudden shock I realized he was oblivious of the movements taking place in the Jebel Ali area. 'Mike,' I screamed, my voice rising above the noise and confusion raging around us, 'look over there!' My left arm pointed towards the running figures. Mike spun around and stared in the direction I was pointing. He squinted into the acrid fog of fumes and mist and white phosphorous smoke wafting over the undulating ground in the middle distance. His blank stare remained fixed. His face registered no reaction.

I was confused, my concern growing by the second as I waited for a response. After a few moments his right hand slowly came up to the pocket in his OG shirt, undid the button and withdrew a pair of thin-rimmed spectacles. He pushed his face forward into the glasses and leaned over the parapet of the sangar as if some invisible force was drawing him towards the hottest part of the action. He carefully removed his glasses, wiped off the dust on his loosely flapping shirt-end, unhurriedly replaced them, peered into the distance once more and said slowly, 'Don't open fire yet, it could be the Firks returning.' His voice sounded calm, steady and deliberate amid the tumult of the moment. Still the figures on the plain swept on unhindered. They looked confident, inspired. Then their weapons came up into the fire position. A split second later, a Bren gun rattled out its deadly rhythm from the Wali's fort. A short pause followed, then the whole of the ramparts suddenly exploded into a frenzy of action.

* * *

Lofty went through a last-minute visual check. Completely satisfied that G Squadron were now prepared and fully equipped for battle, he walked swiftly towards the transport waiting to whisk them off to the airfield at RAF Salalah. As he jumped into the driver's seat of the nearest Land Rover, he could see that over by the armoury the same character was still there doing his boots up. 'Hey, Scouse,' shouted Lofty, leaning out of the window as he eased the Land Rover down a gear and drew level with the armoury steps, 'you can stop doing your boots up now, it looks like we're going into combat.'

* * *

'Open fire!' screamed Mike urgently above the chatter of machine-gun fire and the crackle of the old Lee Enfield .303s. The calmness of his voice had given way to ruthless urgency.

The moment that battle is joined. The moment that the days, the weeks, the months of training have all been leading up to. The moment that seems to stand still, but is only as long as the split-second pause at the end of a pendulum's swing. Only a split second, but one that holds in its brief passing a thousand thoughts, a million feelings. The moment that battle is joined. My first major battle, but my mind is drilled to precision. The steel shutter has crashed to the floor; humanity is locked outside beating its fist on the cold, hard surface. No sound, no cry of compassion can penetrate within. I am now ruthless and single-minded. It's a kind of insanity. You have to be insane to survive. It's me or him. At our level, at the sharp end, when the whistle blows, it's not politics, it's not heroics or war-games, it's not the big picture of world affairs. It's me or him, it's kill or be killed, it's the quick and the dead, the law of the jungle. Over the top and into no man's land. Brutal, efficient killing. We take them out, we root them out, we blow them away, we pick them off, we eliminate them. We don't really kill them. It's something we block out of our minds completely. We don't even talk about it among ourselves. The enemy are not human beings. They are everything else – a threat, an attack, a movement in a rifle sight, a running, lunging, shouting, adrenaline-charged shape. You don't think of them as real people, as fathers, family men, with a picture of the wife and kids in the back pocket. You can't afford to. It's me or him. They are to be eliminated, it's as simple as that. That is my duty, my role. At this moment, my only concern is to not let my mates down. I am determined to not be a weak link. In the split second that battle is joined, we are together, we are a team, the sum is now greater than the parts. We have fire in our eyes, ice in our veins and metal in our hearts. The highly lubricated precision machine bursts into life. The moment that battle is joined.

We opened fire simultaneously, unleashing a hail of GPMG and .50-calibre bullets at the assaulting Adoo troops. The running figures became a focal point where the red tracer and exploding incendiary rounds converged in a frenzied dance. It rained fire and lead. Where moments before there had been an orderly advance, parts of the line now faltered and collapsed. Figures staggered under the impact of the heavy .50-calibre rounds, falling, twisting, screaming. We traversed the machine guns right, a burst of fire scything a lethal harvest among the exposed enemy. But still the Adoo kept coming. Wave upon wave on the plain, dull shapes advancing at speed. They were in groups of ten and well spread out. They were moving steadily, relentlessly, towards the DG fort and the town. A nightmare scene, with bodies appearing to fall and get up again like homicidal zombies, there were so many of them.

Machine guns chattered, rifles cracked, yells, curses and explosions echoed across the plain. But still the Adoo kept coming. They reached the perimeter fence and tore with bare hands and blind zeal at the vicious, razor-sharp barbed wire as if it was tinsel on a Christmas tree. A Carl Gustav rocket-launcher spat death, the rocket impacting against the fort wall and showering the immediate area with shrapnel and flame. In the gun pit, the gleaming figure of Laba applied the gun drills with slick precision, like a sweating stoker feeding a boiler in the smoky bowels of a steamship. Laba worked feverishly to load and blast the big gun at the fanatical enemy struggling through the fence only a few metres away. The twenty-five-pounder was traversed through forty-five degrees and used in the direct-fire role, dealing death at point-blank range. The breech detonations threw up clouds of cordite. A pall of acrid fumes hovered over the firing mechanism, growing bigger by the minute. Dead Adoo were soon hanging over the perimeter wire like ragged crows strung out along a farmer's fence.

Back at the Batt House, Tak received an ominous message on his walkie-talkie. The strained voice of Laba informed him that a bullet had grazed his chin. He added that otherwise he was all right, but Tak, his fellow-countryman, was not convinced. He knew Laba too well – a huge man with huge courage and huge modesty; a man of few words when the going was tough. The radio then went dead and defied all Tak's attempts to re-establish communications.

In an instant, Tak had decided he must join his Fijian brother at the twenty-five-pounder. Still wearing his flip-flops, but with a pair of desert boots dangling round his neck, he grabbed his SLR and, with the sharp staccato of the Adoo Spargen MGs ringing in his ears, started his 500-metre run towards the DG fort. Even with high-velocity rounds cracking and popping around him, with explosions to the front and rear of him and with shells screeching overhead, all he heard was the roar of the crowd, the shrill scream of the whistle, all he saw was the flash of the cameras. He was back on his favourite rugby field at home in Fiji, and he was going for the greatest try of his life. He had been a top-class flank forward in his time, and long swerving runs were his speciality. Taut lines of hot tracer zipped across in front of him as he surged forward, bobbing and weaving.

Two hundred metres to go. He was still going strong, the breath burning in his throat. One hundred metres to go. Bullets threw sand and dirt all around him as they hit the ground close to his feet. He swerved around the lunging tackles. Fifty metres to go. He could see the try line, nothing could stop him now, his determination was incredible. A mortar bomb burst nearby. The roar of the crowd became louder. A piece of shrapnel made him duck instinctively. He tucked in his head to avoid an out-thrust hand. Ten metres to go. The try line was within reach. In a final lung-bursting sprint he ran up the last incline that led to the DG fort. He launched into the air, his body arching across the line. He was up and over the sangar wall. Miraculously, he had reached the gun pit without so much as a scratch. He had scored the try of a lifetime.

Tak steadied himself, the rasp in his throat slowly subsiding. Through a mist of perspiration, he surveyed the chaos in the gun pit.

Laba was firing the gun on his own. He had looked around briefly, nodded an acknowledgement, pointed to the unopened ammunition boxes and turned back to the gun. Tak squinted through the smoke and dust at the broken ramparts of the fort. If there was any firepower left in the fort, if he could organize and motivate the DG to help out in the gun pit it could make all the difference.

Tak carefully eased himself over the sandbagged wall of the sangar and, crouching to the lowest profile possible, sprinted across the short distance to the great doors of the fort. Grasping the large metal handle in his left hand, SLR at the ready in his right, he twisted the locking mechanism and pushed. Nothing. He swore in Fijian, and shouted at the DG. Surely they would recognize his voice – he was always up there drinking tea with them. Impatiently he cranked the mechanism again before putting the full weight of his muscular shoulders behind the next push. Still nothing. The door was solid. He cranked the mechanism a third time. Every moment he remained in this exposed position he was in mortal danger. Suddenly, he heard the heavy metallic sound of a bolt being withdrawn. The door creaked open and there, to his relief, in the small opening he recognized the dark features of the Omani gunner. Tak motioned him over.

Just then a burst of HMG fire hammered into the fort wall above Tak's head, sending small stone splinters whining viciously past his ear. He sprinted back to the cover of the gun pit. As he jumped over the side of the sangar wall, he glanced around to see the Omani, who had started to follow him, spinning around and around, pirouetting like a ballet dancer with an insane grimace on his face, then falling to the ground clutching his stomach.

The big gun continued to belch flame. It looked brave and defiant, spitting death at close range. It wasn't called the artillery machine gun for nothing – and in the hands of Laba and Tak, the Adoo must have thought it was belt-fed! They were now working as if possessed, shovelling the shells into the breech like madmen. Open breech, slam a shell in, ram it with baton, fire. Open breech, eject hot spent cartridge-case, kick it away. The same mechanical sequence repeated time after time after time. Laba, covered in sweat, the front of his clothes blackened with cordite, had no time to think. He just kept laying the sight – bubble up, line, bubble up, line. On. Fire! And still the Adoo kept coming. As one group reached the wire and was gunned down, another replaced it almost instantaneously. Wave after wave surged up behind their fallen comrades, willingly following the same fate, a relentless waterfall of human beings plunging over the precipice of life.

The heat from the red-hot breech made sweat run down Tak's face in dirty rivulets. Open breech, slam one in, ram it, close breech. Fire! A small group close to the wire disappeared in a rain of shrapnel, smoke and dust. Open breech, slam one in, ram it, close breech. Fire! Tak was soon surrounded by piles of empty ammunition boxes and spent cartridge-cases. He searched frantically for another shell. His hand closed around a dull brass case – and in that instant he tumbled backwards and sideways. The pain in his shoulder exploded into his brain as he slumped against the sangar wall. He looked towards Laba without uttering a sound. Then another round parted his thick black hair and ploughed a bloody furrow through the skin on top of his skull. 'Laba, I'm hit!' he shouted violently in Fijian, the whole of his upper body suffused with the pain of the 7.62mm round lodged somewhere in his back, perilously close to his spinal column. Another millimetre, and his spine would have been snapped in two.

The mighty twenty-five-pounder now stood silent. Without Tak to feed the beast, the situation was desperate. The gun pit was in real danger of being overrun. Laba looked around in despair. Tak was propped against the sangar wall, his shirt soaked in blood, somehow, with a supreme effort, summoning up the strength to take well-aimed shots with his SLR at the figures near the wire. We've got to have more firepower, thought Laba. His eyes darted anxiously from left to right. He knew what he was looking for.

There it is, there's the firepower we need, he thought triumphantly. He began to crawl through the piles of spent shell-cases towards a 60mm mortar leaning upright against the sandbagged wall of the gun pit. The sweat ran down his face, stinging the wound on his chin. The noise of Tak's SLR made him flinch momentarily and then he was moving again, oblivious to the hot brass cases burning his hands and lower arms. A Titan figure, seemingly immortal, he was now dangerously beyond the cover of the twenty-five-pounder's bullet-riddled armour shield. He stood up and reached out for the mortar. Bullets whistled all around him. He seemed driven by a superhuman energy, possessed by a single-minded duty to fight his fight, to stand by his comrades. Above the din of the battle he could just make out Tak's voice shouting in Fijian, 'Get your head down, get your head down!'

Laba didn't hear the bullet that killed him. His only sensation must have been an intense burning pain on his neck, as though someone had stabbed a red-hot needle through his jugular. And then he was falling through darkness, lost forever. The mighty Fijian warrior had breathed his last. Tak was on his own.

'I don't like it. It's gone too quiet. Something's happened over at the fort. If the gun position goes we've got big problems. I need a volunteer, someone to watch my back. I must find out what the situation is over there.' Mike Kealy's terse request cut through the tense atmosphere in the radio room. Gone were the boyish features of the young, inexperienced troop officer. His face now had a grim, grey-edged, hard-bitten look about it that none of us had seen before. We were standing before him in a half-circle, Bob in the centre, me to the right, and Tommy, his stocky frame resting casually on the SLR propped up by his side, to the left. I had just finished keying out the 316 radio to Um al Gwarif requesting an airstrike and a casevac chopper, and I now joined the other two in agreeing that we should all share the risk. This was the ultimate Chinese parliament. We argued our case vehemently, but Mike's mind was made up. He would only take one man, the Batt House medic, Tommy, who could give medical assistance to any casualties we had taken at the gun pit. Mike reasoned that Bob would be required to take over command of the Batt House and control the air strike, and I was needed to give covering fire on the .50-calibre and also to man the radio set.

Disappointment and feelings of guilt swept over me as I removed my belt kit. Why had I not been chosen to go with Mike? Was I not good enough, not experienced enough? I desperately wanted to get over to Laba and Tak. In a short space of time I had grown to like the two Fijians enormously. I felt a bond with them as if they were my own brothers. I admired their great courage, their fortitude and stamina, their laconic understatement in the face of real danger.

I swept aside the negative thoughts worming through my brain and considered the worsening situation. I looked down at the luminous face of my watch: it was just 0700 hours. A short time ago we had heard high-velocity gunfire passing over our heads from the south of Mirbat town. That could mean only one thing – a co-ordinated attack from the north and the south. We were surrounded. It was shit or bust now. Once more, I sat down at the radio table and repeated the request for Startrek on the 316. The jets were really going to be at a premium now, if only the wretched monsoon mists and low cloud would lift.

Unexpectedly, we gained a temporary respite when a strange lull descended on the battlefield. The Adoo troops had faltered and fallen back into the shallow wadis that interlaced the plain leading up to the fort. The heavy concentration of automatic fire they had earlier employed had emptied their magazines, and in the excitement and desperation of the assault, some had forgotten to carry out their magazine changes. Others had not had time to reload from the bandoliers of ammunition they carried across their chests. The firing had become spasmodic; only the mortars kept up their relentless bombardment. More ominously, though, there was a lack of return fire from the twenty-five-pounder and the DG fort. Bob and I tried to raise them on the walkie-talkie several times, but it remained silent. Maybe they had discarded the walkie-talkie in the heat of the moment. Maybe their set had been blasted apart by a bullet. Maybe Tak and Laba were taking advantage of the temporary lull to replenish their ammunition from unopened ammunition boxes. Or perhaps the silence was more sinister.

'And don't forget to change into your desert boots.' Bob's parting words to Mike as he left the radio room for the roof interrupted my increasingly busy train of thought. I looked across the room at the two figures preparing themselves for the mercy dash to the fort. Mike had retrieved his dusty desert boots from under his camp bed against the far wall, and was kneeling down and pulling very tightly on the laces. Tommy stood patiently watching Mike, steeling himself. He had a calm, totally committed look on his face. All his doubts, his fears, his private thoughts had retreated far within. Between his index finger and thumb he held the cocking handle of his SLR. He eased the breechblock back slightly to confirm that he had chambered a round. He fingered his belt kit and the patrol medical pack slung across his back.

Just then a long burst of machine-gun fire from the GPMG on the roof above us shook the room violently, adding renewed urgency to the situation. 'OK Tommy, it's time to go,' said Mike quietly. They were through the door and gone without another word.

Racing back up to the .50-calibre Browning, I noticed Roger disappearing down the steps to the front door. He must be going to the beach to retrieve the casevac chopper, I thought, as I flipped the safety-catch on the machine gun to 'fire'. My mind settled on the task in hand. It was my job to give covering fire. The palms of my hands began to sweat. For the next few minutes the lives of two of my comrades rested on my shoulders. I prayed I would be switched-on enough to carry the burden. I watched intently as Mike and Tommy began edging their way past the mortar pit. Once around it, they sprinted for a shallow wadi about ninety metres on the right. The wadi ran roughly in the direction of the fort and would afford some cover from the machine guns outside the perimeter wire. Bullets were still zipping by. They came in flurries, but the fire lacked intensity and direction. So far, the Adoo had not noticed Mike and Tommy. I held my fire. I did not want to draw attention to the two running figures. I felt the belt of incendiary resting easily in my left hand. I feathered the cold metal of the trigger with the index finger of my right hand. I watched nervously as the two figures worked their way towards the fort, moving in short rushes, ten or fifteen metres at a time, pepper-potting forward, one man running, one man covering. So far so good. Their luck was holding. My grip on the ammunition belt became tighter.

They had gone about halfway to the gun pit when the whole battlefield erupted. The Adoo had spotted them. Where minutes before the firing had been spasmodic and half-hearted, there was now a delirium of noise: the crack of rifles, the rattle of machine guns, the crump of detonating mortar bombs. A heavy machine gun barked over to the east of the fort, the taut lines of tracer zipping across the path of the two moving figures. Like a dragon belching fire, the gun spat hot tracer closer and closer to its prey.

I had to act quickly and decisively. There wasn't a moment to lose. I lined up the sights of the .50-calibre on the tongues of flame sparking from the flash-eliminator of the Adoo machine gun. My breathing got quicker – short, sharp and controlled. The skin on my forehead tightened. The pressure of concentration felt like a thumb-press on my third eye. I took careful aim and squeezed the trigger. The gun jerked and ejaculated its seeds of destruction, and I watched with professional satisfaction as the Adoo machine gun disappeared under a stream of red tracer and exploding incendiary rounds. My body relaxed with relief. There would be no more trouble from that quarter.

The inferno of fire raged on. The two figures were surging outwards in short rushes across the bullet-swept plain. The closer they got to the gun pit, the faster they ran. Onwards, onwards, stop, cover, rush. The bullets hissed and spat around them; the breath rasped in their windpipes and burned their lungs. They ran faster than they had ever run in their whole lives, their limbs pumping like pistons in full-throttle combustion engines. Then Tommy was up the slope to the fort and vaulting the sandbagged wall into the sangar, with Mike hot on his heels.

A quick look at the chaos in the gun pit told Mike that there was more advantage to be gained by making for the ammunition bunker a few feet to the right. As he jumped down into the bunker bottom, he felt something soft and fleshy under his desert boots. He glanced down. To his horror he realised he was standing on the mangled body of a DG soldier, his foot squelching in the bloody peach-pulp of guts where the stomach used to be. He shrank back in disgust as if he had just turned back the sheets on a lover's bed and found a rotting corpse crawling with maggots. A movement caught his eye. Squinting through the dust and smoke that hung in the air dirtying the lenses of his glasses, he discovered he had company. Wide-eyed, trembling and half paralysed by fear, a DG soldier cowered in the far corner of the bunker like a snared rabbit. The Omani was shaking in every limb. 'Pull yourself together and move the body,' snapped Mike as he stared across the gun pit, already assessing the situation.

The battle reached a crescendo, the air thick with splinters of steel and lead. A hurricane of fire whirled and roared across the Mirbat plain. Flash followed flash followed flash, as bright as the flares from an arc welder's torch. Before one explosion of light had travelled down the optic nerve and burned itself on to the brain, another followed in instant succession, creating a stroboscopic display of agonizing intensity. Tak, totally resigned, his face misshapen with pain, was still propped against the sangar wall, his SLR still hurling hot lead. A short, stocky guerrilla straddled the perimeter wire, his snarling mouth hollering and gesturing towards the fort. The silver whistle around his neck made an excellent aiming marker. Tak's rifle kicked. With a scream of pain, the man slumped across the wire, lifeless like an old rag, still holding his AK-47 in the grip of death.

The twenty-five-pounder, though silent, was still under concentrated fire. The hail of bullets sparked and ricocheted off the barrel and armoured shield as if the gun had just been cast in a foundry and was being smoothed off by heavy-duty abrasion wheels. Tommy was crouched attending to the body of Laba. He straightened slightly and half turned towards the medical pack. It was his last, fatal movement. If the medical pack had been an inch nearer, or if it had been lying to his right instead of his left, or if he'd checked Laba's wounds for a split second longer, his head would not have crossed the path of the murderous Kalashnikov round spinning its way faster than the speed of sound. A casual stoop saved de Gaulle from the assassin's bullet. Tommy was not so lucky. His time had come. He tumbled forward, scattering the spent shell-cases, and then lay motionless.

Screams of agony filled the air. The swishing roar of a Carl Gustav rocket arcing over the position deafened Mike and Tak. Then the Adoo broke through the wire, a ragged line of desperate, yelling figures, their faces distorted with hate. They dashed in ones and twos, all notion of formation now cast aside, towards the cover of the north wall of the fort and the dead ground to the rear. Tak's rifle kicked twice in quick succession. A figure fell twitching to the ground. Like crabs on a beach scrambling for a dead fish, the Adoo worked their way round the fort walls, hungry for possession of the big gun. No words were exchanged between Mike and Tak. Each man knew instinctively what he had to do. On either side of the fort, Kalashnikovs disgorged death. And still the Adoo kept coming. The most courageous among them were now only six or seven metres away at the two front corners of the fort wall. Mike and Tak were looking death in the face.

* * *

Halfway to Salalah, and Lofty Wiseman, sensing a big battle in the air, was driving like a man possessed. He careered the Land Rover over the rough desert track pitted with potholes. The men in the rear cursed in full technicolour with every crash and jolt. Clutching in one hand the twisting steering wheel like a Wild West rancher gripping the saddle on an unbroken horse, Lofty bent down and felt between his feet for the three cardboard boxes that were sliding around the floor in rhythm with the madly lurching vehicle. With his head level with the dashboard, he alternated his gaze rapidly between the road and the boxes as his fingers pulled back the tape that secured the contents. He flipped open the lid on the first box and his hand dived in like a mechanical grab in a fairground booth. Straightening up, he passed the first handful of morphine syrettes over his shoulder as though he were giving Smarties to impatient kids. 'Here you are, lads, grab these syrettes.' Another handful found their way into the back of the vehicle. 'Inject the morphine straight into the upper thigh – instant nirvana.' The patrol in the back scrambled for the syrettes and stuffed them into every available empty pouch they could find.

* * *

Mike and Tak picked off the swarming Adoo as fast as they could double-tap. A fusillade of LMG fire ripped into the ground just in front of the ammunition bunker. A round cracked so close to Mike's skull he could feel the vibration of the bullet as it sped over him. Then came the green pineapple. It sailed gracefully through the air and landed smoking on the parapet of the bunker. As Mike ducked down in the confined space, the grenade exploded. An agonizing ringing drummed in his ears, and the acrid smoke of detonation ripped through his lungs. Miraculously, he was uninjured. He eased himself back upright, trembling slightly. Through the smoke and confusion he could just make out the pathetic figure of a DG soldier. You're no bloody good to me grovelling down there, he thought. He did a quick magazine change and threw the empty magazines at the frightened man. 'Fill those!' he barked, kicking the cringing soldier violently on the soles of his boots. And then he was up and firing again.

He squeezed the trigger twice, as near simultaneously as is mechanically and humanly possible, and caught the guerrilla at the corner of the fort wall full in the face. Blood, brain and hair exploded in a crazy stain across the whitewashed wall. The guerrilla slumped to the ground, arms spreadeagled by the shock, with the remains of his head sliding down the wall after him. Then came a salvo of grenades. They arced over towards Mike and Tak like clay pigeons; several exploded nearby with a dull crump. More grenades – and then Mike and Tak froze in horror, their minds switched into a slow-motion nightmare. A grenade hit the parapet at the far end of the ammo bunker and, after what seemed like an age, rolled over the edge. Mike could clearly see the black smoke from the six-second safety fuse as it burned its way towards the detonator. He watched, mesmerized, unable to move as the smoke curled upwards. One... two... three. He counted the seconds, each one booming in his head like a chime from Big Ben. Four... five... six. He steeled himself for the impact of the explosion that would do to his body what his bullets had just done to the head of the guerrilla by the fort wall. Seven... eight... nine. He prised open his rigid eyelids. The smoke fizzled out. Ten... eleven... twelve...

Mike stared in disbelief at the matt green object that should have been the last thing he saw on this earth. It was a misfire, a damp squib. He thanked God in the briefest manner possible and searched the immediate area for the next target, more determined than ever to defeat the Adoo now that he had survived the hand grenade. Cursing aloud, he took a bead on the camouflaged figure at the corner of the fort, squeezed the trigger, saw the figure fall and reached for the two-way radio.

* * *

'Laba's dead, Tak and Tommy are very seriously injured.' The sound of Mike Kealy's voice on the walkie-talkie cracked the atmosphere in the command-post sangar like obscenities mouthed in the middle of a hushed church service.

I was stunned. I couldn't believe it. Laba! Dead! The din of the battle receded like surf on a distant shore, and my eyes seemed to go out of focus. The next thing I knew, I was re-experiencing my grandfather's death, the first time I'd lost someone close. A wave of desolation, loneliness and separation had engulfed me then. I had hardly been able to believe that this warm-hearted, laughing, noisy man was now stretched out cold, stiff and lifeless in his grave; the same man whose morning ritual I used to watch with unending awe. He would pour boiling water straight from the kettle into his shaving mug, and then, with a flourish designed to impress me even more, he would plunge his dishevelled shaving brush into the scalding water. After a quick wipe around the stunted remains of a stick of hard shaving soap, he would jut out his jaw, open his mouth and with a half-smile, half-grimace apply the dripping brush to his chin with rapid circular movements. I would always wince at this point, feeling sure that the boiling water must hurt terribly, secretly hoping I wouldn't grow up to be a man for a very long time yet if that was what grown men had to do.

'Get on the set and call for reinforcements.' Bob turned and looked at me, his face still amazingly calm, his voice quiet and steady. I was back in my first major battle, well and truly bloodied, my initiation into manhood brutally complete.

Without a word, my resolve stiffened to ruthlessness by the news of Laba's death, I pushed the safety-catch on the .50-calibre to 'safe' and raced down the steps to the radio room. I began hammering the key, pushing out the message in clear, precise morse. 'Zero Alpha. Zero Alpha. This is 82. Message. Over.'

'82. This is Zero Alpha. Over.'

'Zero Alpha. This is 82. Laba dead. Sekonia VSI. Tobin VSI. Situation desperate. Send reinforcements. Over.'

There was a brief pause, and then the reply boomed in my ear. '82. This is Zero Alpha. Roger your last. Send wet rep. Over.'

'Wet rep!' I shouted aloud in great exasperation to no one in particular. A weather report at this stage of the game! My mind was so filled with the exigencies and emotions of the moment that I didn't realize the implications of this request from base. I jumped up quickly, jarring the radio table with my knee and sending the chair teetering across the floor. I poked my head out of the door. Cloud base must be about 150 feet, and the flags were limp on the flagpoles. That would do. '0815 hours. Heavy cloud. No wind.' I hammered out the wet rep, waited impatiently for confirmation, then sprinted back to my position in the command post.

As I brushed past Bob to get at the .50-calibre, the high-pitched roar of a jet's exhaust filled my ears. Two Strikemaster jets broke into view through the mass of sullen cloud and monsoon mist. The speed at which they appeared meant that they must have been in a holding pattern circling immediately above the battlefield. The jets streaked over the town and raced eighty feet above the plain, contour-flying on a low-level ground-attack mission. The bravery of the pilots in these weather conditions and in the face of sustained fire from the Adoo was awesome.

'Who's controlling them?' shouted Bob urgently.

'Must be Roger,' I screamed in reply above the noise of the howling jet engines. 'He thought another casevac chopper was arriving and took the blue sarbe to direct it to the beach helipad. He must be controlling the jets with it.' I broke off as the ammunition-box pyramid behind me rattled violently. I spun round to see the sweating face of Roger appearing over the lip of the sandbagged wall.

'The Seventh Cavalry has arrived!' he shouted triumphantly. 'Here's the sarbe; I'm going to help with the wounded on the ground floor.' And with that he was gone again.

Bob grabbed the ground-to-air radio and settled down to control the jet strike. 'Hello, Red Leader. This is Batt House. Enemy left and right of the fort. Over.'

'Roger, Batt House. How long have they been going at you?'

'Since dawn,' Bob informed them.

The pilot gave away no sign of reaction to the feats of resistance taking place below him. 'Roger, Batt House. They are like ants down there – I can see hundreds of them.'

The jets began wheeling and swooping like hungry gannets searching for prey. The enemy now ceased firing on the fort and the town and, throwing themselves behind the nearest cover, concentrated the firepower of their light machine guns on the flashing jets. Hot green tracer flurried upwards in a blizzard of burning steel across the sky. The first jet went into a vertical dive, spraying bullets and death around the perimeter wire to the left. The second jet, amidst a barrage of machine-gun fire, stabbed two rockets into the wadi to the right. The wingtips of the aircraft seemed to brush the walls of the DG fort as they sped past. And then they pulled up violently, twisting and dodging, stretched to the limits of their capabilities, to escape back into the mist. Moments later they reappeared, plunging out of the cloud across Mirbat Bay. They streaked around the contours of Jebel Ali, with lines of HMG in hot pursuit and closing. Then they headed low-level back into the maelstrom to start their strafing run over again.

All along the wire, rockets and lead cascaded from the sky. The Strikemasters tracked each other. More bullets, more rockets, and then the jet on the right spawned a 500kg bomb. The large black object plummeted earthwards and buried itself among the enemy massing in a shallow wadi just east of the fort. The smoke-filled air was rent asunder by a blinding flash and a thunderous explosion. But disaster followed triumph. One of the jets caught a burst of HMG fire in the tail as it made an impossibly low pass at the enemy. It banked steeply and then, subdued as if ashamed of the jagged hole in its tail section, it drifted away to the north, limping into the cover of the mist. The remaining jet circled for a while, then swooped downwards into one last steep dive, hammering the Adoo along the perimeter wire. Finally, its ordnance totally expended, it followed its partner into the clouds on its way back to Salalah.

The pressure on the fort area had been momentarily relieved, but for how long? At this point a new and disturbing dimension crept into the battle. Heavy firing could be heard behind us, well over to the east. Scarcely able to withstand the enemy frontal assault, our nerves began to pulsate at crisis level with the realization that the Adoo had regrouped and were counter-attacking from the east. That meant only one thing: not only had our air support gone, but we were now completely surrounded.

* * *

The pilot of the first Huey 205 chopper with G Squadron reinforcements on board just glimpsed the rear half of a Strikemaster jet being swallowed up in the mist as he flew the 205 on a ground-assault mission, heading for the south side of town.

Crammed into the confined space behind him were Doug, Scouse, Ian, Dave, Dennis, Neil, Ian, Eric and Stonker. They carried with them a formidable array of weaponry: five GPMGs plus at least 1,000 rounds per gun; an M79 plus 100 bombs; and SLRs with 100 rounds of 7.62mm per man. As they broke through the mist, Doug looked through the window and saw five heavily armed Adoo dragging a body. Hell, Doug thought, they're going to open up on the chopper! 'Adoo! Adoo!' He grabbed the pilot's shoulder, shook him and screamed in his ear to make himself heard above the racket of the rotor blades, emphasizing his words with a pointed finger jabbing down at the figures on the ground. To his surprise, as the chopper banked and came down, the Adoo disappeared into the mist.

Once on the ground, the fighting patrol rapidly went into all-round defence 3,500 yards from the town to secure the LZ for the arrival of Alistair Morrison, the squadron commander – who in 1977 would make a name for himself during the hijack of Flight 181 at Mogadishu, advising the German GSG 9 commandos who stormed the jet – and Wilbur Watson, the troop corporal. Minutes later they arrived in the second chopper, bristling with firepower and carrying 10,000 rounds of back-up ammunition for the gimpies. With G Squadron reinforcements fully deployed, twenty-four men in all, Alistair assessed the situation and made an instant decision. Allocating one group to secure the LZ for the second wave of reinforcements, he directed Stonker and Doug's group to move towards the east of the town to flank the fort and winkle out pockets of enemy resistance on the way. Just as they were moving off, four figures appeared out of the mist, calmly looked in their direction and walked over a rise no more than seventy metres away. Ian squinted at them through the powerful binoculars and shouted, 'They're Adoo, they're Adoo! They've got AK-47s!' They ran forward tactically to the top of the rise, engaged the four figures – who by now were running furiously in the direction of the Jebel – and downed them in a hail of machine-gun fire. The exchange attracted the attention of other Adoo east of Mirbat. Stonker and Doug's group now came under sustained fire.

* * *

The walkie-talkie crackled into life and cut though our anxious thoughts. It was Mike again. For one trembling moment I thought it was more bad news. With relief I learned that Mike and Tak were still clinging onto their position by the fort. Mike was requesting mortar fire support. In calm, measured tones he asked Bob to put down a ranging bomb in the wadi, seventy-five metres to the right, and then he would make corrections. Bob did his mental arithmetic – a quick estimation of range and charge. He gave a long, low whistle. This was going to be tricky. He would have to do a line-of-sight shoot based on estimated range, charge and elevation. Bob shouted on his first fire mission to Fuzz, who by now was firing the mortar on his own. He watched anxiously as Fuzz pulled the bipod legs backwards, set the mortar at an extreme angle, bubbled up the sight and slid an HE bomb down the barrel. I watched the performance with growing frustration and alarm. The .50-calibre was causing big problems. I was down to single shots, and after each one I had to recock the firing mechanism myself. The breechblock and slide had become clogged with brass shavings, the result of firing the gun over a long period without a number two to feed the heavy belt.

Fuzz's mortar bomb whooshed over the plain in a blurred crescent and exploded harmlessly 800 metres away on the far side of the fort. Mike's correction crackled over the air and Bob relayed his estimated fire mission to Fuzz. Each correction after that brought the exploding mortar bombs closer and closer until Fuzz reached maximum elevation on the bipod. At the next correction from Bob, Fuzz hesitated for a moment, glanced at Bob as if he'd asked him to summon a heavenly army of angels from the clouds and then, with one determined movement, clasped the mortar barrel to his chest and raised it until the bipod legs dangled clear of the ground. 'Frag them,' roared Bob. Fuzz looked like some demonic dancer in a drunken two-step as he hugged the barrel as tightly as he could and sent bomb after bomb spilling down on the enemy position.

The welcome drone of aircraft engines filled our ears again. Two more Strikemasters pounced down out of the clouds in a shallow dive across Mirbat Bay. They banked, levelled off to obtain greater accuracy and, hugging the contours, screeched across in front of us at the start of their strafing run.

Bob clicked on the blue sarbe. 'Hello, Red Leader. This is Batt House. Enemy HMG on Jebel Ali. Also rear of fort.'

'Roger, Batt House. It looks hot down there.'

'Roger, Red Leader. Sheets of lead! Sheets of lead!'

The two jets split in a scissor-like manoeuvre. The first one, in a low pass, went for the fort. The second banked round steeply, plunged like an out-of-control kite, levelled off at the last moment and streaked towards the HMG positions on Jebel Ali, going for a gun kill with its two wing-mounted GPMGs. Death and destruction sluiced down from the skies. The sangars on top of the hill disappeared in a hail of red tracer. The Stikemaster screamed past Jebel Ali and out across the bay. After banking round lazily like a condor on hot thermals it began its next run in, fifty feet above the water, this time going for a rocket kill. It roared over the top of Jebel Ali sticking rockets into the circular sangars like darts in a dartboard. The top of the hill disintegrated in a huge ball of flame. As the jet disappeared back into the clouds, surging masses of black smoke climbed up into the mist, then began to drift as the force of the upper-air breeze overcame the impetus of the explosion. The two Strikemasters returned for one final low pass, fifty feet above the perimeter wire, just to one side of the fort. Smoke and flame belched from their wings, and rockets and tracer rained down on the now-retreating enemy. The high-pitched jet whine deafened the occupants of the fort as the two aircraft shrieked overhead in a spectacular display of firepower. Then they pulled upwards, climbing steeply through the mist until they were both swallowed up by the heavy monsoon clouds.

The second wave of 205 helicopters, carrying the other ten G Squadron men, a doctor, two medical orderlies and a mound of ammunition, hovered down onto the LZ like giant sycamore seeds. It was 1020 hours. Alistair Morrison decided he and his group could now move forward to clear the enemy from the south of the town. They closed on three Adoo and a GPMG concealed in rocks on the beach. After a brief exchange, the enemy were killed. Five more Adoo were spotted in a wadi behind a ridge. Alistair's group advanced to within 200 yards. Three of the five were gunned down and two wounded. A third party of Adoo opened fire from another clump of rocks. All six died. As with the others, their bodies were searched and their weapons removed. Many more enemy still remained between Alistair and the town. The group pushed forward with fire suppression and flanking attacks, capturing a small hill on the way. More Adoo fell. Two RPGs and a number of rockets were recovered. A helicopter, flying tactically, brought over a platoon of the Northern Frontier Regiment to join Alistair's group. Then, as one body, they moved in disciplined formation towards the Batt House.

* * *

As I watched the two Strikemasters race away into the distance, my tired, bloodshot eyes were drawn to the landscape east of the fort about 2,000 metres away. I could see figures appearing on the skyline. They looked a disciplined and determined body of men as they surged forward at a brisk pace, methodically working their way across the undulating ground in extended-line formation. Now that the frontal onslaught of the Adoo had been broken by the jet strikes, a tiny voice inside me reasoned that we had just a chance of surviving if this new threat from our rear could be overcome. Mechanically, my body reduced by fatigue to functioning only as a well-programmed automation, I lined up the front sight blade of the .50-calibre on the lead figure. I might be down to single shots, but that was all I would need to take the officer out. Who were they? I wondered. At this range it was impossible to tell. They appeared merely as black dots in an expanse of dull brown sand and rock.

Around the fort and Jebel Ali area the cacophony of battle had decreased significantly. Only the occasional burst of machine-gun fire cracked over the Batt House. All our attention could now be focused on the new developments in the east. I looked at Bob. He was switched on to the same direction. He seemed to be agonizing over a decision.

At a signal, the figures suddenly swung off to the right flank and disappeared into the shallow wadis on the far side of the town. Heavy firing in the area erupted almost immediately.

'Go down to the radio and get a sit rep from base. Find out what's happened to the reinforcements,' shouted Bob suddenly, his voice taking on a new urgency.

A few moments later, the morse crackled over the headset. The message was music to my ears. I hardly dared believe it. My mind struggled to prevent wishful thinking from overtaking cold logic. I looked at my watch: it was just 1030 hours. I did a quick time appreciation, fearful that my initial calculations might prove wrong. Twenty minutes by chopper from RAF Salalah to Mirbat, five minutes to shake out on the ground. It was like finding the last piece to a puzzle. Surely I was right. My conclusion fitted the facts perfectly. The figures on the skyline must be the second wave of G Squadron reinforcements. I was now convinced of it. Even though I was exhausted and seemingly drained of all emotion, a warm surge of exhilaration swept up from deep inside me. I was jubilant as I raced up the sangar steps with the good news.

Bob's face remained as cool and impassive as ever as I relayed the contents of the message. 'I guessed as much,' he said quietly, then added, totally professional to the end, 'I've sent Fuzz up to the gun pit with the other medical packs to assist with the wounded. I don't think we need the mortar any more.' With that he grabbed his SLR and, leaning on the parapet of the sangar, began sniping at the retreating Adoo. Following his example, I cocked the .50-calibre, cursing the stoppage, chambered a round and searched the perimeter wire for a target.

Across the battlefield the orgy of violence and killing had diminished. The Adoo were in full retreat, shoulders bowed with the humiliation of defeat. They slunk away in ones and twos across the shallow wadis of the plain, heading towards the ignominious safety of the mist-shrouded Jebel. The sad, quiet debris of battle lay everywhere: abandoned weapons, clothing and webbing, the dead and the dying. It was a forlorn and desolate scene.

Dark thoughts began to drift through my mind as we continued to snipe at the occasional exposed guerrilla. How could all this have happened? Why had we not been warned? It was later revealed that the green slime had received Grade A reports that groups of Adoo had been seen massing in various parts of the Jebel over the last few weeks, many of the reports coming from our own local Firqat. Perhaps they had chosen to ignore them. My critical ruminations were interrupted by the heavy thudding noise of a helicopter's rotor blades. A Huey had landed minutes before in the area of the twenty-five-pounder gun pit, and now it hugged the contours of the plain as it made its way across to the Batt House. The chopper went into a hover as it flew level with the main door of the house. Then, amid swirling clouds of dust and sand, it landed fifty feet away from the side of the building.

'Go down and help Roger with the casevac.' I could only just hear Bob's voice above the noise of the helicopter blades. I scrambled my way quickly down the two flights of stairs to the ground floor. As I got to the bottom and began making my way to the front door, I thought that I had stumbled into an abattoir refuse-room. The whole area was covered with wounded men, either lying down or propped up against the walls. The floor was littered with bloodstained shell-dressings. The stench of blood, sweat and urine was everywhere. Clusters of flies buzzed frenziedly around, feeding greedily on open wounds and bits of flesh and bone. Roger knelt, trying to force a drip into the trembling arm of a man with a gaping hole in his throat. The man's rapid breathing made a terrible whistling and bubbling noise.

I looked past Roger and through the front door. The pilot of the casevac chopper had his arm out of the cockpit window and was beckoning me towards him. The rotor blades thudded above my head as, doubled up, I ran quickly towards the cockpit and stuck my ear into the open space of the window. It was a struggle to make sense of the pilot's words through the noise, like trying to have a conversation with a loom-operator in a clatter-filled weaving shed. 'Go and check the bodies in the rear!' he shouted slowly and deliberately, his face an inch from my ear. 'Confirm to the loadmaster which bodies belong to the BATT.'

I didn't relish the task. Moving carefully along the side of the Huey, I came to the passenger compartment. The sliding door was already open and the loadmaster was kneeling. He nodded grimly at the recumbent shapes in the back and said nothing. There were six bodies covered by blankets on the stretcher racks. This wasn't going to be easy.

I started with the three racks to the rear. Bending down, I pulled the blanket off the body on the bottom stretcher. The man looked as if he had been hit by a large piece of shrapnel. One ear had been ripped away and the side of his head was caved in. But his facial features were intact and he was clearly a Gulf Arab. I covered him quickly with the blanket and moved on.

The body on the stretcher in the middle was also an Arab. He looked about seventeen. His head was uninjured and his eyes stared back at me with a glassy expression. A cold shiver ran up my spine and I threw the blanket back over the staring eyes. Give me combat any time, I thought as I stood up to look at the top stretcher.

I peeled the blanket back nervously, wondering what horror this one concealed. The man lay face-down, his right arm crooked upwards, his forehead resting on his wrist. The face was obscured. I swallowed hard and grabbed the arm. To my horror it felt solid. The flesh was as cold and rigid as the barrel of a GPMG. The hair prickled on the back of my head. I paused a moment and tightened my resolve.

Then, with both hands gripping the elbow, I levered the whole body upwards and over. I was sledgehammered by the shock. I stared at the face. Even with part of the chin shot away and with sweat, blood and grime matted down one side, I would recognize those dark contoured features anywhere. It was Laba.

I finished checking the other three bodies as quickly as I could and scrambled out to suck in some fresh air. It was now 1230 hours. I had been on the go for seven hours solid. With the sharp taste of bile still in my mouth and the stench of death in my nostrils, I stared out over the plain of Mirbat, smouldering and broken, like a fire-ravaged pine forest. I watched a column of grey smoke slowly rising from above the fort, unsure whether I was glad to be alive or not. It was a day I would never forget, a carnival of carnage; a lifetime of experience crushed down into a few hours. I stared out over the flat expanse of Mirbat plain.

10

Belfast

The night sea was waveless but full of motion, crawling and glinting like a swarm of bluebottles on a cowpat. Faintly flashing lights gathered around the harbour, a handful of frozen sparks kindling brighter as we drew nearer. A depressingly heavy rain slanted through the sky and hissed onto the ferry foredeck. 1974. What a start to the New Year! It was enough to make even the most resolute of resolutions slide into the sewers with the next pint of beer or evaporate into thin air with the next cigarette.

I looked out over the dark water that separated us from the port. In my mind's eye, all I could see was the flat, smouldering expanse of Mirbat plain. The battle of Mirbat was a hard act to follow. Had it really been just two years ago? I felt dull. After the adrenaline high of Dhofar, the monotony of routine training and tours of duty was beginning to take its toll. Maybe, just maybe, this trip would be the breakthrough back into real action. We didn't expect to come face to face with the enemy in open battle; we were too tightly bound by the restrictions. And yet, here, anything could happen.

Belfast. The home of barricades, bombs and marching bands. The graveyard of the professional soldier's ambitions, the career charnel house of the military intelligence officer. We were heading into the gutters and backstreets, bowed under the weight of bergens loaded to overflowing with Whitehall edicts and Rules of Engagement to be obeyed like the Ten Commandments. We were to face an opposition unfettered by constitutional laws and diplomatic niceties. It seemed we were completely pinioned, like men buried to the neck in sand, watching the rising tide of political confusion, intelligence confusion, military confusion and legal confusion. Belfast! A nervous breakdown just waiting to happen.

To most of us mere soldiers the answer was simple. All you had to do was take out the ringleaders and the rest would fold like a pack of cards, putting the 'revolution' back twenty or thirty years. The Head Shed could not see this, and kept banging on about the democratic society and working within the law of the land. I began to have a sneaky suspicion they could smell easy medals, but I couldn't prove it. One thing I did know: with its sinister streets and alienated population, Belfast was no place for highly trained special forces. This was a job for armed police – switched-on operators who knew the law and could pick their way through the minefield of rules and regulations.

We hadn't got off to a good start. When we passed under the red-and-white striped security barrier at the main gate to Bradbury Lines on our way to the ferry terminal at Liverpool, our regular freelance journalists were encamped as usual a few metres from the main gate. It was a public highway so we were powerless to stop this. God only knows what they made of our sudden departure and it was no doubt the cause of much journalistic musing. Absolute secrecy would be the key to our very survival, let alone our success, so it was crucial we weren't tailed.

Thankfully we weren't, but things continued to get worse. By the time we arrived at the departure lounge of the ferry terminal, a late-night hush had descended all around. The lounge consisted of two linked rooms. The one further from the door – the larger of the two – was completely deserted. Dimly illuminated, the faded holiday-resort posters peeling from the walls failed miserably to cheer it up. In the corner of the smaller room by the entrance, a young couple in their early twenties huddled together. The woman was half asleep, her head lolling on the man's shoulder.

We split into ones and twos and drifted into the corners, trying not to appear too conspicuous. Easier said than done – we didn't exactly look like holidaymakers. Even though we were dressed down in our Oxfam reject specials to give the impression of itinerant building-site workers or casual hotel kitchen staff, and even though we assumed a nonchalant, bored air as if to say we'd made the journey so many times that we could afford to relax into indifference, it was hard to remain unnoticed. We studiously avoided all conversation, other than the occasional whispered remark, in order not to fill the rooms with telltale English accents. But in spite of all the obvious precautions it was extremely difficult for a team of highly alert men who had spent weeks and months as a family, eating, sleeping, drinking and training together, to melt unobserved into the background. We tried hard not to let the bond, the group consciousness that mates in a team create automatically, project and spill over into the confined space of the departure lounge.

Suddenly the door at the end of the room rattled open and in trudged a soldier dressed in full combat gear. I recognized him immediately. A year earlier he had been attached to the Regiment as part of the administrative support team, and six months ago he had been posted back to his parent unit. He must have been returning from leave to rejoin his regiment in Northern Ireland. He took one look round the room, his eyes twitching with recognition, and promptly darted into the toilets. Christ, I thought, this will be all round the NAAFI in Palace Barracks, Holywood by tomorrow night – our cover blown and we haven't even set foot in Northern Ireland yet!

The crossing brought a further twist of complications. We'd all assumed false names and adopted new regiments for the duration of the passage. One of the lads had a passion for painting wild flowers, believe it or not. In between operations in the more remote exotic locations, he would often search out an especially rare specimen, display it in a beer bottle and do a quick pencil sketch to take home with him. He had chosen the suitably horticultural pseudonym Orchid and completed his disguise by promoting himself to Sergeant. Unfortunately, he'd also decided to attach himself to the Royal Tank Regiment. Halfway across the Irish Sea, as fate would have it, a major from the Royal Tank Regiment decided to check the passenger list. He spotted the name Sergeant Orchid and put in a request for a meeting over the ship's tannoy system.

'Sergeant Orchid, Sergeant Orchid, Royal Tank Regiment. Report immediately to Major Jones in the Bursar's office.'

The tannoy boomed through the night air above the hissing sound of the bow-split waves rushing down the side of the ship. We were in the bar, riveted in our seats. No one dared move. One or two looked up and glanced at the others, saw their impervious, stony expressions and quickly lowered their gaze once more. Sergeant Orchid swallowed a mouthful of beer and continued to read the day-old newspaper he had picked up in the departure lounge. He betrayed not a single flicker of emotion. Without speaking a word we all knew one another's mind. We'd decided to sit it out in the hope that the major would eventually lose interest and conclude that there had been a clerical foul-up. It paid off. After one repeat of the message and a further agonizing wait, the tannoy fell silent. Our trip was beginning to look like the roughcut of a *Carry On* film, a real comedy of errors.

The final dangerous farce was played out on the ferry terminal in Belfast. As we disembarked, the pungent smell of diesel fuel, decaying seaweed and gutted fish flaring in our nostrils, a creased photo of our Belfast contact man was produced. The passport-size colour photo was of a young and impressionable-looking Rupert with short, slick black hair and an old school tie. It had probably been taken when he was serving with the Eton Rifles. We scanned the disembarkation area looking for a likely candidate. Nothing! Just a rather seedy-looking character with long, straggly hair. He was hunched into a well-worn donkey jacket, smoking a cigarette and looking distinctly furtive. With one arm crooked he was leaning heavily on a red sign marked with white lettering, 'Passengers only beyond this point'. It tilted at a precarious angle under his weight, even though its base was set in a concrete-filled tyre to prevent it from blowing over in the wind. The man gave no sign of recognition and looked more hostile by the minute.

I began to feel anxious. Our first time in Northern Ireland and already we were drawing attention to ourselves – a dozen heavies with long hair and second-hand clothes trying desperately to look inconspicuous. A movement caught my eye. It was Kevin. He'd just drawn out a grey, crumpled, elephant's ear of a handkerchief and was unconcernedly flapping it about. He trumpeted loudly into it, sniffed, then stuffed it unceremoniously back into his trouser pocket, finishing off the job with an exaggerated wipe with the back of his hand. My heart sank. Nicknamed the Airborne Wart, with a face like a blistered piss-pot, Kevin would look suspicious at a memorial dinner for Al Capone! What chance of passing himself off as an innocent traveller arriving in Belfast in the middle of a bleak January night!

I shivered violently and turned up my collar against the incessant rain. Where was the contact? The only sign of life was a pair of cats quietly growling at each other from either end of a piece of bacon rind. I glanced at my watch. Five minutes had ticked by. I looked out to sea. A series of red and green pilot lights glowed in the distance beyond the harbour entrance. Within the harbour itself, long thin concertinas of light shimmered on the surface of the water opposite the lamps on the far side of the docks. The harbour walls, dirty brown smudges on the black of the night, loomed up out of the water. They were topped by a rambling collection of offices, warehouses, huts and tanks. As I gazed at the buildings, the desolate cry of an unseen seagull pierced the night air, reinforcing the stillness and quietness.

I felt another wave of unease. Where was the transport? I blew into my hands and shuffled my feet, getting increasingly alarmed by our impossible attempts at inconspicuousness. I walked over to the exit door and squinted through the glass. All I could see was row upon row of empty cars lined up in the floodlit car park. Another five minutes had passed. My gaze returned nervously to the shabby figure still leaning impressively on the sign as he exhaled a cloud of cigarette smoke and flicked the dog-end into the water.

At last, Arthur, the team leader, realizing it was too dangerous to wait any longer, seized the initiative and made a decision. It was a risk, but there appeared to be no alternative. Looking incongruously smart in a houndstooth jacket and cavalry twills, the rain dripping from his check tweed cap, he walked over to the donkey jacket still leaning on the sign. In the dull, dingy surroundings he looked like a member of the aristocracy approaching a purveyor of pornography. We all tensed, ready for immediate action. A brief exchange of veiled speech followed, and then suddenly it was all over and we were being hurriedly ushered through the exit door into the back of a blue minibus. Contact had been made.

The rain hit the windscreen like a jet from a high-pressure hose as we sped through the grey, depressing streets of Belfast. It felt strange to be driving on the left. Whenever I had caught a boat or flown across a stretch of water in the past, I had always ended up driving on the right-hand side of the road. Now I was in limbo, neither at home nor abroad. The road signs were not in an exotic foreign language as my mind half expected – but the place-names were almost culturally strong enough to qualify as foreign: Larne, Ballymena and Ballymoney going north; Lisburn, Lurgan and Craigavon going west. I rubbed the sleeve of my jacket over the condensation on the side-window and peered out. The night rain had oiled the glistening streets and slicked the pavements with dark puddles. Rows of derelict buildings dripped with angry graffiti: 'Touts will be shot'… 'Provos rule'… 'Smash the

H Blocks'… 'No surrender'… 'Brit bastards out'. Whitewashed gable-ends flashed past publicity hoardings in the battle for hearts and minds – raw, powerful murals, created by tragically skilled hands, depicting clenched fists, sectarian insignia and sinister hooded figures clasping lethal weapons.

What a far cry from the deep wadis, the open rolling plains and the blue skies of Dhofar. As the minibus turned onto the M1 taking us south I reflected on the events of the last few years. Since the battle of Mirbat in 1972 my troop had been decimated. Laba and Tommy lost, Tak was still convalescing, Bob was an instructor on training wing, Fuzz and Roger had left the Regiment, and Mike Kealy, his three-year tour of duty as a troop officer completed, had been posted back to a desk job at Group Headquarters. You have to be good at pushing paper to be promoted to field marshal.

I looked around the faces in the bus. Our composite team had been drawn from all four troops in the squadron; misfits who just happened to fit together. But there was not a Fijian in sight. After long and hard deliberation, the best brains in the Kremlin had finally decided in their wisdom that the Fijians, with their swarthy features, short black curly hair and heavy accents, wouldn't quite blend in with the local population, especially on the Falls Road and the sprawling estates of West Belfast. Valdez in Andy's Town – no way! It was perhaps just as well. I recollected that when we'd been at Otterburn taking part in a fire-and-movement exercise just before going to Dhofar, Valdez had joked about how his team had occupied their spare time by improvising a Ouija board. Whether they'd meddled with something they shouldn't have is a matter for speculation. What is certain is that during Operation *Jaguar* all four of Valdez's team were wounded. Stranger still, there had been a fifth man in the room there, Sam, who had refused to take part. He came through Operation *Jaguar* completely unscathed. We had a difficult enough job in Northern Ireland as it was, without having to contend with the supernatural as well!

As the memories drifted and eddied I must have dozed off. My next sensation was one of confusion as I was abruptly awoken when the minibus suddenly jerked to a halt. In an instant I was alert, rubbing at tired eyes, a stiff muscle in my neck making me wince with pain. The side-door slid noisily open and I was given my first view of the SF base that was to be our home for the next few months. In the bitter January dawn, the base looked squalid and claustrophobic. We were surrounded by high corrugated-tin walls topped by wire netting to thwart attack from RPG-7s, the Russian-manufactured rocket-propelled grenades. Concrete sentry boxes at regular intervals and camouflage nets stretched across sandbagged roofs gave added protection. The interior of the base was an untidy clutter of Portakabins serving as both accommodation and admin offices. Soldiers dressed in combat gear and a few uniformed police were milling around amongst a line of Saracen armoured cars. I felt strangely disorientated in this cold grey world. At this time of morning in Dhofar the sun would be growing more powerful by the minute; waves of heat would be spreading across the terrain. The quivering shapes of the hills would be melting into the blue of the sky generating an upsurge of morale. Here there was only damp, gloom and depression.

Over the next few days, I became more and more convinced that I had to get out of this place. We thought we'd come here to take out the opposition; in reality we were armed with the latest Japanese camera technology and told to photograph them. The green slime, the ink boys, were building an empire and using a mountain of photographs to justify it. I could feel the beginning of a new and dangerous frustration: the frustration of not being able to get to grips with the enemy. After Dhofar you could call it post-operation depression.

* * *

'Alpha from Zero. Radio check.'

It was the duty operator. I gripped the volume control on the radio and turned the sound down, then pressed the speak button with my index finger. 'Zero from Alpha. Read you. Fives.'

'Alpha from Zero. Roger. Out.'

As we finished the radio check I nodded to Taff and the car lurched forward with a squeal of rubber. The high corrugated-tin gates swung open with an electronic whine, the CCTV camera relaying our exit to the duty operator in the operations room. We were sitting in a four-year-old Vauxhall Viva that must have had a dozen number-plate changes in its short existence. The green bodywork was battered and there was rust everywhere – along the crumbling sills, on the jagged door bottoms, disfiguring one corner of the boot and eating into the dented towing hitch. A casualty of the constantly damp, saline air, it looked like a typical working vehicle: thoroughly neglected through lack of interest, lack of ambition and lack of money. The car would blend in nicely with the traffic. The last thing we wanted to do was draw attention to ourselves around the streets of West Belfast. I glanced at Taff, the driver. He looked as battered as the transport. A lean man with long, dirty-blond hair, he was wearing a scruffy overcoat and a face as sour as last week's wine. To the casual observer he could have been anyone – a farm labourer, a navvy – but he was as watchful as a hunting heron. Taff had been kicking around Ireland a long time and had served in the mobile reconnaissance force. Experienced, dependable, he had the nerve of a New York steeplejack. He was to be my guide for today's familiarization exercise. He knew Belfast like his own backyard.

We were each armed with a 9mm Browning automatic pistol. The four thirteen-round magazines gave me a feeling of security. The pistol grip of the 9mm protruding from the Len Dixon holster dug uncomfortably into my ribs as we drove out through the heavily reinforced gate sangar. We passed the perimeter lights and the coils of Dannet barbed wire and turned onto the main drag, heading straight for the M1. Once we got under way I removed the pistol, placed it on my lap between my legs and concealed it under a copy of the *News of the World*. As I read the latest 'Gay Boys in Bondage Scandal at Guards Depot', I held the pistol at the ready, thumb on safety-catch, trigger finger resting on the trigger guard.

Having consumed the sensational revelations, I brought my mind back to the day's job. With my free hand I clicked open the glove compartment, rummaged among an assortment of screwdrivers and fuses, a couple of torches and an old fan belt and took out a well-thumbed Ordnance Survey map of the area. The M1 looked like a blue artery, carrying the flow of life-blood straight into the beating heart of Republican West Belfast. This was our second week, and the last couple of days had been spent driving around various locations throughout the province, familiarizing ourselves with them, getting the feel of the place. Today, the big one: Belfast, the worst urban guerrilla battleground in the Western world.

The night-time temperature had dropped well below zero. The frost had spiked the grass verges with glinting feathery crystals and fossilized the trees into frozen wayside sentinels. As we drove through the dawn, the tyres of the vehicles in front of us showered our windscreen with speckles of road grime. Taff flicked on the wipers to clear our view, but succeeded only in smearing multi-arced lines across the glass. The wash liquid had frozen solid in the hopelessly narrow plastic feed-tubes. Then the low-lying early morning sun hit the filthy screen, momentarily blinding us. As we neared the city, Divis Mountain rose through the haze like a giant submarine coming to the surface in a sea of mist. The haze almost completely obscured the scramble of houses that jostled for position on the Republican estate at the mountain's base.

We turned off the motorway and took the west link to the Grosvenor Road roundabout. Following the left-hand lane up Grosvenor Road, we then headed straight for Provo land – past the Royal Victoria Hospital, through the traffic lights and on up the Springfield Road towards Turf Lodge. Taff navigated the area with practised ease, giving a running commentary as he drove. He had a story for every street. 'They fired an RPG at an armoured pig from behind that wall.' His voice drifted over the crackle of a radio transmission. 'They command-detonated a dustbin full of explosives from across the wasteland.'

Everywhere I looked there were reminders that this was a highly dangerous environment. Row upon row of terraced houses had had their doors and windows bricked and boarded up, their gardens reduced to bombsites. It reminded me of the photographs I'd seen of London after the Blitz. The pavements outside the pubs were barricaded with huge concrete blocks. The pub windows were caged in heavy-duty wire netting as protection against car bombs and petrol bombers. The people on the streets looked cold and hostile. The dickers were out: bands of youths stood on street corners giving us maximum eyes as we drove past, as threatening as black gangs in the Bronx. Hyperactive, they had the air of mescalin-crazed marionettes: their eyes darted up and down, their heads jerked from side to side, and every now and again their arms shot out, hands flat and outstretched, palms upward.

We were now driving through Ballymurphy estate, heading for the Bullring. We hit the Whiterock Road and turned left, the sprawling Belfast cemetery on our right. The final RV. We drove on through the bleak winter day. And then we were turning left into the Falls Road, the Provo heartland, the centre of the deadliest killing grounds in Northern Ireland. We joined the stream of traffic heading towards Divis. The volume of black taxis seemed to increase significantly, their passenger compartments crammed to overflowing. A grey-painted RUC mobile, travelling just in front, swung left up Beechmount Avenue. The hard, alert faces of the two officers in the rear scanned the rooftops and upper windows for possible sniper positions.

We swept up on the Falls past the spot where an RF guy had been shot in his car. 'He forgot his counter-surveillance drills,' explained Taff simply. I peered through a hole in the condensation on the side-window, past the inside lane of traffic, at the dilapidated building on the corner of the junction with Springfield Road. Two youths lurking suspiciously in the doorway attracted my attention. I had been in Ulster only a short time, but already the same instincts that had been able to detect a presence of the Adoo in Oman had been tuned to a new level of alertness to cope with the altogether more sinister threat posed by this environment. These youths signalled danger. I felt sure something was going to happen. What, and exactly how I could not tell, but something was going to happen. Without apparent movement, I adjusted my grip on the Browning pistol, and with my other hand, quietly located the exact position of the spare thirteen-round magazine. My breathing became imperceptibly quicker as the adrenaline began to flow. I glanced at the two youths out of the corner of my eye. The first youth was standing in the shadows, his head jerking swiftly from side to side as he observed the line of traffic. His mate stood slightly forward, more exposed. He was tall and arrogant-looking, his square stocky body clothed in an old bomber jacket. Both sets of eyes zapped like tracer into the rows of cars.

Then suddenly it happened.

In an instant, the tall youth was through the inside line of vehicles and around the back of the Viva, and was wrenching the driver's door open.

'Get out the cahr, or I'll blow yer fecking head orf.'

The coarse, rasping West Belfast accent cut through the silence in the car. It sounded as if the ligaments in the man's neck and throat were being stretched by some massive effort. My heart thumped and the pumping of blood beat in my ears. A flash-flood of adrenaline surged through my muscles as my hand tightened on the pistol grip of the 9mm. Only my eyes moved as I glanced over my right shoulder. The youth was standing next to Taff, jamming the door open with one leg. He tilted his head down from above the level of the car roof so that his voice would carry into the car and not alert passers-by or other drivers. All I could see was his bread-dough gut framed in the rear window of the Viva – a perfect target for a one-second double tap. I realized he could not see me from where he was. I thumbed the safety-catch on the Browning to fire, then hesitated, my breathing coming in short, shallow gasps. Where was the shooter? Show me a shooter, you bastard! Show me a shooter! His right hand was inside the unzipped bomber jacket. What happens if it's a bluff? What happens if I shoot and kill an unarmed man? I'll be up for murder and the Regiment will have fucked up as soon as it has arrived.

But there was also the other possibility. What if we had been tailed leaving the SF base? What if the whole thing was a carefully planned operation? What if we had been set up like Figure 11 targets? Did they think we were civvies on the way to work, or did they realize we were the Army doing an altogether different kind of job? Were we the target, or did they simply want the Viva for a car bomb? In a microsecond, I unspooled the whole of the morning's journey in my mind, desperately scanning every single frame, reassessing every minor incident, seeking the tiniest clue towards the solution of the dilemma I was facing: to shoot or not to shoot.

Nothing came. There wasn't even the vaguest hint of anything sinister. But was the observation merely a reflection of my own inexperience of this urban battlefield, rather than an accurate conclusion? The thoughts ran amok through my pulsating mind. Show me a shooter, you bastard! Show me a shooter! I screamed the words so loudly inside my head I was surprised no one heard me. The youth's hand remained stubbornly jammed inside his bomber jacket. There was only one possible thing to do. If I could catch a look at his mate, I might be able to read some sign in his facial expression, or his posture might give some tell-tale indication of focused aggression. But it was risky, very risky. If he eyeballed me he would realize at once what I was up to. He would recognize the soldier's training and the soldier's reaction. Our cover as civvies would be completely blown.

There was no choice. We were otherwise caught in a split-second, deadly stalemate. Quick as the snap of an alligator's jaw, I turned my head a fraction to the left, pumped my eyeballs as far into the corner of their sockets as they would go, shuttered the youth and returned my gaze to the front. Shit! Nothing! Not a single clue as to his intentions or his state of mind. Back to square one, back to the biggest choice of my life so far: to shoot or not to shoot. Time had run out. The pressure, the urgency swelling inside my head, was about to explode through my head like a bursting tyre. No more reflection. No more option assessment. No more hesitation. I had to make a choice! Now!

'You can fuck off, you wanker.'

At that precise split second I was catapulted free of my agonizing deliberation. Taff, his lean face set hard, had made the choice for me. He gripped the Viva's door handle, and, with a violent whiplash movement, yanked it momentarily towards himself, then instantaneously outwards with all the force and speed he could muster. He hit the hijacker square in the guts with the edge of the door, cracking his knee and jolting his gun arm. The man reeled back, floundering and stumbling with surprise, his mouth twisted in a grimace of pure hate. His right arm, flailing as he steadied himself, exposed an empty hand. There was no telling whether it had been clutching a gun inside the jacket or not. That's something I'll never know.

I had experienced fear before, in Dhofar: the nervous gut feeling at the beginning of a contact before the surge of tingling warmth, the adrenaline-induced relief, gradually took hold. But this was a different kind of fear. Never before had I experienced this sudden shock effect on my mind like the jolt of ice on a raw tooth-nerve, this drawn-out agonizing hesitation, this frustration of not finding relief in the smooth, efficient operation of the trigger. 'Go, go, go!' I heard myself shouting. 'Get the fuck out of here!'

Taff rammed the Viva into first gear and jabbed his foot down hard on the accelerator. The rear wheels spun viciously, spurting gravel, steam and burning rubber. 'Come on… Come on… Come on!' screamed Taff, frantically urging on the old car. The Viva suddenly lurched forward. Taff wrenched at the steering wheel and swung the car into the oncoming lanes, the still-open door flapping wildly like a pegged-out sheet on washing day. The 1300cc engine screamed to destruction pitch as we shot through the red lights at the junction, playing a life-and-death game of chicken with the screeching, swerving traffic hurtling crosswise towards us. We took a right turn up Grosvenor Road and straightened out towards the city centre. Taff leaned out, grabbed the flapping door – miraculously still on its hinges – and banged it shut. As I stabbed the speak button on the radio, I felt a tightness in my throat, I felt the waves of fear and indignation suddenly harden into savage realization. My mind was now in gear. Professionalism had taken over.

'Zero. Alpha. Over.' The transmission was clipped, hurried.

'Alpha from Zero. Send.'

'Alpha. Attempted hijack corner of Springfield and Falls.'

'Zero. Roger. Lift-off. Will send other call sign to investigate.'

'Alpha. Roger. Out.'

As the Viva roared up the Grosvenor Road, driving towards the west link and the M1, I sank back in my seat. I looked down at the hand holding the 9-milly. It was shaking slightly. I eased the safety-catch to 'safe' and replaced the copy of the *News of the World*. I could have been the lead story in next Sunday's edition, I reflected, if I'd pulled the trigger. The fame would have been as instant as the hijacker's death.

The uniformed policeman guarding the detention block at Castlereagh directed us into the shadows of the covered car park at the rear of the building. Taff eased the Viva to a halt and switched off the engine. It was evening. We both sat silent, expressionless, our heads turned, straining to see through the rear window. It was to be a covert identification parade. After the hijack incident, the local commander from Springfield Road Barracks had initiated a sweep of the area. Foot patrols and mobiles had trawled the Falls and Springfield areas, personnel-checking and lifting any suspicious youths. The haul was then transported to Castlereagh for further questioning. We now sat patiently, blacked out in the darkness of the car's interior, waiting for the ID parade to begin.

An arc light high up on the far wall flared into life, bathing the floor of the block to our rear in brilliant white light. A uniformed officer appeared and prodded four recalcitrant youths into our line of sight. The brightness of the light cascading down made them stare at the floor in front of them. Further prodding with a baton, accompanied by gruff, guttural threats, persuaded the youths to raise their eyes and look straight ahead to facilitate identification. The scene was stark and eerie. The sharp light trepanning into the dark of the night had eliminated all superfluous colour. All that remained was harsh black and pure white.

I studied the pale, hate-filled faces, my hand hovering over the car horn. The arrangement was that if I got a positive ID I would sound the horn once. I scanned the defiant faces again. 'Do you recognize anyone?' I asked Taff.

'Nope!' came the clipped, emotionless reply.

'Then we might as well lift off,' I said, barely able to keep the frustration from my voice. I jabbed the horn three times in quick succession, terminating the parade. The light went out and we were once more cloaked in darkness.

The Belfast winter slipped by, dark, desultory and depressing. More observation, more photographs; every day the camera shutters clicked with monotonous regularity. Hardened IRA men immortalized in grainy black and white. The green slime would be having a field day piecing together the big picture. And still the killing went on. An armoured pig was hit by an RPG-7. The married corporal inside was very seriously injured, losing his testicles. A part-time member of the Ulster Defence Regiment was shot dead while operating his JCB tractor. A foot patrol in the Turf Lodge came under sniper fire and one member of the patrol was killed. Month after month, on and on it went, and all the while we were seemingly powerless, unable to take part in the action, our cameras our only weapons.

Then everything suddenly changed.

Remington pump-action shotgun, oiled and ready to go; a box of cartridges, ideal for blowing Yale locks out of flimsy doors; Bristol body armour guaranteed to stop anything up to .357 Magnum; high-velocity inserts to give protection against 7.62mm; assault waistcoat with elasticated pockets to take a selection of stun grenades; and finally the Len Dixon belt kit, genuine leather, with the thumb-break, quick-draw holster.

I looked down at the assault equipment laid out neatly on my bed. After weeks of routine patrols, the leash had finally been loosened: we had been put on standby for a possible house assault in the Andersonstown area of the city. A tout had informed the green slime that four armed PIRA had taken over the top flat of a block of flats and were preparing to carry out a snipe on an Army foot patrol.

I picked up the 9mm Browning on the bedside locker, removed the magazine and, gripping the knurled slide with index finger and thumb, cocked the action. The oiled working parts slipped back smoothly, revealing the empty chamber. Satisfied with the weapon's safety precautions, I released the slide, allowing it to snap forward, replaced the fully loaded mag and secured the pistol in the holster on the belt kit. I was just reaching for my personal radio, hanging by its harness on the wardrobe door, when the outside door of the basha flew open.

'Get tooled-up lads, we're going for it!' The urgency in the team leader's voice cracked through the steadiness of our methodical preparations and whipped us into a frenzy of action. We had moved from standby to immediate. We staggered into our body armour, threw on our assault kit, loaded and cocked our weapons, and double-checked our gas-masks for serviceability.

I was lost in a sea of struggling, cursing assaulters as we made for the two armoured pigs that would transport us to Andy's Town. I scrambled into the first pig. Jake, Ginge and Bob were already seated in the cramped interior. Jake, hard and intense, a Jock from the Highland Light Infantry and second-in-command of the assault team, was straightening the splayed ends of the safety-pin protruding from his stun grenade to facilitate quicker withdrawal. The other lads were checking their Heckler & Koch MP5s and adjusting their gas-masks. I took a handful of cartridges from the map pocket of my combat trousers and began feeding the Remington. The pigs lurched forward out through the main gates of the RUC station and into the Springfield Road.

The two pigs turned into the Falls, trundling along at normal patrol speed, heading for Andy's Town. Then we took a right, up Kennedy Way, getting close. Each man was tense, not talking, going over the assault plan in his mind. No orders would be shouted. The drill was automatic. Nothing could stop the ball once it had started rolling. Right turn into Andy's Town, the high whine of the pig's engine in our ears.

'Two hundred metres,' came the terse message from the front. 'One hundred metres.' I could feel the adrenaline start to pump. 'Fifty metres.' The man nearest the back twisted one of the rear door handles and disengaged the securing rod. Gripping tightly onto both door handles he pushed the doors slightly outwards to check that they were moving freely, then swung them closed again. His fingers stayed clenched around the handles, ready for instant action.

The pig jerked to a halt. 'Go, go, go,' was the only shouted order. The rear doors burst open. I counted them out. One out. Two out. I was three out. Four out. I looked up. We were hemmed in on two sides by the pre-cast concrete frontages of two bleak rows of flats, whose dirty and neglected windows looked all the more bizarre and hostile for having their frames painted bright garish colours, totally out of keeping with the dismal greyness of the rest of the scene. A muddy grass verge littered with broken bottles, pieces of masonry and dog shit led up to each row of flats, like a rubbish-strewn sea lapping at a harbour wall. The two blocks were connected by a low-sided, open concrete walkway to our front, blackened by the weather and disfigured by graffiti – an ideal position from which an old car engine could be levered over the low walls onto a passing Army patrol. Two ten-year-olds standing at one end eyed us with hate and disgust. They dashed to alert the occupants of the flats that the SF had arrived.

Running hard, we slithered over the grass and headed for the block of flats on the left, gas-masks restricting breathing, eyepieces beginning to mist over. We crashed through the front door. All I could see was the heaving back of number two as we mounted the stairs. The bare concrete steps were in flights of eight, zigzagging up the central stairwell in alternating directions and connected by small, rough-surfaced landings. Our momentum was halted momentarily at each landing as we lurched around in an acute reversal of direction, wrenching at the rusty handrail to aid our progress upwards. First floor, second floor. No problems. So far so good. I could feel the urgent presence of number four pushing behind me as we approached the target flat on the third floor.

The safety-catch on the Remington came off as I hit the third floor and made for the target door. Number one and number two were already in position at the hinges, waiting for the door to swing open. I squeezed the trigger on the shotgun. The shot hammered through the Yale lock, splintering the wood surround into a thousand slivers. A heavy size-nine boot finished the job and the door crashed open. Number one and number two disappeared inside.

I took up a crouched position just inside the door, ready for the shooting to start. Shouts and screams reverberated around the interior of the flat. A stun grenade went off, the force of the detonation cracking the cheap plaster on the ceiling and walls. I waited for the last blinding flash, then moved deeper into the room. Through the fog I could see shadowy figures. A man and a woman sat doubled on the settee, coughing, vomiting and babbling incoherently.

A gas-mask came towards me, a gloved hand gripped my arm. 'The bastards aren't here.' His voice sounded strangely distorted through the mask. 'We're going for the flat across the landing.' With that he darted past me and rocketed towards the other door, his number two hard on his heels.

I followed fast, the Remington coming up to the aiming position. In a blur of movement the shot hammered the Yale and the door splintered and sprang open. In one fast and practised movement, the two assaulters cannoned into the flat.

I stood near the doorway, covering the entrance to the living room. A bedlam of sound pounded my ears: hysterical voices… Irish accents… the deafening explosions of the stun grenades… but still no gunfire. The bastards have got to be in there this time. For fuck's sake pull the trigger and let's get the job over with.

The earpiece of my Pyephone radio crackled into life. 'All stations. This is Jake. The birds have flown. Endex. Lift off.'

Bastard, I thought, all this pissing about for nothing! The sharp acid of frustration started to well up and corrode my insides. My skull seemed to grow tighter and press in on my brain. The fucking tout had got it wrong. How much was the green slime paying him anyway?

I couldn't stand much more of this, I had to get out of this place.

* * *

Then the frustration of not being able to take out the enemy exploded into a scandal that rocked B Squadron and brought to an end the Regiment's mission to support the fledgling 14 Intelligence Company known as the 'The Det'.

The first incident occurred when four members of B Squadron had gone into a well-known Republican bar in Londonderry for a drink and a quick look around. When they were there they recognized a senior IRA player from source photographs. This made him a legitimate target for an official operation. Trouble was this was not an officially planned lift. This was a spur of the moment recce. Tension about the whole Northern Ireland situation was running sky-high and this was no ordinary IRA player but a known IRA killer – drinking in broad daylight!

Inflamed by their frustration at constantly having their hands tied thanks to bureaucracy and politics, they allowed their impatience to get the better of them. Seizing the opportunity they pistol-whipped him in the car park in an attempt to subdue him so they could get him in the car and drop him off at the nearest SF base for interrogation. But just at that moment all the Republican drinkers happened to stream out of the bar. In the face of a large, hostile crowd the B Squadron men jumped into their car and only just managed to escape before they were surrounded by the mob.

They were traced through their car's number plate and immediately RTU'd. This began to play on my mind. How could the number be traced when the plates were false and changed on a weekly basis? It should have been simple for them to be able to bluff their way out of it unless someone wanted the SAS to take the fall. I was starting to suspect that the higher chain of command didn't relish special forces troops running loose in the region.

The situation only got worse when two Irish members of Seven Troop snapped – in spectacular fashion. These two guys had become sick of simply taking photographs of hardened terrorists when they should have been slotting them. What made it worse was that some of the IRA were regularly raiding post offices and filling their boots full of cash. Tony, a Bogside boy and now a Seven Troop man, had gone to school with some of these criminals, and was now forced to take photos of them living the high life while he and his mates struggled on Army pay. One night it got too much for them. Quite simply, they lost it.

They went out and did an armed robbery on a post office themselves, more to relieve the boredom and frustration than for any serious mercenary desires, and snaffled a load of cash. This was lunacy especially since the Regiment wasn't even meant to be in Northern Ireland!

If it got out that the SAS had been involved in the robbery the reputation of the Regiment would be mud. Besides the usual suspects there was also an unexpected, silent enemy lurking in the background, waiting for their opportunity to attack with the big guns – the senior officers of the British Army themselves. Many of them didn't understand the concept of special forces and couldn't hack that a bunch of renegades and mavericks could achieve what the traditional order couldn't. After the debacle with the bar snatch, Tony and his mates' escapade was the final straw. They were quietly arrested and later jailed although the whole thing was officially hushed up. But of course it signalled the end of B Squadron's time in Northern Ireland, and we were unceremoniously ordered out of the province. At the time the GOC even went so far as to remark that the SAS would never return to Northern Ireland.

He was wrong. All it took was a prolonged killing spree by the PIRA down in South Armagh. In response, on 7 January 1976, Prime Minister Harold Wilson publicly announced that the SAS would be committed to Northern Ireland. At least this time we thought we would be able to put the cameras away and take up our weapons. But some things never really changed. Our hands were still tied by the policy of minimum force and we were given specific orders to 'capture' terrorists, not to kill them.

By 1978 I was back in Londonderry myself operating out of a secret SF base. We spent four months patrolling, setting up ambushes and providing surveillance, but we had only one kill to show for it – an IRA man caught retrieving a hidden weapon, under the muzzles of an SAS ambush team.

Once again the frustration started to boil up. The desire to escape was as primal as that of a spawning salmon trapped downstream by a storm-fed torrent. Then, out of the blue, I got the order to go and see Maurice, B Squadron Officer Commanding.

11

Hong Kong

It was with some degree of trepidation and a vague, elusive feeling of guilt tightening my lips that I approached the OC's office. Why had he called for me? Surely I couldn't be blamed for our recent lack of success. It was the green slime who identified potential targets – we were just following orders. There had been a rumour that the IRA had used a scanner to lock onto our frequencies during an operation and had made an audiotape. Was my voice on the tape? Was I compromised?

I felt sure that I was in for the mother of all bollockings. Four years of bullshit regulations in Northern Ireland was obviously starting to make me paranoid. As I closed the door firmly but quietly behind me, my thoughts became even more paranoid. Was I being singled out as a scapegoat? Was I going to be sacrificed on the altar of political expediency, watched from afar by the hooded high priests of Whitehall?

'Sit down, Sergeant.' The tall, slim figure behind the desk remained firmly upright. Only his head tilted slightly as he scanned the report in front of him, making occasional pencil notes in the margin.

Power play, I thought. Making me wait, creating the impression that his paperwork is more important than me, gives him the upper hand, reinforces his authority. Psychological-warfare tactics. I braced myself for the worst.

'Right.' The OC looked up, giving nothing away. His swarthy

features had not yet been washed away by the Belfast rain. He eyed me closely for a moment, then his gaze relaxed into a hint of a smile. 'Pack your bags, Sergeant. You're going to the exotic East!'

* * *

Kai Tak airport is unique amongst the world's major international airports in that it is limited to a single runway. But then that is not surprising. Everything in Hong Kong is restricted, hemmed in and squeezed by the lack of space. Like an overcrowded refugee ship, the country has a population a tenth the size of Great Britain's crammed into a tiny land mass of small islands and mainland territories, in all just two-thirds the size of London.

The concrete stick of runway was clearly visible in the distance as the military transport plane throttled back its engines. I felt a warm tingle of pride when I brought to mind my mission. I was here to professionally train the Special Duties Unit of the Royal Hong Kong Police in anti-terrorism tactics. It was one of the perks of being in the SAS. Our specialist skills were much in demand among security forces throughout the free world.

As we began our final descent, I looked out over a sea churned by a thousand vessels, large and small. Flying fish-finned junks jostled for position with lumbering freighters. Tiny yachts sailed impertinently close to huge ocean-going liners. Nearer to shore, beetle-shaped sampans scuttled along wearing protective belts of old car tyres around their hulls. They wobbled precariously on top of the water, buffeted by every passing swell, their human cargoes sitting unconcernedly beneath the coarse sun-bleached calico awnings.

The fierce sun liquefied the high-rise buildings hedging in the airport. Planes parked up in bays at the side of the runway soaked up the blistering heat like lizards on sun-drenched rocks. This is the life, I thought. Sunshine and training with the Royal Hong Kong Police to help create an elite counter-terrorism unit – the best possible antidote after nearly four years of rain-sodden boredom in Northern Ireland. I was as eager to get into it as a thirsty, callous-fingered labourer striding into a lunchtime pub for a pint of foaming beer. Things were really going my way at last.

* * *

I obviously hadn't yet learned the lesson: beware of over-optimism. The previous training jaunt to exotic places had been considered a jolly too, a bit of R & R after the rigours of operational duties. Little had I known that that trip would nearly cost me my life, that it would prove more dangerous even than Mirbat. We'd taken a C-130 from Brize Norton to Khartoum, then travelled overland to the coast just below Port Sudan. We set up camp by the Red Sea, very close to Jacques Cousteau's diving school.

The trip was to last six weeks. It wasn't long before a certain amount of boredom set in, particularly as alcohol was illegal in Sudan. But we soon found a way of solving the boredom problem. One of the lads dug out the Admiralty charts and gave them a closer look. Near to where we were diving was a place marked on the chart as a large square block labelled 'restricted, dangerous'. It was like a red rag to a bull. Further enquiries revealed that it was the site of the wreck of the SS *Umbria*, a Second World War Italian ammunition ship. We immediately sniffed booty! Ignoring all dangers of unexploded ordnance, we dived in eagerly and quickly located a hold full of unexploded bombs. They were unarmed. That gave us a clue. Further searches uncovered a stash of nose-cone mechanisms – all made out of pure brass. That would do nicely! Back in Hereford, they would bring a tidy sum in scrap.

We then began to focus our attention on the huge propeller: phosphor bronze, worth a fortune, nearly as valuable as gold! The nose-cones represented loose change compared to this! We first tried to slice off one of the leaves of the propeller, but abandoned the idea when we had difficulty with the cutting tool. Further exploration revealed a spare leaf, bolted to the side of the cargo hold. Perfect! We quickly unbolted it from its housing and laid it on the ocean floor. We then went back to shore, assembled two dozen Burma Oil drums and freighted them out over the wreck, towing them behind our three Geminis. We lashed the Burmoils together, filled them with water and sank them over the wreck. Having attached the propeller leaf to the Burmoils, we used our airlines to blow water out of the drums, and slowly they began to rise to the surface. In no time at all there were twenty-four Burmoils bobbing on the surface with the huge one-and-a-half ton propeller leaf suspended on ropes underneath.

The flotilla headed back for shore. As the Geminis chugged along, the Burmoils unfortunately began to fill with water and started to pop under the surface one after the other. We were quickly down to two or three Burmoils. The sheer weight of the propeller began to pull down on the rear of the Geminis and lift the bows up into the air, threatening to tip them over at any moment. The shout went up: 'Cut the ropes!'

Ginge, who was steering my boat, cut what he thought was the main rope. Unfortunately, he had not noticed that there was another rope attached to the propeller leaf whose other end was coiled loosely in the bottom of the boat. The heavy hemp rope snaked out and snapped tight around my upper leg.

As I struggled against the muscle-tearing pull of the rope, a mental picture of Geordie, the jungle survival expert, flashed into my mind. 'You are only as sharp as your knife,' he used to say in his heavy Newcastle accent. I reached for my diver's knife, fitted to my leg. The blade glittered in the sun as I hacked away at the hemp. The pain in my thigh was becoming unbearable. I could just feel my hip-joint beginning to dislocate as I cut through the final strands. The relief was immediate. The propeller leaf plummeted to the depths of the ocean. As it disappeared, I don't know which was more painful: my thigh or the thought of the thousands of pounds sterling lying on the ocean floor!

The OC turned a blind eye to the escapade. He knew it was going on, but after all, it was good training – something for us to focus our minds on, instead of aimlessly paddling around looking for fish. However, there was no way he could ignore what was about to happen in Hong Kong.

* * *

'Let's go for a boogie at BMH and work up a thirst,' said Clint as he stuffed his rugby kit into a battered holdall.

'Work up a thirst! I must have lost a gallon of sweat this afternoon. I need an ale transfusion quick. I'll be fainting from dehydration.'

'You can get a drink at the disco.'

'I'm not into discos. I've got some serious drinking to do.'

'Me too. But we can go down town later. Think of all those gorgeous nurses, those black-stocking beauties just waiting for us. Right little ravers, no inhibitions. They're seeing naked bodies all day long. It builds up the passion, especially in this heat. Can't you just feel those well-practised hands getting to grips with you already? They can give me a bed-bath any time they want.'

'Hey, Clint, remember I'm a married man!'

We were in the changing rooms, Buffalo, Clint and I, discussing the evening's entertainment. Buffalo and Clint were inspectors in the Hong Kong police. They'd co-opted me into their local league rugby team. That afternoon's match had been particularly hard, but we'd just scraped a win. I was feeling the effects of the humidity; having been in Hong Kong only three weeks, I was still not fully acclimatized. The thought of several hours' dancing did not exactly fill me with excitement. However, as I did up my last shirt button, I resigned myself to the BMH detour.

We finally left BMH around midnight and to my relief headed for Tsim-Sha-Tsui, a bustling shopping, bar and restaurant district situated in the shadow of the mountain known as the Peak, which towers like a high-swell wave crest over the trough of Hong Kong city. We were aiming for the renowned Bottoms Up bar to get on with the real business of the night: beer and men's talk.

As we turned into Hankow Road, I looked up eagerly to see if I could spot the entrance to the bar I'd heard so much about. A flashing neon ticker tape of matchstick Chinese script showered right down to street level. The occasional English sign emphasized the cosmopolitan nature of the city: 'Golden Dragon Company – Wholesale and Retail', 'Jimmy Sung – Tailor', 'Golden Fountain Restaurant'. The road itself was lined with high-class boutiques, their window displays expensively draped and spotlit to attract passers-by, who even at this hour were thronging the pavements. The trademarks of Sony, Omega and Nikon assailed window-browsers from all sides.

In spite of the neon snowstorm, the sign for the Bottoms Up bar stood out a fair distance down on the right-hand side of the road. Box-shaped, the sign had a thick black border engraved with white Chinese writing. The centre was a rich purple colour. It featured a prominent white bottom cleverly designed to resemble a heart.

It was 2.00am by the time I finally made it out of there and through the door of the Red Mill Inn. This was a conventional late-night drinking den. It was the early hours of the morning and as the conversation wore on and the sporting exploits grew in stature with each alcohol-infused repetition, my concentration began to wander. I gazed around the bar, then momentarily tensed, consciously halting the drift of my mind towards weariness-induced torpor. Something wasn't quite right. I didn't feel comfortable. There was something in the atmosphere of the bar that seemed to convey a vague sense of danger, some unstated aura of threat – not especially aimed at me or Clint or Buffalo, just generalized, floating around the room, seeping through the air like a gas escape. It was as if all it would take was a misinterpreted gesture, an ill-timed comment or a glance in the wrong direction, and the casual strike of a match would trigger the explosion. I was sure the feeling had not been there before we came in. Something or someone had precipitated it since we'd arrived.

More alert, I scanned the room seeking clues. Everything seemed normal – normal that is, for a late-night bar in the early hours of the morning in downtown Hong Kong, a bar peopled by a potent racial mix drawn from the Portuguese, Chinese, British and Filipino subcultures. The general bar area seemed quiet enough; just two neat-looking Chinese men sitting by the door talking softly and a sprinkling of other nondescript faces scattered around in ones and twos.

After a while the general calmness began to allay my fears. It must be my hyperactive imagination, I thought as I did a mental search-and-destroy mission inside my body to locate and unwind the tension-cramped muscles. By the time Susi Soriano appeared and I had recognized her as a nightclub hostess and singer from the Speakeasy Club, a seedy downtown drinking den that Clint, Buffalo and I had recently started to frequent, all notions of latent hostility had completely evaporated. I felt I needed some female conversation. Nothing more, just friendly conversation. It gets lonely when you are separated from the wife.

'Hello Susi, got the night off?'

'Yes, that's right.'

'Come and join us for a drink.'

'No thanks. Not just now. I'm with my sister.'

'Better still. Bring Chai over too.'

'Maybe later.' And with that she disappeared into the toilets.

We continued drinking, but the sight of Susi had made me restless. Not one to be put off easily, I decided to see if I could persuade Susi and Chai to be more sociable. I wandered over to where they were sitting in a semi-private booth. The two sisters were sitting with a group of Portuguese men. They were obviously engrossed in something more than social pleasantries, so I decided to leave them alone for a little while longer. Ten minutes later, I thought I would try again. I went right up to where they were sitting and gestured. Susi glanced up and nervously gestured for me to go away. The nervous look did not register with me and I simply thought she was playing hard to get. One more drink and then I would go right up to their table. I turned and headed back for the empty stool at the bar next to Clint.

As I had my back to the booth area, I didn't see the three characters behind me whisper something urgent, get up, move their chairs swiftly to one side and head for the steps by the jukebox. The first I knew of anything being wrong was when the unmistakable sound of breaking glass cut through the bar and jolted the place into high tension. Instinctively I spun round, and saw the lead character of the three, tense-armed, gripping a broken bottle held menacingly low and pointing directly towards me.

Clint swivelled round, saw the bottle, leapt off his stool, jutted out the index finger of his right hand and shouted, 'Police! Put the bottle down!'

The three paid no attention whatsoever and continued to advance. At this point Clint went for the guy with the bottle. He evaded the first threatening swing of the vicious, jagged weapon, grasped the man's wrist in a vice-lock, forced the bottle to the floor and threw him against the jukebox. As he crashed spreadeagled into the machine and slumped to the floor, a wild screech and scratch followed by a rumbling sound emanated from the loudspeaker and then, incongruously amid the mayhem, the soft romantic ballad began to play again a few bars further on. Out of the corner of my eye I could just see Clint putting the boot in to finish off the job, when the man's companions both grabbed bottles from the nearest empty table, broke off the bases with a practised flick of the wrist and advanced to within striking distance of Buffalo and me.

As they had paid no heed to Clint's warnings, I decide to throw the system out of the window and go solo. I reached into my back pocket for the insurance policy I always carried with me in case of trouble – a First World War trench-fighting knuckleduster issued to British troops for hand-to-hand combat. A lovely piece, worn smooth by age, I'd obtained it from my brother-in-law who runs a military museum. Years before, while serving with the Royal Engineers in Germany, a mate of mine had been jumped by a gang of Italian *Gastarbeiter* thugs. They put their knives into him and he never walked again. I was determined that no one was going to turn me into a vegetable at any cost, and I carried the knuckleduster with me everywhere I went. Now it was about to come into its own.

I felt for the reassuring hard touch of the metal and drew the weapon out into the open. I jammed it into my hand, pointed it directly at my would-be assailants, flexed my fingers conspicuously and snorted in a cold, rock-steady voice, 'Right! Let's have you, lads.'

As they came forward I struck the nearer one full in the face. He went down. I swung my arm back and caught the other on the side of the temple. He dropped his broken bottle and went down. A fourth person, later identified as Didier Peres, a well-known drug-pusher, then came from the booths area and lunged at me with a crude form of rugby tackle. He was very quick. Before I could strike him with the knuckleduster, he grabbed me around the throat and pushed me into the bar, sending two or three stools clattering to the floor. At the same time his considerable strength enabled him to turn me around so that I was facing towards and was bent over the bar. He then thrust his hand up to my throat and held me in a windpipe pinch. The pain was excruciating, as if I were being gripped by a rabid Dobermann. The precise positioning of the thumb and index finger had all the hallmarks of a professional street fighter. It was the throat equivalent of getting your hand jammed in a bank's time-locked safe door when all the staff have gone home for the weekend.

My position was now serious. By shaking forcefully from side to side, I managed to free my knuckleduster arm and swing it around. Peres was bent low into my shoulder, so the duster cracked him on the top of the head. To my dismay, the blow had no effect except to make him tighten his grip on my throat. By now my eyes were beginning to blur; the bottles behind the bar were swimming. There was a heavy thumping in my head and a high-pitched whistling in my ears. I was desperate. I had to do something quick. By now I was having trouble breathing. I could feel my temples beating to bursting point. I was virtually paralysed. I frantically scoured my brain for a solution, going on fast-forward through all my years of training. A flash of inspiration! I had to try it! It could be my last chance. I worked up my left hand, grabbed hold of Peres's thumb, snatched it away from my throat and put it straight into my mouth. I bit down as hard as I could until I felt the solid resistance of the bone. Peres, taken by surprise, squealed like a stuck pig, released his stranglehold and ran out of the bar.

I looked around. Clint was still over by the jukebox slugging it out with someone who later turned out to be a Portuguese-American sailor on forty-eight-hour shore leave. Clint swung his arm, the man crashed backwards, smashing the glass cover on the jukebox, and the music was silenced for good. Buffalo was arguing with the barman about using the phone to call for help. The barman refused, saying, suspiciously, that it was out of order. So Buffalo dashed out to phone from the restaurant across the street. At this point I decided to get out of the bar as quickly as I could. I was on a sensitive job and didn't want complications.

I pushed past another character who tried to stop me. He dropped like a ton of muck as I cracked him with the duster. I was staring freedom in the face when suddenly I was jumped from behind at the door. We rolled around, the momentum carrying us straight through the door and into the street. As we continued to roll around on the pavement, a crowd gathered to watch the spectacle. Suddenly someone ran out of the gathering, kicked me straight in the face as I wrestled with my assailant, then mingled back into the crowd.

Undeterred, I continued the struggle. I heaved the man over and managed to get on top of him. Just when I thought I had the situation under control, he put his hand up, gripped my testicles and twisted them violently beneath the thin material of my lightweight tropical trousers. It blew my mind. The anger exploded in my brain. There was only one answer to this. I grabbed his hair with my left hand and rapped him across the forehead with the knuckleduster, splitting the skin from eye to eye. Like a heavyweight boxer in a title fight who goes on punching beyond the bell, I just did not hear the high-pitched wailing of the police siren. As the character slumped unconscious to the ground and I began to think I might have overdone it, I suddenly felt a heavy hand on my shoulder.

'Police! You're under arrest.'

There is something strange and frightening when in the course of a single moment you realize that your life has irrevocably altered. It is the moment when a young wife, joyfully looking forward to her husband's return so she can reveal the news of her first pregnancy, is told by the grave-faced policeman at the door that she is now a widow; when the champion jockey, who only a moment ago was soaring high over the jumps, wakes up in hospital to be told that his vertebrae are so badly smashed that he will never ride again. The moment is strange because it is so sudden and disorientating, and it is frightening because you are cast headlong into a situation where a completely new order reigns and a new set of rules prevails. Your unsuspecting emotions are cruelly whiplashed into a vicious reversal of direction. No matter how loud you scream inside, 'This can't be happening, this can't be true,' no one will ever hear you. Events are propelled forward with an absolute and remorseless energy.

Under arrest! I used to have a recurring nightmare about being at the wheel of a car careering out of control downhill with its accelerator jammed full on. No matter how hard I struggled to disengage the clutch with one foot and ram the brake down hard with the other, I could do nothing to stop the vehicle. It wasn't the fear of crashing that made me wake up in a sweat, it was the terrifying powerlessness to stop the forward motion, the deeply unnerving experience of sheer relentlessness.

The nightmare had now come true. I looked up and saw the khaki drill, the dark leather of the Sam Browne cross belt, the black shiny peaked cap and the drawn pistol. Just behind, the flashing light on top of the Land Rover seemed to gyrate crazily like an out-of-control lighthouse beacon. I was about to start the B-movie dialogue of, for want of something more original, 'You've got the wrong man,' when Clint beat me to it. Waving his police warrant card to try to emphasize his authority, he shouted urgently, 'There's people in the bar who should be held for questioning.'

Even as he spoke, Peres and the bottle boys, the real culprits, were slinking out of the bar. As soon as they were at a safe distance they broke into a run down the street and away into the night. The hyped-up inspector, who by this time, having confiscated the knuckleduster, was cautioning me and hustling me into the rear of the Land Rover, completely ignored Clint's warnings. He was young, inexperienced and totally out of his depth.

The next thing I knew I was being driven to Tsim-Sha-Tsui police station, with Clint and Buffalo in hot pursuit in their own car. At the station I was processed through the system, searched, cautioned and interviewed and my statement taken down by a clumsy typist. It was written in uncultured English, heavy with police terminology, which tends to reduce an infinite variety of real-life happenings to a limited series of categorized events. After reading the statement I was told to initial in the margin the errors and crossings out and to sign and date it at the bottom.

Since the knuckleduster was classified as an illegal weapon and the possession of the weapon constituted an offence contrary to the Public Order Act, my case was transferred to the CID. I could not escape the charge of possession of an offensive weapon – POOW as it was referred to – since I'd admitted in my statement to having it in the first place. I'd had no choice, I had been caught with it literally red-handed. To my dismay, I learned that self-defence was no defence. As for the fight,

I felt that the charge would be the relatively minor offence of causing an affray. No such luck. I was to be prosecuted under the Public Order Act for the much more serious offence of assault occasioning actual bodily harm – AOABH for short. Around 4.30am, with my spirits ebbing away, it was decided that I should be taken into mess arrest. I was driven in a police Land Rover to Gunclub Barracks – the resident Hong Kong battalion headquarters – where I was to remain for the next two weeks until the case came up in court.

Clint and Buffalo had arrived at the station a few minutes after me. Ken Jones, a friend of Clint's, happened to be the inspector on duty. He'd recognized me from the rugby club, so when Clint came dashing in to see what was going on, Ken said to him, 'We've got one of your mates. I think you should look at the report book.'

Clint flipped the pages and found the relevant entry. It read: '0200 hours: Red Mill Inn, Ashley Road. A European male attacked a Chinese male with an offensive weapon, namely a knuckleduster.' Clint was incensed when he read this, and insisted on changing the book. He later got a severe reprimand for this, but he was determined to see the truth come out even if it meant putting his job on the line.

Clint and Buffalo decided right at the outset to take the unusual step of appearing for the defence. A policeman is only ever expected to appear for the prosecution – even more particularly in instances such as this, when the case for POOW was cut and dried. Buffalo was sticking his neck out even more than Clint. He had crossed swords with the police establishment in the past and was already considered something of a renegade. What made them dig their heels in even further was when they were called into the office one day and told bluntly, 'You are strongly advised not to appear for the defence.' Without their support my case would have been severely weakened. To ensure the co-operation of the police authorities, my solicitor sent a subpoena requesting the presence in court of Clint and Buffalo simply because they had facts material to the case. The police couldn't legally refuse the request.

Clint came to visit me in Gunclub Barracks. 'They're determined to nail you,' he said. 'They are pressing ahead with the AOABH despite what Buffalo and I have told them. With a half-decent judge you might get off, but there is still the charge for the POOW. Do you realize what you are looking at? You are going down for six months, more if they make the AOABH stick. You're convicted even before the trial.'

'But I didn't start anything. It was self-defence. Surely the judge will see that.'

'Makes no difference. It's mandatory. No matter what the reason, POOW is an automatic six-monther. No appeal.'

I didn't know what was the greater blow: the contemplation of a minimum six-month stretch locked up inside some humid rat-hole in Hong Kong, or the prospect of a certain end to my career in the SAS and the Army following a jail sentence. 'Is there nothing we can do?' I asked.

Clint looked at me. He seemed hesitant, reluctant to continue. 'Well there is something. A mate of mine in the CID has been doing some research for me on the quiet. There's a procedure for requesting corporal punishment as an alternative. What do you think?'

'What does it entail?'

'Bamboo across the backside. A short sharp shock, then you're back in business.' I was too relieved by the thought of escaping prison to notice the shadow of a frown that flitted across Clint's face.

'Sounds OK to me. Anything's got to be better than being cooped up in prison. I'd die of boredom. Yeah! Let's go for it.'

'OK, but don't count on it. It's entirely at the discretion of the judge.'

* * *

The judge was about to return after considering his verdict, and I'd been called back into the dock. While awaiting the reappearance of the judge, the policeman sitting to my left unconcernedly brought a newspaper out of his pocket and began to read it. This informal motion contrasted starkly with the gravity of the surroundings. But then to him it was just another case in a long line of such cases. As far as he was concerned, familiarity bred irreverence. I shifted nervously in my seat and looked round as the court began to reconvene. My gaze finally came to rest for no particular reason on the dull brass bars surrounding the dock, and just for a moment or two I had time for my own thoughts.

I'd spent two weeks at Gunclub Barracks before the trial came up. Then, on the appointed day, the police Land Rover had come to pick me up at dawn to bring me to court. As we drove in, I scanned every detail of the city scene, things I would not normally cast a second glance at, knowing it could be my last visual stimulus for six months: a van parked up unloading boxes, a hotel worker emptying the leftovers from the morning's breakfast into the refuse bins. As we drew closer to the centre, the sheer compactness of so many buildings in such a small space began to press on me. And once inside South Kowloon Court, the institutional solidity, the implacable process of the law gripped me even tighter.

Waiting for the case to be called, I could not feel comfortable for more than a few minutes in any one position: sitting down, standing with hands defiantly in pockets, pacing up and down the corridor, staring blankly out of the window and inwardly contemplating the impending loss of freedom. Even my cast-iron digestion was beginning to weaken. I asked to go to the toilet. When I saw the white pan already besmirched by the day's nerve-churned stomachs, the call of nature struggled with the urge to turn straight round and get back as quickly as I could.

Before I knew it the case was under way. The first two days flashed by in a blur of formalities and feigned politeness. The charges were read out. I pleaded guilty to POOW. The prosecution constructed their case for AOABH. Witnesses came and went. My defence lawyer, the colonel of the Army legal services, countered at best he could each of the points that were raised. Clint and Buffalo, the only defence witnesses, appeared to give their evidence, but they had some difficulty giving a coherent story. They were constantly interrupted by Harry Reynolds, OC CID, who kept telling them to speak more slowly. He was taking down what they said word for word. Their evidence was going to be minutely compared with their previous written statements. The Hong Kong police, still smarting from the two men's insistence on appearing for the defence, were all out to trip them up. One slip-up, one discrepancy between the two accounts and they would be up for perjury. When they had finished they took their places in the spectators' gallery to see if their interventions would make any difference.

The first two days had raised more questions than they had answered. The proceedings had become increasingly bizarre, the story of what had happened increasingly disorientated. I was beginning to feel my freedom slip away.

* * *

'All stand!'

Mid-morning on the third day, and Justice Ferguson was returning to deliver his summing-up and pronounce his judgement. The policeman sitting next to me hurriedly folded his newspaper as the judge came in, bowed stiffly to the court in mock obeisance and took his seat on the dais.

At the beginning of the trial, the first thing I had noticed was that there were no windows in the courtroom. This had emphasized to me the falseness of the proceedings, the separateness from the real life of the city. Now, at the end of the trial, I was aware that somewhere along the line, my view had done a volte-face. Now, the outside world had faded to unreality. The only real and tangible thing was this courtroom, the only thing that mattered to me was this quaintly berobed representative of the legal process sitting before me sipping a glass of water and adjusting the position of several weighty tomes of law on a ledge in front of him.

'This being a criminal case, the defendant is presumed to be innocent until proved guilty…'

The use of the word 'until' had an ominous finality to it. Was this a Freudian slip? Had he given the game away right at the start of his summing-up? If he had said 'unless' instead of 'until', his pronouncement would have a much less fatalistic ring to it.

I was surprised at how much time the judge spent on seemingly irrelevant or minor details, such as the amount of light in the bar at the time, the sound level of the jukebox, the background noise of the city itself, and the exact distances between the bar, the booths and the jukebox – and here witnesses were asked to select two points in the courtroom to illustrate how far apart they estimated these items to be. I glanced at the clock high up on the wall. Already three-quarters of an hour into his summing-up, the judge didn't appear yet to have said anything concrete or to have given any indication as to which way the case would swing. My stomach still felt uneasy. I shifted in my seat again and crossed my right leg horizontally over my left knee. The policeman next to me leaned forward with his hand on his forehead and appeared to doze off.

'Being cross-examined is not a very pleasant experience…'

By now, the judge's voice had become strangely monotone, his manner remote and detached, and his delivery had lapsed into a seemingly automatic style. A lull seemed to descend on the court. Attention began to wander. The only person who maintained his level of concentration was the court stenographer, inconspicuously sitting a few feet to the judge's right, furiously tapping away at what looked like a desktop calculator. I found myself staring blankly at the reflected shine of the neon lighting in the varnished wooden rail in front of me. My reverie was interrupted by a noise as someone walked in front of the spectators' gallery. There was so much ancient-looking wood in the room that the slightest movement anywhere in the court was accompanied by an intrusive creaking sound.

'Indeed, excessive anxiety against a charge falsely brought can lead to false evidence being given…'

False evidence! There was certainly plenty of false evidence being given, but not through any sense of anxiety or nervousness! Quite the contrary. It was a cold, deliberate attempt to pervert the course of justice, to set me up and to deflect attention away from the truth about what had really been going on in the bar. And the source of this false evidence? Who should appear as star witnesses for the prosecution? None other than the thugs who had started the fight in the first place: Peres and his bottle boys, all smartly turned out and looking distinctly uncomfortable in their Sunday-best suits designed to impress the court and project an aura of probity and integrity. The young Chinese inspector, completely misreading the situation, had tracked down Peres and his gang and brought them in to make out a case against me.

I had been utterly astonished. I wouldn't have been more surprised if, to make pronouncement on the proceedings, the judge had called in a jury consisting entirely of a vanload of day-tripping psychiatric patients from the local asylum. To add weight to the gang's story, a Chinese doctor was wheeled in to testify that in his professional and considered opinion the wound on Peres' head had indeed been caused by Exhibit A – the infamous knuckleduster, which lay all along in the middle of a large table below the judge, tagged with a small white label. It looked faintly ridiculous – like an unwanted sale item – and totally innocuous. You couldn't fire it, throw it, detonate it, cut with it. If a machine gun or a pistol or a ten-inch bladed knife has been lying there, then the severity of the court proceedings would have been justified. But a knuckleduster, a lump of inert metal! To add insult to injury, the thugs were aided and abetted in their evidence by the meek and mild Soriano sisters, who looked as if they'd been given time out from the nunnery specially to appear in court that day. I daresay they were under some kind of duress to turn up. To me they seemed essentially decent types who somehow had lost their way, who somewhere along the line had naively been caught up in the petty-crime scene.

'Now to the evidence itself…'

Justice Ferguson picked up a large red notebook, adjusted his spectacles, coughed, flicked through the pages to refresh his memory with some of the handwritten notes he'd taken and proceeded to read out his version of the events. The sight and sound of the learned judge describing in reverent tones the details of a fight that was clearly totally alien to someone of his status bordered on the comic.

'Kicked the assailant in the groin… struck him a blow to the temple… head-butted the second man… grappled with the broken bottle… split his scalp with a blow to the head… rolled across the floor… a scuffle ensued…'

A scuffle! More like a life-or-death struggle. I glanced over at the policeman next to me to see what he was making of it all. He was still leaning over with his head on his hands, but contrary to what I had at first supposed he was not dozing. The newspaper had been folded in a strategic manner and he was actually doing the crossword! So much for his concern for the drama that was gripping me.

As I looked around again I realized I'd be glad to be out of this place, no matter what the outcome. The courtroom was much smaller than such rooms appear on TV and in films and, with all its dark wood, it was beginning to press in on me.

'I have weighed all the evidence and completed my deliberation…'

The last three words were like a whip-crack. One and a half hours had passed since the summing-up begun, but now the courtroom was fully alert once more. I leaned forward in my seat, partly in anxiety, partly in an attempt to catch the judge's fading voice.

'In the matter of the case for AOABH, the prosecuting counsel together with Mr Reynolds representing the CID have not covered themselves with glory. Far from it. Their performance borders on the shameful. I have not heard such an ill-prepared case in a long time…'

I couldn't believe what I was hearing. Relief was sweeping through me. Vindicated! Not only was their case not good enough, but they were being actively criticized for putting it together so poorly. 'The evidence was atrocious. All the stories were false, nobody told two accounts the same, no two pieces of evidence were consistent…'

At this point the prosecution barrister rose to protest. 'If it please your honour…' The judge glared down at him over his glasses. The barrister quickly lost courage, mumbled something in a tone of voice hushed to the point of obsequiousness, then sat down, disheartened.

'The only independent witness,' Justice Ferguson continued, 'should have been the barman. He wasn't part of Peres' party, he wasn't police, he wasn't with the defendant. But the only time he told the truth…' Here the judge paused regally in mid-sentence, poured himself a glass of water from the carafe, drank half of it and then went on, '…was when he said that when it was all over he went round and collected money from everyone for the drinks. The only two prosecution witnesses who consistently spoke the truth were the two Chinese detectives who happened to be having a quiet drink in the bar. Even though they were appearing for the prosecution, their evidence undermined the very case the prosecution was attempting to establish…'

It was going my way. Maybe the due process of law had some merit after all! The tension in my shoulders had noticeably relaxed, and I eased back slightly in my chair.

'I rule therefore that the charge of AOABH should be struck out…'

Wonderful! I could have been looking at a long stretch for that. Justice Ferguson is not as senile as he looks. One down, one to go. Because of the prosecution's bungling on the first charge, the judge might have some sympathy with me on the second – possession of the duster. He might, after all, accept my argument of self-defence. I was in for a shock.

'As for the charge of possession of an offensive weapon…'

Here Justice Ferguson reached forward for one of the large volumes of case history that lay before him, adjusted his wig slightly, shaded his eyes with his left hand, turned the pages of the book with the other and proceeded to cite the case in 1974 of a Chinese civilian who had got involved in a punch-up in a bar in Kowloon. He'd ripped an ornamental sword from where it was displayed stapled to the wood above the bar and used it to defend himself. He was arrested, charged with POOW and sentenced to six months. My euphoria was quickly dissipating.

'In spite of the considerable extenuating circumstances surrounding this case, I have still been given no valid reason why you should have about your person an offensive weapon, namely a knuckleduster. Even if it formed part of your training – and who am I to question these things? I leave that to the judgement of the military authorities – even if it was part of your official equipment, you should not have been carrying it, let alone using it in a public place. Before we know it we will have off-duty members of the forces walking down the street with rifles and machine guns. That is something that just cannot be tolerated.'

All hope was fading. How would I cope with a prison sentence? Would I be able to bear the strain of the claustrophobic routine? What would I do when I got back to the UK? Would the RE have me back? If they wouldn't, it would be a dishonourable discharge and into Civvy Street to try to get work with the only trade I knew: driving trucks.

'Taking everything into consideration I have no alternative but to find you guilty as charged…'

Here the judge paused. He was sitting with a large ledger before him, pen poised. The pen was just coming down to write me off for six months when my lawyer, the colonel, stood up. 'My learned judge, before you pass sentence…'

The judge looked at him with a certain benign curiosity.

'There are certain mitigating circumstances in this case.'

There was a moment of silence. The judge looked over his half-glasses, pen still poised, and said in a slow, enquiring voice, 'Yes, Colonel?'

The colonel proceeded to launch into a well-prepared plea of mitigation covering five full sheets of paper. Not only did he repeat every aspect of the case that was in my favour, but he also went into every detail of my family background, placing special emphasis on the fact that I had a seven-month-old son to look after. He brought forward an impressive list of character references. I was almost embarrassed. The essential thrust of the pleas was an endeavour to demonstrate that basically I was not criminally inclined and therefore was not a suitable candidate for jail, but rather that as a man who had served in the forces I must be deemed to have some substance. The incident in the bar had simply been a temporary and uncharacteristic aberration, which could be penalized with a short, sharp sentence. The colonel ended by making a strong plea for corporal punishment.

'Well…' said Justice Ferguson, a little bemused, 'it certainly didn't do me any good at school, but I sentence you to six strokes of the cane. The sentence will be carried out at Stanley Jail. Take the prisoner away.'

Thank fuck for that, I thought as I was led down the stairs in the dock that disappeared below court, that's great. At least I've got a fighting chance of saving my Army career now. My mind was hardly on the sentence at all. When I heard the judge refer to the cane, I felt as if I was back at school. It felt like nothing more serious than a visit to the headmaster's study.

I was taken to a holding area beneath the courts which consisted of one large transit cell full of pimps, prostitutes and drug-pushers – the fallout from that day's hearings, the dross from the seething social cauldron that was Hong Kong. It was midday. I would have to remain there until late afternoon when the courts rose and the full complement of convicts had been assembled ready for onward transport to their appointed place of punishment. I didn't relish the prospect of five minutes in that cell, let alone five hours. Hardened faces looked up and took my measure as the door clanged shut behind me and the key clicked in the lock. The inside of the cell consisted simply of a concrete block running around the edge, a hole in the middle of the floor serving as a primitive – and very public – latrine for both males and females, and nothing else. The floor was filthy and stank of urine and human faeces. There was no ventilation and it was unbearably hot.

I suddenly realized that I was very thirsty. Not only had I not had a drink all morning, but the heat and tension had combined to make my thirst all the more fierce. I called to the guard. 'You! Get me some water!' I was in no mood for playing the part of the humble prisoner.

Fortunately, the guard, although little surprised at my forthrightness, appeared to comply with my demand. He wandered off down the corridor and came back a moment later carrying a plastic cup of water. His face broke into an ugly, malicious sneer as, deliberately dangling two fingers in the water, he passed the beaker through the bars.

I looked at it in disgust. The rim was cracked, chewed and dirty and a film of grease scummed the surface. God knows what bacteria were swimming in the filthy liquid ready to infest my already tortured guts. I grabbed the beaker from the guard's hand, and shouted angrily, 'You must be fucking joking,' and threw it full in his face with all the venom I could muster.

He reeled back incensed and, with water still dribbling from his chin, said menacingly, 'I'll have you, I'll have you my boy. No one does that to me and gets away with it. My mates at Stanley will deal with you, my boy.' He would have been even more incensed if he had realized that I was not going to be incarcerated at Stanley Jail, that it would be all over in a few hours and that his mates would never have a chance to get near me. I strode defiantly over to the concrete block, stared fixedly at one of the prisoners sitting there until he reluctantly shuffled over to make room for me, and sat down to wait.

Late in the afternoon, a Black Maria with two Chinese warders arrived. The guard muttered a few more threats, prodded me in the ribs with a truncheon and handed me over to the warders. The warders frogmarched me up the stairs to the back of the court, out into the high-walled courtyard, where I quickly gulped in welcome lungfuls of fresh air, and into the Black Maria along with several other dangerous-looking characters. We drove in complete silence through the city streets, into the cross-harbour tunnel and over to the south side of Hong Kong Island.

The Black Maria backed into the courtyard of Stanley Jail, the door was opened and the prisoners filed out under the guard into the reception area. I was first in the queue. The other characters who had been brought with me watched somewhat sullenly as I was processed through the jail system. I was stripped naked and searched, all my valuables were removed, placed in a brown envelope and put into a locker, then my clothes were given back, minus belt and shoelaces. I was then stripped by the same two warders who had brought me there and marched across the courtyard. It was early evening. All the prisoners were lining up holding pitifully small wooden bowls to collect their supper of rice and scraps of meat. Far from feeling nervous about the impending punishment, I could focus my mind only on the size of the bowls. Thank God I'm getting out quick, I thought, I wouldn't last six weeks here, let along six months. I'd starve to death!

We entered a building and walked down a long corridor. As we went along I imagined that the person who would administer the caning would be a normal-sized Chinese. Thank fuck they're all small in China, I thought with relief. I pictured a diminutive figure with a copy of a holy book under his arm to prevent him from raising the cane too high – just as I'd seen at public floggings in the Middle East. I was in for a shock. There, at the end of the corridor, I saw him. Stripped to the waist, wearing PT shorts and pumps, with big muscles, broad shoulders, hands like shovels, his arms folded across a barrel for a chest, the monster was waiting. A mountain giant from north Mongolia. I felt the first shivers of fear clutch my stomach.

We turned left at the bottom of the corridor into a large, windowless room. At the back of the room was a long desk at which sat six stern-faced prison officials: governor, deputy governor, head warder, a psychiatrist, an Indian doctor and finally a nurse. Over the left stood a vaulting box with a thick leather strap dangling loose from each of the four legs. Behind the box there was a rack of solid rattan canes lined up like snooker cues. The monster went over to the rack and started to examine the canes. It was a scene straight out of some Dark Ages dungeon. The knot in my stomach drew tighter.

'Prepare the prisoner.' The governor had spoken.

The warder to my left ordered, 'Strip down naked. Sit in a chair while the doctor examines you.'

Once more I suffered the indignity of standing naked in front of a row of officials. The Indian doctor came over and gave me a cursory examination. He looked at my eyes and my tongue, prodded his stethoscope over my chest and took my blood pressure. With my heart beating at a rate of knots, it was no surprise when the doctor exclaimed, 'My goodness! Your blood pressure's high! Have you been taking any sort of drugs recently?'

I saw my chance. I clutched at the straw. 'Yeah, I've been on Mogadon and Valium for the last four months.'

The doctor stepped back in horror and went for a whispered conversation with the governor. However, it did no good. They saw through the ruse. The doctor returned, shook his head and sat down.

The two warders then hauled me over the bondage apparatus so that my legs were completely off the ground. As I lay spreadeagled I caught the ominous odour of stale vomit left by previous detainees. I screwed my nose up in disgust and started to breathe through my mouth to avoid the noxious smell. It brought to mind something I'd read about torture sessions in medieval chambers. When the prisoner, through the sheer weight of the pain, was beginning to lose consciousness and black out, the torturers, intent on extracting every last drop of suffering, would set light to a greasy rag and hold it below the prisoner's nostrils. The acrid smoke from the flames would sting the unfortunate man back to wakefulness, make him vomit and thus revive him for the next round of torture. As the warders unceremoniously hauled me further forward on the box, I deepened my resolve not to show any signs of reaction to the punishment, not to yell out or show any emotion whatsoever. It would be stiff upper lip to the bitter end. This would be my way of resistance, of maintaining my dignity, of showing them they could not really get to me. I would end up winning this particular contest, this battle of wills, at all costs. They could beat my body but they could not beat my mind.

My legs were strapped in, then two canvas pads were placed across my back – one to cover the small of my back to protect my kidneys from any badly aimed blows and one across the top of my thighs to protect my testicles. As my wrists were strapped to the front supports, I thought, sod it, every day is a bonus after Mirbat.

The doctor came round, brought a chair and sat next to my head. He whispered almost apologetically, 'Oh, for goodness sake make sure your tongue is well back, make sure you keep your teeth clenched, make sure you keep your head still. I will hold your head to keep it from whipping back.' Experience had taught him that victims of this barbaric punishment are quickly broken by the beating rod, their reserves of willpower soon overwhelmed by the pain. And that the pain itself bites deeper with each stroke, giving greater and greater impetus to the overwhelming reflex action of jerking the head back.

The governor nodded his head. The chief warder, in a high-pitched, near-hysterical voice, shouted out, 'Number one.' The monster swished the cane twice in the air to build up momentum to let me know it was coming. The next second it bit into my flesh like a branding iron. My body jerked involuntarily upwards to try to relieve the pain, but the spasm fell back on itself. There was nowhere for my body to go. I was completely immobilized. The straps bound me tight and dug cruelly into my ankles and wrists.

The first stroke had been delivered with unnerving ferocity. It was as if the monster was taking revenge on me for some grave personal insult. With nowhere for my body to move, the agonizing pain simply stabbed deeper and deeper, with a strange shuddering motion like the aftermath of an earthquake. With the first strike the blood vessels immediately beneath the surface of the skin were completely ruptured. My lungs convulsed and sucked a sharp intake of breath through my clenched teeth. With my eyes watering and my head reeling, I was in a state of semi-shock. The intensity of the experience was beyond description. I hadn't expected anything remotely like this. I needed something to focus on, something to hold my senses together. I began to count off the strokes, thinking, every one is one step nearer freedom.

Swish. Swish.

Thwack.

The second blow seared into my flesh and racked my body. I barely resisted the impulse to scream out. The bleeding from the dozens of torn vessels was already welling up into a large, crimson contusion.

'Take some deep breaths. Try to relax. Try to absorb the cane. Don't resist the strokes.' The feverish tone and rising urgency with which the Indian doctor delivered his well-meant advice seemed only to convey a sense of incipient panic. I strained to hold my focus: number two, four more to go to freedom. My brain felt tightly compressed, my teeth were firmly clenched.

Swish. Swish.

Thwack.

The impact of the third stroke jolted down and made my legs kick outwards, wrenching at the leather straps in the process. Each one was searingly more painful than the last. The monster was an expert. They were all DCs – dead centres. Each blow landed on exactly the same spot as the previous one, intensifying the torture tenfold. The third one had split the skin right across. The pressure that had been building up from the damaged vessels below now found a sudden release. The blood began to flow freely. Three down. Three to go.

Swish. Swish.

Thwack.

The next hit thrashed into me with a strange slapping sound. With unerring accuracy the fourth stroke again hit the wound dead centre, causing blood to splatter up onto the small of my back and over my upper thighs. Since I was unable to move, all my insides seemed to be writhing around trying to release the suffering.

'For goodness sake, don't move your head. Take some deep breaths. Come on now, deep breaths.' The doctor was now gripping my head like a wrestler, tighter and tighter with each successive stroke. He was leaning forward, his face right next to mine, his mouth babbling directly into my ear.

The fourth impact had made my tongue jolt up to the roof of my mouth. This was swiftly followed by a burning sensation in my nose as a corrosive taste curdled up through my throat and into my mouth. A feeling of nausea flooded through me. I willed myself not to capitulate. I was determined not to give in, not to show any sign of weakness. The urge to vomit beat through me like storm waves on a beach. I was saved only by the fact that having been in court and then in the holding cell I hadn't had anything to eat all day. If there had been any undigested food in my stomach, by now it would have been strewn over the floor.

Swish. Swish.

Thwack.

Jesus! I inwardly screamed. It felt as if the fifth blow had bludgeoned and torn right into the muscles. The deep groove was now a mass of blood and gore. I felt feverishly hot. I was sweating profusely. The leather beneath me had become slippery with perspiration and allowed a fraction more movement. I had thought carrying the tripod on the death march during Operation *Jaguar* was bad enough, but I have never to this day experienced such excruciating pain. It was as if somehow the pain was bolted onto me. It was so intense it felt as though it couldn't be part of my own body; it felt alien, sinister. I had a tremendous urge to rip it off. I felt that if only I could tear it off I would be free of it.

'Breathe. Don't resist. Breathe. Don't resist.' By now the doctor sounded almost incoherent.

Five down. One more left. I tensed for the final stroke.

Swish. Swish.

Thwack.

Bastard! The sixth stroke seemed to bite down to the bone. Every muscle was jarred rigid. My whole body was consumed in a furnace of pain. I took some rapid breaths. For a moment I couldn't move. I was totally paralysed, then I felt the influx of relief sweep down my spine and lighten my whole body. Number six! I'm a free man! They can't touch me now!

'Release the prisoner.' The governor barked the command and two warders came forward. They unstrapped my wrists and ankles, undid the canvas pads and yanked me roughly to my feet. As I stood up, another wave of nausea and dizziness hit me. I felt like spewing over the pair of them. I started retching violently, but managed to hold it back. The agonizing sensation in my buttocks was overwhelming. The movement of my muscles and the change of gravity had forced more blood to the lower half of my body. Only one opiate thought eased the pain: I'm free – they can't do any more. In a few minutes I'll be out of Stanley Jail forever.

The doctor, now somewhat calmer, handed me my clothes and told me to get dressed. It was an agonizing operation. Every slight movement, every minor lift or twist of my body, altered the configuration of muscles and sinews around my buttocks and redoubled the intensity of the pain. I struggled into my shirt first. I then looked at my underpants. The very thought of having anything tight upon the wound made me feel faint. The underpants were filthy anyway. A nerve-racking, three-day court case in the humid atmosphere of Hong Kong had left its mark in no uncertain terms. I paused, then slung them into the corner of the room as a farewell gift to the prison authorities, thinking, 'Those tossers can clean that up.' I eased myself into my lightweight trousers. Having got the waistband as far as the buttocks I could hardly pull any further, so I left them hanging down at the back, unzipped at the front and loosely held together just enough to avoid being arrested for indecency. The thought then suddenly came into my mind – what am I going to do now?

The decision was made for me. The torture-chamber door opened and in came a man in a white coat pushing a stretcher on wheels. The doctor said, 'You'd better get on here now and we'll take you to the prison health centre where we'll give you some medical aid.' No one offered any assistance as I struggled onto the stretcher and lay face down.

We trundled back down the corridor to the medical centre. I was becoming stronger and more rebellious the further away from the torture room we went. I kept on thinking, they can't do anything more to me now – I'm free. In the medical room I saw an orderly standing around appearing to do nothing. I pointed at him and said, 'You! I want a jab for tetanus straight away!' The startled orderly looked around for some assistance, but the two warders had already gone. 'Yeah, you! I want a jab for tetanus right now! Move!'

He scuttled away to the fridge and got out a little phial, found a syringe, filled it up and gave me a jab in the arm. He then proceeded to dress the bloody wound. 'I cannot dress this wound – it is far too severe, too open. It will be too sore for you. All I can do is put on some antiseptic powder.' After he'd ministered to me, he pointed down the corridor to the prison reception where I'd come in and said, 'You can go now.'

I eased myself off the stretcher, still grasping the waistband of my trousers, trying to keep them up, still in extreme pain and still thinking, what am I supposed to do now? My thoughts had changed from savouring freedom to wondering about practicalities and feeling anxious about how I was going to get back to Gunclub Barracks. All I got from the reception staff were unsympathetic sneers as they handed over the brown envelope and pointed me towards the little door in the corner of the huge prison gates. I was thinking hard. It must be at least five miles to Gunclub. How am I going to get back? There's no way I can sit down in a taxi.

As I stepped through the gate, a rickshaw driver gestured to me. I winced violently at the thought of being clattered through the streets on the hard seat of that solid-wheeled springless contraption. 'You must be fucking joking, mate,' I said to him, but I doubt he understood. I stood there, my rear end throbbing like a cross-Channel ferry's engine. Suddenly I saw a movement out the corner of my eye – and there they all were, waiting for me: an ambulance, CBF, the colonel of the legal services. I nearly collapsed with relief.

CBF approached. 'Hello, Sergeant. Did it hurt?'

The understatement of the decade. I just looked blank, didn't answer.

'Right! You'd better get on this ambulance and we'll take you to BMH.'

My entrance into BMH was made in total secrecy. I was taken round the back to the tradesmen's entrance, and up in a service lift. At the top, the stretcher was wheeled into a sterile wing of the private officers' suite. They did not want it to become known that a member of the SAS had been in trouble.

I was put into bed face down. A medical orderly told me, 'The hospital dermatologist will be along in a few minutes to investigate the wound.' And with that he disappeared. I was still in acute pain, but the friendliness of the surroundings began to act like soothing balm.

When the dermatologist arrived, he looked down at the wound and exclaimed, 'I've never seen a wound like this in the whole of my Army service! Can I take a photograph of it for my records? It really is a unique specimen.'

'Well, I've been humiliated enough already today, so I suppose a photograph won't make any difference now. You can send a copy to Reg the medic back at camp for his photo album.'

The dermatologist went away and returned a few minutes later with his camera. He took shots from different angles, at one point placing a biro pen on my thigh to get the scale. As he flitted around the bed he muttered, 'This is a real prize specimen.' Snap. 'This is definitely one for the archives.' Snap. 'My colleagues must see this one.' Snap. I consoled myself with the thought that if I didn't do anything else with my life, at least I'd made medical history. As for treatment, all the dermatologist could say was, 'There's not much we can do, I'm afraid. It's got to heal on its own. You'll have to spend a few days in BMH on your stomach. There's no point putting any dressing on it. It needs plenty of fresh air. Do you want any painkiller?'

'Yeah, give me a shot of morphine, but make sure it's in the lower thigh.'

After he'd gone, the medical orderly returned and said, 'CBF's coming to see you.'

CBF in all his glory duly appeared. 'Do you realize what you've done, Sergeant?'

'How do you mean?'

'What on earth possessed you to become involved in this escapade? Do you realize the publicity it could attract?'

I just looked at him and said, 'Yeah, I know. It's real headline material: the only sergeant in the British Army with twelve stripes – three on each arm and six on the backside. I'm going to sell my story to the *News of the World* when I get back!'

CBF looked rather shocked. 'I hope you are not serious, Sergeant.' His voice, ringing with uncertainty, tailed off. He disappeared, unsure of whether I was joking or not.

I remained there a further week, being looked after by my own personal captain from the QA's – the Queen Alexandra's Nursing Corps.

My own personal nurse. She really had the tender touch. It was almost worth getting whipped for. Apart from the captain I saw no one else. I was left to my own devices and my own thoughts. After a week I was told that I was fit enough to make it back to the UK and that I would leave on a hospital plane from Kai Tak airport the next day. I drifted off to sleep, happy at the prospect of going home.

12

A Visit from the Colonel

I awoke to hear voices in the distance. I was lying face down on the bed, hot, not quite sweating, but covered in a fine film of body moisture. My nose was blocked, pressed into the pillow. I'd been breathing too long through my mouth; my throat and lips were like burnt cardboard. I turned my head to one side and coughed away the congestion in my chest. The voices were closer now. Must be the orderlies coming to prepare me for the journey to Kai Tak airport and then back to the good old UK.

Good old UK? I wasn't so sure that I was relishing the prospect after all. First there would be an extremely uncomfortable flight lasting several hours, throughout which I'd be lying on my stomach on a stretcher strapped to a rack on a medical C-130. Then, once I was home and had had a couple of weeks' R & R, I'd have to face the wrath of the Colonel. The big interview! My future in the balance after the drama of Hong Kong.

Doors were banging. The orderlies were shouting. I couldn't quite make out what they were saying. I shifted slightly on the bed. The muscles in my buttocks and upper thighs were locked solid, as rigid as ships' girders. Something wasn't quite right. Something was out of sync. It was like hearing a blackbird, fooled by a neon streetlight, singing its morning song in the dead of the night. I began to prise my eyelids open.

'Come on, you lot, out of the pits! Every able-bodied man to assemble in the yard at 0600 hours. You've got five minutes.'

'What the hell…?' I finally managed to lever open my bleary eyes and look around. The room was full of coughing, cursing, fumbling shapes. I slid my hand down the side of my body and gingerly fingertipped my buttocks as if feathering a sleeping baby's head. Nothing! Satin smooth. Not a mark. Then it dawned. Ward 11! The early-morning run!

This I was going to relish. Thursday. Action at last after six days of lethargy and boredom! I jumped into my trainers and shorts and trotted to join the rest downstairs. They were all there: doctors, male nurses and patients. That was the system. The doctors had to be seen to be leading from the front. They had to show a good example – a healthy mind in a healthy body and all that. It was part of the occupational therapy.

Twenty minutes and three miles later, I'd outstripped the lot of them, I was on the finishing line way ahead of the rest. I grabbed my chance. As the first of the medics puffed into sight around the last hundred metres, I gave it Sickener 1 for all I was worth. 'Come on, you lazy bastards! You should be fitter than me. You do this every morning. I'm supposed to be a burnt-out alkie and I've left you standing!' I beasted them like a veteran instructor, relishing my moment of glory. 'What kept you? I'm thirty-eight. I'm fifteen years older than some of you guys and I still came in way ahead of you. You should be fitter than me. I haven't been running for ten days.'

They weren't amused.

Nor was the doctor I bumped into coming down the corridor later in the day. He looked tired, stressed and overworked. I said to him, 'What's up, doc, got problems?'

'This job is really getting to me,' he muttered. 'I'm up to here with the pressure of work.'

He had fallen headlong into the trap. I lowered my voice, and with a concerned look and in hushed tones of mock-sympathy I enquired, 'Do you want to sit down and talk about it?'

A psychiatrist! Depressed! And we were the ones who were supposed to have the problems!

A sense of humour works wonders – the best therapy imaginable. I didn't fancy lying there for days on end like an inanimate cabbage. That would be too much like toeing the line – far too boring, far too predictable. I sensed another opportunity a few days later, when the hospital Colonel was about to make his weekly visitation. He would normally sweep around the ward in magisterial style, his sycophantic entourage clucking behind him, enquiring of people lying on their beds or sitting in their chairs how they were feeling. I secretly had a word with the other lads in the ward, then primed the newly arrived lance-corporal from the Royal Irish Rangers, who'd been given the bed nearest the door. 'Hey, Shaun. When the Colonel comes in, bring the ward to attention. He expects that. It'll go down well on your report.'

I went back to lie on my bed, thinking Shaun would forget all about it – he was after all looking a bit dazed. I was wrong. Half an hour later, the Colonel marched in. Without a moment's hesitation, Shaun leapt to his feet, roaring, 'Ward! Ward! Shun!'

As one man, all the alkies shot to attention with a stiff salute and stood there rigid. The Colonel, an astonished look on his face, was rendered nearly speechless. 'Er... Oh. Very good, chaps. Very good. Carry on.'

You didn't need a sense of humour for the videos they showed us, they were funny enough in themselves. They were meant to convey the evils of drink and inspire us to mend our ways. It was difficult taking them seriously. There was the Jimmy Greaves' story – a famous footballer hits the net, then hits the bottle. Then the Glasgow rubber men – drunks staggering down Buchanan Street in broad daylight. When this particular one was shown I used to play 'Spot the Jock'. Jimmy the Jock who'd saved Ginge on the death march claimed that he had a leading role in one of the street scenes. And finally, the third video, the main attraction, the X Certificate horror film: cirrhosis! Full technicolour close-ups and cross-sections of gory livers – dark red healthy ones wobbling on mortuary slabs and then alcohol-sodden ones looking like jellies at a kids' party that someone had been sick over. Aversion therapy, they called it – just like a scene from *A Clockwork Orange*. Or it would have been if anyone paid any attention.

'The liver becomes congested with blood, first grows very large, and then begins to shrink and harden…'

The film quality was poor – the soundtrack scratchy, the pictures flickering and popping.

'Haemorrhage from the stomach may arise, the blood being vomited or passed through the bowel…'

It was like an out-of-date training film for student doctors, the medical equivalent of Mrs Beeton's cookbook.

'The urine becomes scanty and turbid. Ascites or dropsy of the peritoneal cavity is very often present…'

I looked around the room at the other half-dozen lads in the audience. Two were asleep, one was staring out of the window, one was reading a magazine and the other two were watching the film with dramatic indifference.

Phase two of the treatment was nearing its end: ten days of lectures, videos and interviews, and an LFT count every morning. The results of the count were transferred to a graph. If the line dropped below the critical threshold and stayed below, they considered you fit enough for release – physically fit, that is. If any psychological stress fractures were detected, that was an altogether different matter. And they were clever. They shifted, prodded, probed, searched the defences, sought the chink in the mental armour, X-rayed the brain for hairline cracks. If any cracks were found and they were serious enough, the brain would be stamped 'Rejected' and cast down the chute into the Stygian depths of Ward 5 below.

Twelve per cent of casualties in any major battle are psychiatric cases, soldiers suffering from combat stress. For many, the symptoms are temporary and manageable. The rest are the ones with unseen wounds. You can see an arm in a sling, a leg in plaster, but you can't see their wounds. They are shunned by society with even greater revulsion than those who have obviously horrific wounds – severed limbs, faces grossly disfigured by burns, sightless eyes. The ones with the mental wounds are often the ones who have done and seen things that the ordinary man in the street couldn't even begin to conceive of, in order to safeguard the well-being of that same man and to allow him to continue walking down that same street in freedom. Their reward is to be entombed in their own minds, like a dead Pharaoh's followers doomed to remain in their master's burial chamber, deep in the centre of a pyramid, listening in horror as the sand that held the great building blocks in check trickles away and the stones come crashing down to seal off the passageways to the world outside.

Some of the characters in Ward 11 looked like prime candidates for demotion to Ward 5, first-class specimens just waiting to slide down the chute. One of them had built up an irrational grudge against his orderly officer. One day, while the officer was doing his regular rounds, he'd jumped on top of him out of a two-storey window and broken his collarbone. Another character was worse still. He'd attempted suicide by slashing his wrists. He'd been in Northern Ireland and couldn't stand the stress. The crazy thing was, when I questioned him further, I discovered he hadn't even been on the streets: he was a mechanic with the REME! Yet a third bloke, only about twenty-three years old, had a severe case of the DTs. He had to be kept locked away. He was only ever let out to go to the toilet, when two orderlies would march him through the ward, his feet dragging along the floor, his body shaking like a leaf.

My case seemed minor compared to these people's. I should never have been there in the first place. I'd already proved I was physically fitter than the rest. I now had to prove I was mentally fit. Tomorrow, I would face the big one. My interview and assessment with the chief psychiatrist. It all now depended on one man.

13

The Embassy Siege

The interview was preying on my mind. I'd tossed and turned all night, and now a fog of tiredness clouded my brain. I took some deep breaths of air to try to clear my thoughts. When I reached the office I knocked on the door sharply and confidently, just once, summoning up some strength by doing so, letting the person inside know I was a force to be reckoned with.

'Enter.' It was more formal, more authoritative than the polite, 'Come in'.

I went inside. The owner of the voice was speaking on the telephone. I looked at the chair. He caught my glance and gestured to me to remain standing exactly where I was. That was ominous. He continued with the seemingly leisurely conversation on the phone. Delaying tactics. Power games. I'd seen it all before. They try to belittle you by showing who's in control. The big desk, the impressive chair, your small chair, lower than his – it's all part of the strategy.

The conversation finished and the Colonel put the phone down. He paused for a moment, then picked up a thick sheaf of papers from his desk and waved them furiously in the air. 'Look at these, Sergeant! These signals from Hong Kong, they're all about *you!*' As he spoke the word '*you*' his voice rose several decibels. He flung the signals towards the rear of the room. They hit the back wall with a crash and fluttered to the floor in an untidy heap. 'We are the people who go into these places, do the job, keep quiet about the job, and at the end we leave the job silently, and we return to the UK as if nothing has happened. What do you have to say in your defence?'

I launched into my plea of mitigation modelled on the one in Kowloon Court, focusing on the self-defence angle and ending with, 'You don't have to go to the jungles of Malaya to find a jungle.'

The Colonel pondered for a while, then said, 'Well, Sergeant. You should not have been there in the first place. But there are certain mitigating circumstances surrounding this case. Therefore, although I could RTU you for life and you would never return to the SAS, I am going to RTU you for only eighteen months.'

So it was back to the Royal Engineers, back to Southwood Camp.

I decided to start off as I meant to go on. I would seize the psychological initiative and gain the upper hand. I knew the very first thing they would do would be to order me to get a short back and sides. This was their way of humiliating people, suppressing the individuality. I beat them to it by having my hair shaved virtually down to the wood before I left Hereford.

As I strode confidently through the gate of the RE depot, a regimental police corporal bawled, 'Hey, you! Come here!'

I thought, he can't be shouting at me. I haven't been shouted at for ten years! I looked behind me. I couldn't see anyone else.

'Yes, you! Come here!'

I looked behind me again. Still no one there. 'Right, you bastard,' I thought, as I walked up to him. He was in his little sentry box, behind his little pigeonhole. He opened the window, about to say something more, but before he could utter another word I grabbed him by the throat, looked him straight in the eye and snapped, 'You! I'm a sergeant from the SAS. Where's the RSM's office?'

He suddenly turned pale. 'Sorry, Sarge. I thought you were one of the new recruits,' he mumbled apologetically as he furiously dusted himself down.

I strode into the RSM's office and announced boldly, 'I'm posted in from the SAS.'

The RSM looked up slowly from the carefully printed duty roster he was studying. 'You mean you're here on a course, are you?'

'No. I'm posted in.'

'You mean you're on a course.'

'No. I'm posted in.' I was determined to give them a hard time.

'Where are your documents?'

'Have they not sent them yet?'

'No. We haven't got any documents. Wait here.'

He went off to check with the Colonel.

'Right. Come in and see the Colonel.'

I strode into the Colonel's office, and it started all over again.

'Are you here on a course?'

'No. I'm posted in.'

'Where are your documents?'

'I haven't got any documents.'

'Where are you from?'

'I'm posted in from the SAS.'

'Are you on a course?'

'No, I'm posted in!' I must have seemed like a PoW giving only name, rank and number.

'Oh, well, what rank are you?' The Colonel was struggling to inject some logic into my presence.

'I'm a sergeant in the SAS.'

'No, in the RE.'

'I don't know. I haven't been in the RE for ten years.'

'Right. We'd better find out what your rank was in the RE.' He rang up RE records at Brighton, put the phone down and said, 'Well, Sergeant. I've got some bad news for you.'

'What's that?'

'You're now a lance-corporal in the RE.'

'I can't be a lance-corporal at my age. I'm thirty-three! I'm a substantive sergeant in the SAS. You can stuff that idea for a start!'

I argued all the pros and cons for the next fifteen minutes, emphasizing my point of view by banging on the table at regular intervals. In the end, the Colonel couldn't hack it any more. He called out, 'Captain Edwards. Come in here. Send this man on three weeks' leave while we sort out his case.'

They would no doubt soon find my precious documents. Without documents the British Army would grind to a standstill. From when you join the Army to when you leave, or die in between, every single second of your life is documented. Every precise detail is recorded. More effort goes into keeping accurate files than went into winning the Second World War.

The irony is that no matter how thorough the paperwork, like everything else it is subject to human error. While I was away on leave, word obviously got around the RE depot about the new upstart recently arrived from the SAS, and the spineless wonders in the sergeants' mess evidently decided to try and teach the new boy a lesson. They tried to recall me from leave and put me on guard duty on Christmas Day 1977. There's no way I'm going to work Christmas, I thought. There's no way they're going to rip me off. I'll beat them at their own game.

I ignored the phone calls and stayed at home. Conveniently catching flu, I made damn sure I got my insurance. They'd obviously decided to put the recall in writing so that it could be entered in my documents for a potential future disciplinary hearing. An OHMS telegram duly went out on the morning of 24 December saying, 'Report back to Southwood Camp for duty by 0830 hours 25th, repeat 25th, December 1977.'

The trouble was they addressed the telegram not to me but to my sixty-six-year-old father, a Dunkirk veteran. He'd been on the Reserve for ten years after the war, but he certainly wasn't expecting anything like this at his stage in life. He took the telegram to the local police station and asked them to sort it out. The military wires started buzzing, and an hour later he received a message from the embarrassed authorities to say that he wasn't needed after all and that the telegram was really meant for his son. They'd tried to knock my morale and it hadn't worked. They'd ended up looking complete fools.

I returned to Southwood three weeks after Christmas and once again stood in front of the Colonel.

'We have now got the blueprint of your career.' His voice sounded enthusiastic, as if he'd been primed by a higher authority. 'I have looked in your documents and I have found that you have done an HGV 2 driving course. Do you realize that with that HGV licence, if you do a month's theory study on MT regulations and pass the Driver REB1 course, you'll be qualified up to Regimental Sergeant Major in the RE?'

'That's all very well, but what's my rank right now?'

'Well, for the duration of the course, we'll make you up to Local Sergeant.'

'Thank you very much.' Local Sergeant unpaid and unwanted, I thought as I quietly closed the Colonel's door behind me.

I passed the course with ease. I was then called back in to see the Colonel.

'We've got a little job for you. We've had an officer cry off from running a recruit troop. Would you like to become an acting troop officer to run the troop?'

I quite fancied the idea of playing God. It meant that I had beaten the career boys back in Hereford to a commission. Visions of going down to the station with a four-tonner to pick up a batch of Sid Vicious lookalikes with purple socks, leather jackets and razor blades and safety pins through their ears, and then beasting them into shape, were rather appealing. I said, 'I'll run a mini-selection. Their feet won't touch the ground.'

'Carry on, Sergeant.'

I must have achieved some kind of record. I went from sergeant in the SAS down to lance-corporal Royal Engineers up to acting troop officer. All within two months!

After eight months as acting troop officer with a sergeant, a corporal and three lance-corporals pandering to my every whim, I was told an officer was moving in to take over my role and I would then be second-in-command. The character turned up: warrant officer second class. He wasn't a bad bloke really, but I resented his authority. I decided to short-circuit the developing personality clash; I took him to one side and said, 'I can't hack this. I've been running this troop very well without you for eight months. I'm off.' I went to the nearest telephone, rang up the second-in-command of the SAS and said, 'You've got to get me out of here or else I'll throw another wobbler. See what you can do.'

He contacted Group HQ. A meeting was arranged. I discussed it with the Colonel, who said, 'Right. We'll get you on next selection in January 1979.'

I was pitched straight into test week. I was given the option of missing out the endurance march if I got A grades in each of the first two marches. It was a great incentive. I didn't stop running for two days, and duly got the grades. I was back in the Regiment, back in business! There was just one catch. Having left the SAS as a sergeant, here I was at the age of thirty-four rejoining as a trooper.

8.30am, Wednesday 30 April 1980. Fifteen months had passed since my return, fifteen months of routine, boredom and lack of action. The rugby-club hangover combined with the noise of the other team members pulling on equipment, filling magazines and cocking weapons made me feel as cheerful as an abattoir-bound pig. I resented that upon my return to the Regiment I'd been unable to get back into my old troop, Eight Troop, the lads I'd fought at Mirbat with. There were no vacancies.

My separation from my old mates in Eight Troop had been made all the more acute when in February of the previous year I'd heard the news of Mike Kealy's death during a forty-mile endurance training march in the Brecon Beacons. The hero of Mirbat six years before, a major and DSO, he died of exposure during a cruel combination of snow, ice and fog. It was a tragic loss and saddened me deeply.

With an ill-disguised lethargy I pushed open the door to the Killing House. My mind was barely in focus as I threw down my holdall of assault kit and began pulling at the wire seal on the box of 9-milly ammo. I broke a fingernail in the process as it stubbornly refused to open. I cursed. When you're not in the mood for a job, even inanimate objects conspire against you. They seem to assume a life of their own and to frustrate your efforts at every turn. I tore off the loose piece of fingernail. It came off at a deeper angle than I'd expected, biting into the skin at the side and drawing blood.

Another routine day was in prospect, a day of shooting neat holes in Figure 11 targets. I was beginning to get bored with this place: the oppressive sameness of the range practices, the same six rooms, the target paste-pots always empty. And the Figure 11 targets themselves. In the old Operation *Jaguar* days, they came properly trimmed with the corners neatly cut off so that they fitted the wooden veneers exactly. Nowadays, the picture of the sinister-looking Russian storm trooper was stamped onto an oblong sheet of brown paper and you had to fuck and fart about fitting the target facing to the trimmed veneer. And then there was the problem of lead in the enclosed atmosphere of the killing rooms. Firing our submachine guns on automatic over long periods of time filled the small rooms with lead fumes. It occurred to me more than once that breathing the thick smoke couldn't be doing my lungs any good. Only yesterday I had coughed up a large black ball of phlegm at the end of the day's training.

As I pulled on my assault kit, a pain in my temple throbbed continuously. I looked down at the heavy Bristol body armour lying on the bench-seat next to my holdall. Fuck the high-velocity plates! I thought, I'm not in the mood for training with that ton weight today – and I threw the ceramic plates back in the holdall. With the now much lighter body armour secure in place, I drew on my skin-tight aviator's leather gloves, cocked the action of my Heckler & Koch MP5, introducing a live round into the chamber, applied the safety-catch, carried out the same operation on my Browning pistol and realized I had begun to sweat. It was going to be a long, tedious day.

* * *

9.00am. Six Arab revolutionaries – Makki, Ali, Shai, Faisal, Hassan and Oan, the leader – assembled on the blood-red carpet in the foyer at 105 Lexham Gardens in Kensington, London. They belonged to the Mohieddin al Nasser Martyr Group, fighting for the autonomy of Arabistan, an oil-rich province in the south-west of Iran, annexed by the country in 1926. In their small, lightweight holdalls they had a veritable arsenal. It included two 9mm machine pistols, accurate up to 150 metres and firing 700 rounds per minute; three Browning automatics with thirteen-round magazines loaded with Winchester hollow-point ammunition; one .38 revolver and several Russian hand grenades. They bade farewell to the handful of unwitting residents who had befriended them and headed for their rendezvous with destiny.

* * *

11.20am. 'Split down into three teams of four again.' Tak's voice boomed across the small changing room, his beetle-black eyes, the eyes of a deep thinker who weighs up the options carefully before acting, slowly scrutinizing the assembled team members.

My one consolation amid all the monotony of routine training was that Tak, my brother-in-arms since Mirbat days, had also found his way into Six Troop. A powerful bond of friendship had developed between us. In his assault kit he looked large and menacing. With his big hands he took a firm grip on life, with his wide feet and muscular toes he stood his ground unyieldingly, and with his broad forehead he faced the world square-on. In his solidity and steadfastness he was extremely placid. When fooling and rolling around with the Firqat children in Dhofar he had been like a cuddly teddy bear. Nothing appeared to bother him. He would take everything in his stride – or so it seemed. Yet there was a distant point, a point that was rarely reached, but once it was, Tak would explode with an awesome temper. He would then become as ferocious as a grizzly bear.

'The game plan is the same. Head shots – double taps or single only. Limits of exploitation are your allocated rooms.' He pointed to the blackboard, circling every individual's responsibility with the barrel of his 9-milly. 'Be on your doors in five minutes. I will initiate with a burst of fire into the long gallery. Any questions?'

'Will there be any distractions this time?' My voice cut through the tedium.

'Yeah, I got a thunderflash on ISFE for this one. I'll detonate after the burst of MP5,' replied Tak, replacing his 9-milly pistol in the quick-draw holster, snapping closed the securing stud on the thumb-brake with a well-practised ease.

* * *

11.25am. The terrorists worked quickly. Shamags were pulled tight across dark Arab features, holdalls were unzipped, weapons produced. Then they were up the steps and bursting in through the slightly ajar main door of 16 Princes Gate. Oan, well-built, square-bodied, the first man in, made straight for PC Lock, who was standing by the door to reception at the bottom of the stairs.

* * *

11.25am. The combination of the twenty-round burst from the MP5 and the deafening explosion of the thunderflash on the ISFE rocked the Killing House. My number three on the Remington blasted the lock of the small combat room with a blank cartridge and then kicked the door in. Drag – the range warden – will go mad if he finds that one, I thought, as the door flew open. In I went and headed straight for the cluster of Figure 11 targets propped up in their rickety stands in the far corner. Usual thing, I thought quickly, my eyes doing a radar scan of the room. Four terrorists and three hostages.

'Ba-bang, Ba-bang, Ba-bang'. Three double taps in less than three seconds, six neat holes in three terrorist heads.

'Ba-bang'. My number two neutralized a kneeling target behind the chair in a corner.

'Paste up,' shouted Tak from the door, adding to the tedium of the moment.

* * *

11.26am. 'Don't move! Don't move!' screamed Oan in Farsi. Then came a deafening burst of submachine-gun fire. All Trevor Lock could see was confusion, disorder, chequered shamags and automatic weapons. A hand came forward and ripped the radio out of his tunic.

'OK, OK,' he found himself saying, as he brought up his hand to investigate a sharp stinging pain in his cheek. The Iranian Embassy siege had begun.

* * *

11.40am. I applied the safety-catch to my MP5, pushed the S6 respirator onto the top of my head and reached for the paste-pot and patches. As I pasted over the neat holes with a grubby Woolworth's paste-brush, a thin, gluey, poorly mixed paste wormed down the handle of the brush and slithered over my fine leather gloves. I cursed inwardly and began applying the one-inch square brown patches to the bullet-holes.

* * *

11.44am. At the precise moment that the first blob of sticky white glue slicked into contact with the smooth black leather gloves, a telephone rang in the Kremlin. Dusty, ex-D Squadron and now serving with the Metropolitan Police, was ringing the Head Shed to warn them about the developing drama. His information was sketchy: a group of armed men had taken over the Iranian Embassy in Princes Gate, and a police constable from the Diplomatic Protection Group was being held at gunpoint. More disturbingly, a burst of submachine-gun fire had been heard. That was all the information he could offer.

* * *

11.48am. 'Be-be-be-be-bee-beep'. I had just finished patching up my second double tap when the whole building was filled with the sound of a dozen electronic bleepers.

'The scalybacks have pressed the wrong button again,' shouted my number two.

'Or it's another lemon,' I added sarcastically. My thoughts went back to the last lemon, a couple of years before, when we had roared down to Stansted Airport to stop Idi Amin getting access to the UK. He had allegedly been circling the airfield in his private plane asking for permission to land.

Suddenly Rusty's harsh voice, calm with certainty, pierced sharp and clear through the high-pitched electronic bleeps echoing round the rooms and corridors of the Killing House. 'From Crocker. This is the real thing. Pack your gear, then move into the hangar for a brief.'

As I dashed for the door, I watched with satisfaction as the cheap Woolworth's paste-brush arced through the air and hit the paste-bucket with a watery splosh.

* * *

11.55am. 'We are members of a democratic revolutionary front for the liberation of Arabistan. We are the Martyrs.' Oan's cold, chilling voice penetrated the tense atmosphere of Room 9 on the second floor. Before him were gathered twenty-six frightened hostages: seventeen Embassy staff; eight visitors, including Harris and Cramer, two BBC men who had been visiting the Embassy to secure visas, and Ron Morris, the chauffeur; and Embassy security policeman Trevor Lock. Oan viewed his captives with satisfaction, his dark eyes beneath the frizzy Afro hairstyle darting from one figure to another. He felt well pleased with himself. He had struck the first blow for the freedom of his beloved Arabistan.

The terrorists' demands were now issued. 'One: we demand our human and legitimate rights. Two: we demand freedom, autonomy and recognition of the Arabistan people. Three: we demand the release of ninety-one Arab prisoners in Arabistan. If all three demands are not met by noon on Thursday 1 May, the Embassy and all the hostages will be blown up.'

* * *

11.30pm. 'Toad, how are we doing for time?'

'We're doing just fine. Keep the speed down,' replied Toad, an assault-team leader, the bowl of his meerschaum pipe sparking and glowing in the darkness.

I eased my foot off the accelerator and watched the needle of the speedo drop to a comfortable seventy miles per hour. I was experiencing the usual tight feeling, the strange tingling alertness I always got when I was heading into a situation where a real enemy might be waiting. As my right foot pumped fuel to power the engine, my heart pounded adrenaline to fire my body to peak alertness.

As we reached the outskirts of the capital, Toad suddenly sat upright and reached for the London *A to Z*. We had come off the M40 and hit the Marylebone Road. The meerschaum pipe had disappeared and the flexi map-reading light had been switched on. 'Once we're past Madame Tussaud's, take the next main road on your left. That will lead us to the barracks.'

The signpost for the A4201 appeared and I swung the Range Rover left into Albany Street. We motored along for 300 metres and then turned right in through the main gate of Regent's Park Barracks, the holding area. The guard checked our IDs, the barrier went up and I eased the vehicle into the parking zone. We unpacked the assault kit in the sparse surroundings of the holding area. The weapon bundles were laid out, boxes of live ammunition broken open and magazines charged. By now it was the early hours of Thursday morning. We had arrived.

* * *

8.00am, Thursday 1 May. 'Oan is beginning to experience a growing feeling of irritability. He has shown good faith by releasing a sick woman, Frieda Mazaffarian. The police have not reciprocated to his request for a doctor to come to the Embassy and examine one of the male hostages. He is becoming increasingly frustrated at the negative response to his demands. He has managed to put an international telephone call through to the Foreign Ministry in Tehran, only to be told by Iran's Foreign Minister, Sadegh Ghotzbadeh, that his group are the agents of President Carter and the CIA and that the hostages would consider it an honour and a privilege to die as martyrs for the Iranian Revolution.'

The holding area at Regent's Park Barracks was like any other holding area: large, derelict and draughty. The toilets were blocked and there was only cold running water. Grey powdery dust clung to the floors, window ledges and washbasins, turning the whole building into a health hazard. I was lying on an Army camp bed, going over in my mind the details of the early-morning green-slime brief we had just received. I was wearing my black overalls, belt kit and Northern Ireland lightweight boots. The rest of my assault kit was close at hand. My MP5, body armour and assault waistcoat loaded with stun grenades were on a chair next to me. My respirator was in its olive-green container. The waiting had begun.

* * *

11.00am. Inside No. 16 Oan was wrestling with his first problem – the sick British hostage. Chris Cramer, the BBC sound organizer, was lying on the floor, doubled up with severe stomach pains. The sweat ran down his face in rivulets as he rocked back and forth, imploring Oan, 'Get me a doctor. For God's sake, get me a doctor.'

'But your British police have refused permission,' replied Oan.

'How do we know this?' interrupted Sim Harris, the BBC sound recordist.

'Come, I show you,' said Oan.

Harris was led downstairs to a green radiophone that the police had passed through a ground-floor window in a shoebox secured to a long pole. Harris talked to the police negotiator, pleading for a doctor for Cramer. The negotiator replied that his request was being considered. As the negotiations became more heated, with the negotiator telling Harris to persuade Oan to release Cramer, and Harris once again pleading with the police for a doctor, the now seriously ill Cramer was helped downstairs and laid on the floor of the Embassy foyer.

At the sight of the sick BBC man writhing about on the carpet, Oan thought that his most productive course of action would be to release him. So finally, at 11.15am, the Embassy front door opened, and Cramer, still doubled up in pain, stumbled to a waiting ambulance. It was Oan's first mistake. The thorough debriefing to which Cramer was subjected after his release was to prove crucial to the planning of the coming operation.

* * *

7.30pm. I readjusted my position on the floor of the Avis hire van to ease the cramp in my left leg. The rear stowage compartment of the van was packed to the roof with personal kit, assault equipment and team members. In the restricted space it was impossible to get comfortable. We were travelling through central London on our way to the new holding area, a location in the heart of South Kensington. Owing to the events of the day, the Head Shed had decided that it would make sound tactical sense for us to be in the vicinity of No. 16, in case of the imminent slaughter of the hostages. It would cut our reaction time down to almost zero.

The situation was deteriorating. Oan was becoming increasingly tense and unpredictable. He had allowed the deadline – and a new one of 2.00pm – to pass without incident. But his demands were changed. He now wanted three Arab ambassadors to act as mediators and negotiate a plane to take him and his group out of Britain.

The Avis van rumbled to a halt. It would be a relief to leave the claustrophobic atmosphere of the rear stowage compartment. We grabbed our holdalls and bergens and jumped out. Our three vans were parked in a side-street east of Princes Gate. This really was the concrete jungle, a million miles away from the tall greenstuff.

* * *

9.30am, Friday 2 May. 'I know what's going on. Your British police have cut off the telex and the international telephone. Your secret police want total control over what the outside world knows about our demands. I am now forced to apply pressure. I must kill a hostage.' Standing in the doorway of Room 9, Oan surveyed the male hostages. They looked devastated. 'You, bring Dr Ezzatti to me,' ordered Oan, pointing his submachine gun at journalist Mustapha Karkouti. Karkouti helped the unfortunate Cultural Attaché to his feet.

'This could be a counter-productive move,' said Lock, staring directly at Oan. 'Why don't we have another talk with the police negotiator?'

Oan hesitated. 'OK. But no tricks or I will kill the hostages,' and he brought his gun up to Ezzatti's head to emphasize the point.

'There is a hostage about to be killed unless you allow Oan full use of telephone and telex.' Lock's voice boomed out over the forecourt from the open window on the first floor.

'Impossible,' came the negotiator's reply.

'But a man is about to be killed,' pleaded Lock.

'What do they mean, impossible?' cut in Oan, sensing a challenge to his authority. He forced the gun harder into the side of Ezzatti's head. He stared fixedly at the terror-stricken man and then appeared to relent, pushing the Cultural Attaché to the rear of the room. 'I want to talk to a man from your BBC, a man who knows Harris.' Oan spoke slowly but could not veil the threats. 'I set a new deadline in a few hours.' And with that, all went quiet at the first-floor window.

* * *

3.00pm. The police had finally produced Tony Crabb, the managing editor of BBC TV News and a personal friend of Sim Harris. Crabb scribbled the hurried statement shouted by Harris from the first-floor window into an old notebook. Oan demanded a coach to take gunmen, hostages and an Arab ambassador to Heathrow. The non-Iranian hostages would be released at the airport. An aircraft would then take the remaining hostages, gunmen and ambassadors to an unspecified Middle Eastern country, where the last hostages would be released. Oan also wanted his aims and grievances broadcast by the BBC that night.

* * *

8.30pm. 'The whole of the ground-floor and the first-floor windows are armour-plated. I know because I cleaned up after the contractors had finished. Behind the wooden door at the front there is an ornate steel security door.' The caretaker's voice cut through the silence of the briefing room like a chainsaw.

We were all sitting around a scale model of the Embassy which had been hastily constructed in quarter-inch plywood the day before. It had taken us twenty-four hours to locate the caretaker, who had been enjoying a day off when the siege began. And here he was giving us our best target brief to date. He knew every nook and cranny in the

Embassy, every storeroom and broom cupboard. I could only speculate as to what he was feeling, suddenly catapulted into the limelight from the anonymity of his humble occupation. All eyes were on him. His was the last job anyone would have chosen if they had wanted to make an impact on the world scene. But from the security forces' point of view, it was the ideal job to enable someone to give an intimate portrait of the structure of the building. Hell! What a stroke of luck locating this guy, I thought. Without his information, our initial response to the threatened slaughter of hostages could have turned into a real can of worms. The original plan had been to run out of No. 14 and batter in the ground-floor window and main door of No. 16 with sledgehammers. Christ! With the armour plating, the sledges would have bounced off. It would have been like trying to knock down a concrete wall with a toffee hammer.

There now followed a hectic period of replanning. Orders were rewritten, we were rebriefed, demolition equipment was issued. I began to get a feeling that this nut was going to be even tougher to crack than we'd anticipated.

* * *

11.30pm. The final outrage for Oan. He had sat right through the evening listening to the regular news bulletins, growing more and more frustrated as each successive broadcast drew a blank. He had become obsessed with hearing his aims and grievances broadcast. The BBC had indeed now transmitted a brief broadcast stating the new demands – but to Oan's disbelief and anger they'd got it wrong. The BBC had stated that the British Government wanted the Arab ambassadors to negotiate with Iran. In fact, Oan had demanded that all negotiations be conducted through the British Government. He rose slowly to his feet, his eyes ablaze with fanaticism and hatred. A chill of fear swept through the hostages.

* * *

6.05am, Saturday 2 May. Beeeeeeeep. The single shrill tone of the field telephone penetrated the operations centre of Alpha Control, the police forward operation room situated in No. 25 Princes Gate – the Royal School of Needlework. A surreal setting if ever there was one! The duty negotiator, a tall, slim, refined man, rubbed his tired, gritty eyes and lifted the receiver. 'Good morning. This is David,' he said politely. 'How…'

'You are liars!' Oan's angry voice scythed into the attempt at exchanging pleasantries. 'You have cheated and deceived me over my demands.'

It was a perfectly clear line. The duty negotiator sensed the extreme agitation in Oan's voice. He tried again to calm him down, to divert his mind from the high tension. 'Oan, what would you all like for breakfast?'

'I'm not hungry. I want to talk to the Arab ambassador.'

'Oan, we are doing our best, but this all takes time.'

'I have no time left. You bring one of the ambassadors to the phone now.'

The negotiator gripped the telephone receiver tighter at the sound of the rising hysteria in Oan's voice. 'Oan. The Foreign Office are dealing with your demands right now, but it all takes time.'

'You are not dealing with my demands at all. You are sitting on your fat bottoms in your warm offices doing nothing. I tell you now. Because of Britain's deceit, your British people, your British police – they will be the last to be released. And if you do not send the BBC man back to talk to me, the one who was here yesterday, someone will have to die.' With that, the phone went dead and silence descended on Alpha Control.

3.30pm. Tony Crabb, the managing editor of BBC TV News, finally turned up. He was bollocked by Harris for putting lives at risk by delaying the broadcast of the gunman's statement and by not ensuring that the statement was correct in every detail. At this stage, the police negotiator, standing close to Crabb, decided to intervene.

He agreed to take down Oan's statement and personally ensure that it was correct. He took out his notebook and pencil and began recording Oan's statement as it was shouted down from the first-floor window by Mustapha Karkouti. The final clause of the statement demanded a guarantee that the BBC put out the demands totally accurately and on the next news bulletin. This was another mistake. It gave the negotiator a bargaining point. He seized his opportunity. 'OK, Oan. I will give you your guarantee if you show us some good faith and release some hostages.'

There was a pause, a movement by the curtains. The air was charged with tension.

'We give you one,' came Oan's reply from within the room.

'We need more,' said the police negotiator impassively.

Another pause. Another tension-filled minute.

'I give you two.'

The bargain was struck.

Two hostages were chosen for release. First, Ali-Gholi Ghazan-Far, a Pakistani educationalist, the man who snored loudly at night and kept everyone awake. That was why he was chosen. They wanted to get rid of him. And second, Haideh Kanji, an Embassy worker who was pregnant. Oan demanded that his statement be broadcast accurately before the release of the two hostages. The police demanded the hostages be released first. Result: stalemate.

On receipt of the police demand, Oan threw the phone to the floor in anger and frustration, threatening to kill a hostage at 9.00pm if nothing was heard on the Nine O'Clock News. At this latest threat, Karkouti went completely to pieces and sank to his knees, pleading with Oan not to carry out the execution. Karkouti's pleading must have struck a humanitarian chord in Oan's fanatical brain, or perhaps it was just a psychopath's cunning that led to the terrorist leader's change of heart. No one will ever know. In the event, Oan decided to meet the police halfway and release the pregnant woman before the 9.00pm deadline.

'We swear to God and to the British people and government that no danger whatsoever…' The voice of Scotland Yard's Head of Information drifted over the airwaves of the BBC at exactly 9.00pm that evening, relaying Oan's statement of demands word-for-word to an anxious, waiting world. It was precise and word-perfect. The hostages and the gunmen were jubilant, kissing and hugging each other, tears of joy running freely down their flushed cheeks. Only one man was absent from the celebrations. Oan. He stood to one side, nursing his machine pistol in the crook of his arm, alone, poker-faced.

A short while later, Ali-Gholi Ghazan-Far was led downstairs to the ground floor. He stepped through the main door of the Embassy and walked across the road to freedom and a waiting ambulance.

* * *

11.00pm. It was a fine, starry night. The sun had vanished, abandoning London to the evening's dark embrace. The air was exquisitely clear as we carefully picked our way across the rooftops towards No. 16 Princes Gate. An eerie silence had descended on Knightsbridge and South Kensington. No noisy rush of traffic, no late-night revellers lost in search of Chelsea. The rustle of clothing, the leather creak of belt kit, the scuffing noise of a running shoe on a bit of loose guttering were the only sounds that stirred the hush of that tranquil May evening.

Suddenly – crack! The sound of a pistol going off. We froze for a few seconds. One of the lads was pointing to his foot; he'd broken a slate as he'd stepped on it. We gave the thumbs-up to the D11 sniper in his concealed position on No. 14 and moved on.

I looked out across the rooftops in front of us. It was a veritable aerial farm, with a jungle of telescopic poles, wires and satellite dishes. About five metres ahead of me was the dim, shadowy figure of Roy, the recce-party leader. He was pointing at something by his feet. As I drew level with him, I caught a glint of moonlight on glass. It was the Embassy skylight. 'This is it. The skylight of No. 16,' whispered Roy, looking down at the glass frame. 'Let's see if it will open.' He knelt down and gripped the wooden surround and attempted to lift it, but it seemed to be locked solid. He swore under his breath and stood up.

We were staring blankly at the wooden frame when Pete, the third team member, whispered quietly, 'Let's peel the lead back,' and with that he knelt down and began picking at the strip of lead waterproofing around the edge of the glass. After fifteen minutes' careful work he had removed most of the lead and was able to lift one of the glass panes clear of the frame. He reached through the hole and after a few seconds stood up with a lock in his hand. 'It wasn't even locked, just pushed through the clasp,' he whispered triumphantly, having once more gripped the skylight and slowly eased it open.

Moonlight immediately flooded the small room beneath us. We found ourselves looking down into a cramped bathroom. Directly below us was a large white enamel bath. In the left-hand corner was a grimy washbasin, and opposite it was the door that could lead us to the top landing of the Embassy and eventually to the terrorist stronghold. I felt a sudden rush of excitement, a surge of adrenaline, at the thought of the options this new development offered. I had to stifle an urge to become the first SAS man into the Embassy. It would have been quite easy to grip the wooden surround of the skylight base and lower myself down onto the edge of the bath. But thoughts of immortality were interrupted by a hand on my shoulder and by Roy's voice whispering, 'Come on. Let's get back to the holding area. We can tell the boss we've got a guaranteed entry point.' A small team carrying silenced MP5s and using night vision equipment could easily have entered in pitch darkness, ghosting along the upper corridors until encountering the terrorists. The idea was discounted, however, because there was muttering about the use of silenced weapons seeming too much like an assassination and so it was back to the drawing board for us.

* * *

8.00pm, Sunday 4 May. The next day, things seemed to go much better. Oan's hardened resolve appeared to be softening. The news bulletins were full of optimism. The Arab ambassadors had agreed to attend a meeting of the Cobra committee in their basement in Whitehall. Oan, in return, had agreed to reduce his demands. He now wanted only one Arab ambassador to negotiate the safe passage of the gunmen. He also agreed to release Mustapha Karkouti, who was suffering from some kind of fever. At about eight o'clock on Sunday evening, Karkouti stepped through the main door of the Embassy, took a deep gulp of fresh air and walked to freedom.

* * *

9.00pm. Malcolm was a nervous, white-faced RAOC clerk, the squadron scribe. He was not deep-chested or strong in the arm, and with his pale, thin face and sympathetic eyes he could have been any mother's favourite son. Being involved in the Embassy siege was a definite event in his life, a step forward, he felt, towards the most coveted badge of rank: the Chief Clerk's crown and laurel leaves. Like some of the damned in legend, he dwelt in a middle void, hung between the elite of the SAS on the one side and the crap-hats on the other. Now as he stood in full assault kit before the plywood scale model of the Iranian Embassy, waiting for room combat brief, he must have felt that he finally belonged.

Earlier in the evening, as, feeling remote and out of touch, he sweated and fussed over the squadron ration indent, Del, one of the assault-team leaders, and I had approached him. 'Malcolm, one of the lads is in a bad way. The doc has diagnosed lepto. He must have caught it in Belize earlier in the year. That leaves us a man short in one of the assault teams. We're on standby. We haven't time to get a replacement down and brief him. Do you think you can stand in?'

The cheap stationery-office pen came to an abrupt halt on the ration-roll, and for a split second Malcolm looked as though he had been asked to partake in a bank robbery. A strange, tortured look flashed across his boyish features, then vanished as quickly as it had appeared. He had led a tedious and mediocre life and had been resigned to his daily mountain of paperwork. Now, with this unusual offer, he had a chance to achieve something out of the ordinary, a chance to be above average, a chance to dare and to win. His decision was made.

He concentrated his attention on the plywood section of the Embassy's second floor. His hands, resting across the front of his body, held his S6 respirator and his fingers shook visibly as he attempted to adjust the securing straps.

'You will be my number two.' Del's voice was precise and to the point as he gave Malcolm his assault pre-brief. 'Once I've gained entry, you will take out targets to my left and right. Remember, if you get hit I will have to leave you. The medics should find you within half an hour.' Del's voice tailed off as he withdrew the hand-held pointer from the plywood corridors and returned it to the briefing pack.

The respirator now shook violently, but there was no look of fear in Malcolm's eyes. For the first time in his life he was doing something positive, and his mind was in overdrive, leaving behind any weak thoughts. He was pumped full of adrenaline, punching the air, shouting, 'Yeah, let's do it!'

I was wondering exactly what kind of psychopath we'd let out of the stationery cupboard.

A creaking door and a muffled cough at the rear of the room interrupted the tense, businesslike briefing. 'From Crocker. The Colonel's main briefing in five minutes.' It was Rusty. He was now third-in-command of the operation. With a final request for any questions, and an extremely efficient 'Synchronize your watches,' Malcolm's assault pre-brief was complete and he was now fully operational.

The large main briefing room in the holding area was buzzing with rumour and gossip as Malcolm, Del and I took our seats. The Colonel launched into his badged-personnel-only briefing, which covered such gory details as the removal of the dead bodies from the Embassy.

Malcolm avoided his hawkish gaze by staring intently at the eyepiece of the respirator resting on his knees, as though he were looking for signs of weakness and fear in the reflected image of his face in the small glass lenses. As the Colonel continued, Malcolm shifted uncomfortably in his seat. By the time the Colonel had finished his brief and left the room, Malcolm had developed severe facial flushes. His head sagged forward as if he was carrying some huge invisible burden on his shoulders, and his fingers twitched feverishly as he worried and fussed over the tightness of the filtering canister on his respirator.

I was just about to suggest that Malcolm should take part in a daylight raid on the Embassy via the skylight entry point, when out of the corner of my eye I noticed the Jester, one of the team leaders, making a rapid cutting motion with the tips of his fingers across his neck. 'Malcolm,' I said quietly, 'you're on *Candid Camera*.'

For a moment, nothing registered on Malcolm's flushed face. He was on his feet, clumsily readjusting the equipment that hung on his slight frame. His hands jerked uncontrollably as his fingers travelled like a spider over belt, holster and pistol grip.

'You're on *Candid Camera*,' I repeated.

As the situation began to register, Malcolm shook his head and slowly straightened his sagging shoulders. A look of total bewilderment spread across his face and his eyes began to blink violently. 'You mean it was a stitch?'

'Yes, Malcolm, it was a stitch, a rubber dick.' For just a split second a look of disappointment seemed to hang heavily on his face, then his eyes stopped blinking. The taut muscles in his neck and jaw seemed to relax and his mouth broke into a huge grin. For Malcolm it was the end of a great adventure.

* * *

6.30am, Monday 5 May. Just when things seemed to be going well, the situation worsened.

The name's Winner, Pete Winner. Prince Charles' close-protection instructor poses with his charge's Aston Martin.

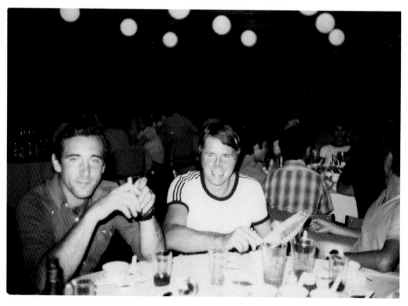

Hong Kong, 1978. Pete (right) with Clint, the inspector in the Royal Hong Kong Police's Special Duties Unit.

The SAS seven-a-side rugby team, with Pete, their coach and manager, at the far right. Here, just after an Army Cup victory, the team poses in front of the clock tower at Stirling Lines.

Prior to the siege, B Squadron practices house assault tactics at the Combat Village at Elm Farm near Hereford, a compound of half-a-dozen buildings used for combat training.

Training at the mock-Embassy, built to resemble a small British Embassy of the type often found in global troublespots. In an emergency the SAS expected to be deployed to defend such embassies, as they did in Zaire in 1991. To the right is the Methods of Entry wall, where troopers practised blowing in windows and doors.

In this rare image, the assault team is briefed in front of a scale model of the Iranian Embassy, in the SAS's Forward Holding Area next door, at No. 14–15 Princes Gate. At the far left of the model are the cellars, where Pete's team entered the Embassy.

Fast-roping from a helicopter in full assault kit, onto the roof of the mock-Embassy training building, Elm Farm. Pete is the figure in the foreground.

The abseil team prepares on the roof, ground scouted by Pete's team on the evening of 2 May.

The second-floor balcony of the Iranian Embassy. At far left in the top photo, Tommy Palmer is about to enter the building, his gas-mask and hood burned off, while Tom the Fijian dangles in the flames at top right, his abseil rope jammed. Before he was cut down, Tom suffered serious burns, but he still entered the Embassy with his team – an action for which he was awarded the George Medal. In the small world of ex-SAS private security, Tom and Pete would later do another job in Kensington together, but this time guarding diamonds.

A   No.14-15 Royal College of General Practioners
B   No.16 Iranian Embassy
C   No.17 Ethiopian Embassy
D   No.20 Polish Institute and Sikorski Museum
E   No.23-24 Montessori Nursery School
F   No.25 Royal School of Needlework

Opposite:

1   Perched on the roof, assault teams abseil down the rear of the building, in the course of which a trooper inadvertently breaks a window with his boot, arousing the terrorists' suspicions that something is amiss.

2   As a diversionary tactic, SAS explosives experts lower a powerful charge through the central glass dome, detonating it moments before simultaneous assaults are launched against the front and rear of the embassy.

3   A team leader's abseil rope becomes snarled, abruptly halting his descent, suspending him helplessly above the second-floor rear balcony, and thus obliging the other members of his team to forego the use of frame charges and smash their way through the windows with hooligan bars. Stun grenades set fire to the curtains and carpet, causing flames to emerge from the windows and burn the entangled trooper.

4   An assault team crosses into the garden, smashes its way through the french doors leading into the library and proceeds to clear the ground floor and cellar, which are discovered unoccupied.

5   Crossing from an adjacent building, an assault team detonates frame charges against the armoured windows on the front balcony, throws in stun grenades and enters the building amidst billowing smoke.

6   While PC Lock and the terrorist leader, Oan, are locked in mortal combat in a room on the first floor, an SAS trooper from the front assault team bursts in, warns the constable off and shoots Oan with a burst from his MP5.

7   One of the rear assault teams, shooting dead one terrorist as he flees towards the front of the embassy, reaches the telex room, where three terrorists have managed to kill one hostage and injure two others only moments before. The SAS men dispatch two terrorists with automatic fire but fail to recognise the presence of the third, who masquerades as a hostage and retains possession of a hand grenade.

8   The female hostages, discovered unguarded in a room on the second floor, are hurriedly joined with their now liberated male counterparts and manhandled downstairs for evacuation out of the rear of the embassy.

(Artwork by Howard Gerrard, © Osprey Publishing)

9   Clutching a hand grenade and still concealed amongst the hostages as they are hustled downstairs, the
    undetected terrorist from the telex room is recognized by Staff Sergeant Pete Winner who, unable to
    open fire for fear of inflicting casualties on the hostages or his colleagues, strikes the terrorist on the
    back of the head with the butt of his weapon, causing his victim to tumble to the base of the stairway
    where other SAS men riddle him with machine-gun fire.

10 (Not visible) Frightened and confused, the rescued hostages emerge into the garden at the rear of the
    embassy, where their SAS escort place them face down on the ground, secure their wrists, and identify
    them, thus discovering and arresting the only surviving terrorist of the original six.

Tak, a long-standing comrade-in-arms. This photo was taken around the time of the battle of Mirbat.

Lesotho, 1991. Training South African special forces as a mercenary, two years after leaving the SAS.

In the cold light of dawn, Oan and the rest of the gunmen seemed to be nervous and jittery as they woke the hostages in Room 9. Oan complained to Trevor Lock that during the night he had heard strange noises, and he was convinced that the police had gained access to the Embassy. He ordered Lock to search the building while he woke the rest of the hostages. The strangeness of this order was a reflection of Oan's agitated state of mind.

Sim Harris and Ron Morris wiped the sleep from their eyes, struggled to their feet and set about the usual early-morning chores. They washed the cups from the previous evening and prepared the Spartan breakfast of biscuits and tea. As Morris passed round the biscuit tin to the women in Room 9A, Trevor Lock returned from the recce of the building. He could be overheard telling Oan that he must be mistaken and that apart from themselves the Embassy was empty.

10.00am. A telegram arrived from Iran's Foreign Minister, Sadegh Ghotzbadeh. It was addressed to the hostages, and it declared that Iran was proud of their steadfastness and forbearance over the situation and that tens of thousands of Iranians were just ready to enter the Embassy with cries of 'Allah Akbar,' bringing final judgement to the mercenaries of Ba'athist Iraq. The final line reduced the hostages to a shocked silence: 'We feel certain that you are all ready for martyrdom alongside your nation.'

11.00am. Oan, enraged and extremely suspicious, called for Trevor Lock to join him on the first-floor landing. 'What is this? Are your British police trying to break in?' he shouted, pointing to the unmistakable bulge in the wall separating the Iranian Embassy from the Ethiopian Embassy next door.

'Of course not,' replied Lock.

'I do not believe you. Your police are up to some trickery.'

'Don't worry, Oan, the police won't break in here.'

'What do you mean, the police won't break in here? Where will they break in?'

'What I meant was, if the police were planning an attack, it would not be imminent,' replied Lock, trying to retrieve the situation.

'Your police, they are up to something, I am convinced. I'm going to make new arrangements for the hostages.' And with that, Oan stormed off upstairs to the second floor to organize the movement of the hostages.

The gunmen now looked alert and extremely agitated. Their weapons at the ready, chequered shamags pulled tight about their heads, they moved the male hostages from their room along the corridor to Room 10, the telex room. Oan and his comrades could sense that something was happening. The whole situation was as taut as a piano wire. They were all tired, tired of this psychological game. The operation had been planned to last only forty-eight hours at the most. They couldn't go on forever sheltering under this political umbrella. They had to break out. They had to play the final scene.

12.00 noon. Lock, tired, resigned, his face haggard with exhaustion, continued his efforts to pacify the terrorists. 'Oan, we must talk to the police.'

'Why should I?'

'The situation is serious. We must have a chance to talk to them.'

'OK. I give you five minutes with them.'

Lock and Harris made their way to the first-floor front balcony and made contact with the police negotiator. 'Now listen to me,' said Harris urgently. 'Lives are at risk, time is running out.'

'We are doing all we can,' replied the police negotiator, his voice sounding calm amidst the rising drama.

'Something has got to be done,' urged Harris. 'The Foreign Office is not moving.'

'It all takes time,' said the negotiator.

'I told you, time is running out. Where is the Arab ambassador who is going to mediate? We've got to have answers.'

'Things are moving along as quickly as possible. The Foreign Office is still in discussion with the ambassadors, and if you listen to the BBC World Service you will get your confirmation,' said the negotiator finally.

1.00pm. The news bulletin provoked a response that effectively drove the final nail into Oan's coffin. He was infuriated by the fact that the meeting between Cobra and the Arab ambassadors was still continuing and that a final decision as to who would mediate had not been taken. Incensed and expressionless, his mind clouded with frustration and loathing, he put the telephone receiver to his ear. His lips formed the words that would seal his destiny: 'You have run out of time. There will be no more talking. Bring the ambassador to the phone or I will kill a hostage in forty-five minutes.'

1.40pm. The duty negotiator seated by the field telephone in Alpha Control drummed his fingers on the table serving as a desk and glanced nervously at the clock on the wall. The minutes since the last conversation with Oan had flown by, and there was still no news from Cobra, still nothing positive to bargain with. Intuition based on years of experience of dealing with criminals told him something was wrong, something had changed. It was as if he had been sitting dozing by a fire and had suddenly awakened to see the last flickering flames die away, just as a chill wind outside began to rattle the window panes.

A moment later the shrill tone of the telephone buzzer cut through the silence. The negotiator lifted the phone off the cradle and in a voice filled with a calm he did not feel spoke into the receiver. 'Hello, it's Stuart here.'

'Stuart, they have a hostage and they are going to kill him.' It was Trevor Lock. 'They have him at the bottom of the stairs. Something terrible is going to happen. They are tying his hands behind his back. They are tying him to the banister.' Lock's voice still sounded calm, he still seemed in control; only his rapid breathing betrayed him.

'If you don't accept my demand, I will shoot him.' The voice had changed; it was more urgent, more threatening. It was Oan.

'Oan, this is Stuart. Don't do anything that could be counterproductive.'

'I told you, I have waited long enough. You have deceived me. Someone will die.'

A whole minute passed.

'I am one of the hostages.' The voice came in short, rapid gasps. It was inarticulate, as though the owner was fighting for control. 'I am one of the hostages. My name is Lavasani.'

Another pause, another tortured moment.

The voice that cut in next was high-pitched, immediate and threatening. 'No names. No names.'

At that moment, the whole tense atmosphere dissolved into the distinct, unmistakable sound of three low-velocity shots. It was precisely 1.45pm.

* * *

1.46pm. After four days of restless inactivity, the holding area was becoming decidedly claustrophobic. Even the monotonous routines of the Killing House began to seem appealing: at least back at base there was noise, movement and action – and the chance of decent food and a few pints afterwards. I was lounging on my camp bed, bored, uninterested, aware of a cynical resignation creeping in. All this effort. All this activity. All this waiting. All for nothing. I could see that we would soon be packing our bags and heading back to Hereford.

Suddenly there was a shout. The news of the hostage's death hurricaned through the room. I reach for my MP5, removed the magazine, cocked the action and caught the ejected 9-milly round. I then stripped the weapon and began to clean the working parts meticulously. This is it, I thought as I lightly oiled the breechblock. There could be no going back now. A hostage had been murdered. Direct action would have to be taken. As I threaded the metal beads of the Heckler & Koch pull-through down the barrel of the machine pistol, I let my mind wander through the problems of attacking a building with over fifty rooms. We would need speed, we would need surprise, we would need aggression. I thought of the words of advice from Paddy Mayne, one of the founders of the SAS: 'When you enter a room full of armed men, shoot the first person who makes a move, hostile or otherwise. He has started to think and is therefore dangerous...'

With one final smooth tug on the pull-through, I finished cleaning the MP5. I reassembled the weapon and replaced the magazine of thirty rounds. There was the usual reassuring metallic click as I snapped home the cocking handle. I applied the safety-catch and returned the MP5 to the chair next to my assault waistcoat, then cast a quick glance over the rest of my kit. Satisfied with its condition, I picked up the copy of *Colonel Paddy*, the biography of the late Lieutenant-Colonel R. Blair Mayne DSO (3 Bars), that I had been reading earlier, and settled down to wait for the final orders before movement into assault positions. I knew from experience they would not be long in coming.

* * *

7.00pm. 'We put the body on the doorstep. You come and collect it. You have forty-five minutes. Then I give you another one.' Oan's chilling message rippled over the airwaves in Alpha Control. The atmosphere was electric. A short while before, a second burst of shots had been heard, and now all eyes were glued to the television screens relaying the growing drama to a worldwide audience. The main Embassy door swung open and the police watched as a lifeless bundle was dumped on the steps.

Twenty minutes later, the field telephone rang on the first-floor landing. Oan picked up the receiver. 'Yes, what do you want? The time is running out.'

'Yes, we know that,' replied the duty negotiator. 'That's why we want to discuss the arrangements.'

'What arrangements? What are you talking about?' snapped Oan.

'The arrangements for the coach to take you to the airport. How big do you want the coach? How many hostages will be going to the airport? What sort of guarantee do you require?'

There was a brief pause. The negotiator could almost sense the questions running through Oan's mind.

'I require a coach big enough for twenty-five people, and Mr Trevor will drive it.' Oan's voice was still cautious, but it had a more confident tone.

'Shall we park the coach at the front of the Embassy?'

'That will be fine. But I want a guarantee this is no trick.'

'Oan, this is not a trick.'

'I want the guarantee from your police chief.'

'Oan, I repeat, this is not…'

Boooooooom!

7.23pm. The deafening explosion of the diversion charge was like a thousand wind-slammed doors. It rocked the Iranian Embassy and shattered the eerie silence. Two call signs from Zero Delta located behind the high wall at the front of the building began pumping CS gas through the broken windows. Orange-yellow flames burst through the windows and licked into the mellowing gold of the early-evening sun which layered the Roman columns and ornate balustrades with a soft coat of creamy light.

My troop was waiting, counting the microseconds, in the Royal College of General Practitioners next door to the Embassy. Shortly before, I had stared in disbelief as John Mac – ex-Royal Engineers and as tough a Jock as they come – had been making his way to his final assault position on the front balcony when he held up a novelty cardboard frog suspended on two pieces of string. As the black-clad figure pulled on the ends of the string, the frog's green-coloured legs made a ridiculous leaping motion. This act of pure pantomime cut through the tension like a hot knife.

Now, the voice in my earpiece screamed, 'Go. Go. Go.' There was no turning back. We were on our way. I was number one in the crocodile.

The rest of the call signs were strung out behind me. Hell, I thought, what am I doing at number one? The new boys should be at number one. I've done my time under fire. I should be at the rear with Tak, my Mirbat mate with whom I have a sixth-sense intuitive understanding in the operational field. Damn the RTU! Damn the demotion! I was pushing open the French windows at the rear of No. 14. As I led the crocodile out of No. 14 towards the rear of No. 16, I glanced up at the block of flats to our left. It was bristling with snipers.

We took up a position behind a low wall as the demolition call sign ran forward and placed the explosive charge on the Embassy's French windows. It was then that I saw the abseiler swinging in the flames coming from the second-floor balcony window. It was all noise, confusion, bursts of submachine-gun fire. I could hear women screaming. Christ! It's all going wrong, I thought. There's no way we can blow that charge without injuring the abseiler. Instant change of plans. The sledge-man ran forward and lifted the sledgehammer. One blow, just above the lock, was sufficient to open the door. They say luck shines on the brave. We were certainly lucky. If that door had been bolted or barricaded, we would have had big problems.

'Go. Go. Go. Get in at the rear.' The voice was screaming in my ear. The eight call signs rose to their feet as one and then we were sweeping in through the splintered door. All feelings of doubt and fear had now disappeared. I was blasted. The adrenaline was bursting through my bloodstream. Fearsome! I got a fearsome rush, the best one of my life. I had the heavy body armour on, with high-velocity plates front and back. During training it weighs a ton. Now it felt like a T-shirt. Search and destroy! We were in the library. There were thousands of books. As I adjusted my eyes to the eyepieces, the thought occurred to me that if we had blown that explosive charge we might have set fire to the books. Then we would really have had big problems: the whole Embassy would have been ablaze in seconds.

The adrenaline was making me feel confident, elated. My mind was crystal-clear as we swept on through the library and headed for our first objective. I reached the head of the cellar stairs first, and was quickly joined by Tak and two of the call signs. The entry to the stairs was blocked by two sets of stepladders. I searched desperately with my eyes for any signs of booby-traps. There wasn't time for a thorough check. We had to risk it. We braced ourselves and wrenched the ladders out of the way.

Mercifully there was no explosion. The stairs were now cleared and we disappeared into the gloom of the basement. I fished a stun grenade out of my waistcoat and pulled the pin. Audio Armageddon, I thought as I tossed the grenade down into the darkness. We descended the stairs, squinting into the blinding flashes for any unexpected movement, any sign of the enemy, and then we were into the corridor at the bottom. We had no sledge, no Remington with us so we had to drill the locks with 9-milly, booting the doors in, clearing the rooms methodically as we went along. Minutes turned into seconds; it was the fastest room clearance I'd ever done.

It was when I entered the last room that I saw the dark shape crouched in the corner. Christ! This is it, I thought. We've hit the jackpot. We've found a terrorist. I jabbed my MP5 into the fire position and let off a burst of twenty rounds. There was a clang as the crouched figure crumpled and rolled over. It was a dustbin! Nothing, not a thing. The cellars were clear. I was now conscious of the sweat. It was stinging my eyes, and the rubber on the inside of the respirator was slimy. My mouth was dry and I could feel the blood pulsing through my temples. And then we were off again, no time to stop now, up the cellar stairs and into the Embassy reception area. As we advanced across the hallway, there was smoke, confusion, a tremendous clamour of noise coming from above us. The rest of the lads, having stormed over the balcony at the front and blasted their way into the first floor of the building with a well-placed explosive charge, were now systematically clearing the upper rooms, assisted by a winning combination of the stunning effect of the initial explosion, the choking fumes of CS gas, the chilling execution of well-practised manoeuvres and the sheer terror induced by their sinister, black-hooded appearance. We were intoxicated by the situation. Nothing could stop us now.

In the telex room the terrorist Makki had begun the executions with the words, 'Now I have a chance to get you, Afrouz!' He opened fire at the chargé d'affaires in the centre of the room, shooting in a psychopathic rage. The wild hail of gunfire hit Dr Afrouz in both legs.

Sitting next to Afrouz was the assistant press attaché, Ali Akhbar Samadzadeh. He received multiple gunshot wounds to the chest and died instantly. Ahmed Dadgar, the medical aide, was sitting on the other side of Afrouz and was also shot in the chest. The Embassy doorman, Abbas Fallahi, was also hit by Makki's hail of fire. But miraculously, a 50p piece in his pocket deflected a lethal bullet and saved his life.

For Red Team, who had just abseiled down onto the second-floor balcony, there was no time to lose. They had to get to the telex room. Tommy Palmer and the rest of the team swarmed through the windows and raced to the telex room. The team included Tom the Fijian, whose legs had suffered serious burns as he dangled helplessly above the window, his rope jammed, with flames taking hold below him. Despite his injuries, he raced into the Embassy with his team.

The terrorist Shai, standing in the doorway of the room, surveying the carnage, fished a grenade from his pocket and reached for the pin. He didn't get a chance to pull it. Tommy shot him in the back of the head.

Makki now tried to hide among the hostages. He lay face-down on the floor. But when confronted by another member of Red Team, he made a suspicious movement and was instantly shot dead. When he was turned over he was found to be holding a Russian fragmentation grenade.

Back on the ground floor, I stared through the swirling smoke and gloom in reception. I could see the masked and black-clad figures of the other team members forming a line on the main staircase. My radio earpiece crackled into life. 'The hostages are coming. Feed them out through the back. I repeat, out through the back.'

I joined a line with Tak. We were six or seven steps up from the hallway. There were more explosions. The hysterical voices of the women swept over us. Then the first hostages were passed down the line. I had my MP5 on a sling around my neck. My pistol was in its holster. My hands were free to help the hostages, to steady them, to reassure them, to point them in the right direction. They looked shocked and disorientated. Their eyes were streaming with CS gas. They stumbled down the stairs looking frightened and dishevelled. One woman had her blouse ripped and her breasts exposed. I lost count at fifteen and still they were coming, stumbling, confused, heading towards the library and freedom.

'This one's a terrorist!' The high-pitched yell cut through the atmosphere on the stairs like a screaming jet, adding to the confusion of the moment. A dark face ringed by an Afro-style haircut came into view; then the body, clothed in a green combat jacket, bent double, crouched in an unnatural pose, running the gauntlet of the black-hooded figures. He was punched and kicked as he made his descent of the stairs. He was running afraid. He knew he was close to death.

He drew level with me. Then I saw it – a fragmentation grenade. I could see the detonator cap protruding from his hand. I moved my hands to the MP5 and slipped the safety-catch to 'automatic'. Through the smoke and gloom I could see call signs at the bottom of the stairs in the hallway. Shit! I can't fire. They are in my line of sight, the bullets will go straight through the terrorist and into my mates. I've got to immobilize the bastard. I've got to do something. Instinctively, I raised the MP5 above my head and in one swift, sharp movement brought the stock of the weapon down on the back of his neck. I hit him as hard as I could. His head snapped backwards and for one fleeting second I caught sight of his tortured, hate-filled face. He collapsed forward and rolled down the remaining few stairs, hitting the carpet in the hallway, a sagging, crumpled heap. The sound of two magazines being emptied into him was deafening. As he twitched and vomited his life away, his hand opened and the grenade rolled out. In that split second my mind was so crystal-clear with adrenaline it zoomed straight in on the grenade pin and lever. I stared at the mechanism for what seemed like an eternity, and what I saw flooded the very core of me with relief and elation. The pin was still located in the lever. It was all over, everything was going to be OK.

But this was no time to rest, this was one of the most vulnerable periods of the operation, the closing stages. This was where inexperienced troops would drop their guard. The radio crackled into life. 'You must abandon the building. The other floors are ablaze. Make your way out through the library entrance at the rear. The Embassy is clear. I repeat, the Embassy is clear.'

I joined Tak and we filed out through the library, through the smoke and the debris. We turned left and headed back for No. 14, past the hostages, who were laid out and trussed up on the lawn ready for documentation, past the unexploded explosive charge, past the discarded sledgehammer and other pieces of assault equipment – all the trappings of battle in the middle of South Kensington. It was 8.07pm.

As we made our way through the French windows of No. 14, the Gonze, ex-Para, a new boy in the Regiment from one of the other call signs, removed his respirator and asked the Irish police sergeant on duty at the door what the Embassy World Snooker score was. A look of total disbelief spread across the policeman's face and he just stood there shaking his head from side to side.

I crossed the room to my holdall, and as I began pulling off my assault equipment I could feel the tiredness spreading through my limbs. It wasn't just the energy expended on the assault, it was the accumulation of six days of tension and high drama, of snatched sleep in a noisy room, of anxiety and worry over the outcome of the operation. I looked to my left. The Toad had just returned. He looked tired, his face was flushed and he was out of breath. He looked at me and shook his head. 'I'm getting too old for this sort of thing.'

'So am I,' I replied.

Within fifteen minutes most of the team members had stripped off their assault kit, packed it into their holdalls and parcelled their MP5s into plastic bags to be taken away for forensic examination. Before moving out through the front door of No. 14 to the waiting Avis hire van, we had a dramatic visit from Home Secretary William Whitelaw, old 'Oyster Eyes' himself. He stood before us, tears of joy unashamedly running down his cheeks, wringing his hands in relief. He thanked the assembled team members for what they had done for the country that day. 'This operation will show that we in Britain will not tolerate terrorists. The world must learn this.' It was a fine personal gesture and rounded the operation off perfectly.

* * *

The day would live forever in Regimental history, of that we were sure, even though barely two hours had passed since the first explosion. Out of a total of twenty-six hostages taken in the Embassy, two had died, five had been released before the assault and nineteen had been rescued. The dramatic events were still reverberating through my senses: the first ear-stinging detonations, the bedlam of screaming women and snarling, yapping police dogs, the blanketing throb of 9-milly, the intense searing heat of the blazing Embassy. The tensions and stresses of the six-day siege now began to evaporate like a late-monsoon mist on a Dhofar morning, as a great feeling of relief and gladness washed over me, a feeling of anticipation of better things to come. Maybe the RTU and demotion was not such a bad thing after all. Maybe life with Six Troop was going to be better than I'd thought. I wouldn't have missed this action for a dozen overseas jaunts.

We were in London, the heart of the nation, the centre of excellence. You can't go any higher, I thought to myself. This is where the spotlight is. This is where the top people in their professions are to be found: actors, politicians, businessmen… and soldiers. We had been involved in a triumphant day; we had restored the nation's pride and morale. I felt light-headed, intoxicated by the powerful atmosphere pervading the conference room of Regent's Park Barracks. We stood around in small groups, sipping lukewarm Foster's lager straight from the can. Some switched-on character had stacked the hall with cartons before we arrived, and they stood in great piles around the edges of the long room. Tak's voice cut through the roar of elated conversation. 'A total success! The operation is a total success.' Team members, the Head Shed, the green slime, the whole war machine was milling around, faces flushed with victory.

I reached for a fresh can of lager and looked at the label. The red Foster's logo brought back memories of blue skies, clear water, golden sand dunes and beautiful nude female bodies. On a trip to Australia a few years earlier, we basha'd up at the Aussie SAS camp in Perth. The southern camp perimeter backed onto a beach, and there amongst the sand dunes were dozens of nudists, beautiful long-legged Australian girls, their shapely bodies bronzed a deep golden brown, their pubic hair bleached almost white by the sun. As that area of the beach was army property, the civvy police had no jurisdiction. It was the only place along that part of the coastline where the nudists could sunbathe without being disturbed. The army certainly had no intention of moving them off, that's for sure. Each afternoon we would have our daily run along the beach and over the sand dunes. It was the most interesting running circuit I'd ever known. And it gave a new meaning to physical fitness!

My thoughts of golden-haired beach beauties were interrupted by the sudden appearance of a well-dressed character at the main door of the conference hall. He was wearing a sharp pinstriped suit and an old school tie. He reeked of the Establishment. Oh God, I thought, not the red-tape wallahs, the bureaucratic brigade. Surely the form-filling and statement-taking weren't going to start already. Surely they could leave us in peace for a couple of hours to drink the excitement pitch down a few degrees.

The man moved forward to speak. 'Gentlemen, the Prime Minister.' The unexpected announcement boomed out across the full length of the room. Heads turned and the buzz and chatter of conversation dropped like a stone as an air of expectancy descended on the gathering.

In swept the Prime Minister, magisterial, like a triumphant Caesar returning to the Senate, 'Gentlemen, there is nothing sweeter than success, and you boys have got it.' Her voice rose above the resounding cheers and the crack and hiss of newly opened lager cans. She expressed pride and joy at the brave and brilliant management of the Embassy assault, stressing that victory was gained not only through faultless teamwork and infinite patience, but also through immense physical courage and flexibility. As she continued, I stared at her with growing admiration. She definitely had the Nelson touch. At the battle of Cape St Vincent, Nelson had led the decisive charge when his sailors boarded the Spanish three-decker *San Josef* with a battle cry of 'Westminster Abbey or victory!' I could just imagine the thought that had run through Mrs Thatcher's mind as she made the decision to send in the SAS. 'Back benches or victory!'

As the heady atmosphere generated by the Prime Minister's dramatic entrance stabilized, the cool authority in her personality took over, and without a moment's hesitation she proceeded to wander freely about the conference room, meeting each individual team member and thanking us all personally. Denis, ever the faithful companion, followed in her footsteps. He asked me about my parent unit and told me he'd served in the artillery in the Second World War. They both expressed concern for Tom the Fijian, the abseiler who had suffered severe leg burns and who had been admitted to St Stephen's Hospital in Fulham. They learned that his abseil rope had become hopelessly tangled, that his legs, clothed in non-flameproof overalls, had dangled helplessly in the flames licking out of the window below; that he had eventually been cut down by other members of his team and that, even though suffering from serious burns, he had reorganized his assault team, gained entry to the Embassy and converged on the telex room. Tom was later awarded a high decoration for his actions.

As the clock on the wall moved rapidly to 10.00pm, a colour television was wheeled into the hall. It was suggested that the assembled company, including the Prime Minister, watch the news broadcast of the rescue.

'What an excellent idea,' exclaimed Mrs Thatcher. 'Come, let us all move to the viewing area.'

As the first dramatic newsreel shots of the explosive charge blasting the first-floor balcony window exploded onto the screen, we crowded round the TV set shining in the darkened corner of the room. 'Sit down, you in the front, and let the rest of us see it,' ordered a gruff Jock voice from the rear. Glowing with pride and contentment, the Prime Minister obediently sat down and joined members of Alpha Assault Group sitting cross-legged on the floor. The scent of her Chanel No. 5 filled the air as we stared, mesmerized, at the day's events unrolling with lethal ferocity on the screen.

* * *

There is nothing more threatening to the advancement of civilization than the man who thinks himself God. The Roman conqueror, riding victorious through a defeated city, would employ a jester to walk beside his horse and degrade the military glory through lampooning and buffoonery. With this historical perspective in mind, I walked up the gravel drive of one of Hereford's best hotels to collect a top 1980s jester and TV star, Jim Davidson. Being a keen student of military history, Jim had secretly agreed to put in a mystery appearance at the celebration thrash marking the siege victory. A champagne party was to take place at a well-known Hereford watering hole, and my job was to infiltrate Jim covertly into the pub.

He arrived in reception wearing a grey double-breasted two-piece suit, looking, with his slim figure and slightly suntanned face, as though he'd just come off a team job abroad. I shook Jim's hand and we made small-talk. I was impressed by his enthusiasm and I knew instinctively he was going to be the right man for the evening. We passed a few minutes in light conversation, then left the hotel and made for the car park. As I swung my legs into Jim's Mercedes 220SE, he shot me a conspiratorial glance. 'Have you got all the gear?'

'Yes, it's in the hotel room,' I assured him.

'What time do we start?'

'We'll kick off at 9.00pm prompt.'

Jim turned the ignition key and the engine purred into life. He put the Merc in gear and we glided out of the car park. I looked at my watch. It was just 8.00pm. That left plenty of time to organize the evening's cabaret. Feeling quite pleased with phase one of the operation, I settled back in the luxurious comfort of the car's passenger seat and proceeded to direct Jim to the location of the party.

By 8.15pm we were in downtown Hereford. We let ourselves into a hotel bedroom adjacent to the hall where the festivities were taking place. I could hear the clink of beer-mugs and the buzz of conversation from the early drinkers. The sound of Ricky Sickit and the Vomits on the downstairs jukebox was deafening. 'Who the hell's that?' said Jim as he closed the bedroom door. 'It sounds like the second coming of Sid Vicious!'

I glanced around the room. It looked like the duty NCO's bunk in a seedy NAAFI. The mattress and sheets on the single bed were only slightly cleaner than the olive-green holdall resting on top of them. I went over to the holdall, unzipped the top and checked the contents. Everything was there.

Time to get ready. Jim stripped to his underwear and reached for the first article of assault kit. In a matter of seconds he climbed into the black flameproof overalls and fastened the zip. We both sneezed as the

CS gas trapped in the creases of the material was released into the atmosphere. With tears in my eyes I handed him the Northern Ireland lightweight boots. He immediately recognized the para-cord bootlaces and told me a great joke about his charity parachuting days. Choking back the tears and the laughter, I helped him strap on the Len Dixon belt kit and checked that the 9-milly Browning was unloaded. He fastened his leg-strap like a seasoned gunfighter and holstered the shooter. He then threaded the abseil rope round his waist and secured it with a Karabiner. Finally, he lifted the respirator off the bed and, with a professional touch, checked the tightness of the canister and adjusted the mask's securing straps. With a last impish grin and an enthusiastic thumbs-up, he pulled on the respirator, coiled the abseil rope over his forearm, opened the hotel door and stepped out into the darkened corridor.

With cat-like stealth, we moved down the corridor, opened a concealed door near the fire exit and began climbing a rickety staircase. 'You go first, Jim, and I'll cover you.' Jim grunted through the rubber of the respirator and snaked his way tactically up the narrow stairs. I could have sworn he imagined he was on operations.

The staircase led to a minstrels' gallery which overlooked the bar and cabaret lounge. The bar was now filled to capacity with team members and percentage players quaffing their thirst gratefully on case after case of champagne sent in by the public, including one from an old lady in Torquay, who'd been saving it for years 'for a special occasion'. Earlier in the day, I had blocked off the safety-rail running across the gallery front with plywood sheeting. We were totally hidden from the crowd below. As we crawled into position across the wooden boards of the balcony, desperately trying not to make them creak, I looked at my watch. 8.55pm. Five minutes to go. I tapped Jim on the shoulder and showed him five fingers. He gave me the thumbs-up and handed me the wire that was connected to the small explosive charge I had put in position that afternoon. I took the two bare ends of the D10 wire and pushed them into the shrike exploder. I pressed the test button and got the green light. Good, complete circuit, we're ready to go.

I took a look at my watch. Thirty seconds to go. I tapped Jim on the shoulder and pointed towards the safety-rail. As he moved into position, I pressed the priming button on the shrike. The red 'fire' light flashed in the gloom. At precisely 9.00pm I pressed the firing button. Bang! The small stage charge took the drinkers completely by surprise. Heads whipped round and the odd Walter Mitty gatecrasher reached for a non-existent shoulder holster.

Jim jumped to his feet and threw the abseil rope over the balcony. For a few tense moments he trod the gallery boards, shooting menacing glances at the crowd below. Then, in one quick, efficient movement, he removed his respirator and, to roars of applause, launched straight into his first joke.

'A man dies and goes up to the Pearly Gates. He sees St Peter standing there with rows and rows of clocks behind him. When asked the purpose of the clocks, St Peter replies that every person on earth is given an allotted span of time and the clocks keep a record. Suddenly one of the clocks goes round a full hour in a couple of seconds. "That man has just slept with his neighbour's wife," explains St Peter with a frown. Then another clock jerks round a full two hours. "That man has just mugged an old lady in the street," intones St Peter. At that moment, the newly arrived man sees a clock immediately behind St Peter frantically spinning round at high speed. "Ah, that clock," says St Peter…,' and here Jim paused a moment, looked me straight between the eyes, then continued, '" …that clock belongs to a certain member of B Squadron SAS. We use it as a fan to keep us cool in the hot weather."'

* * *

Better to be tried by twelve than to be carried by six, I thought, as I waited in the corridor outside Westminster Coroner's Court. The jokes and the back-slapping were over. Nine months on from the siege, now it was into the serious business of the inquest. I was more nervous at the prospect of doing battle in the legal cut and thrust with clued-up solicitors and highly paid barristers than I'd ever been before going in to tackle Oan and his band. I'd been away for nearly a year, travelled twice around the world on training missions, and here I was being called to account before the cold, impassive power of the law for actions whose precise sequences were already beginning to blur in my mind. Worst of all, I was to bare my soul and that of the Regiment in public. I was to give details of an SAS operation before the massed ranks of the media crammed into the public galleries, at least five dozen hardened journalists, pens poised in excitement, awaiting with schoolboy eagerness the unfolding of tomorrow's guaranteed bestseller. I'd spent eleven years of total anonymity and secrecy with the SAS. But since the television exposure of the siege had blown our cover, the Head Shed felt compelled to go against all their normal instincts. We now had to be seen to be accountable. Democracy in action. It marked a new stage in the Regiment's history, a new dimension in the psychological warfare against terrorists.

I was one of the chosen four due to appear in court – the ones who'd drawn the short straws. I'd spent three days in court in Hong Kong and was deemed to have the necessary experience. A legal veteran! It was thought I was better equipped to withstand the pressure than some of the other lads. I was to be a star witness. A real patsy, a scapegoat for the percentage players! This sort of exposure can't go on, I thought, this must be rectified for the future. Some precautions had been taken. The coroner had ordered that no photographs or sketches be taken in court in any circumstances whatever. Furthermore, it had been agreed that we could be identified by alphabetical designations to avoid the use of our real names. The cover was scant in the extreme. It offered little consolation.

My confidence in the system had already been severely dented by events prior to our reaching court. There were four of us: Sam, the superstitious one who'd refused to play the Ouija board with Valdez just before Operation *Jaguar*, Steve, Tom the Fijian abseiler – now recovered from his burns – and myself. We'd been at Group HQ, awaiting the arrival of a Black Maria to spirit us unnoticed to the court. What should turn up but a bright red Vauxhall Viva!

Worse still, on arrival at the court, instead of being taken to the back entrance we were driven up to the front where all the press were waiting. They spotted the car immediately and came running towards us, cameras flashing. 'Get to the back! Get to the mortuary door at the back!' Sam was yelling at the driver as we all ducked down. Luckily the police driver was well trained. With tyres squealing, he did an emergency reverse and about-turn and, with Fleet Street's finest in hot pursuit, roared towards the rear entrance, through a large gate and into a courtyard. We were through the back door before the perspiring gentlemen of the press were able to catch up with us.

Just inside the mortuary door we were faced with a gruesome sight: the naked body of an old man laid out on a trolley. He had recently been subjected to a post-mortem. A huge cut stretching from breastbone to navel had been peremptorily sewn back up with large blanket stitches. The crown of his shaven head had been lopped off like the top of a hard-boiled egg and it, too had been clumsily sewn back on again. The stench of formaldehyde was sickening.

While I was waiting outside the courtroom to be called, my spirits rose a little when one of our senior officers, who'd come to meet us for our final brief, revealed that the member of the jury nearest the witness box was a very pretty young thing no more than twenty years old. I decided that when I was asked to relate how Faisal had ended up with thirty bullet-holes in him, I would tell the story directly to her personally, gory details and all. A nice intimate conversation, just she and I. At least it would take my mind off the court ordeal.

I came back to reality with the rumour that newspaper reporters were climbing onto the roofs all around the building to get pictures of our exit. I just hoped to God the police would get it right this time and reverse a Black Maria right up to the back door.

The usher nodded to me to get ready. I got up and waited just outside the swing door that led into the court. I pushed the door open a few inches with my foot to try and get a feel of the atmosphere inside so I could be a little better prepared when I entered the arena. I eyed the young female juror with expectation. Then the coroner looked up from his notes and said in measured tones, 'We will now hear evidence from the military personnel who brought the siege to a conclusion.'

With eyes like hawks, everyone present spun round to face the door where I stood. A deathly hush descended on the court.

A voice boomed out, 'Soldier I: take the stand.'

14

The Falklands

'She was squirming in her seat, giggling with excitement, wide-eyed and eager. I fixed her very deliberately with my best macho stare as I related the unsavoury details of Faisal's demise. She wasn't put off. Far from it. She was hanging on every word, raring to go. One thing is for certain: if I hadn't been married I could have got her number and I would have had a guaranteed jump that night – and I'm not talking about parachuting.' I took another gulp of beer. 'But the funniest part was when I'd just finished giving evidence and was stepping from the witness box. Ron Morris came charging across the courtroom, his arm outstretched. He gripped me by the hand and said to the coroner, "Excuse me, sir, but I must shake hands with this man. I want to thank him and his mates for all they did for us." I was quite taken aback, embarrassed, almost.'

The alcohol was flowing freely. I was sitting reminiscing about the Embassy inquest in the Volcano Club, an American airmen's gin palace that clung like a limpet to the edge of Wideawake airfield on Ascension Island. If you draw a cross whose horizontal axis links Brazil in South America to Angola in West Africa, and whose vertical axis bisects the island of Ireland from north to south, in the centre of the cross you will find Ascension Island, a scab of volcanic rock and dust in the middle of the South Atlantic Ocean, a British telecommunications centre,

US airbase and US space-research station. It was 1982. We'd not long since flown out from Hereford; the Falklands War was in full swing.

'Take No Prisoners!' The name of the newly christened cocktail was shouted to the rafters as several half-pint glasses of a milky-coloured liquid appeared on the plastic-topped table in front of the troop hierarchy. The lethal-looking concoction had just been invented by an ex-Para called Paul. Before joining the Army, Paul had worked as a croupier in a South Coast casino, until he got fed up with the well-heeled punters, who would blow clouds of smoke from expensive cigars in his face as a distraction. Young, hard but amiable, a rebel from the maroon machine, he was the troop new boy. 'A warmer in the bank before the Last Supper,' he would announce invitingly as he raised his glass.

Disorientated by the octane rating of this Molotov-strength cocktail, the troop would then await with mouth-watering relish the arrival of the Volcano's special grill. The steak was a joy to behold. It was so vast it overlapped the plate at both ends. It must have been at least one inch thick and came generously garnished with garlic butter. With the passing of each evening, and our departure for the Falklands becoming more and more imminent, this gastronomic delight really did become known as the Last Supper. It helped clear the mind of gremlins after a day of green-slime briefings.

As this particular day's Last Supper entered its closing stages the lads in the troop, actively encouraged by Big Fred the Fijian and aided and abetted by Tak – once again setting off on a great adventure alongside me – were required to take part in an initiation test steeped in ritual. Each member of the mission had to finish off the evening by drinking a flaming Drambuie. Big Fred would half fill a standard spirit glass with the liqueur, and Tak would step forward and ignite it. A nine-inch Bunsen flame would then shoot upwards from the surface of the liquid. The initiation test required the drinker to place the flaming spirit glass to his lips, drain the Drambuie, then put the empty glass back on the table with the blue flame still leaping off its rim. (This ritual was an

SAS refinement of the 'dance of the flaming arseholes' – a custom peculiar to the crap-hats – in which pieces of newspaper were rolled up tightly and inserted into the anal orifices of two rookie squad members. Both were then set alight. The first man to pull out the flaming roll bought the drinks.) The last time the SAS attempted this before abandoning it as childish was back in 1972, when Del, the guy who was later to help me stitch up Malcolm the clerk during the Embassy siege, decided to liven up the proceedings by throwing a glass of Drambuie over the back of a Nine Troop man called Frenchie. It burst into flames and badly burned Frenchie's back.

Big Fred, solemn and dignified, had the bearing of an MC at a Fijian kava ceremony. Kava is a narcotic drink prepared from the root of the Yagona tree and is drunk from coconut shells. It numbs the lips, gums and tongue and acts like dental cocaine, rendering the drinker high as a kite. An evening in the Volcano Club had a similar effect. Fred handed the first flaming Drambuie to Tommy, a tough Scot from the Highlands. Tommy was no stranger to the dangers of fire and flame. At the Embassy siege in 1980, during a desperate attempt to get access via a window into an already burning room, his gas-mask and gas-hood had got so badly burned they had to be discarded. In spite of having no protection whatsoever from the thick fumes, he continued to carry out his duties in the smoke- and CS gas-filled rooms. His bravery was later recognized by the award of the Queen's Gallantry Medal.

With a knowing wink, Tommy gripped the stem of the glass, tipped his head back at just the right angle, and with practised ease quickly drained the contents before the glass became too hot to handle. A group of REMFs in the far corner of the bar began chanting 'Napalm sticks to spics' as we each took our turn with the fiery liquid. Most of us were past masters in the art, and not an eyebrow had been singed, not a nose-tip burned by the time the REMFs launched into the latest chant.

Then it was Paul's turn. He accepted the offered glass from a still-solemn Fred, then glanced briefly at the flickering blue flame before raising the glass warily to his lips. The flame was now gathering momentum and Paul hesitated slightly before tilting his head forward to meet the glass. A dangerous mistake. As he gulped at the burning liquid, the flame licked around his upper lip and nose and singed his eyebrows. He spluttered and attempted a recovery, but to no avail; he was forced to spit the fiery Drambuie from his mouth, spraying a two-foot sheet of flame across the table, hitting Nish down his left-hand side.

With the smell of singed eyebrows in my nostrils, I settled back in my chair. Another Last Supper was drawing to a close and the REMFs were on an all-time high with their next chant, 'Jump-jet the Junta'. The troop was busy discussing Paul's facial burns. The whole room vibrated with jingoism. But I was far from happy.

As the alcohol in the cocktails and the flaming Drambuies began to take hold, it helped tranquillize the negative thoughts that had invaded my brain since our departure from the UK. They say history repeats itself, and it seemed that the Head Shed were about to prove it. Back in the briefing room at the Kremlin in Hereford, they had outlined a plan to crash two C-130s containing a heavily armed B Squadron onto the runway at Port Stanley with the aim of bringing the Falklands War to a rapid conclusion. It occurred to me they were making the same mistake as Monty when he sent the Paras into Arnhem in an attempt to short-circuit the Second World War. As in the case of Arnhem, the Head Shed wouldn't believe the intelligence reports presented to them. The airfield at Stanley was ringed by General Joffre's Tenth Brigade, 7,000 fighting men, and, worse still, the 601 Anti-Aircraft Battalion equipped with surface-to-air missiles. Coming in to land with a full load of men and equipment, the C-130s – not the quickest of planes at the best of times – would have been slow and lumbering, sitting duck targets for the anti-aircraft guns. The Argentinian troops may not have been of the same calibre as the four divisions of SS Panzers surrounding Arnhem, but they were well armed, with plenty of reserve ammunition, and they were dug in.

At the end of the briefing, the Head Shed had asked a stunned B Squadron for any questions. Give me a blindfolded tightrope walk in a Force 10 gale any time, I thought. I decided to take the bull by the horns and give them the solution. 'Put a conventional warhead on a Polaris missile, and send it onto the Argentinian mainland airbases that are servicing the Mirage III and the Super Etendards,' I offered. The Head Shed were not amused, although Colonel Mike Rose conceded it might be an option.

To make matters worse, as a parting gesture prior to embarking on the coach taking us to Brize Norton, an Army Pay Corps sergeant, hovering like a death clerk, had been on hand to issue life insurance to anyone who didn't have it. 'Come on lads, this is your last chance. Sign on the dotted line.' Valdez, that tower of Fijian strength – along with Laba and Tak one of the original three Fijians I'd met at Otterburn in 1971, who were to inspire in me a lasting affection and respect for that friendly South Pacific people – proved the only light at the end of the tunnel. As we settled into our seats on the coach, squadron morale soared when he fished out of his battered Barbour jacket pocket a faded copy of *Rules for War*, written in the early 1950s. A mischievous grin cracked his dark features as his index finger traced Rule 762: SAS troops are not suicide troops. As he replaced *Rules for War* in his pocket, I kept my fingers crossed he wouldn't bring out a Ouija board to pass the time on the journey. I wasn't superstitious, but the Ouija board and the death clerk would have made an ominous combination.

That had been the morning of 19 May. By 20 May we had arrived on Ascension Island and were about to receive the worst Regimental news since the Second World War: a chopper had gone down, killing twenty of the lads from D and G Squadron. Crocker read out the list of dead – fine soldiers all of them, and irreplaceable in terms of experience and expertise. A total of twenty-one soldiers – senior NCOs, junior NCOs, troopers and signallers – had been killed when the Sea King they were travelling in had crashed into the sea off the stern of the assault ship *Intrepid*. In a small regiment like the SAS, one death in the family causes ripples. To lose so many was a major disaster.

The sound of the riotous assembly brought me back to the present with a jolt. The REMFs had finally gone over the top and were in fine vocal form as they offered a grand finale to the snake pit: a cannibalized version of 'Summer Holiday':

We're all going on a summer holiday,

We're all going to kill a Spic or two,

We're all going on a summer holiday,

We'll get them with our GPMGs...

As the singing reached a crescendo, I decided it was time to leave. Most of the troop had thinned out anyway.

'Cos there ain't no fucking trees,' screamed the REMFs as I levered myself into the upright position, pushed the table to one side and picked my way through the smoke-filled bar. Cliff Richard would be proud of us, I thought, pushing through the exit door into the warm night air.

* * *

'Come on boys, get your kit together. The trucks are outside. We're going for it.' The urgent voice cut through the alcohol-induced dream. I prised my eyelids open and attempted to focus on the blurred figure of the SSM.

My head thumped round like the centre hub of a helicopter's rotor blade. I now knew why I had done selection and had been tested to destruction. I felt as if I was back on Sickener 1. My body ached and my mouth tasted like a gorilla's armpit. The suicide mission had begun.

'Get all the weapons and ammunition onto the trucks. We're moving out immediately,' repeated the SSM. The room burst into life as the squadron began rushing around packing their personal kit and getting ready to load the Bedfords. The short, sharp, shock – it's one way of curing your hangover, I thought, as I glanced at my watch. It was just after 0500 hours.

We began checking weapons, priming grenades, breaking open liners of GPMG link, removing the M202s from their cardboard transit boxes. The thought of the 202 cheered me up — four 66mm incendiary rockets, box-mounted, operating from one trigger mechanism. We were anxious, raring to go, eager to get the job done. We applied green and black camouflage cream to our faces and pulled on our fighting order, heavy belt kits weighed down with 5.56mm ammunition and 40mm high-explosive bombs for the XM203. This was an Armalite with a single-shot, breech-loaded, pump-action grenade-launcher attached to the underside of the stock – hence the nickname 'under and over'. 'Thank Christ we've got these; now I don't have to stand up to throw a grenade,' I thought as I checked the quadrant sight, then depressed the barrel-locking latch and slid the barrel forward to check that the launcher was clear. Happy with the safety-check. I snapped the barrel backwards, the tube latch locking the barrel and receiver together.

I joined the line of squadron members moving purposefully towards the Bedfords parked on the road outside the basha. The REMFs singing 'We're all going on a summer holiday' turned around my brain like a pig on a spit, but I wasn't in the mood to burst into song. We pulled ourselves onto the Bedfords already jam-packed with kit and weapons, and made ourselves as comfortable as possible amid liners of 7.62mm link, bergens, cases of M202s and GPMGs. A famous First World War general once said that the machine gun is a much-overrated toy, but experience in the Dhofar war had taught us how vital it was. We made sure we took every GPMG we could lay our hands on. No wonder there was no room to move.

The convoy was now ready. It was just a matter of driving across the airfield and loading the waiting C-130s. The squadron fell silent, each man left to his own thoughts. This was the biggest operation the Regiment had been committed to since the Second World War. If B Squadron pulled this off, we could name our own medals. We were anxious for the success of the operation itself. Would we manage to land on the airfield at Stanley or would we be blown out of the sky by surface-to-air missiles? And if we did indeed land, would we be annihilated on the runway by the radar-controlled 35mm anti-aircraft guns used in the ground role?

I blocked the negative thoughts out of my mind and looked at my watch. The minutes ticked by. Five, ten, fifteen agonizing minutes. Come on, let's get going. I looked up and down the stationary convoy. Where the hell was Crocker? We were supposed to be on operation immediate. The waiting was getting to me; it was a bad fifteen minutes. A murmur of conversation had broken out in the rear Bedford. One or two of the fitness fanatics were standing on the mountains of kit, stretching their stiffened limbs and looking bored.

I looked at Tommy, who was sitting quietly on a box of smoke grenades. His grey face looked like how I felt. He shrugged his shoulders and went back to the oily flannelette he was using to clean the 5.56mm rounds before easing them into the thirty-round magazine of his 203. As I settled back once more I could feel the slow regular thump of a headache beating across my temples. It was 0630 hours.

Crocker suddenly appeared from the direction of the signal shack. He had a scowl on his face. He looked at the convoy but said nothing. He walked over to the lead Bedford and spoke quickly and with calm authority to the SSM. The message flashed down the full length of the convoy: scrubbed! The operation had been scrubbed. 'Thank fuck for that,' I said to Tommy. 'Good old SAS common sense has prevailed. Come on, let's hit the Volcano and get stuck into one of those steaks.'

* * *

The synchronized flash of the navigational lights of the USAF Starlifter cut into the grey of the overcast dawn as we plodded in silence across Wideawake airfield, dressed in camouflage OGs and each carrying a diver's dry suit, a set of fins and a lifejacket. It was 0430 hours. After the previous day's reprieve, we had been re-tasked and re-briefed. We were to fly south towards the Falklands in two C-130s, rendezvous with HMS *Andromeda*, a Type 21 frigate, and carry out a para-drop into the South Atlantic. Pick-up and delivery to the ship was to be by Rigid Raider. *Andromeda* would be our host until we reached San Carlos Water, where we would rendezvous with the depleted ranks of D Squadron.

This was to be a reinforced jump, so it was classed as operational. I briefly entertained the idea of asking the Brigadier on our return to the UK if he would endorse the Second World War rule on parachuting, which stated that any squadron member who has made an operational jump is entitled to wear his SAS wings above his medals, rather than on the shoulder where they are normally worn. The recollection of the look of horror on the Brigadier's face when I'd asked him at the opening of the new Pal-U-Drin Club back in Hereford in 1981 about a bar to the General Service Medal commemorating Princes Gate quickly changed my mind.

The early June morning was cool on Ascension as we picked our way through the clutter on the airfield, past rows of aircraft, Vulcan bombers, Victor tankers, American Starlifters and Nimrod recce planes, towards the two C-130s. Everywhere the ironmongery of war choked the tarmac: stockpiles of rations, fuel, medical supplies and ammunition, advance communications equipment, forklift trucks – thousands of pieces of equipment. Wessex and Scout helicopters droned like bees overhead. The Royal Corps of Transport were working flat out organizing the movement of war material, the servicing of airlift pallets. War fever was in the air.

After what seemed like an age, we finally arrived at our C-130s. I noticed with interest the in-flight refuelling probe over the flight deck. The transporter would be one of sixteen models converted especially for the Falklands War as in-flight refuelling tankers/receivers. Inside the cargo and passenger holds of these converted planes were two long-range fuel tanks. Apparently one of the converted C-130s created a world record for duration of flight by remaining in the air for twenty-eight hours during an operational flight.

We boarded the two cramped aircraft and prepared for take-off. Practised eyes and hands went through a familiar routine. I checked the main and reserve parachutes for serviceability. Happy with the brake ties, elastic bungees, cape-well releases, static-line stowage and leg-strap adjustments, I placed the two parachutes and the diver's dry suit on the floor between my legs, strapped myself into the uncomfortable web seat and awaited the roar of the four Allison turbo-prop engines. The crew carried out their final flight checks, and at 0500 hours the two C-130s began taxiing rapidly across the airfield. The constant-speed, fully feathering props were revved up to take-off speed, and without another minute's delay we thundered down the runway and lumbered into the dawn sky.

As I felt the lift of the aircraft wheels, I settled back in the cramped seat and removed my seatbelt. I was feeling exhilarated but somewhat daunted by the change in plan. My first operational jump into a war zone. Alongside me in the womb of the aircraft sat several newly badged members of the Regiment. I thought of the slick precision and ruthless timing required by our plan. I looked at the fresh faces of the new recruits, the young men who had so enthusiastically applied for selection, who had passed with flying colours but who, as yet, were untried in battle, and I wondered…

'Actions stations. Prepare equipment.' The parachute-dispatcher's voice was quick and urgent, barely audible over the noise of the aircraft engines and the added roar of the slipstream rush now coming from the rear, where the tailgate door was being lowered. 'Here we go,' I said feelingly to no one in particular. I reached for the diver's dry suit under my seat and climbed into the zipped opening. I swore under my breath as I pulled on the awkward rubber garment, bending my ears painfully as I forced my head through the skintight neck seal. 'Zip me up, Tommy, and make sure you fasten the last quarter of an inch.' In about half an hour we would be in the South Atlantic, where a man could freeze to death in a couple of hours. Even an unzipped quarter of an inch could prove fatal.

A few minutes later, with arms outstretched and convulsing like a cat coughing up a fur-ball, I had cursed and struggled my way into my dry suit. I stowed my fins where they could be easily accessible for fitting once I was in the water. Next, the parachute. It was already adjusted to my personal measurements, so it was simply a matter of hoisting myself into the harness – not an easy task in the cramped passenger space of the Hercules. Finally, I strapped the distress flare to my wrist.

I began to sweat as I pushed through the crowded fuselage towards the chaos of the tailgate area. Someone had stitched the RAF dispatcher by telling him there was a missile on its way and that we must eject chaff immediately. He was panicking, desperately trying to contact the pilot and find the chaff button at the same time. The tailgate ramp of the Hercules was now fully down. I gazed out over the air-drop pallets crammed onto the ramp, over the edge of the ramp itself curving away into space and into the Atlantic swell 800 feet below.

Up in the cockpit of the C-130 the pilot pressed the button. A green light pierced the sparsely lit cargo hold. The RAF dispatcher, who by now had regained his composure, and two corporals from the RCT dispatcher team, all three fully kitted out for an operational jump (zip-up flying boots, olive-green flying suits, DPM jackets, white leather PGI gloves, and safety harnesses attached to the fuselage), began moving the heavy air-drop pallets containing our personal kit, weapons, bergens and advance-signalling equipment over the edge of the tailgate. There was a clatter as the pallets moved over the rollers fixed to the tailgate floor and a twang as each one dropped off the end. I watched fascinated as the parachutes' static lines ran clear and the canopies deployed. The plane bucked in slight turbulence, and I realized with a palpitating heart that this was the moment of truth. I took a deep breath, clipped on my reserve and moved into position.

I was number one in the stick, standing on the edge of the tailgate, adrenaline-charged, aching for release. It's fearsome, being number one: you see everything in front of you – and worse, everything below you.

When you are number three or four in the stick, all you see is the pair of shoulders and 'chute of the guy in front of you. You can shuffle forward almost with your eyes closed, as easily as a blind man being led off a cliff.

I was in the ready position: right hand gripping the parachute static line, left hand resting on the top of my reserve. Far below was the grey wash of the sea. I moved closer still to the edge. The deafening roar of the aircraft slipstream made all conversation impossible. My head was raised and turned to the right, watching, waiting for the red warning light to turn green. My rear leg was braced, ready to launch me over the edge of the tailgate.

'Red on. Green on. Go!' screamed the dispatcher, slapping me on the back. Automatically I leapt into space, forcing my right hand down on the top of my reserve to improve my exit stability. For an instant I was carried violently forward in the blast from the Hercules slipstream. Then I felt the reassuring tug of the parachute harness and the profound relief that the canopy had deployed. Almost immediately, I looked up and carried out my main canopy check for malfunction, ensuring it was deployed correctly.

My hands began to feel for the release hooks of my reserve. I looked down, and for one wild moment I saw I was directly above the dull, blue-grey shape of HMS *Andromeda*. If I released the reserve now, it would hit the ship square on. I took avoiding action. I pulled down violently – too violently – on my steering toggle. This caused air to spill out of my canopy, upsetting the stability and trim of my flight. I began to oscillate through 180 degrees. I spiralled downwards, my rate of descent decreasing. I swung back and forth, but at least I managed to clear the ship. I pulled down on both steering toggles, and this had the effect of breaking the forward speed of the canopy; the swinging was reduced. I had unclipped the reserve hooks from the D-rings on my main harness and watched the reserve plummet into the sea below. Now I was conscious only of the water rushing up to meet me and of the constant buffeting from eddies of wind all around.

Judging distance in poor light when making a vertical descent into a high swell can be difficult. So I decided to jettison my harness without delay. I hit my cape-well releases and the shoulder straps fell away – but only just in time. I was suddenly immersed in water. At least the harness was free, there was no drag and the canopy did not envelop me. The parachute fell away at an angle, blown away downwind. I was now exhilarated, switched on. I struggled into my fins to help me tread water. Then I pulled down on the toggle and popped my lifejacket. I watched the full-green canopies of the other troop members, many of them kicking violently out of twists as they drifted slowly down and hit the water.

I looked up and saw the lone C-130, its cargo now bobbing about in the South Atlantic, disappearing into the clouds. The second C-130 had turned back earlier because of fuel resupply problems with a Victor tanker, and would now be sitting on the tarmac on Ascension Island, its occupants in the Volcano Club, seething with an imperial frustration that even the arrival of a gargantuan steak would do little to alleviate. I was lucky. My disciplinary misdemeanours were working in my favour again. The same fate that had put me in the Killing House when the balloon went up for the Embassy siege, and subsequently allowed me to take part in an uniquely glorious episode in the Regiment's history, had now ensured that I was on the first C-130 and not on the second one, containing my old troop, Eight Troop, which had had to turn back.

Bobbing about in the ocean, I could feel the adrenaline pumping. I was at the sharp end, heading for action. The Atlantic swell was tremendous. At the crests of the waves I could see all around me. In the distance I could just make out the grey superstructure of HMS *Andromeda*. Then I disappeared into a trough and there was no view, no horizon. I was surrounded by a vast ocean of grey, foam-flecked waves. I became aware of the cold. The dry suit protected my body heat, but my hands and face were exposed to the elements. I had to tread water with my hands held clear of the bitter, near-zero temperatures of the South Atlantic. Where was the pick-up? The light was failing and the frigate seemed a long way off. Having been the first out of the Hercules, I was furthest from the ship and would no doubt be the last to be picked up. Like a piece of battered flotsam, I rose back to the crest of the wave. In the poor light I could just make out the Rigid Raider about 250 metres away. A member of the troop appeared to be struggling over its side, then it headed back for the *Andromeda*.

I had now been in the water fifteen minutes, and my hands and face were numb. I began to wish I'd only partially inflated my lifejacket, by mouth, rather than popping the automatic inflater. The bulky shape was straining my neck, pressing it back at an awkward angle. I cracked the plastic tube of the chemical distress flare attached to my wrist. The two chemicals mingled and the tube began to glow. I disappeared into a trough and realized it was pointless waving my flare – no one could see me. I couldn't even see the ship. I would have to wait till I was back on the crest of the wave. I kicked with my fins to gain height. I waved my flare arm, but to no avail. The Rigid Raider was returning to the mother craft with another full load. My vision began to go grey in the gloom. The camouflaged superstructure of the *Andromeda* disappeared from sight, and once more I became engulfed in the dark trough of a huge wave.

Anxiety began to gnaw at my insides. I had been in the water thirty-five minutes and had begun to shiver. There were two dangers now: exposure and exhaustion. Already I was having difficulty keeping my hands out of the water. Perhaps fate was not so kind after all. I would have been better off in the Volcano Club with Eight Troop.

I seemed to be aimlessly paddling around, going nowhere, getting weaker. The South Atlantic was taking its toll on me; serious fatigue had set in. I rose again on the crest of another wave. At last, the familiar shape of the Rigid Raider crawled into view about a hundred metres away. I waved my flare arm wildly as the small boat surged forward.

They'd seen me! They were heading in my direction, an olive-green shape bucking violently in the Atlantic swell.

'We'd thought we'd lost you,' said the big Marine boat-handler.

'So did I,' I replied. 'I'm starving. Got any scran?'

As they hauled me over the side, they burst my lifejacket with a diving knife to make it easier to get hold of me and pull me into the boat. The tension fell away, and as the Rigid Raider sped over the waves towards *Andromeda*, a surge of weariness and a longing to be on dry land swept over me.

No sooner had I got on board than it was realized that an air-drop pallet was missing. A radar scan of the immediate area proved fruitless. A Sea King helicopter was due to arrive any minute to cross-deck the troop to HMS *Intrepid*. The Navy called off the search for the missing pallet. It was decided that I and one other would stay behind and persuade the Navy to continue the search. We would then remain on *Andromeda* until its arrival in San Carlos Bay.

I went to the petty officer and requested a resumption of the search. I was told that no way was that possible. 'Fuck you,' I said and strode straight into the Captain's cabin.

I was struck by the homeliness of the tidy room. Going through the door was like walking into the warm, secure atmosphere of a comfortable study. The Captain, pen in hand, looked up from a desk cluttered with paperwork. With his steely-grey hair and steady gaze, he reminded me of a favourite uncle. When he spoke he had the dignity of a housemaster at a public school. His whole persona radiated power and authority. 'We have got to get under way, we must be in San Carlos Bay by the morning,' he replied quietly to my demand. His dignified features had taken on the expression of a patient negotiator handling a siege situation.

I took a deep breath. 'What's the point of putting the RAF to the trouble of bringing us all this way to do a reinforcement jump into the South Atlantic when we'll be a liability to D Squadron if we go into the field without the proper kit and equipment? We might as well have stayed on the piss on Ascension.'

For a split second the steady non-committal gaze was replaced by a far sterner look, as though the Captain was turning over some crucial piece of information in his precise naval mind. 'OK,' he announced, 'I'll give you a couple of hours.'

A period of intense activity followed. Time and time again I had to fight back fatigue and persuade the Navy to continue the search. I had to locate that pallet. We chugged on through the night, the radar search providing the eyes, Chalky – the other troop member – and I providing the concentration. Lashed by spray, freezing cold and near exhaustion, we stood with a group of naval ratings on the bow of the ship, peering into the starlit night. As *Andromeda* lumbered through the seas and the hours slipped by, I was becoming increasingly strained. The continuation of the search seemed to hinge on my resolve and determination to keep going. I shivered and looked at my watch. It was just past midnight. The naval ratings were looking towards their bunks, and I was expecting at any time to be called up to the Captain's cabin and given the bad news.

Then word came down from the bridge that something had been picked up on the radar. Suddenly, a rating on the starboard rail of the bows shouted that he could see something in the water. I grabbed the petty officer of the watch, who was in possession of a dragon light. We made our way over to the starboard side of the ship. As the powerful beam of the dragon light cut through the night Chalky shouted, 'There it is!' as the beam played on a set of rigging lines, a parachute canopy and a large, dull-brown packing box. It was the missing air-drop pallet.

Sleep. That was all I wanted now. The ship was extremely crowded, every berth taken. One of the Navy lads showed me a bed that someone had just vacated to go on duty. 'There's your bed for the next eight hours.' It was lovely and warm. I went out like a light.

* * *

The Falklands! Two small islands to the north-east of Tierra del Fuega, two specks floating in the sea, like tiny scales dislodged from the great curl of the scorpion's tail that is South America. With a coastline as long as Norway's circumscribing a land mass no bigger than Wales, the Falklands are subject to relentless winds and the hazards of wind-chill factor that accompany them. The islands are the same latitude south of the equator as London is to the north. They are doggedly British and are determined to stay so.

I was deeply impressed as I stood on the forecastle of the Royal Fleet Auxiliary LSL *Sir Lancelot* and surveyed the anchorage at San Carlos Water. There hadn't been so many ships around the Falklands since the days preceding the first battle of the Falklands in December 1914, when dozens of colliers arrived to fuel the battlecruisers HMS *Invincible* and *Inflexible* and the other ships that made up Admiral Sturdee's original Falklands task force, sent to root out von Spee's Imperial German fleet hiding around the islands.

San Carlos Water bustled with activity. Aboard the frigates, acting as goalkeepers at each end of the waterway, anxious eyes scanned radar screens for the expected air attacks. In front of me, across the bay, I could see RFA *Blue Rover*, SS *Atlantic Causeway*, MV *Norland* and, faintly ridiculous amid the camouflage grey, the brightly coloured *Nordic Ferry*. Anchored at the southern end was the assault ship HMS *Fearless*. On the high ground overlooking the water, the Rapier batteries formed a defensive ring of steel. Like hungry seagulls circling a freshly churned refuse tip, helicopters wheeled and dived as they carried out routine cross-decking sorties and undertook offloading operations. A Sea King 5 vet-repped drums of petrol swinging beneath its matt green belly.

It was just after 1600 hours and, with dusk gathering, I gave my belt kit, personal weapons and ammunition a final check, ready for the mission ahead. At that time of the year it would be dark at 1630 hours, ensuring a covert insert into enemy territory. We had to be in position by 1800 hours. The plan, like all good plans, was simple. We were to take a night flight to enemy-occupied West Falkland by Sea King helicopter. We would deploy a linear-type ambush on high ground overlooking the target area. Intelligence received had indicated that three Argentinian C-130s were going to do a reinforcement drop of an elite company of Paras at 0100 hours the following morning. Members of D Squadron, boosted by Six Troop B Squadron, would provide the DZ reception party.

The cocking handle of my XM203 snapped forward, chambering the first 5.56mm round. I applied the safety-catch. My fingers checked the smooth metallic cases of the 40mm bombs located in the pockets and the bandoliers criss-crossing my chest. Cradling the loaded rifle in the crook of my left arm, I stood motionless in the growing darkness. As my eyes adjusted to night vision, taking the inkiness out of the purple-black surroundings, my thoughts turned to the achievements of British forces over the last few weeks. In very little time, a task force of over a hundred ships had sailed 8,000 miles and landed between 9,000 and 10,000 men on an enemy-occupied coastline, and the men had fought to within an ace of total victory.

The overloaded Sea King helicopters of 846 Squadron took off at precisely 1800 hours. They flew low and fast, skimming across the darkness of San Carlos Water, heading for Falkland Sound. The Navy pilots wore passive night goggles – image-intensifiers enabling them to see at night in conditions of low light. In the cramped, blacked-out passenger compartment of the chopper, the noise of the rotor blades, specially coated to withstand the harsh weather conditions, was deafening. We swept across the undulating terrain of East Falkland and then enemy-occupied West Falkland. We hugged the contours and hedge-hopped the sheep fences; we dipped over hillocks and swooped down re-entrants. Finally, after a gut-lurching, hair-raising short dash up a pitch-black gully, we reached our objective. We put down on an area of high ground amid lumps of tussock grass and soggy peat. A blast of fresh, crisp air hit me as the loadmaster slid open the door. The clear, starlit night was bitterly cold as we struggled out of the helicopters, pulled on our heavy bergens weighed down with 7.62mm link, and went into all-round defence.

The drone of the Sea Kings spiralling upwards into the moonlit night signalled the move out. In the distance, the relentless pounding of 4.5-inch shells from the Type 21 frigate could be heard bombarding the Fox Bay area. We moved off silently on a preset compass bearing. Because visibility was good we travelled in staggered file, well spaced out. We carried a formidable array of weapons: GPMGs, XM203s, L42 sniper rifles with night sights, 66mm LAWs and the new, American-supplied Stingers – lightweight heat-seeking surface-to-air missiles. For a while, we followed the gently rising spur running north. The brilliant full moon bathed the jagged rocks on the high ground in front of us. We made good time on a steadily climbing, steepening slope, picking our way quietly and patiently through the semi-frozen boggy hillside strewn with unyielding rock.

Shortly after 2030 hours, we began to drop off the high ground to avoid the slab-sided razor-back edges that formed the crest lines of most of the unmarked ridges of West Falkland. A slight right hook took us below the craggy crest. As we gained the lower slopes, we began to cross extensive stone runs, cursing under our breath as we scrambled across huge slabs of rock covered with wet, slippery lichen.

We reached the final rockfall that overlooked our objective at 2130 hours. It was a perfect position for a linear ambush. The high ground we were standing on was covered in quartzite blocks in all shapes and sizes, running in narrow parallel lines hundreds of metres long. The bleak hillside fell away sharply into a grass-covered valley bottom. The huge open space was ideal for a drop zone. It was also ideal for a killing ground.

After a short, silent pause for a tactical shake-out, forty heavily armed men wormed their way into ambush positions in the rock run. The only noise was the occasional clink of stone, the rustle of equipment, a stifled cough. No orders were given. We had all studied the plan. We all knew that each man was preparing his firing position, choosing his arc of fire, unsplaying grenade pins, going over the 'ambush sprung' signals in his mind.

We hid silently in the security of the rocks: bodies and minds alert, eyes and ears straining for the slightest sign of movement, trigger fingers resting along trigger guards, safety-catches off. Moonglow clouds scudded soundlessly across the night sky while the icy chill crept slowly through the camouflage material into our immobile limbs. The silence in the valley was intense, overpowering, as still and deep as the voiceless hush of a post-explosion shock. The long cold wait took us well past midnight, past the estimated drop time, past the point where the moonlight was at its brightest before beginning to fade. I unzipped my Gore-Tex jacket, pulled out the para-cord necklace around my neck and looked at the luminous dial of my G10 watch. It was 3.30am.

Time passed slowly through the hours of uncertainty. Gradually the moon and stars disappeared and the cold, clear darkness gave way to the grey damp of dawn. And still we waited, tense, shivering, the tiredness clinging to our limbs, like ivy entwining a dying tree. The first misty glimmer of daybreak broke into a bright, frosty morning. We lay motionless for a further hour until finally the 'ambush scrubbed' signal was passed down the line, Tommy, a part-time poacher, was totally in his element, lying a few feet away looking as if he was sizing up a salmon pool on the River Dee. He seemed disappointed, depressed almost, as he made a cutting motion across his throat with the index finger of his left hand. Another lemon!

Throughout the long day we remained hidden, with only our Gore-Tex bivvy bags as protection against the bitter cold. Above us, unidentified high-flying jets sliced through the tight blue of the sky trailing thin vapour scars, red-edged and inflamed in the rays of the low-lying winter sun. We were all conscious of how exposed, how cut off from the rest of the task force we had become. We were on hard routine: no eating, no brewing, no talking, no nothing. We went to extreme lengths to ensure that no small sound or movement would betray our presence to the enemy. Our exhausted minds lengthened the seconds into minutes, the minutes into hours. There were periods when even the turn of the globe seemed frozen still. Finally darkness came, and with it – the relief was immeasurable – the clattering sound of the Sea Kings coming to take us back to base.

We returned to the *Sir Lancelot*. The old tub had been hit on the morning of 24 May by Skyhawks and abandoned with two unexploded bombs aboard. The bombs had crashed straight through the steel-plate decking, leaving gaping holes, and burrowed deep into the bowels of the ship like maggots through cheese. A naval bomb-disposal team had finally removed the bombs the week before the linear ambush and it now made an excellent base for an SAS QRF. Covert teams could now move at a minute's notice to locations on East or West Falkland.

Over the next few days we undertook several clandestine, precisely targeted operations. Like acupuncture needles stimulating the flow of energy through the body, our activities quickened the pulse of war and hastened the drive for victory. Tumbledown fell. Two Sisters fell. The Gurkhas took control of Mount William. It was during one of our secret sorties that the radio burst into life: 'The white flag is flying over Port Stanley.' Endgame! The Argies had surrendered.

We made our way to Stanley to take part in the celebrations. The first thing we saw at the airfield gates were the prisoners. Now that the big guns had fallen silent, a vast army of beaten, dejected but relieved men stood clustered around field kitchens waiting to be embarked on the *Canberra*, now anchored in Berkeley Sound. They were dazed, tired and starving. Their combat fatigues were thick with congealed mud that looked like the solidified dribbles of wax down the sides of restaurant candle bottles. Some were draped in rain-soaked blankets and ponchos as protection against the southerly gales blowing across the peninsula from the Antarctic.

Huge piles of discarded weapons and helmets lay rusting in the damp air. Only the officers had been allowed to keep their 9-milly Browning pistols – to protect themselves from their own men. They needed them. Some of the officers, besides handling the battle itself with a disastrous ineptitude that had cost many lives, had shot their own men in the legs to stop them running away when fortune had turned against them in the closing stages of the war.

I was sitting in the driving seat of an Argentinian Army four-wheel-drive Mercedes jeep on the tarmac outside Stanley airport control tower and terminal building. I had just dropped Tommy off to meet one of his contacts. Besides being a part-time poacher, Tommy, ex-Royal Engineers and a fugitive from D Squadron, was the best full-time scrounger in the Regiment. I stared through the jeep's windscreen. A blustering wind teased fibres of rain from the dirty fleece of cloud that hung low over the desolate scene before me. Over at the air terminal, the walls of the buildings were pockmarked by hundreds of bullet holes and cannon-shell hits. The broken windows were boarded over against the bitter cold. Across the airfield the litter of war was strewn: ragged tents, burnt-out skeletons of vehicles, Pucará bombers upended and devastated by Harrier cannon fire. When I was a small boy, my father had told me of his experiences on the beaches at Dunkirk, and I imagined that this was what it must have looked like.

I was just watching a glint of metal in the sky that must have been a Harrier making a return flight to one of the task force's aircraft carriers, when the sound of Tommy heaving himself into the passenger seat made me turn my head. 'Get what you came for?' I asked briefly.

'Yep. I got the name of the ship that provides the booze.'

'Did you get the name of the contact men?'

'It's all arranged. We'll pick up the stuff tomorrow. I'm going to turn the Ross Road Guest House into the best-stocked drinking den in town.'

'OK, are you hot to trot? We've got to meet Alastair in the Upland Goose in a couple of hours.' I started the Mercedes engine and engaged first gear, and the jeep leapt into motion. We drove through the chaos and shambles and out through the main gate of the airport.

A few yards down the road, I pulled up at a huge pile of Argentinian-made 7.62mm FN rifles with folding butts. I lifted one off the pile and worked the cocking handle a few times to make sure it was clear. 'Throw it back,' said Tommy in his broad Scottish accent. 'You'll never get it past Ascension. And besides, the Argies have removed all the firing pins.'

I quickly stripped the FN, and sure enough the firing pin was missing from the breechblock. I threw the rifle and its working parts back on the pile and we continued our three-mile journey back to Port Stanley. Driving along the metal road, we were aware of the mine problem. Every approach to Stanley and the airport was crawling with incorrectly planted minefields. Although the Argentinians had kept some basic charts and records, they were not very precise, with the result that one unit had often overlaid another unit's minefield. A few own goals had been scored in the process.

In Stanley itself, the danger would be even more immediate. Here, the Argies had played really dirty. Grenades on one-second fuses, with their pins out, had been found hidden everywhere: under inverted teacups, jammed between bales of wool – just waiting for someone to lift the cup, to part the bales.

We moved on past the unmistakable signs of defeat scattered on either side of the road: 7.62mm FN automatic rifles, .45 American submachine guns, .50-calibre Browning HMGs and Argentinian-made GPMGs, all piled in great heaps; hundreds of combat helmets lying where their owners had abandoned them; vast quantities of boxed ammunition awaiting disposal; abandoned artillery positions – Italian-built 105mm howitzers that could throw a 95lb shell thirteen and a half miles – carefully concealed in their turf and peat bunkers; a land-based Exocet missile, complete with launcher and generator, parked on wasteland. And all along the windswept route, groups of unarmed Argentinian prisoners could be seen huddling like refugees around burning piles of rubbish or toiling slowly along at the side of the road.

Port Stanley. This small, neat town had, in the short space of time since the surrender, developed a massive traffic problem. Hundreds of vehicles were crammed into small streets. Land Rovers, trucks and Mercedes jeeps churned up a sea of mud. We turned right into Philomel Street and headed towards a line of brand-new French-built Panhard armoured cars. Clothes and loose ammunition lay strewn across the road. The detritus of war was visible everywhere. So was the damage of war. The demoralized Argentinians, avalanching towards defeat, had succeeded in turning the town into a disaster area. Houses had been broken into and looted, rooms left smeared with human excrement, fences chopped down for firewood. In Port Stanley West, where a seaplane hangar had been used as an Argentinian medical dressing station, amputated limbs had been tossed onto the roof of a shed inside the hangar and left to rot. Continuing on along Philomel Street, we passed shattered houses with gaping holes in their roofs, and the still-smouldering ruins of the Globe store, set on fire by rioting prisoners. We turned left into Ross Road, ignoring the large white direction arrows painted on the road – an attempt by the Argentinians to impose a drive-on-the-right policy upon the Falkland Islanders. We drove along the seafront, past houses with large red crosses on their roofs masquerading as hospital dressing stations, which had been used to stockpile ammunition.

We pulled up outside the post office. The Falklands are famous for their stamp issues. Philatelic sales account for about 14 per cent of the islands' income. Every year they produce four or five attractively designed high-quality sets, which become much sought-after by collectors. Tommy, ever the wise old bird, had heard that a philatelic war between Argentina and Great Britain had been raging since 1936; and that on 5 April 1982, when the Argie postal staff took over the Port Stanley post office, they had taken the opportunity to give all waiting mail the Malvinas treatment. Stamps had been crossed through and envelopes marked with the special legend '9409 Islas Malvinas'. Tommy reckoned that if he could acquire some of these specially marked stamps they would be worth a fortune in years to come. A group of Gurkhas, well wrapped up against the cold, passed the jeep as Tommy jumped out of the vehicle into the mud of the street and disappeared into the post office. I watched the Gurkhas make their way down Ross Road to Government House, looking to see if I could recognize any of them from my training days in Hong Kong.

When Tommy re-emerged from the post office, he didn't look too happy. He glanced quickly up the street, as if looking for an escaping intruder, before wrenching the jeep door open and jumping into the passenger seat.

'Get what you were looking for, Tommy?'

'No chance! The Ruperts were there before me. All I could get was the standard first-day issues. Come on, let's get down to the Upland Goose.'

As we strode confidently into the Upland Goose, Des King the proprietor, a man on the verge of a nervous breakdown, looked up briefly from his defensive position behind the bar. His look blackened when he saw our green duvet jackets and ski-march boots. We ignored his verbal broadside and headed for the restaurant. Alastair McQueen, a reporter with the *Daily Mirror* and our host for the evening, had acquired the corner table commanding a good view of the whole restaurant, now full of Paras and Marines in camouflage clothing. Alastair was already seated with Big Fred the Fijian, Crocker, Stonker and Gary. We pushed past the drunken hacks at the bar, took our seats and awaited developments.

Alastair was the perfect host, regaling us with stories of his days on the *Mirror*, while quietly emptying the wine cellar of its stocks of champagne. We troughed our way noisily through a three-course meal, reminiscing about the events of the past three months.

Throughout the festivities, Gary remained quiet, even morose. Just as a second Drambuie arrived, he decided he had had enough of it all and curled up on the floor for a quick kip in front of the amazed hacks. Dave Norris of the *Daily Mail*, well tanked up by this stage and making a spectacular effort to stagger out of the restaurant, paused for a moment and gazed down on the snoring figure. 'If there's one thing I can't abide,' he hiccupped, 'it's drunks,' and he delivered a swift kick into the backside of the sleeping Gary.

All round the room, knives and forks were quietly laid down. All conversation stopped. 'Fucking hell, Norris, you'd better leg it!' suggested Alastair helpfully to his fellow reporter.

The advice had come too late, Gary, as a testament to his training, sprang to his feet like a coiled spring and, scowling straight at Fleet Street's finest, advanced menacingly. 'Norris didn't mean it,' pleaded Alastair, 'he's drunk.'

'Forget it, Gary,' I shouted through the growing tension, 'he's just not worth getting upset over.'

Gary, awake and alert, his clenched fists relaxing slightly, glanced quickly around the silent bar. 'Serves me right for kipping in a nest of vipers.' And with that he walked calmly through the door of the restaurant and past the horrified Des King – who was by now definitely having a nervous breakdown – and disappeared into the darkness of Ross Road.

The conversation picked up again, just a murmur at first as people slowly digested the incident that had just taken place, then building into an excited babble, louder than before, as the onlookers began to work off the rush of adrenaline the scene had precipitated. But just as the festivities were getting into full swing again, I suddenly no longer felt part of the celebrations. I seemed to have stepped back from it all, as if I were in the room next door listening to the party through the walls. Twenty men lost! Twenty of the lads from D Squadron had been killed in one brief moment. It seemed so stupid and senseless – they hadn't even come under enemy fire. Engine failure? A seagull sucked into the rotor blades? What did it matter? The result was still the same. Good friends had perished. I had played rugby with Taff Jones and Paddy O'Connor; I had served in Dhofar with Sid Davidson; I had worked in Northern Ireland with Phil Curass. The sadness was rising higher and higher. I needed another drink, and quick!

15

Fallen Comrades

'Two pints of bitter and a draught Guinness.' I really needed a drink,
I was choked with emotion. It happened every year, the same gut-
wrenching feeling, the same sad thoughts that lay too deep for words.
It was 1984, two years after the Falklands. As usual, I'd gone home to
spend the morning with the people I respected most in my life: my
father, a veteran of Dunkirk, Burma, Italy, France and Germany, now
in his seventies, a man of traditional tastes and pleasures, passing his
days content to look after his canaries and take his evening tot of whisky
– 'Good for the heart, thins the blood' – a man who said little but
missed nothing, a man of wisdom, simplicity and quiet dignity; and
Archy, Boy Bugler, naval rating, submariner, holder of the Croix de
Guerre – the French VC – a man of great tenderness, relentless good
humour and single-minded bravery.

Armistice Day. At this hour on this day a great tidal wave of
melancholy and heavy emotion sweeps the land. The same ceremony
takes place at the same time in every town throughout the nation,
and has done so year after year. As I stood facing the Cenotaph, I
experienced a powerful sense of history, a deep continuity of tradition.
I felt part of a process going back to Agincourt, to 1066 and beyond.
I was aware of a sense of duty to safeguard the nation, to safeguard my
friends, my family, my son. In performing that duty, I had found a

fulfilling role in life. Some people are still searching for a role, an identity, when they are forty or fifty. When you join the Army you gain an instant identity. The three of us wore our medals with pride.

The sun was just breaking through the clouds, but a chill wind was blowing. At measured intervals, a tannoy announced each of the veterans' organizations and a representative came forward with a wreath.

'Submariners and Old Comrades Association.'

The sombre silence between each announcement was broken only by the persistent cough of a young child somewhere at the back of the crowd.

'Royal Air Force Association.'

As each wreath was laid on the Cenotaph, one by one the bearers stepped back, paused very stiffly for a few moments, saluted sharply, turned on their heels and, belying their years, marched briskly away. One of the oldest wore the thick dark glasses of the blind and had to be guided by one of his comrades, but he was none the less precise in his movements.

As the time approached eleven, the band struck up, slightly out of time for the first few bars but quickly falling into line:

'O God, our help in ages past,

Our hope for years to come…'

As the last bars played out, the officiating priest came in too early, with 'Let us remember…' The band played a ragged 'Amen' and the priest began, slightly flustered, then quickly regaining his composure, began again.

'Let us remember before Almighty God and commend to his keeping those who have died for their country in war…'

A baby started crying as, on the stroke of eleven, the standards dipped. A plaintive Last Post was sounded, one of the most forlorn and evocative of all sounds. Standing beside me, Archy listened intently. The priest continued:

'They shall grow not old, as we that are left grow old;

Age shall not weary them, nor the years condemn.
At the going down of the sun and in the morning
We will remember them.'

Two minutes' silence followed, and I remembered them: Laba, Tommy, Taff, Paddy, Sid, Phil and the rest who had perished. Reveille sounded and the standards rose again. I shifted my feet slightly to position the flags between myself and the winter sun to get some relief from the low-lying orb, now shining blindingly in my eyes.

'The Grace of our Lord Jesus Christ, the love of God and the fellowship of the Holy Spirit, be with us all, evermore.'

As the service drew to a close, people emerged from the crowd in ones and twos and gently laid single red poppies alongside the wreaths, symbols of their own private sorrows, grief-laden tokens for a brother, a father, a son, a husband.

'Eyes… left! Eyes… front!'

The band and procession of veterans marched off past the Cenotaph, the trombones momentarily seeming to blow stronger, and away down the road. The music faded along with the memories until the only sound was the regular thump of the bass drum, a distant echo of the big guns pounding Fox Bay on the night of the linear ambush.

I drove back to Hereford in a cheerless mood. When I arrived, I felt strongly impelled towards a church a short distance down the road from camp. I hadn't been there for a long while. Why I should feel particularly drawn there this Armistice Day I didn't know. Maybe all nostalgia was growing stronger with the passing of the years. All I knew was that I wanted to visit some old friends.

St Martin's – the final RV, the last basha for the lads who didn't make it. The graveyard was to the rear of the church, enveloped in peace and tranquillity, away from the traffic grinding up the road from the city centre. It was staked out with six sturdy yew trees. Between the trees I could clearly see the square tower of Hereford Cathedral about a mile away. An air of late-autumn decay pervaded the atmosphere: flowers wilting and faded; fetid water greening in vases; urns weatherworn and chipped; a gathered pile of leaves mouldering in the corner. A helicopter clattered overhead, returning to camp, its young occupants, full of life, vigour and vitality, completely unaware of the disconsolate scene below.

I went over to Tommy and Laba. They lay in adjacent rows beneath the trees and outside the Regimental plot. They had died before this area was set aside. They had only each other for company. I stood at the foot of Laba's grave. The mound seemed far too short. I wondered how such a small plot could possibly contain such a colossus of a man. A neat winged dagger was carved into the top of his headstone, and below it the inscription:

> 23892771 Sergeant
> T. Labalaba BEM
> The Royal Irish Rangers
> 22 SAS Regiment
> 19 July 1972 Aged 30 years

19 July 1972! The battle of Mirbat. It seemed like another lifetime. And yet, I could see Laba again, as clearly as the cathedral tower. The soundless scenes flitted through my mind. Operation *Jaguar*: a mortar aiming post under his arm, taking the young Firqats on a mock drill parade to roars of applause from the onlookers; appearing over the rise after the death march, 500 rounds of GPMG link wrapped around his shoulders, two precious jerrycans of water splashing in his hands. The siege of Mirbat: sweat pouring off him, feeding the twenty-five-pounder for all he was worth, the enemy just yards away. Then the bullet cut him down and he breathed his last. I read the words at the base of the headstone with a mixture of pride, gratitude and sadness:

> Greater love hath no man than this,
> that a man lay down his life for his friend.

There must have been two or three hundred civilian graves in the main cemetery, but I hardly noticed them as I walked across to the Regimental plot, twenty yards to one side and semi-enclosed by a low wall. A neat line of white headstones stretched down the centre of the plot – a linear ambush of graves! Walking down the line I was suddenly overcome by a deep sense of awe that I had been spared where so many had fallen. Death roams eagerly during battles. A split second, a microsecond, that's all it takes to die in combat, that's all it takes to blast the spirit from the body, to destroy years of loving work building family, friends and future.

The line of headstones was so straight, so disciplined, it was as if the men were still on parade, backs rigid, eyes front, forever waiting to be dismissed. An equally ordered row of urns stretched out in front of the headstones, each engraved with a single name: 'Tony', 'Steve', 'Frank', 'Dave', 'Ginge'. The effect was powerful, they were so heart-rendingly simple. I sensed an aura of grief, of shock, immediate, still beating. There was some essence of the men that was still alive, still whispering through the trees. A spirit of restlessness, of startled disorientation roamed around the headstones. I glanced across at the civilian graves. Over there was a sense of peace. Those people had lived their lives, they'd run their course, they'd seen out their allotted span of winters and summers. Around the linear ambush lives had been too abruptly snatched away, souls too suddenly ripped from wounded bodies. The psychic shockwaves still lingered, still rippled through the air.

The last grave in the line was a new one. I stooped down. The man's camouflaged webbing belt had been folded in four and laid carefully between two urns of flowers across the freshly dug soil. I picked up the belt and felt the solid, reassuring weight of the canvas weave. For a moment, the distant roar of the traffic penetrated my awareness again. Then just as quickly it faded away. I folded the belt into four again and placed it gently back on the mound.

I stood up and walked back towards the stone wall at the end of the plot. A large winged-dagger plaque was set into the wall, and on either side a row of ten smaller plaques. As I drew nearer, I could see a crop of tiny white balsa wood crosses planted in the grass just in front of the wall. Silent Valley! The sight of the crosses sparked a flash of recollection of that sombre graveyard scene in Aden all those years before when I was a regular soldier with the Royal Engineers. I'd come a long way since then. I was lucky. The sand was still trickling through my hourglass.

To the left of the winged dagger and lower down, a quote from the Regimental clock had been reproduced, a quote I'd glimpsed as I scrambled out of the training-wing theatre after the Colonel's opening address on the first day of selection. I now read the words slowly and deliberately, letting the meaning sink deeply within:

We are the pilgrims, master; we shall go
Always a little further: it may be
Beyond that last blue mountain barr'd with snow
Across that angry or that glimmering sea.

I'd been across that angry sea, I'd been beyond that mountain barred with snow. The pilgrimage continued. But for these lads the journey was at an end. They would go no further. Back at camp, their names were inscribed in white lettering on the bronze panels at the base of the clock: it was a mark of utter finality. In Regimental terminology, they had been unable to beat the clock.

I looked at the moving messages inscribed on the urns.

To the world you were a soldier;
But to me you were the world.

The fresh flowers in the urns swayed slightly as I read the words. Each inscription was like a thump in the chest.

Your love lies within my heart.
Until our spirits touch.

A breeze sprang up as if from nowhere. The skin across my cheekbones was drawing tight with the cold and my hands were going numb.

Loving husband and Daddy.

I thought of my own son, now eight years old. What would he have been feeling now if I'd gone down with them, if I'd not come back?

The inscriptions on the small plaques were uniform, stark in their simplicity: number, rank, name, date of birth, date of death. A relentless sense of tragedy gripped me as my eyes read from left to right and saw, repeated again and again, the same date of death: 19.5.1982. The Falklands helicopter crash.

The sadness was welling up. It tightened my throat. I kept on swallowing unconsciously, trying to get rid of it, as if it were a piece of food stuck in my gullet – but it refused to go away. I knew there was only one way to relieve the feeling. I needed a drink and a chat with the lads to get things back in perspective.

* * *

The warm, bustling, smoky, beery atmosphere of the pub was a great comfort as I carried drinks to the table and sat down with Paddy and Iain Thomson – the strangest variation you could imagine on the theme of the Englishman, Irishman and Scotsman! The beer quickly took effect and the stories started to flow. This was what I enjoyed the most. A couple of pints to release the tensions, and the world suddenly seemed a better place to be. With the stories came the glow of reminiscence; with the recollections came the warmth of camaraderie.

'Iain, you never did tell me the full story on those thirteen morphine syrettes in Borneo. How come you took so many?'

'Ah yes. The Borneo ambush. I remember it as if it were yesterday. Mind you, it's thirsty work telling stories. It'll cost you a double Grouse.'

'Yer on,' I said without hesitation.

Iain took a sip of beer and settled back. 'It was at Gunong Rawan, Sarawak. We were on patrol against the Indonesian KKP, myself and seven other lads from D Squadron. I was lead scout. I'd been in Malaya on a trackers' course with the Maori SAS. Being a non-smoker, I could smell scents in the jungle very easily. It was seven o'clock in the morning and we'd just come across a track leading to a clearing. I had a bad feeling about it, a premonition.

'The next moment the world erupted. Rounds were hitting the ground at my feet and ricocheting off the rocks into the trees. Bits of branches were falling on my head. I felt a terrific thump in my thigh and went flying backwards through the air. As I hit the ground, an Indonesian KKP popped up. I was lucky – I hadn't dropped my Armalite when I got hit. I swung it round and blew him away. As I crouched back down, a spurt of blood hit me in the face. My femoral artery was severed and I was already feeling very weak. I whisked off my face veil, wrapped it around my leg as far into my crotch as I could get it, pulled it tight and tied it off. I whipped out my commando dagger, twisted it around the veil, then stuck it through the leg of my OGs. The bleeding stopped!

'The firing continued, pushing the rest of the patrol down the valley, leaving me stranded. By this time, I'd already banged in my second syrette. I was lucky. I'd spotted a pile of morphine just as I was leaving the Gurkha base at Kuching before the patrol. Being a canny Jock, I'd stuck it into my breast pocket.

'I started to crawl in the direction of the emergency RV. I wasn't going to stay there and rot if I could help it. I could feel the femur crunching together. There was no pain; the morphine had started to take effect. By nightfall, and four morphines later, I crawled into a pig-hole under a tree to hide from the Indos. I covered myself with mud and pig shit as camouflage. I couldn't smell anything, I was too high on the morphine.

'I crawled throughout the next day. My thirst was terrible. Every time I tried to drink water, I spewed it up again. My system just couldn't accept it. About 1630 hours, I reached a stream. I was hugely relieved. It was the watershed of the border. I rolled about in the water to get rid of the maggots which covered me from knee to waist. The fish must have had a field day! I started to fire shots in the air, three at a time, the emergency signal. Suddenly I spotted a movement above me. I rolled behind a rock and somehow managed to get my Armalite pointing in the right direction. Someone ran behind a tree. Indo bastards, they've found me! I made my mind up to have a go as much as I could, then banjo myself. I remembered what had happened to Paddy Condon when they caught him.

'It was then I saw the red hat and the Bren gun. The Gurkhas! Salvation! Then I saw Kevin, the airborne wart, as large as life and twice as ugly! I cried my eyes out against his broad Yorkshire shoulder. Never was I so glad to see a fellow Para.

'That night, Kevin slept cuddled around me to keep me warm. As I fell into a deep sleep, I worked out that in thirty hours of crawling I had taken twelve syrettes of quarter-grain morphine. Plus one the next day, waiting for the casevac. That makes thirteen!'

'I don't understand it, Iain,' I said. 'Thirteen syrettes! You should have been dead! A medic stood up in training wing and told us that the human body can only take three syrettes of morphine. One more, and you would be dead!'

'What a way to go though! Quite a pleasant death really – beautiful surroundings, no pain, mind floating, lying back and thinking of Scotland, all of that lovely McEwan's Export I would never taste again, wondering if anyone would ever find my body!'

The night wore on and Iain left for home. I got up and headed for the bar to get Paddy and myself a last drink. I brushed against Jim

Mackay – the mayor of Hereford and a prominent local businessman – who was propping up the bar. This man was rather unusual in that, while taking full advantage of the benefits of free enterprise, he retained staunch socialist views. He saw no contradiction – he was practising the revolution from within, a subversive hearts-and-minds campaign, death by a thousand cuts to the capitalist culture. He never lost an opportunity to spread the gospel. As I placed my order, he picked up a collection tin from the bar and rattled it under my face. 'Are you not going to make a contribution to the miners' strike fund?' He began to bait me right away.

In a flash the glow of camaraderie and humour was gone. I was back into the cold reality of my career, the daily confrontation with danger that the last few hours had reminded me of only too vividly. 'Not on your frigging life. Do you think I've been fighting the Queen's enemies for the last twenty years, watching my mates get wounded and killed, risking my neck daily to make Britain a safe place to live in, just so that the Arthur Scargills of this world can hold the country to ransom!? I was biting like a hungry salmon – a dangerous mistake.

'Risking your neck! Your lot didn't do anything in the Falklands!'

'Didn't do anything! We played a crucial part in the whole thing, and what's more, we lost twenty lads down there!' I was now on the hook.

'You shouldn't have been there in the first place. It was just a bluff, a political manoeuvre by Maggie Thatcher.' He was beginning to reel me in.

'I suppose your crowd would have let the Argies run riot in the Falklands like yer darling Harold sold us down the river in Aden and let the Commies take over.'

Just as I was nearing the net, he lost his nerve, ran out of brain and began to resort to brawn. 'Come on outside, we'll settle this on the lawn.'

Paddy was now at the bar and tried to intervene. 'Don't be stupid, fella. If I were you, I wouldn't go outside, even in a tank, with my mate here.'

'He doesn't scare me,' sneered the businessman.

'You're too old,' I said sarcastically as I paid for the drinks.

'Who's too old? I'll bloody well show you who's too old,' roared the businessman, taking his jacket off.

At this point, thoughts of the Red Mill Inn and all the drama in Hong Kong flashed across my mind. More importantly, so did the more recent events that had taken place at the B Squadron OC's wedding a few months earlier. The OC was marrying one of the daughters of David Shepherd, the famous artist who had done two fine paintings of Mirbat and the Embassy siege. All of B Squadron had been invited. It was a very smart occasion – everyone in ceremonial uniform and finery. The reception was in full swing when I spotted Carl, on whom I'd been looking for an opportunity to exact retribution for some time. Carl had been on the piss one night, staggered into the basha and for no reason whatever decided to set about Malcolm, the clerk, nearly veteran of the Embassy siege. He just beat him up while he was sleeping in his bed! If there's one thing I can't stand, it's bullies. So at the wedding reception I decided to take Carl unawares, just as he'd done to Malcolm.

I went over to him and challenged him to a friendly arm-wrestling contest. We sat down, rolled up our sleeves, locked our hands and started to grapple. After a while I let Carl think he was getting the better of me. I allowed my arm to be pushed nearly onto the table. Just as he was eagerly scenting victory, I brought up my free hand from under the table and punched him square in the face. 'That one's for Malcolm,' I said. Carl crashed over backwards. A big punch-up ensued. Tables and chairs were sent crashing and women screamed as we rolled over the floor and out through the marquee entrance into the garden. I taught Carl a lesson he wouldn't forget in a hurry.

To commemorate the occasion, I later thought of suggesting to David Shepherd that he might like to do a wedding portrait of the OC and his new bride holding hands, standing at the marquee entrance gazing romantically into each other's eyes, with Carl and me in the background slogging it out in the rhododendrons. I don't think David Shepherd would have been amused. The OC certainly wasn't. He had me up on Colonel's orders for the second time. I was given a severe warning and put on probation.

Since I was on probation, the scenario now developing with the businessman did not look at all healthy. I've been in this situation before, I thought to myself, I've got to get out of here. I pushed the businessman's shaking fist abruptly to one side and, like a bull going for a red cloak, I started for the door. As I stormed blindly past Paddy, I knocked his shoulder. Paddy lost his balance, crashed into a partition and ended up on the floor with blood streaming from his nose. By this time, I was out of the door, into my Capri and away into the night.

The next morning, I was on Colonel's orders for the third time! If looks could kill, the Colonel would have been convicted of mass murder. He was incandescent with rage. He stabbed his forefinger angrily on his desk to emphasize his outrage. A note of incredulity sounded in his voice. 'You assaulted and verbally abused a respected member of Hereford society. You struck one of your colleagues a blow to the face…'

It was no use protesting. On paper, my case looked hopeless: RTU'd for Hong Kong, put on probation for the OC's wedding fracas and now this. Surely I was finished? I interjected a sharp 'sir' at appropriate moments to show a reaction, to show acceptance of the point being made, and a softer 'sir' to intone a note of query or a request for further classification.

'…and before you even try a plea of mitigation, you can forget it. I don't want to hear any feeble excuses. I don't want to hear any litany of extenuating arguments. What I expect from the men in this regiment is nothing short of the best – at all times, in all places, in all circumstances. Anything less that that and we fail. And if we fail, we call attention to ourselves, and in our book, that's the worst possible crime…'

He leaned forward across his desk. 'You are irredeemable. Your behaviour makes Neanderthal Man look like the epitome of sophistication…'

He leaned back in this chair again, arms folded, decisive, his voice lower now. 'You are a time bomb, trooper, a time bomb just waiting to explode. I'm taking a risk, a huge risk, I know that. You seem determined to ruin yourself. But I'm sending you down to Woolwich Hospital to see if the medics can make any sense of you, to see if they can take your brain apart bit by bit until they find the fuse.'

He let out a deep, weary sigh and reached for a pen. His voice now took on a more threatening tone. 'I'm warning you. One false step at Woolwich and you are finished – finished for good this time.'

16

Frustration

Finished for good? Not if I could help it. I was lying in my bed in Ward 11, going over the game plan in my mind. Tomorrow was the big one, the chief psychiatrist. It all depended on one man, a civilian at that – a civilian in charge of the mental health of the British Army! I was determined not to give in, not to let go of the values and ideals I'd lived for all this time, my identity, my self-respect, forged in the flames of the battlefield. I owed it to my fallen comrades to pull through.

The bloke in the next bed stirred. He'd come in two days before and hadn't said a word yet. He's just lain on his bed, staring into space, eyes as dead as pebbles. He was saying, 'It was the tooth that killed him. The gunshot wound was the start of it, but it was the tooth that killed him.'

I glanced over. He was looking straight at me. His eyes had become moist, human again. Tears were rolling down his cheeks.

'I was a trained medic. I'd worked in three hospitals. I should have known better. A jagged piece of filthy, decayed tooth must have gone into the lung tissue and just festered. That's what killed him. It wasn't the gunshot wound, it was the miserable piece of rotten tooth that killed him.'

He lay back on his pillow and stared ahead again, but the tears continued to flow. 'He was my best mate. He'd caught a high-velocity in the jaw. He was lying on his back, choking – not with blood or vomit, he swallowed his tongue. I yanked his tongue forward and pulled every bit of mess out of his mouth I could find. I was sure I'd got everything out of his passageway. I was sure I'd completely cleared the cavity of all the bits of teeth. He made it back to the UK all right, but he was having increasing problems with his breathing. Pneumonia or pleurisy, I don't know. They were pumping him full of penicillin, trying to get him better from the infection.

'I used to visit him in hospital as often as I could. It gave Jean a break. She had her hands full as it was with the kids. This particular day, he seemed fine one minute, a bit pale, but fine. The next minute he was no longer seeing what I was seeing, hearing what I was hearing. His eyes had glazed over, his ears somehow stopped up with the effort of trying to get his breath. I called the nurse.

'He twisted his head fiercely from side to side, his mouth working away as if he was chewing a piece of leather. Suddenly he would lie still, and his mouth would gape open for a while at the point of some momentous inner struggle. Then the head would start again. Strange sounds, not of this earth, emerged from his mouth and spoke of deep, agonizing distress. He strove to turn and lever his body off the bed, driven by some deep instinctive urge, as if he could pull through if only he could get himself into an upright position.

'He lifted and twisted his head one last time, more slowly now, and he looked at me, fear and questioning in his eyes. Questioning in his eyes. Then, slowly, slowly, he sank down with a rasping sigh, the life visibly draining away from him. I stared at him in complete and total helplessness, such impotence to alter the course of events as I'd never before experienced. A few last twitches and then his body was still, as if some great sinking battleship had finally come to rest on the bed of the ocean.

'The doctor came and went. I sat there for an age, staring at his silent form, hoping for an eyelid to rise, for a flicker of movement in the chest, staring for so long that my eyes began to play tricks on me and I imagined I saw a tremor of movement in his solar plexus. Eventually, I slowly got up, stiff from staring, and walked away. I was feeling heavy. I knew I had to tell Jean.

'She was laying the table for tea when I came in. She had a plate of buttered sliced bread in her hand. Her two kids were shouting excitedly, running around, tugging each other's sleeves. Her eyes met mine and she knew straight away. The welcoming smile faded and in an instant turned to dawning horror. She didn't rant, she didn't rave. She didn't burst into tears, she didn't shake with rage. There were no silent mouthings of incredulity nor any desperate fist-clenched challenge to the heavens to explain why. She neither fainted nor slumped in a chair, nor gripped the edge of the table. She was rigid, transfixed by a charge of emotion that overpowered her ability to think, feel or speak clearly, that seemed for an instant to have chased the very soul out of her body. She simply, slowly and deliberately, closed her eyes, was silent for the eternity of a moment, then whispered with a voice that was not her own, "Please go." With the two kids now silently staring at me, uncomprehending but sensing that something momentous was taking place, I turned, opened the door and quickly left. I hadn't spoken a word, not a single word.'

'Maybe the shock of the high-velocity bullet that hit him made him suddenly catch his breath and inhale the piece of tooth into his lungs,' I suggested, trying to offer some comfort.

'How could you tell them what it was really like down there?' he continued, apparently without hearing what I'd said. 'They all wanted to buy you drinks in the pub and ask you how it was, but how could you tell them what it was really like? To most people, the war was just an interesting diversion, something that happened each night for ten minutes on the Nine O'Clock News. Some people thought the Falklands was an island just off the coast of Scotland.' He leaned back over in my direction and fixed me with his eyes. 'I didn't want to leave when it was all over. That's where the lads had fought and died. That's where you'd been through it together. How could anyone else possible understand? No one could possibly know what you had been through.'

'That's true, mate, that's true.'

'They told me I'm suffering from POST.'

'POST, PTSD, ABR! Bullshit! It's all bullshit!' I exclaimed angrily. 'It's just names, boxes. They think if they can put a name on it, put it into a box, then everything's explained, that's all's well with the world. You've gone psychosomatic. There's nothing wrong with you. It's just shell shock. That's all you've got. Good old-fashioned shell shock.'

I looked at him. He could see from my eyes that I'd been there too. We were mates together, mates who had never met. A veil of gloom and fear seemed to lift off his face.

'You know something? They can't really cure you in here,' I went on. 'All they're after is your mind. You're just a case study, one for the archives, a bit of research for the thesis they're writing. They've got a tape recorder hidden on the desk. There's a little red light when it's on. You'll see it. They record everything you say so they can have a good laugh with their pals afterwards.

'If you think you're Napoleon now, nothing's going to stop you waking up when you're ninety-three and still thinking you're Napoleon. There's only one way you can be cured, and that's from within yourself. It's got to come from inside. You've got to get a grip on yourself. No one can do that for you.'

As the evening wore on I finally dozed off to sleep, the man's words spooling through my mind on an endlessly repeating loop tape. 'How could you tell them what it was really like?'

*   *   *

'How could I begin to tell you what it was really like?' It was the next day and I was struggling to get through to the psychiatrist. 'I could describe to you the terror, the disorientation, the sheer loneliness of being caught in a blizzard late at night driving across the mountains, when the road disappears, when everything is eerily hushed, when you don't know what is ditch and what is road or even which side of the road you're on, when the snow is so heavy the windscreen wipers begin to slow down under the accumulating weight, and the flakes stick to the screen even though the heater is trained full onto it, when you can't stop because to stop would be even more dangerous than to carry on, when you feel like a man slowly sinking in quicksand as you are sucked into the centre of the snowstorm, when your mind tells you there are other people in the world but your heart tells you are the only one there.

'I could tell you all this, and this is something within the spectrum of your own experience. We've all been in a snowstorm, we've all driven late at night through rain and snow and mist. I could tell you all this. But unless you had been where I was at the precise time I was there, you could not know, you could not feel, you could not be completely submerged in that total terror, that incipient suppressed panic. Your mind could not have been stretched taut in that relentless nerve-strain. Now look at that gap between my experience and your reaction to my relating it. Multiply that gap by ten, by twenty, by a hundred and you have some idea of the experience of war, the sense-crush of combat, the mind-blast of battle, the trauma of violent death.'

I looked at the psychiatrist and he showed no reaction. I wasn't getting through to him. I was frustrated, angry. It felt as though I was trying to run through waist-deep water.

Suddenly, there was the sound of a detonation, a huge, cataclysmic detonation. The next moment I was coming to, lying there, dazed and confused, for what seemed like an age. I prised my eyes open. A shaft of light came in. I heard the sound of voices. It felt hot. I could smell the sweet, sharp, prickly smell of cordite. My mouth tasted dry and dusty. My hands were working, fists slowly clenching and unclenching. I felt the rough woollen material of a blanket.

A blanket! I sprang up with a start. Christ, I've been dreaming! A full technicolour dream complete with stereophonic sound. It was dawn. The ward was stirring into life. My new-found mate in the next bed had lit up a cigarette and was waving the match in the air to extinguish it. Red phosphorus – the smell of cordite! The nurse was pushing a metal trolley full of surgical equipment rattling on steel trays down the middle of the ward. The doors through which she'd just exploded were swinging violently, neon light glinting on their aluminium panels.

* * *

I walked slowly down the corridor towards the chief psychiatrist's office.

'You are a time bomb, trooper, a time bomb just waiting to explode. But we can defuse you!' The Colonel's words rang through my mind as footsteps echoed off the bare walls. I thought of Tommo the Scouse exploding with anger on selection all those years before. It hadn't done him much good. Or maybe it had. Maybe he wasn't meant to be in the SAS – he might never have made it past Operation *Jaguar*. That explosion might have saved his life. Maybe he was better off out of it after all. Maybe he'd got himself a nice little number back with the Royal Fusiliers and done very well for himself. Perhaps he'd found the secret: expression of emotion rather than suppression. Why bottle up all your feelings, build up the pressure, build up the stress until your heart fails, your stomach ulcerates, your liver collapses or your brain gets blown apart by a stroke?

The Colonel thinks I'm going to explode. Maybe I should explode, get it off my chest, go out with a bang rather than a whimper. I've fought my fights, I've waged my wars. Perhaps it would be a fitting end to a drama-filled career. Shit or bust! Attack – the best form of defence!

One thing is for certain. I'm not going to play second fiddle to some jumped-up civilian psychiatrist who doesn't know the first thing about combat. I've never let the system get me down before. If I had, if I hadn't shown initiative and self-confidence before, I wouldn't be here now. If I hadn't broken the rules at Mirbat and sent the first radio message to Um al Gwarif in plain-language morse, crucial time would have been lost; if I hadn't used the knuckleduster in Hong Kong, I would have been dead on the street; if I hadn't demanded that the hospital orderly in Stanley Jail give me a tetanus jab, I could have had serious health problems; if I hadn't stood my ground with the RE colonel back at Southwood Barracks, I would have spent an unpleasant twelve months as a lance-corporal rather than a sergeant; if I hadn't insisted on seeing the captain on the *Andomeda*, we would have lost a pallet full of vital equipment. I had never grovelled to another man in my life and I didn't intend starting now.

I strode into the office without knocking. The psychiatrist looked up, slightly startled. He was as ugly as an iguana. Folds of yellow-green skin clung to his prominent facial bones, he had dark rings around his eyes and his expression was as bleak as a wind-ruffled winter puddle. He lit another cigarette from the remains of one he'd just finished, and screwed the bent dog-end into the layer of ash in the bottom of the ashtray amid the burnt-out remains of a dozen other cigarettes. Christ! Not only a civilian in charge of the mental health of the British Army, but a chain-smoker at that! What have you got to hide, mate? What's gnawing away at your insides? Why do you need to smoke so much? I've no problem going three months in the jungle without a drink. You wouldn't last three days there without cigarettes. You'd be crawling up the trees!

A thick blue haze hung in the room like a morning mist. I'm not having this. I'm used to the great outdoors. Plenty of fresh air. Without saying a word, I marched over to the window, rattled it open and took some deep breaths of the air wafting over Woolwich Common. He didn't like it. It was late November and he got an icy draught on the back of his neck. I sauntered back round to the front of the desk and, without waiting to be asked, sat down. I was in a defiant mood. The psychiatrist picked up a folder, his eyes not leaving me for a moment. He placed it before him and grasped a pencil from a plastic container. Then he looked down. The pencil hissed across the page as he furiously scribbled notes on my report.

17

The Final RV

In the days before steam, when tall-masted clippers plied the tea route between China and Europe, speed was of the essence. The ship that reached port first got the benefit of the markets. Moreover, the quicker the journey, the better the condition of the cargo and the higher the price it could command. The speed of the ship depended on the skill of the seamen in unfurling and reefing the sails. The men with the most dangerous job on board were those who worked on the uppermost masts, hauling the huge sails in and out. Safety was not of paramount concern. It was not unknown for one of the topmost riggers, subjected as they were to the highest winds and the greatest pitch and roll of the swell, to lose his grip and go plunging down a hundred feet or more. If he hit the deck, it meant almost certain death. If he fell into the sea, he might just escape with shock and bruising. A seaman who survived the fall intact was encouraged by the older hands to climb straight back up to the top of the mainmast so that he might not lose his nerve forever. This was exposure therapy of the most immediate kind.

BET they call it today – behavioural exposure therapy – a legacy of post-Freudian psychoanalytical theory. I learned all about it in Ward 11. They gave me pills to break down the barriers and allow the traumas of my operational experiences to come to the surface. Through being exposed and confronted, the traumas could hopefully be cured. As I drove back from Woolwich to Hereford, I thought I would undertake a bit of freelance BET myself. I decided to pay a visit to the scene of my so-called crime. I would have a pint in the pub where the argument with the mayor had taken place. Not only would it satisfy my self-willed bloody-mindedness, but it would have the additional benefit of allowing me to re-orientate myself into familiar surroundings after the wasteland of Ward 11 before facing the Colonel on camp.

It was lunchtime and the tap-room was surprisingly busy. I was hoping to find Tak there. A drink and talk about the old days, a bit of exposure to his laconic Fijian humour would be just the aftercare I needed. I sat down at the bar, ordered a pint of draught Guinness and quietly smiled to myself. No one said anything. It was as if nothing had ever happened. I relaxed and let the normality flow over me.

I was halfway through my pint when I spotted the infamous Lynda. She had become almost as much a part of the Regiment as the clock tower itself. The night I'd seen her all those years before, tumbling in the sheets with Geordie before Sickener 1, had not been her first visit to camp, nor her last. She'd had as many willing partners as there are daisies on an uncut lawn. Now in her mid-thirties, the passions of youth tempered by the pummellings of experience, she had acquired a hard, no-nonsense manner which on the few occasions when I now saw her I found an irresistible challenge.

I gave her a wave and she breezed over, exclaiming jauntily, 'Hi, soldier. How're you keeping? I haven't seen you in ages. Where've you been?'

'I've just returned from down south – training exercise, that sort of thing. What are you doing with yourself these days, Lynda?'

'I'm training to be a psychiatric nurse.'

'A psychiatric nurse! I know all about them. They're all as mad as hatters. What made you choose that career?'

'It's a case of if you can't beat them, join them.'

'When you qualify, you should set up a therapy clinic on camp.'

She completely missed the veiled reference to her erstwhile penchant for helping the lads release the tensions of Army life. 'Why? Are you all screwball down there?'

'Yeah! Didn't you know there's a chopper on constant hover 500 feet above the camp to make sure no one escapes?'

'I can believe it.'

'If you opened a clinic, they'd be queuing up at the door to see you – especially if you had your black stockings on!'

'Oh yeah, and my whip?' A hint of anger was creeping into her voice. She was beginning to take me too seriously.

'Why not? I had the whip in Hong Kong. It didn't do me any lasting harm.'

'Physically or psychologically?'

'Physically. You'll have to analyse me to see if I suffered any brain damage or not! I'll be your first patient if you'll have me.'

'Sure, I'm game.'

'I've no doubt you are! I look forward to meeting you on the couch then, Lynda.'

By now she'd cottoned on to the *doubles entendres*, so I drained my Guinness and beat a hasty retreat. I didn't want to tangle with her new-found temper. She'd recently gone over onto the loony fringe of the women's lib movement. And that was even more dangerous than the loony fringe of the socialist movement!

As I walked through the main gate of the barracks, the tension began to crawl through my muscles. I felt nervous and apprehensive. I wondered what the chain-smoking shrink had written about me. I wondered whether fifteen years' drama-filled service in the SAS was about to end in an ignominious anticlimax, a definitive RTU. The mod plod on the gate gave me a friendly wave. That was reassuring – no urgent call to the telephone, no clipped voice ordering me to the CO's office to be hit by the report.

I pushed through the main door of the headquarters block and turned right into the orderly room. A large oil painting of David Stirling, the driving force behind the foundation of the SAS, hung on the far wall and dominated the office. The clerks looked indifferent. No arrangements had been made. There was no memo ordering me to attend a CO's interview. The chief clerk shrugged his shoulders and looked blank. I closed the door on the paper factory and headed for the operational research department to try my luck there. Still nothing doing. From there I was redirected to admin wing, the last refuge of the Regimental bad boys. At this rate, I thought, I'm going to end up in the stores blanket-stacking.

Just when I was fearing the worst, just when I thought the system had finally caught up with me, the message came down the line: a clean bill of health! The shrinks had given me a clean bill of health! I was elated. The gamble had paid off! Once more I'd brazened my way out of a tight corner. I was back in business with a vengeance. They were going to put my operational expertise to the best possible use: I was to be an instructor in the counter-revolutionary warfare wing. From trainee to tutor, after fifteen years my career in the SAS had come full circle. Being no longer in the field, exposed to the life-threatening situations, I had not only beaten the system, but I had now well and truly beaten the clock. I'd ridden the death-or-glory course and made it to the finishing post.

As the weeks went by, I threw myself wholeheartedly into the job in hand, counter-terrorism team training. As I did so, the realization dawned: I must be well and truly A1 and fit for service. There was no way the Head Shed would risk a training compromise. What was required of troops for these types of operations – even above and beyond all specialist skills – was a cool head, a clear mind and a rock-solid temperament. If the trainer was unstable, what hope for the trainees?

But before I was to close the door on CRW wing for the last time, before I was to face my next big battle – civvy life – I still had a significant contribution to make to the Regiment. I was about to train an SAS team from Northern Ireland whose 'spectacular' would set in motion events that would eventually force the IRA to the negotiation table.

On Friday 8 May 1987, eight IRA men were killed in a gun battle in the village of Loughgall, Co. Armagh. They were members of the lethal East Tyrone Brigade, and had tried to attack the local RUC station with a hijacked JCB digger, loaded with beer kegs containing 500lb of explosives. It was part of an ongoing campaign of intimidation against the RUC, and it was ambushed with deadly effect by the SAS team. One senior policeman said, 'We really needed a victory. It will do wonders for the morale of our men.'

It was a good way to end.

18

When the Camp Gates Close

On 31 December 1987 I retired from the Regiment.

Once that camp gate swings closed behind you for the last time and you stand there in Civvy Street you are on your own. You are Mr Nobody. All you come out with, believe it or not, is a reference – a few pieces of paper in exchange for twenty-six years of risking your life on an almost daily basis. I was shell-shocked. The days of taking part in high-drama, headline-grabbing operations were gone. The indescribable highs and mind-numbing lows, the despair and depression, the exhilaration, the pride, the intense camaraderie, the frustration, the boredom, all the achingly intense emotions that are the daily reality of a soldier's life suddenly drain away and leave you emptier than you've ever felt in your whole life.

A Roman general once talked of a soldier as one who 'knows the great enthusiasms, the great devotions, and spends himself in a worthy cause'. Well, when the cause itself is spent what's left? I sat in my armchair at home staring into empty space. How can anything prepare you for civilian life after twenty-six years in the Army, eighteen of those years with the SAS? 'The culture here is self-discipline, self-motivation. You can use that attitude. It means you can adjust when you come out.' That was the gist of the demob briefing when I left the SAS.

What they really mean is you're on your own. Self-discipline? The only discipline I'd ever known was fire discipline – counting your rounds and making sure every shot counts – and water discipline – metering your water out into the cap of your water bottle so you know not only how much water you have drunk per hour but how much you have left. Crucial survival skills in the Army, but they weren't going to help me now.

When you leave the SAS you're out on a limb, isolated. All you've got is cold turkey withdrawal symptoms after years of mainlining on adrenaline. It's always the same. It's always after the battle that the shock and the sorrow and the trauma of it all comes pouring out, when the adrenaline and fear have gone. It's the eerie silence after a battle. It's as if you've just opened your eyes for the first time in hours and you're suddenly surveying a scene of devastation. Roads, trees, houses, animals all completely blasted. All you're left with is the sad, quiet debris of conflict lying everywhere: abandoned weapons, bits of clothing and webbing, mangled vehicles, the bodies of the dead, the slow, agonized writhing of the dying, pools of blood getting ever bigger. It's desolate and it's forlorn.

And that's how it felt now leaving the Army and looking out on the aftermath of twenty-six years of battles. It's the swing of the pendulum, one extreme to the other. From twenty-six years of superhuman endeavour – in combat, feeling unbeatable and euphoric; out of combat, charged with eager anticipation waiting for the next battle to begin – to this, the intense boredom that could be the rest of my life.

I picked up the *Hereford Times* and broke into a cold sweat. My eyes focused in sharply on the article as if it were a gun-wielding enemy looming up into my line of fire. I felt strangely compelled to read it even though I knew it would stir up a slurry of black emotions. 'Tragic End for Shell Shocked Hero', ran the headline. It was about Private Jones who lived in the Hereford area at the beginning of the twentieth century. He had won the VC for heroism at Rorke's Drift in 1879.

When he got back, he couldn't adjust to civilian life in rural Herefordshire. He was tormented by recurring nightmares of the stabbing, slashing, blood-soaked spears of screaming Zulu warriors. He walked out one day and blew his head off with a double-barrel shotgun.

Will the day finally dawn when all my stress comes bubbling out? How will it show itself? It doesn't take a genius to work that one out. 'These Men are Dangerous' – that was the title of a communiqué from Adolf Hitler to the French occupation forces, directing that all captured SAS troops be turned over to the Gestapo. The Army turns you into a ruthless killing machine. In every battle, instinct tells you to keep your head down, hug the ground, keep a low profile. So what was it drove men to stand up and charge over the top of the trenches in the First World War, sacrificing their lives for another yard of mud? And what drove men to storm full frontal up the murderous beaches of D-Day to face near-certain death? Army training and discipline, perfected through centuries of practice, that's what does it. That's what overcomes fear, confusion, logic and the survival instinct itself. That's what turns you into a killing machine. The trouble is, what turns you back into a human being at the end of it all?

I dropped the *Hereford Times* down the side of my armchair and went into the kitchen to make a brew. I stood gazing out of the window waiting for the kettle to boil, my mind drifting over my turbulent career in the SAS. I recollected the very first day of selection, that twenty-six-week course from hell. The Colonel was addressing the rows of hopeful candidates, 135 of us in all: 'You have a difficult task ahead of you. Twenty-six weeks of exhaustive scrutiny. Half a year of uncertainty.'

He was wrong. It wasn't half a year of scrutiny and uncertainty. The ones that got through, only seventeen of us in total, faced a lifetime of uncertainty, never knowing if we are going to explode with the stress of it all. That niggling thought never leaves you. As it says in the SAS survival Top Ten: all five-second grenade fuses are three seconds. So how long was my fuse? I had survived the stresses of the Army and even the psychiatrists' scrutiny at Woolwich but Civvy Street was another matter.

What was I going to do? I doubted if the NHS could help. Can you imagine it, a group therapy session with the flotsam and jetsam of today's society – alkies, druggies, divorcees? I'm sat there like some fucking freak till it's my turn. What questions would they ask me? Are you married? Do you have any children? What does it feel like to storm an Embassy and kill terrorists? And then they move on to the next case, some sad bastard whose life has been torn apart because his pet dog died... No, I couldn't quite see it somehow. NHS counsellors don't spend time in execution chambers watching people get killed. They're not taken round mortuaries to see the dead. They don't ride shotgun with paramedics to see bodies ripped to shreds in road traffic accidents. They don't get desensitized, they don't get to become immune. What do they know?

What can a civilian possibly know about the unremitting brutality, the violence, the aggression, the twisted and ugly spectacle of a battle zone? Combat in the front line? I'll tell you what it's all about. It's about ruptured arteries spurting out plumes of blood. It's about that frogspawn of scarlet foam, that gurgling and unearthly whistling coming from some poor bastard's throat with a hole the size of a fist ripped from it. It's about that deadly cocktail of looks in a fatally wounded man's eyes – the torment, the urgent plea, the faltering realization, the imminence of his last breath struggling up out of tortured lungs. It's about the shock in the eyes of your best mate lying there staring in disbelief at the oozing sausage-spill of purple-veined innards splashed out over his webbing belt, the ignominious stench of his private sewage consuming the air all around you. Wringing wet, sleeping rough, surviving on hard tack and cheese out of a tube, senses tormented by seeing bodies ripped apart and blown limb from limb, ears seeming to be ringing permanently with some voice screaming

'I'm hit… I'm hit… I'm hit…' – and any moment it could be your turn next. How could a civilian diagnose me and offer me a cure after that?

My trouble was I'd fought the wrong kind of wars. When my father was in the Army during the Second World War, there were no sociological questions about the ethics of war being debated on prime-time TV. There was no hand-wringing and agonizing over hidden political agendas and what the true objective of the conflict was. Where Hitler was concerned it was black and white, good versus evil. And at the end of it all, there were cheering crowds in the streets to welcome you back, to prove you'd righted the wrong, to slap you on the back and tell you what a marvellous job you'd done. My kinds of wars were the bad kind. Nothing was clear-cut. The enemy was not always obvious, there was scepticism and lack of popular support at home, our hands were tied by legal and political constraints. No black and white there, just treacherous shades of grey. No cheering crowds in the streets when you come back. Shrouded in secrecy, we were processed through RAF Lynham or RAF Brize Norton in the dead of night. Whether returning from deadly combat or routine exercise, it was exactly the same.

The Yanks returning from Vietnam soon found out the morale-bursting stress of that particular kind of silence. At least the American public knew about Vietnam. Most of my wars were not only the wrong kind but they were secret too. Covert operations, confidential assignments, anonymous infiltrations. We moved in silently, did our job, and melted away again. No speak, no tell, no profile. The British public were none the wiser. The Sixties and early Seventies – flower power, summer of love, make love not war, better red than dead? Bullshit! I was fighting in the Middle East in the 1970s. The Commies seemed to be taking over the world and we soldiers were the ones tasked with doing something about it. But no one shouted it from the rooftops. That's the culture of secrecy. Everything's clamped up inside, suppressed, bottled up. That's when the time bomb starts ticking.

I could hear the church bells ringing down in the centre of Hereford. I used to dream of days like this when I was undercover in some far-off land preparing for combat. The sun would be shining, the civilians around me going about their usual business, everything eerily normal. I'd suddenly think that back home right now my father would be relaxing in his armchair reading his Sunday paper and drinking a brew of tea, my mates would be going down to the pub for a livener, and there I was about to enter battle and fight for my life. Very weird. But now it was Sunday and it was me that was at home, wishing I was back in combat. I had to face up to the fact I was hooked on the adrenaline hit, the camaraderie, the SAS gallows humour. The hit is so powerful and so addictive that you get withdrawal symptoms sat at home, worrying about mortgages, gas and electricity bills, all the mundane elements of so-called normal life.

I glanced at my watch. Eleven o'clock already. The pubs would be open soon. Time for a shave. At least I still bothered to take some kind of basic care of my personal appearance. Which was more than I could say for the appearance of the bathroom. The bath and loo mats were grimy. The plugholes in the bath and hand basin were matted over with enough hair to weave a rug. A tiny scrap of soap, no mirror, one torn towel, one toothbrush in a holder, toothpaste dribbling down like bird droppings under a perch, a loo seat that had a mind of its own and would come crashing down in mid-piss, and a weird, pervasive smell of decay. Was it the drains, the mould on the shower curtain, a dead mouse beneath the bath panels? I didn't know, and I didn't really care. I'd get round to sorting it one day. My wife had left me and taken my son with her. I didn't need to bother any more on the domestic front.

The downstairs was no better. You could say it was lacking a woman's touch. Curtains always drawn, the television blaring out constantly, half-drunk cups of tea lying around the place like in an under-staffed café, rooms not vaccuumed in months, the garden looking like the Borneo jungle. There were even exotic mushrooms growing under the fridge and getting bigger by the day. I thought of preserving them under glass and taking them down to the survival course briefing room at the camp as an exhibit in the dangerous fungi section. But what can you expect? The SAS is not a school for aspiring ballet dancers. You can't expect us to go in for civilised niceties like cleaning the house. I was even toying with the idea of moving out of my bedroom and getting my head down at nights in the back garden under a poncho to see if that would make me feel more at home.

It was all getting too much. I wasn't sure I could hack it. I was still functioning in this society, but only just. Our mortar man at the battle of Mirbat, Fuzz, had already cracked up in Civvy Street. More would go the same way, I was sure of that. Would I join them? Would I end up burnt out, just another statistic, another skeleton in the nation's cupboard? 'Tragic End for Shell Shocked Hero', would they write that about me too in the *Hereford Times*?

Enough! Enough! This morbid navel-gazing had gone on far too long. I couldn't spend the rest of my life like this. I shook my head and came to my senses. I was disgusted with myself for feeling so edgy and discontented. People should be able to handle their own feelings. I wasn't a civilian under some kind of imminent threat: I wasn't living through some kind of civil war or trying to survive a conflict-induced famine or vicious ethnic cleansing. I was a proud soldier. I'd come through the battle of Mirbat, the Embassy siege, the Falklands War, Northern Ireland. Why should I feel dissatisfied now? I was a pampered Westerner with everything on a plate.

No more self-pity. It was time to pick up the phone.

19

On the Circuit

'Tak. I need a job. I need some anti-boredom pills.' In the Army that was the slang for getting in some money, and I could always rely on my Fijian brother-in-arms to get me out of a fix. He'd done it often enough in the past. He'd left the SAS a bit before me and in typical Tak fashion had quickly risen through the ranks of his new profession to become a director of Kilo Alpha Services (KAS) – a private security firm. KAS were part of 'the Circuit' – a network of companies run mainly by ex-SAS members specializing in close protection, risk assessment, UK and international security and hostile-environment survival training. It's a sphere of operations that demands the same degree of stealth, silence and anonymity that became second nature to me in the Army. As with the world of espionage and secret intelligence, the general public gets only the faintest glimpse of what really goes on behind the scenes. This was familiar territory.

'Get yourself down to London tomorrow. I might have something for you.' The phone clicked and Tak was gone. In all the years I'd known him, Tak had never, ever discussed operational matters over the telephone.

The offices of KAS were at 22 South Audley Street right in the middle of London's Mayfair. I smiled as I clocked the abbreviation of this address – 22 SAS. Familiar territory indeed! As I pushed open the front door I was confronted by an imposing six-foot-six figure. Slightly stooped as if apologizing for his unusual height, his clothes were immaculate, his manners perfect. Softly spoken and of modest demeanour, with an obvious aristocratic background, in the Regiment he had been nicknamed 'the Scarlet Pimpernel' for his actions behind enemy lines in the Second World War. It was none other than Sir Archibald David Stirling DSO OBE, the legendary founder of the SAS and now chairman of KAS.

It was only a couple of years ago that I'd been his bodyguard in the Regiment. He recognized me straight away and shot out his hand to greet me. 'Nice to see you again.' I felt at home already.

I felt even more so when I met the managing director of the outfit, Major Ian Crooke. When I knew him in the Regiment he had been OC of A Squadron, then Ops Officer. He was part of the outside team collating intel and information during the Embassy siege in 1980. When you've been through something like that together, you've bonded forever. Stunning though that episode was, his most daring exploit took place a year later. He and two senior NCOs from B Squadron were sent to 'observe and advise' on a Marxist coup in the Commonwealth nation of the Gambia. It was when he got to the capital, Banjul, that he took the expression 'going beyond the call of duty' to a spectacular new level. Being the loose cannon he was, Crookie proceeded to do a little bit more than observe and advise. He decided to end the coup single-handed.

The rebels had taken control of the key infrastructure in and around Banjul whilst the president, Sir Dawda Jawara, was in the UK as an honoured guest at the wedding of Prince Charles and Lady Diana Spencer. While the happy couple were sunning themselves on honeymoon on board *Britannia*, Crookie and his team flew in to neighbouring Senegal. They casually strolled across the border into the Gambia dressed in jeans and T-shirts and carrying rucksacks crammed with Heckler & Koch MP5s, Browning pistols and an ample supply of ammunition.

Arriving in the capital, they quickly assessed the situation and found the rebels in control of key positions. In particular, members of the president's family and other high-placed dignitaries were being held hostage at the main hospital. Totally undaunted, Crookie and his NCOs acquired white coats and stethoscopes and arrived at the hospital in nothing more threatening than a taxi. With the element of surprise on their side they quickly disarmed the rebels and freed the hostages. Next, they established contact with an elite force of French-trained Senegalese paratroopers who'd also arrived at the request of the president. Crookie introduced himself to their senior officer and promptly took command of the unit. Leading the counter-attack from the turret of an armoured car and with his two sergeants running the assault groups, he routed the rebels and dislodged them from their strongholds in the army barracks, the radio station and the police armoury. Without further ado, he and his team hopped on a plane and headed back to Hereford. Freeing a small African state from Communist rebels – all in a day's work for the SAS! Back home the top brass were spitting blood at how he'd gone beyond his brief. They were on the verge of court-martialling him. In the end they changed their minds and gave him a DSO for outstanding bravery instead.

I had definitely found the right outfit. KAS was obviously the Rolls-Royce of security companies – the right address, the right contacts and the right people at the top. It was like the civilian wing of the Regiment. Another squadron, only better pay. I couldn't wait to start.

I soon found my former comrade. 'What've you got, Tak?'

'Diamonds. Are you interested?' His Fijian features broke into a wide grin.

'I'm interested. Tell me more.'

Tak briefed me on the deal. My first assignment was to be one half of a two-man team providing security for an exhibition at the St James Club, just down the road in Mayfair. And the subject of the exhibition? A mere £3 million of jewellery! Although access to the exhibition was strictly reserved for members of the club itself – a real Who's Who of top society names – this was still a daunting prospect. I pretended to take it all in my stride, but relief swept over me when I heard who my fellow operative would be. My partner for the job of making sure the gems didn't go AWOL was Tak's compatriot Tom the Fijian.

Tom was now fully recovered from the heavy-duty burns he received at the Embassy siege, when his abseil gear became jammed and he swung into the fierce flames coming from the second-floor windows. His legs were very badly burned. But once he'd been cut free, his severe injuries didn't stop him storming the telex room and slotting the terrorist Makki who'd just opened fire on the hostages, killing the assistant press attaché and badly wounding Dr Afrouz, the chargé d'affaires. For his heroism, Tom was awarded the George Medal. I was in good company.

Talk about diamonds are forever! It was like a scene from a James Bond film. The exhibition room was crammed with spotlit glass cases glittering with more jewels than you could shake an AK-47 at. I glanced up, half-expecting a black-clad cat burglar to be abseiling down from the ceiling. We appraised the situation, then took up tactical positions to prevent any smash-and-grab attempt. One man took up station in the corridor by the door, the other in the room overlooking the cabinets.

At first it went very well. We had a procession of high-fliers coming to take a look including Peter de Savary, former owner of the club itself, who'd made his fortune in shipping and oil. He swept in magisterially, surrounded by his entourage of bright young men, had a quick glance at the gems, then marched out again. I imagine he could have bought the lot if he'd wanted to.

All went smoothly until after lunch. That's when the problems started – or should I say staggered in – in the form of Leonard of Mayfair. Leonard Lewis was the UK's first superstar celebrity hairdresser. One of the founder members of the Swinging Sixties, his iconic 'crop' look shot Twiggy to supermodel stardom. His fingers had styled the hair of the most famous celebrities and Hollywood stars of three decades, from the Beatles to Princess Diana. But the pressures of fame and – unknown to me – a brain tumour had taken their toll, and he was now reduced to a pitiful alcoholic.

Each day he would lurch in at 2.30pm on the dot and launch a torrent of abuse at Tom and myself. But his antics gave me real pause for thought. Just how could the famous Leonard of Mayfair end up a drunk? A man who had been a millionaire and rubbed shoulders with the high and mighty? I would have to be careful. Civvy Street was obviously not all plain sailing. You might not end up shot to pieces, but there were different dangers to face.

The first day was uneventful until it came to closing time, when the drama began. To call it a disastrous breakdown in communication would be an understatement. During previous exhibitions, the diamonds had been taken under heavy guard to the Knightsbridge Security Deposit Centre and held there overnight. Unfortunately, the slight matter of one of the world's largest-ever bank heists had recently taken place there, led by Italian master criminal Valerio Viccei. He and his gang had pillaged cash, gold and jewels conservatively estimated at £125 million from over a hundred boxes in the facility. Not only had the raid led to the temporary closure of the facility, but it had also prompted a climate of fear and insecurity amongst the top jewellers in London.

When we queried the overnight arrangements, the near-hysterical owner of the jewels said – and this is the polite version – 'Sort it out. That's what I pay you for. Put them in the club's safe.' One slight problem – the St James Club's management were not prepared to let us use their safe, claiming their insurance wouldn't cover a potential £3 million theft. By this time, the staff at KAS had all left for home. Pre-mobile phones, it was impossible to contact them. As usual, we were isolated, left to our own devices. Some things don't change, I thought, as a picture flashed into my mind of being abandoned and helpless in a prison cell in Hong Kong.

Of all things, Tesco carrier bags solved the problem. Taking a leaf out of Crookie's book, we decided to use our initiative and go over and above the call of duty. After paying a visit to the local supermarket, we split the diamonds into two plastic bags and sauntered off through Mayfair, carrying the priceless contents as if it was the day's shopping. Our accommodation for the week was in the converted attic at KAS's HQ in South Audley Street. Incredibly, there was no safe in the office. That's how I ended up with half the stash – a cool £1.5 million pounds of precious stones – tucked up in bed with me. As I drifted off to sleep, it occurred to me that when Crookie found out, we'd either get the mother of all bonuses or the mother of all bollockings!

It did the trick. The week passed off without incident and the jewels were returned to their relieved owner. Job done. But little did I know this was just my probation. This was my starter for ten.

A bigger job was in the offing.

20

Champagne and Diamonds

'Eighty million pounds' worth of diamonds! You've got to be joking! You really can't be serious.'

'Shouldn't be a problem,' said Tak in his usual laid-back manner. He was a man of few words. Why use fifty when five would do?

Crookie had been pleased at how the St James Club assignment had gone, in spite of the misunderstanding about overnighting the jewels. He went out of his way to thank us for a job well done. Christ, I thought, that was a piece of cake. Easy money. I don't remember getting a pat on the back after Mirbat. But whilst the praise was genuine, I could tell Crookie was leading up to something else.

This was the big one. The contract was with one of the most famous jewellers in the world. He was a real larger-than-life character, an ebullient buccaneer of the diamond trade, fabled for tales of derring-do; secret assignments with clients in the dead of night, negotiations held on a remote airfield in some exotic land with the pockets of his dapper suit stuffed with priceless gems. The son of immigrants, he'd started off from very humble beginnings selling cheap rings at the markets in London's East End. He'd made his money in the Seventies, when high-rolling Arab royalty flush with oil money poured through the doors of his glittering Knightsbridge store, buying up to 400 pieces at a time. A true entrepreneur, he reportedly closed one sale with a Saudi prince by convincing him the diamond he held in his hand was absolutely fated to be his. 'Here, have a closer look,' he had said, handing the prince an eyepiece to peer at the gem. He'd inserted a minuscule photograph of the client into the stone's setting, so when the prince looked into it he saw himself glittering back!

With formidable drive, he had established himself at the head of a business spanning the whole range of the diamond industry, from mining, cutting and polishing right through to the design and production of the jewellery itself.

His major break came when he acquired the one client everyone was after – the supremely wealthy twenty-ninth Sultan of Brunei, then the world's richest man. Our client reserved the very best of his major gems for the Sultan and his three wives. The Sultan's patronage had opened some very heavily guarded doors amongst the mega-rich of Asia and the Far East.

Our job now was to fly out to Brunei and take £80 million of jewellery to the Sultan's palace. Eight-zero millions. A small matter of a wedding gift for the Sultan's brother. Tak was coming with me on this job and I met with him for the security briefing. 'What are we going to use for transporting the diamonds to the airport?' I enquired. 'A Group 4 armoured car? Motorcycle outriders? Two-car convoy?'

Tak's reply, when it came, was short, sharp and to the point. 'Low profile. Two briefcases and a four-door production saloon.' It transpired our cavalier client had picked up the habit early in his career of carrying his wares around in an ordinary-looking briefcase. It was a habit he hadn't kicked. He was coming with us to Brunei and insisted on the same low-key approach.

My heart sank. This was a security headache of gigantic proportions. £80 million of gems in two briefcases. Well, at least it was better than Tesco bags!

A week later, I found myself back in Knightsbridge, pulling up outside the client's Aladdin's cave of a shop in a battered and anonymous-looking old Ford Orion Ghia. I smiled to myself. The last time I'd been in this part of South Kensington I'd been dressed in all-black assault kit, wielding a Heckler & Koch and breaking into the Iranian Embassy. Now I was suited and booted and looking every inch the successful businessman.

Tak and I left the car with the driver and entered the building. We were ushered into a back room past display cases stuffed with fabulous gems. Our client was in there, leaning nonchalantly back in an office chair. On the table in front of him, two briefcases were already packed and waiting. I picked mine up. I couldn't believe it. In my possession I now had £40 million of precious stones. Our client was either a very clever man or a very foolhardy one.

Now came the dangerous bit. If we were going to be hit, chances are it would be while walking to the car outside. Casual, nice and casual. Switched on, every sense on high alert, every muscle tensed and pumping with adrenaline, yet sauntering casually towards the car as if we were mere accountants with briefcases full of invoices and ledgers. We had to look as if we'd just attended a business meeting and were heading back to our office. We were ready for trouble, but nothing, not the merest flinch, not the merest split-second, sharp-eyed glance around the street outside should betray the true contents of the cases. I felt almost naked. We were not even handcuffed to the briefcases, with a raincoat casually slung over the wrist to conceal the chains. Too much of a giveaway. The professional villain wouldn't fall for that one. Absolutely nothing should draw attention to ourselves. Those few steps felt like climbing Everest.

Relief. We were inside the car. Time to go. I had hoped that Tak would source a car with enough power to really shift in the event that we picked up a tail. The old Orion was never going to set the world alight, but I had trusted that at least it would start on the button. The driver turned the ignition key. Nothing. He tried again. Nothing. Shit, it's not going to start! I was as tense as a tightrope. I knew we should have used a BMW.

The driver tried a third time. Suddenly the Orion burst into life. With Tak and our wealthy passenger sitting in the back we glided away and joined the flow of traffic. No dramatics. No wheel spins. There could be watchers with radios waiting to identify us to other gang members waiting in ambush en route. The hijack on the Falls Road flashed back into my mind and I double-checked all the doors were locked. We were very exposed now. As we joined the Cromwell Road heading for the M4, I fished out of my pocket my own stick-on rear-view mirror. I fixed it firmly in place, adjusting it for optimum vision. I wanted to put in maximum mirror time for counter-surveillance during the vulnerable miles to the airport. I sat upright, the briefcase cradled between my feet, tensing at every red light, every junction, every slow-moving roundabout.

We reached Heathrow without incident. This was worse. Still couldn't relax, not for a millisecond. Too many strangers milling around, too many potential threats. Too much ambient noise to pick up quickening steps behind us. Mercifully, we were given the red carpet treatment and were whisked through in no time to the haven of the First Class section of the BA flight to Brunei. We took our briefcases as hand luggage, mightily relieved we were not asked to open them by security staff before boarding.

On board it was like a flying Michelin-starred restaurant. Unlimited free champagne, and vintage champagne at that. One bottle finished, another brought over without even asking. I had to pinch myself. Quite something when you're accustomed to business-class flying being the para seats on a military C-130. Strapped into the hard bucket seats with no arms to rest on, back against the fuselage, staring blankly for hours on end at the high stack of stores strapped down under a cargo net along the centre of the plane, right in front of our faces. Serve-yourself haversack rations – crisps, ham sandwiches and a cold drink if you were lucky. The noise, the vibration, the juddering and shaking indescribable. And now this, the Rolls-Royce of flying experiences. Pausing briefly at the head of the runway, the captain opened up the engines to full throttle and we were away.

Now all we had to worry about was the main threat: arrival in Brunei.

21

The Sultan's Palace

During the flight, I gave a lot of thought to the dangers ahead. At my feet, a harmless-looking briefcase, part and parcel of every businessman's standard equipment. And yet, and yet. I tried not to think about it. So much wealth concentrated into so little space. If some would-be criminal had got wind of this particular consignment, the temptation would be massive. My heart was beginning to sink. Why did I ever agree to this hare-brained plan to go low-profile with such a huge stash of gems? And no weapons to defend ourselves with either.

I did a mental check of 'what ifs'. What if there was an operation in place ready to make the hit in the arrivals hall in Brunei? This prize would certainly warrant planning on an international scale. What if someone in the UK had briefed the advance party at our destination of our flight number and arrival time? What if they'd set up a trigger in arrivals, a spotter to ID the target and let the outside team know? We'd have to run the gauntlet of the paging area, all the chauffeurs and minibus drivers searching for their clients. Not just one or two, but everyone staring at you as you walk out. This would be an ideal spot to eyeball two guys carrying briefcases and with bulging muscles you don't get from pushing bits of paper from one side of a desk to the other.

Then what if we picked up a tail in transit from the airport to our hotel? It would be night-time. A stick-on mirror would be useless.

The dazzling effect of car headlights behind us, even on dip, let alone deliberately on beam, makes it virtually impossible to ID a suspect vehicle in the rear view. And as for identifying the occupants, you could forget that. And yet another 'what if'. What if they'd got to someone in the hotel? Getting out of the car and into the hotel, another key vulnerability. Another serious threat.

The plane taxied to a halt and my pulse started beating faster. My body was telling me it was time to rest. My mind was telling me to stay hyper-alert. I stretched my legs out, fully enjoying the luxury of space in First Class. SAS soldiers come in all shapes and sizes. I come in the extra-large variety.

Off the plane and our footsteps echoed down endless gleaming corridors. We tried not to quicken our pace, though the temptation was great. I gripped the handle of the briefcase a bit harder, though what good that would do with a villain's Beretta poking me in the mouth and threatening to give me some urgent dental treatment I'm not sure.

We reached the main concourse and were hit with a cacophony of sound. It was as if it was purpose-built to maximize the volume. Indoor palm trees reached up to high, vaulted ceilings. Glass, marble and stainless steel everywhere. Bright lights and booming loudspeakers. Cafés, restaurants, currency exchange kiosks and glittering shops jostled against each other. A hubbub of humanity scurrying about like ants. The din, the confusion, the late hour, stacks of suitcases – any one of which could be rammed into our legs to force us to the ground. If you had to invent a worst-case security scenario this was it. The very things that made this a palace of delights for the average passenger combined to make it a hazard-filled madhouse for the travel-weary close protection operative.

Tak whispered an urgent, 'Take a left here.' He'd done a reconnaissance run prior to the real thing. He knew the ropes. He knew every corridor, every door. Before I knew it, we were in the haven of the VIP lounge. Processed in no time at all by hushed and discreet officials, we headed for a nondescript exit on the side of the building.

I took a deep breath and stepped out into the hot night-time air. The heat and humidity clutched at my already-tense chest. The adrenaline was pumping overtime. As any seasoned traveller will know, those first few moments after leaving the airport terminal are the point of maximum disorientation. Jet lag, culture shock, climate differences, and the lack of familiar bearings all combine to play havoc with your internal guidance system. Maximum disorientation means maximum vulnerability. Mercifully, a limo and driver were waiting. Well done, Tak. Going like clockwork so far. Already drenched in sweat due to the extreme humidity, I threw myself into the front seat and stashed the briefcase underneath and out of sight. We quickly locked the doors and glided away.

No sign of a tail, but I wasn't about to lower my guard. Because of the darkness, I'd have to use Plan B and carry out standard anti-surveillance tactics en route to where we staying. I reeled off the instructions to the driver. Stop frequently and suddenly. Speed up then slow down. Jump a red light to see if anyone else does. At a junction, indicate to turn left then move off to the right. On the motorway, come off at an exit and immediately rejoin by the same slip road. Make three turns to box three sides of a square. For the next one I looked for the right place. There it was, a large roundabout with nothing growing on it to obstruct my vision. I instructed the driver to drive twice round the roundabout, two 360-degree manoeuvres. As we went round for the second time, I had a good look across the central reservation. The roundabout was deserted. So was the road that hit the roundabout from the airport. We were lucky. It was late at night and the roads were quiet. We couldn't have chosen a better time.

So far so good. I was more or less satisfied that we were not being followed. But not quite. I decided to carry out one last manoeuvre for final confirmation. I checked the road ahead for a suitable spot. As we came round a sharp bend I saw the ideal place. 'Pull in,' I shouted. The driver acknowledged and pulled sharply into the approaching lay-by.

There was a grating sound and a small cloud of dust as the tyres bit into the gravel. Everything was still. We waited. The occupants of any car tailing us would not see us until the last moment as they came round the steep bend. The only option open to them would be to overtake. We waited some more. Nothing. The minutes ticked by, the road was empty. 'Drive on,' I instructed. By this time, our driver must have been really dizzy. He must have thought he'd picked up three madmen from the airport. That's enough anti-surveillance, I decided. Let's get to the hotel.

We pulled up outside the Sheraton Utama and hit the pavement, moving fast. I felt switched-on, alert. We were exposed here. I was ready for trouble. As we approached the doorman in his smart uniform I checked out his body language. I looked for the usual signs. It was a sixth sense you develop through years of dealing with dangerous men. This guy might be a trigger. He was ideally placed to report back to any waiting gang. The key thing I was looking for was his eye-line. Was he looking at us or did he have laser eyes zapping into the briefcases to ID them? Nothing. Just the usual smiling face and white-gloved hand holding the door open. No problems here. He was looking for dollars, not diamonds. He was only after a tip.

We headed for the reception desk where it quickly became obvious that we were expected. We were given the full VIP treatment with an express check-in, and in a matter of minutes we were whooshing up to our floor in the lift accompanied by an exquisite Malayan girl who was in possession of our room keys. That's good, I thought, she's going to escort us to our rooms. No confusion when we emerge from the lift, no working out whether to go right or left, no potentially fatal hesitation in the lift lobby area where someone might – just might – be waiting.

The girl took us straight to our wing of the hotel. She opened the doors, let us in and handed me the keys. We had two suites side by side – Tak and myself sharing one, our client in the other. The rooms were connected by an internal door. Excellent! That was a real asset. It would simplify liaison and planning of each day's tasks. The 'Do Not Disturb' sign went immediately onto the outside of the door and stayed on for the whole of the five days we were there. Tak briefed me. He wanted me to do three things – familiarize myself with the fire arrangements, find out the location of the hotel doctor, and get the phone number of the head of security. As I checked out the fire escape door, memories of Ward 11 and the visit to the Mirbat gun came flooding back. With my tasks done, I reported back to Tak, ordered room service, and then settled down for the night in what was one of the top suites in the hotel. I soaked up the luxury that surrounded me and broke into a smile. All memories of Ward 11 had disappeared.

Istana Nural Iman, located on a hillside just a few miles from the city centre, is not only the largest residential palace in the world, but the largest residence of any type in the world. The statistics are bewildering – over two million square feet of floor space, nearly two thousand rooms, and a banqueting hall bigger than Wembley stadium. Tak stood in the centre of the suite with the briefcases at his feet, briefing me on the layout like a Fijian property developer. For a development that size, we couldn't take it for granted that even once inside the gates the threat level would be zero.

We weren't taking any chances. The drill was that Tak and our client would go over to the palace each day, taking different samples of the jewellery in one bag, and I would stay behind guarding the rest. This would be the order of the day until the deal was concluded. Divide and rule – always a good principle.

The phone rang. The Sultan's limousine had arrived. Our client wandered in wearing an ultra-sharp Savile Row suit and looking every inch the diamond merchant. He glanced at his watch. 'Let's go.' Tak picked up his briefcase and the two of them disappeared off down the hotel corridor. I closed the door behind them, secured the safety chain and sat down to wait. And wait. The next few days passed by without incident. This was getting more like life in the Regiment all the time. Ninety-nine per cent monotonous routine, one per cent adrenaline-fuelled action.

On the Thursday Tak phoned. The Sultan and his wives had decided to purchase all the diamonds. Job done! Thank fuck we don't have to transport the gems back to London, I thought. Relief surged over me. I could relax now. I went to the bar to celebrate. Tak joined me an hour or so later. He had a surprise for me. He'd been talking to the palace officials. 'You'll never guess who's staying on the tenth floor.' He broke into a wide grin. 'Alfie Tasker, ex-D Squadron.' At first this seemed like a huge coincidence, but over the coming years I would get used to bumping into former members of the SAS working in the world of security. There were so many of us that we jokingly called ourselves 'C' (Civvy) Squadron 24 SAS (21 and 23 SAS being the Territorials and 22 'A', 'B', 'D' and 'G' Squadrons being the regulars.)

The mini-Regimental reunion was soon underway. Alfie explained that he was over from the UK on a liaison visit. He was working with the Sultan's family to beef up security on their expensive portfolio of properties in the south of England after thieves had plundered £20 million of valuables from the Sultan's mansion on Billionaire's Row in Hampstead.

As the drink flowed, Alfie began reminiscing about his time with the ill-fated Edward's Patrol in Aden's Radfan Mountains, near the Yemeni border, in 1964. Russian-backed Communists in North Yemen sneaking across the border and down the wadis into Aden were threatening not only British interests in the region but also the stability of the whole of the oil-rich Arabian peninsula itself. Captain Edwards was in charge, with Alfie as second-in-command. The object of the patrol was to mark out a DZ with Aldis lamps for a night descent by the Paras in the mountains sixty miles north of Aden. Reaching the area in the morning, the patrol had to take cover and lie up in two ancient stone sangars to await nightfall. Things did not go to plan.

In mid-morning they were compromised by a herd of goats, followed by a man and a woman – an eerie echo of what would happen years later to the famous Bravo Two Zero patrol in Iraq. Within minutes a large band of heavily armed tribesmen were on the scene. What followed was a vicious, day-long sniping duel, a struggle that left Captain Edwards and his signaller, Trooper Warburton, dead and two others badly wounded. Under cover of darkness, they decided they had no option other than to abort the mission and make a run for it to try and get the casualties to safety before the enemy, vastly outnumbering them, had a chance to storm their position. With shock and fatigue setting in, they finally reached safety at first light the next day. Seven patrol members had survived, but for Alfie and the others, the worst shock of the mission was yet to come. News filtered through that the heads of two British soldiers had been put on display, skewered on stakes in the main square of the mountain city of Ta'izz. A patrol later found the decapitated bodies of Edwards and Warburton.

As Alfie finished talking, it occurred to me that this could well have been the fate that awaited Tak and myself had we lost the battle of Mirbat. I shuddered at the very thought of it, and ordered a menu and another bottle of champagne. Nah, I thought, I've moved on from all that now. I've had enough of patrols in hostile terrain, hexamine stoves, hard-routine rations, incoming fire zipping millimetres from my head, not knowing if I'll survive from one second to the next. This was the life for me now. Five-star hotels, champagne and steak, first-class VIP travel. I could get used to this. Civvy Street's not so bad after all.

But before I knew it, I was back in a war zone.

22

Aid Convoy

Bosnia. The stench of death, the merciless crimes, the rape, mutilation, theft and murder, the madness of war, proud buildings reduced to rubble, ethnic cleansing, starving refugees with wailing children trudging barefoot and ill-clad across harsh and freezing mountain terrain, and all, unbelievably, right in the heart of Europe. Ten cruel years of conflict, 1991–2001. The former Socialist Federal Republic of Yugoslavia, held together by Tito and communism since 1945, was falling apart under an upsurge of nationalism. The Balkan federation was crumbling. Like some great iceberg, huge chunks were tumbling away. First Slovenia. Crash! Then Croatia. Crash! Then the rest followed in turn, leaving the patchwork quilt of federations and republics that is south-eastern Europe today.

My job? To escort and advise a humanitarian convoy of 150 tons of supplies to north-eastern Bosnia. Mission statement: 'To relieve the besieged city of Tuzla.' Just my luck! Right up to the front line, no less. The aid consisted of medicines, pasta, sugar, yeast, and tinned fish, meat and fruit. Tuzla was in dire straits. Serbia had isolated and besieged the city despite it having been declared a UN 'safe haven'. It was under constant bombardment. Normally home to 130,000 residents, its population had swelled to 400,000 desperate souls with the influx of wave upon wave of bedraggled and penniless Bosnian Muslims, forced to flee from their homes elsewhere in Bosnia by ruthless Serb gunmen. In theory our convoy was to travel under the auspices of the UN High Commission for Refugees (UNHCR), protected by the British contingent of the UN Protection Force (UNPROFOR2), and with the support of the Bosnian Government and the municipal authorities of Tuzla. In practice, we were on our own.

Our convoy was being organized by the great and the good of London society. A worthy or a witless venture? A raw and deeply felt humanitarian impulse, or a *cause célèbre* for rich kids with nothing better to do, a chance to play boy soldiers and go on a romantic mission? I know what my first impressions were.

The main mover and shaker was Orlando Fraser. His family tree was like a page out of *Who's Who*. Son of writer and historian Lady Antonia Fraser, stepson of playwright Harold Pinter, grandson of social reformer Lord Longford. An impressive dynasty. Would his organizing abilities be equally impressive? Other high-profile patrons and supporters included Eric Clapton, Mick Jagger, Bruce Oldfield, Dave Gilmour of Pink Floyd, William Stirling (great-nephew of Sir David Stirling), South African actor Jamie Bartlett (who would later play the role of Ray in the film of *Bravo Two Zero*), and diplomat, soldier, adventurer, writer and politician Sir Fitzroy MacLean – another relative of Orlando's and supposedly the real-life inspiration for James Bond.

As it turned out, I could have done with James Bond to help me out on the trip to Tuzla. Impressive as the list of supporters might be, it was a convoy organized by civilians, funded by civilians and manned by civilians. Not a professional in sight. Apart from me. We were going to a war zone. How could I possibly guarantee the safety of a bunch of civilians on the front line? In war, anything can happen. Any time. Anywhere.

They didn't even have shell dressings! I remember asking Orlando, 'Where's the medical pack?' He handed me a plastic bag full of Elastoplasts, safety pins and a sling straight off the shelves of Boots! Not remotely good enough for a war zone. I decided to give 21 SAS (TA) a ring. They were only a short hop away in the King's Road. By a stroke of luck, an old B Squadron mate of mine answered the phone. He was a permanent Staff Instructor there. He said he'd leave me a full trauma kit and a box of shell dressings in the MoD Police lodge at the main gate.

As the atrocities mounted and the icy grip of winter made life even more intolerable for the sick, the wounded, the starving and the homeless, London was gripped by a wave of humanitarian concern bordering on hysteria. Understandable. This crisis wasn't unfolding in some far-flung country nobody had heard of. This was happening in Yugoslavia, right on our doorstep. An emotive logo was designed, press releases issued, old favours called in. A benefit evening was held to raise funds. At the event, Sandhurst-trained Prince Khalid bin Sultan, the son of a Saudi Crown Prince and Joint Allied Commander in the Gulf War, set the ball rolling by donating £50,000. The cash came pouring in after that and the target was reached. We were on our way.

Rendezvous Dover. That's where the trouble first started. Four of us were travelling together – Orlando, Willie Stirling, Jamie Bartlett and myself. We'd trundled down from London in one of five articulated trucks, ready to pick up the pallets of scoff being assembled in a dockside warehouse. The plan was to drive down through Europe from Calais to Trieste in Italy, then cross the border into Croatia, through Croatia and into Bosnia. We'd only been going a few hours and Orlando was kicking up a fuss already. The artic's suspension was not to his liking. He'd been shaken and rattled about enough. The prospect of several more days rolling across Europe was too much for him. He got on the phone direct to Mick Jagger and explained his predicament. The next moment we were at the Avis office in Dover hiring a brand new Jagger-funded saloon with a smile on Orlando's face. I wasn't smiling though. You get to know people pretty quickly in my game and I was having serious doubts about Orlando already. The fact that he was related to Fitzroy MacLean who had liberated

Yugoslavia in the Second World War could really open doors for us. But I was starting to think that he was a bit too impatient for my liking.

Orlando, Willie, Jamie and myself drove eighteen hours non-stop through Europe and ditched the hire car in Trieste. No breaks. No sleepovers. Orlando was in a hurry. He always seemed to be in a hurry.

In Trieste, he busied himself making last-minute arrangements. We dumped the hire car and had an overnight stay. The next morning our expense account turned up – a briefcase stuffed full of dollars. Grease money. Oh no! For me it was an instant hit of *déjà vu* – another case full of valuables to protect. Another security headache. Mind you, that cash would come in pretty handy on the road ahead.

The plan was for the four of us to catch the bus across the border into Croatia to await the arrival of the artics at a UN warehouse on the outskirts of a town called Rijeka. We climbed aboard this ramshackle bus to head for the border. It was rammed full with locals, a scattering of journalists and ourselves. We rattled along and the terrain got steeper as we headed south. To our right we got spectacular views over the Gulf of Venice glinting in the distance. After a few hours we reached the entry point into Croatia and were waved down to stop. A heavily armed, mean piece of work got on the bus. Dressed head to toe in a black leather coat with huge lapels, he had a peaked cap, gloves and a pistol in a holster. I had to stifle a smile. He looked just like a member of the Gestapo. I half-expected to see David Niven or Anthony Quinn lurking in the shadows. He worked his way slowly down the bus growling in a heavy accent, 'Papers! Papers!'

When he came to me, I thought he was going to say, 'What are you doing here, Mr Bond?' Instead he grunted, 'What is your purpose here, Mr Winner?'

I rolled out my standard cover story. 'I'm a freelance journalist.'

He stared at my passport. 'What are all these stamps from Africa and the Middle East?'

'Conflict zones. I'm an international correspondent. I travel all over the world.'

It took him a full two hours to go through the whole bus and check everyone's papers. Satisfied we weren't up to anything sinister, he eventually disembarked and waved us on.

We joined the artics in Rijeka and drove south along the relative safety and flat terrain of the Croatian coastal plain, heading to a second UN warehouse near Split. We would go on from there to the border-crossing town of Metkovic, down near Dubrovnik. There we were planning to turn east into Bosnia. Our route would then take us north-east up past Mostar, Sarajevo, Zenica and on to Tuzla.

The boy soldiers were having a whale of a time. They were as excited as a cage full of canaries. They'd obviously seen too many films. 'Look at me. I'm in a war zone. Wow!' To them it was a romantic adventure. To me it was a deadly serious operation. I was getting more and more concerned by the minute. As we drove along, I'd been evaluating the weather, the maps and the terrain. Not good. Not good at all. I broke the bad news to Orlando.

'We can't go on the main roads through Bosnia. They won't be safe.'

'Never mind that nonsense. We're only carrying humanitarian aid. No one will attack us. Push on! Push on!'

'I can guarantee you the Serbs will have DF'd all the main roads with their artillery. Nobody will be safe.'

'Push on! Push on!'

Orlando missed his calling in life. He should have been a general because he knew how to drive men on no matter what the situation. I attempted to take control again. 'The main roads will be an open invitation to the Serbs to fire on us with tanks and mortars. We'll have to go over the mountain passes instead.'

He agreed to that, but then I gave him the next piece of bad news. 'Hairpin bends. Steep gradients. Snow and ice. Articulated trucks. Not a good combination.'

He was puzzled. He couldn't see where I was leading.

I spelt it out. 'Artics. They're just not made for going over mountains. They're too big and heavy and they haven't got four-wheel drive.'

He raised his voice a few more decibels. 'What do you mean? We've got to PUSH ON.'

'Look,' I insisted. 'We've got to get all this stuff off the artics and onto four-ton trucks with four-wheel drive. Those mountains are fearsome. Worse than the Brecon Beacons where I did selection. We'll never get over them in artics.'

'And how do you propose to do that?'

'We'll grease the locals in Metkovic and get some smaller trucks.'

'Very well. Push on!'

My words of warning had obviously had their effect on Orlando. He must have got worried about negotiating the roads ahead in artics. After an overnight in Split where we met up with David Rieff, the American journalist, he promptly acquired two luxurious Range Rovers. We drove on in convoy with the artics, turned east and soon reached another UN warehouse in Metkovic.

Orlando, his Range Rover and his suitcase went off to scour the town for freelance owners of four-tonners. It's amazing how persuasive a fistful of dollars can be. We eventually amassed a convoy of around fifteen small vehicles. Not only that, but to my amazement up trundled two Warrior APCs from the Cheshire Regiment to escort us over the mountains. That's impressive. I thought. My opinion of Orlando was rising, perhaps I had been too quick to judge. That must have been some gift of the gab to persuade the top brass in the Cheshires to loan us a couple of APCs.

Now all we had to do was transfer the supplies from the artics to the four-tonners. I went off and did a recce. All the aid material was on pallets. We needed a forklift truck to transfer it. I knew I'd find one in the depot somewhere.

But what I didn't expect to find there was my first Walter Mitty of the campaign.

23

Port and Stilton

The Walter Mitties were alive and well in Bosnia! From the moment the SAS exploded across the world's media with the Iranian Embassy siege in 1980, the Walter Mitties have been crawling out of the woodwork, seeking excitement and reflected glory, their deception made that much easier by the Regiment's policy of never commenting on anything. I have met any number of men claiming to have been on the balcony at the Iranian Embassy without knowing who *I* was. If they'd all been there, the balcony would have collapsed under the sheer weight! Then there are the young thrusters trying to impress the women in the pubs in Hereford, who get themselves a tan in the middle of winter and claim to have just come back from a secret mission abroad with the SAS. These ones are harmless enough. What is more sinister are those who, driven by greed and by the media's ever more demanding requirement for sensational material, exploit a gullible public and publish books and articles telling outright lies and upsetting the families of dead comrades. They show the Regiment in a bad light and make hundreds of thousands of pounds in the process.

The Walter Mitty in Metkovic was one of the harmless ones. I approached the guard on the depot gate. 'Who's in charge of the UN hangar?'

'Go to the office at the end of the line. There's a bloke there'll put you right.'

So I walked into this office and there's this guy. Looked just like a British Army quartermaster – moustache and all! I didn't say who I was, just that I was in charge of the convoy going to Tuzla. I showed him my UN papers and the letter of safe passage from the Mayor of Tuzla, Selim Beslagic. He seemed happy enough with the paperwork. There was a bit of small talk, then I said 'You British Army, are you?'

'Yeah.'

A bit more small talk, then I asked, 'What regiment were you in?'

'Special Forces, mate.'

I still didn't say anything. A bit more small talk, then 'Impressive that, Special Forces. Which Special Forces would that be then?'

'Two Two, mate.' He glanced around importantly as if to check no one had overheard the amazing secret he had just revealed.

Got him! I had him hook, line and sinker now. A bit more small talk, then I went on, 'It's amazing, you know. I don't know if you've been in the UK recently, but there's loads of books out on the SAS.' I paused a moment for effect, then 'I've read a couple of them.' He went a bit quiet at this point. There was more small talk, then I said, 'I read in one of these books there are four squadrons. Which one were you in?'

He fell right into the trap. 'Nine Squadron, mate.'

I couldn't believe it! There isn't a Nine Squadron in the SAS of course, but there *is* a Nine Squadron in the Royal Engineers. It's their Para squadron. He obviously didn't know that I'd been in the RE too. Unbelievable! It took a superhuman effort of willpower to do so, but I had to hold back from laying into him. We needed him, or more precisely we needed his forklift truck. You could not exist without goodwill out there. That's the name of the game in hostile territory. At the end of the day, we got the forklift truck, and got the pallets loaded onto the four-tonners.

Leaving him to his fantasies, we set off for Mostar.

The weather was closing in and the landscape was changing. Grey skies, bare trees, patches of dirty snow, muddy and rutted roads, knocked-out tanks skewed into ditches, roofs with their red tiles blown off, their timbers gaping like wild dogs baring their teeth, smashed homes, and brutalized people wandering along the roadside. In the convoy, the mood had turned sombre. Reality was hitting home. After a few hours, we reached the outskirts of Mostar. I was shocked. This once-proud city, the biggest and most important in Herzegovina, was a complete wasteland. After relentless bombardment, it looked like Stalingrad in the Second World War. Terrible place. I've been in a few war zones, but this frightened even me. It was like entering a nuclear wilderness. The city was completely blasted. As if to welcome us, the first thing we saw was a huge bus depot on our right. There must have been something like two hundred buses there. All blasted. Riddled with bullets, they were resting at crazy angles, wheels all shot away. Without a soul in sight, it was an eerie atmosphere.

Then we came to the checkpoint. The surly-looking guards were obviously trigger-happy. They were shifting about, fingering their weapons. We'd come well prepared. We were primed for this. What they wanted was grease. Out came the bottles of Johnnie Walker Black Label. No other brand would do. And not the large bottles either, but cases of miniatures. This was the currency round these parts. That and the Marlboros. They'd got to have Marlboro cigarettes. Must have seen too many adverts. They wanted to strut around the place all macho, posing and smoking Marlboros. We'd been well briefed. It did the trick and they waved us through.

The seriously big mountains loomed up in front of us on the other side of Mostar. I was relieved in many ways. In Bosnia there were constantly shifting lines of conflict. You never knew when you might get caught up in no-man's land between the Muslim and Serb forces. At least we had the advantage of cover on the thickly wooded mountain tracks. We struggled on into the night, grinding up near-vertical passes on nothing more than mud roads. This was going to be a long haul. And a dangerous one. We were in bandit territory. It wasn't safe to stop. Besides, there was nowhere to stop. It was too remote. You don't get too many Travelodge motels in the middle of the Bjelasnica mountain range.

The mountains here towered up to 7,000 feet high and were cut through with steep-sided canyons 1,000 feet deep. Wolves, wild boar and bears roamed freely around. This would have been a seriously difficult area to traverse in the middle of summer. It was now the middle of winter. Orlando was right – we would certainly need to push on here. No stopping. From now we would be rolling twenty-four hours a day, switching drivers to get a few hours' kip. We were on hard routine – going without all normal ablutions. No shaving. No washing. No cleaning your teeth. All water reserved for drinking and making tea.

Eventually, after several days and nights of torturously slow progress over the mountains, we descended down the other side to the Cheshires' forward operating base, the last outpost of the British Army before Tuzla and the front line. Colonel Bob Stewart – 'Bosnia Bob' – was in charge. Orlando bowled up in his Range Rover and, to my amazement, started to unload cases of vintage port and Stilton. That's how he'd managed to get hold of the Warriors for top cover! This was what I call long-range planning. He'd sourced the goodies in London before we left and brought them with us. It was just before Christmas. He'd promised to deliver port and Stilton to the Officers' Mess!

After resting up overnight at the Cheshires' base, we went to the Ops Room for a briefing. The ops officer, a captain in the Intelligence Corps, gave us the bad news. 'Well, boys. That's it. You're on your own now. We have to pull the Warriors off.'

'Oh, charming,' I thought. 'Thanks a bunch.' I asked him why.

'The roads forward of here are DF'd by Serb mortars. We've had a recce patrol up in the hills overlooking the road and we identified the mortar firing positions.'

I jumped in. 'Why didn't you take them out?'

He stepped back in shock and horror. 'Take them out! We're NATO. We're UN peacekeepers. We can't take anybody out. We're non-aggressors.'

'So what you're telling me is that we've got to go down that road and face those Serb mortars with no covering fire from you?'

'Precisely.'

The world's gone mad, I thought. Wrong kind of war again. Because of tip-toeing around political sensitivities, the lives of our convoy were going to be put at unnecessary risk. I felt the heavy weight of responsibility on my shoulders. It's a lonely place to be when there's only you to make the life-or-death decision. We couldn't turn round now. We'd come too far. Retreating isn't exactly in the DNA of the SAS. The trouble was, I didn't have any backup. In the Regiment, I'd have half a squadron of SAS behind me. Now I was it! I'd get the blame if it all went pear-shaped and lives were lost. I could just see the headlines now: 'Pete Winner, ex-SAS, fucked it all up.'

I came to a decision. It was all about mitigation, about managing the situation as best I could. I can assure you, if you want to miss a mortar you have to be going at speed. So I got hold of a guy from the REME. 'These trucks of ours,' I said. 'They're diesel. They've got governors on the fuel injection pumps. They'll only do fifty miles an hour. That's way too slow. We'll be sitting ducks. Can you take the governors off so we can put our foot down?'

'No problem, mate.'

The governors were fixed and I came up with a plan of action. The convoy would be split into twos and threes and released at ten-minute intervals. Much smaller targets for a start, and with the governors off we could get up to 65mph, maybe even 70mph at a pinch. At least we stood a fighting chance now. I decided to go in the last truck so if there were any casualties I could sort it out.

The convoy set off. It was only a few miles to Tuzla, but the journey was going to be a complete nightmare. I was dreading the tell-tale 'pop' sound that signalled a mortar was incoming. Nothing happened. We were down to the last two trucks to go. Oh no, I thought, they're saving it for the last two. Still nothing. We blasted along the road as best we could. The terrain was flattening out here, so we managed to keep up a decent speed. Two miles. Three miles. So far so good. Then in the distance I saw mortar splashes on the road ahead. Oh no! Time to get the prayer book out. It was a DF position. I thought, 'Here we go. They've got our range and position. That's the place!' The trouble is when you're in a truck roaring along with the engine straining to the limit you can't hear the mortars 'popping'. All you hear is the explosion that kills you. As we got closer, you could even see the ten-finned mortar tails sticking out of the tarmac. Dozens of them. I thought, 'All these years I've got away with it and this is how it's going to end.'

We kept our foot down and blasted along the road, swerving around the mortar splashes to prevent the fins and bits of shrapnel puncturing our tyres. Every nerve strained for signs of attack. Nothing. I'll never know how, but we got away with it. Maybe the Serb forces were tied up elsewhere, on another front. Maybe it was simply a lack of discipline in their ranks. Whatever the reason, it was a minor miracle in my book. Another few hours of gut-wrenching tension, more rusting and burned-out tanks at the side of the road, more houses with their roofs blown off, more ethnically cleansed homes with timbers and tiles strewn into the road, some with bodies still lying stiffly and silently across the rubble, more slithering along the snow and ice, more threatening grey skies. Then, mercifully, we came round a bend and there it was before us. Tuzla. We'd managed to get through and somehow we were still in one piece.

We were the first Western agency to reach Tuzla since the war began. What state did we find the people in? Proud. Resilient. In surprisingly good shape considering their dire circumstances. They were used to it. A lot of the older folk had survived occupation under the Nazis in the Second World War. That they were hugely grateful for the humanitarian supplies we brought goes without saying. They couldn't have survived much longer on their own. What struck me, though, was how dignified they were as the aid was being doled out.

The town itself was less orderly. A bit like the Wild West. That's where we met these couple of clowns – Geordies, ex-Army, freelance zappers. Mad as a bag full of frogs. They were tooled up with AK-47s and spent most of their time down in Sarajevo holed up in deserted blocks of flats taking on the Serb snipers just for the hell of it. Like a rifle range at the fair. They were living off charity and buckshee scoff. To them, it was just like playing darts at the weekend. As they explained in their near-impenetrable Geordie accents, 'Just havin' a bit of fun, like.' Unbelievable! You'd think they were talking about going off to shoot a few rabbits. Crazy place, Bosnia. Full of crazy people.

Anyway, at least I could relax a bit now. Or so I thought. Tuzla wasn't the end of the story. It was just the beginning.

Just beyond Tuzla was where I nearly became a millionaire.

24

My Kingdom for a Stinger

With the aid we had delivered, things, at least in the short term, had improved greatly for the inhabitants of the city. Not for us, though. This was the point when it all started going wrong. Our orders were quite clearly to 'Deliver the aid to the besieged city of Tuzla'. But Orlando had other ideas. He sidled up to me as we were unloading the convoy. 'Pete, I want a word. Keep five trucks back. Numbers one, five, seven, eleven and fifteen.'

One had a load of medical supplies, the others food. 'What do you want these for, Orlando?' I asked, suspiciously.

Without batting an eyelid, he said calmly, 'We're going up to the front line.'

'Fuck it!' I thought. Hidden agendas. 'Orlando,' I protested, 'that's not in my brief. As far as I'm concerned the mission's complete.' I could see my objections were falling on deaf ears. Curiosity got the better of me. 'Anyway, where exactly is this front line you're proposing to go to?'

'About ten k's from here. There's an enclave nobody's been to since the war began. They're in desperate trouble. We're going to deliver these supplies there. It's much smaller than Tuzla. They didn't have the stocks of food to rely on like Tuzla when it all kicked off.'

'And how do you propose to get through the checkpoints, Orlando? You're now heading into serious warfare. They'll shoot you as soon as look at you.'

'Don't worry about that, Pete. Leave that to me.'

Off he went with his briefcase again. I wondered what he was going to turn up with this time. An Apache helicopter gunship? A Challenger 2 main battle tank?

For the next couple of hours I concentrated on overseeing the trucks as they were unloaded into a compound. Suddenly Orlando returned followed by a massive, gleaming black limo. It was a ZiL, favourite limousine of Russian politicians and high-up government officials, their equivalent of the Rolls-Royce. With its prominent square badge on the front and utilitarian, factory-inspired shape, it looked like a slightly upmarket hearse. Could well have been armour-plated judging by the size of it. Sat up front was this Croatian bloke with dark glasses, looking for all the world like he was straight out of *The Godfather*.

Orlando looked very pleased with himself. His friend – let's just call him 'Big Zil' – was going to help us through the checkpoints.

Big Zil got out of the car and introduced himself. Gestapo regulation leather coat, shoulders like an American NFL quarterback. Talk about intimidating. That's good enough for me, I thought. Let's crack on. I'd already decided to go. It's not in my blood to turn down a challenge.

We piled off down the road again in our mini-convoy, Big Zil at the front. Unbelievable! There were all these checkpoints en route. Each time we were stopped, Big Zil simply poked his head out of the window, and growled, snarled and bared his teeth. As if by magic, we were greeted like honoured guests and were waved through before you could say Checkpoint Charlie. It was just as well we had him with us. The gunfire was intensifying and getting ever closer. We had Union Jacks draped all over the bonnets of our vehicles to let people know who we were. We needn't have bothered, thanks to having Big Zil with us.

Officially he was the police chief of the enclave where we were going. Unofficially he was the warlord who ran the place.

We reached the enclave unscathed. It was just like Liberation Day! Unlike the calm and dignified display in Tuzla, here we were absolutely mobbed. Men, women and children crowding round, arms raised with pure joy, waving at us, wanting to shake our hands. I got a real thrill out of it. With the Union Jacks all over our vehicles, I felt proud to be British. It was like reliving something my father did in the Second World War. I thought I would never do something like that. My wars had been much messier, less black-and-white, all undercover. No one ever knew we were even there. I enjoyed that moment like nothing I'd ever done before. That memory will stay with me for the rest of my life.

After we'd unloaded the precious cargo, the mayor and all the local council invited us to a civic reception in one of the few buildings that remained standing. They laid out a feast of the local produce that was still available and some potent home-made plum brandy known as slivovitch. So there we all were gathered in this room and it's all 'Thank you, thank you' with clapping of hands and speeches and 'Now we drink the slivovitch.' I was only intending to have a couple as I knew we had to be up at first light the next day to make our way back to Split through 200 miles of bandit country. 'Down in one,' they instructed. Now, to say I was used to drinking after eighteen years in the SAS would be a slight understatement. I thought I could take anything that was pushed across the table to me, and some more. But this slivovitch was in a league of its own. After one gulp, I thought a flash-bang grenade had gone off in my head.

The party was soon rocking. Suddenly Big Zil reappeared and sidled up to me. 'Who are you?' he demanded, with no sense of humour whatsoever.

I was on high alert. I wasn't dealing with an amateur here. I kept it deliberately vague. 'I'm in charge of convoy security.'

'How did you get that job?' he persisted.

'I'm a professional soldier. Ex-British Army.'

He stared at me with his cold eyes. 'You must have contacts in the arms world, yes?'

I thought, 'Whoa. I don't move in those circles. My name's Sergeant Pete Winner not General Mike Rose.' I was very curious as to where his line of questioning was leading, though, so I answered simply, 'Nah, not really.'

'You must have. I can tell you are an important man. You get me the Stinger. We knock the jets out of the sky like you did in the Falklands, yes?'

I was playing for time. I said, 'But, Big Zil, I thought there was a total arms embargo in Bosnia.'

'No problem. We get anything we want through our friends in Albania. Give them a good price, we get everything. You get me the Stingers.'

I said, 'Give me your contact details. I'll see what I can do.'

'Good. Good. Now we drink the slivovitch.'

My kingdom for a Stinger! If I'd had a contact for Stingers, I could have cleaned up. With a couple of dozen nice shiny missiles nestling in a shipping crate, I would have been writing these memoirs sat by a pool sipping a long, cool drink in my millionaire's villa in Barbados. But it was not to be.

Meanwhile flags were being exchanged and more speeches being made. Willie Stirling started to get delusions of being immortal and in a moment of solidarity with our besieged cousins, he decided to present his body armour to the mayor. I told him to sit down because he was too young to die. In what was one of my more insane moments I decided to give the mayor my own body armour instead. 'Here, you have my body armour. You need it more than me. I can't be shot. I survived the battle of Mirbat.'

This is where too much combat experience plus an excess of alcohol can turn to recklessness. I survived this, this and this, so it's never going to happen to me. You get careless. Now I had to drive 200 miles back to Split without any body armour. At least we could get our heads down in the local lodgings and freshen up before setting off. Or so I thought. Orlando, as usual, had other ideas.

'Right, Pete. Let's get on the road.'

'Orlando! Do you realize what time it is? It's way past midnight.'

'I must be in Split by noon. There's an official reception at the British Embassy and I've got to be there.'

I couldn't believe it. Never mind the slivovitch which I had been imbibing, what really concerned me was the fatigue. That was the potential killer. It's exhaustion that really affects your judgement, your reaction time.

That's when I made the biggest – and only – mistake of my bodyguarding career. I agreed, and in doing so let the principal take control. Of course, to start the journey then was madness. The drink, the fatigue, the nerves frazzled to bits with the constant danger. We should have rested up. It was a decision I would soon bitterly regret.

We left the trucks there and set off in the two Range Rovers. I was in the lead vehicle with Orlando and David Rieff, the American reporter. I thought, 'Sod this,' got the sleeping bags out, laid them over the back seats and fell asleep.

The next minute: BANG! Then rolling, rolling, rolling. The Range Rover was careering over and over down the mountainside. I thought, 'Fuck it! We've been ambushed. We've been zapped.' Our vehicle came to a jarring halt: SMASH! We were upside down. The Range Rover on its roof, wheels spinning in the air. It was pitch black. No light anywhere, a complete blackout. All I could hear was 'Tick, tick, tick' as the wheels slowly turned round. Then came the groaning. It was Orlando, who had come to in the front. I didn't like the sound of that. He was obviously badly hurt. I didn't really know what was going on. I was upside down, exhausted, concussed, my head swimming with slivovitch.

Suddenly I could smell fuel. Got to get everyone out as quick as possible. We could burst into flames at any second. Luckily, my years of training kicked in and I quickly focused. First things first. There was something more urgent even than the danger of fire. The window on my side had been smashed. I kicked out the rest of the glass, crawled through and crouched down by the side of the vehicle, waiting for the gunfire. If this was an ambush, they'd try to pick us off one by one as we exited the vehicle. Even though it was pitch black, chances are they'd have infrared night sights on their weapons. They'd see us clear as daylight. It would be like shooting fish in a barrel. I strained my ears. Nothing. Everything was silent. I looked around and surveyed the terrain, trying to get my bearings. Further up the hillside, I could just make out a large truck on its side. To the right, further away, I could see the headlights of the other Range Rover. Stopped. They thought we'd been attacked. It was only later that I gradually pieced the story together. Orlando, half-asleep, had whacked into a truck coming the other way with only one headlight working – a 'Bosnian motorcycle'.

I set about getting the others out of the vehicle as quickly as I could. Orlando was in a bad way. Collar bone smashed. Nose smashed. Ribs either broken or badly bruised. Bleeding badly. David Rieff, the American journalist who was writing about us, was staggering around. He seemed OK apart from having changed colour. All his extremities were blue – a sure sign of severe shock. I thought, 'What the fuck are we going to do now?' In the middle of nowhere in the middle of the night. No help at hand for miles and miles.

I don't know about being immortal, but the gods of combat were certainly watching over us that night. All of a sudden I saw another vehicle approaching, its lights all ablaze. I scrambled up the hillside towards the road as it overtook the other Range Rover. As it drew closer, I could just make out the insignia on its side. The Red Crescent! I couldn't believe it. An ambulance! What on earth was an ambulance doing here in the middle of the night? It was truly surreal.

I frantically waved it down. It was a miracle it stopped, this being bandit country. Two guys jumped out dressed in medics' gear. Luckily, one of them spoke broken English. It turned out they had just come from the front line. They were transporting an urgent injury back to the nearest hospital. There was just one combatant in the back on a stretcher with a leg half blown off. There was space for one more casualty. We got Orlando in and the medics gave him the once-over. The only thing that had saved him was his body armour. He'd impacted heavily against the steering column. If that had been me driving with no body armour I would have been killed instantly.

But he had lost a lot of blood. If we didn't get him to hospital in time he would bleed to death on the mountainside. David was OK. He was treatable. He could come with me in the Range Rover. I directed the ambulance to drive to the nearest British military hospital in Zeneca approximately 15km away. Off they went, hell for leather down the road. I scrambled after them in the other Range Rover. I was lucky to be able to follow them. I hadn't a clue where we were. I hadn't been reading the map. I'd left that to Orlando. Fatal mistake, almost literally. It was a mistake I would never repeat again. I could excuse myself. It was early on in my bodyguarding career and I'd learnt my lesson good and proper.

Five years later, another bodyguard made two crucial mistakes. Just like me, he allowed one of his two principals to take control of the journey, and he didn't insist they wear seatbelts. He became, in effect, merely cosmetic, a baggage-handler. He had no real control of the job he was supposed to be doing. The consequences for him were far more wide-reaching than my mistakes in Bosnia. This incident was on 31 August 1997, and the principals were Diana, Princess of Wales and Dodi al-Fayed.

In Zeneca, we found a hotel and got a good night's kip. The next morning I went to the British military hospital to find Orlando. He was in a sorry state, all tied up in bandages, tubes and drips. I marched straight up to him and bellowed at the top of my voice, 'I TOLD YOU! I FUCKING TOLD YOU!'

He just moaned over and over, 'I'm sorry, Pete. I'm sorry.' To his credit, he later sent me a letter of apology for making the wrong decision. In spite of everything, I got to like Orlando. Grudging admiration, I suppose you'd call it. More than anything, I admired his balls. Not many people had the bottle to do what he did.

I had the last laugh. After a bit of small talk, I said I had to leave straightaway so I could get back to the UK for Christmas.

'Going already?' moaned Orlando.

'Yep. Got to get back to Split. Can't hang around here. Got to PUSH ON! Got to PUSH ON!' I walked out with a grin on my face as broad as Big Zil's shoulders.

I was on a real high. Job well done! In spite of the injury to Orlando, the trip to Bosnia had been a big success, despite the difficult and dangerous circumstances. I couldn't believe my luck. After the huge stress and pressure of first leaving the SAS and trying to adjust to civilian life, my career outside the Regiment was now going from strength to strength. There I was, rubbing shoulders with the great and the good on a high-profile humanitarian aid mission, guarding an exhibition of jewellery in the hallowed confines of the St James Club, transporting a massive £80 million shipment of diamonds to the Sultan of Brunei. It couldn't get any better than this. I was living the champagne lifestyle. The days of the hard tack routine in the Army seemed a lifetime away. The adrenaline was pumping. I couldn't wait to get back to the UK to see what my next assignment would be.

That's when it all fell apart.

25

Banned and Blackballed

Banned! I was in shock. No more Regimental reunions. No more invitations to SAS functions and anniversaries. *Persona non grata* at the Regimental Association. I was devastated. No more socialising of any kind. I wasn't allowed to set foot anywhere within the perimeter fence of my own camp. My name was on a 'prohibited' list pinned to the guardroom wall at Stirling Lines. The ultimate indignity after years of loyal service. A veteran of Aden, the secret war in Oman, the Embassy siege, the Falklands War and Northern Ireland.

But what was the most cutting of all? Banned from the Armistice Day commemorations. The names of all our dead are on the clock tower in the camp. Friends I fought with are commemorated there. That was the cruellest thing of all. No longer would I be able to pay my respects to my fallen comrades during those agonizing two minutes of silence at the eleventh hour of the eleventh day of the eleventh month. I was not even allowed to lay a wreath. And why did all this happen? Because I wrote a series of articles in the *Daily Mirror*.

The Regiment has traditionally shunned publicity, practising the 'humility, modesty and the avoidance of boasting' as laid down by the founder, David Stirling. We were designed to be a troop of men that came in, did the job, then drifted away into the night. But that all changed at 1923 hours on 5 May 1980, when the Regiment stormed into the Iranian

Embassy in Princes Gate, London, to the deafening roar of explosive charges and G60 stun grenades. It changed the profile of the SAS forever, catapulting the most secret of regiments onto the world stage.

Following the siege there were persistent rumblings in the media about the manner in which some of the terrorists had been dealt with. To counter any negative publicity Tak and I were instructed by the Kremlin to talk to the *Daily Mirror* reporter Alastair McQueen to put the story straight. The resulting article was a huge success. So with my new life as a civilian going so swimmingly I decided to try and replicate the success but without the official backing. I gave Alastair a call. I had been jotting down notes in diaries and on bits of paper for the last seven years of my Army career and I had loads of potential stories for him. But way beyond any thoughts of earning a few quid, I had a much deeper motivation.

I felt that it was necessary to lay down a factual report, an eyewitness testament of what really happened before it became distorted and corrupted by the passage of time and political agendas. I took my lead from my great hero Sir Winston Churchill. As long ago as the battle of Omdurman, on 2 September 1898, he was busy writing about his exploits as a young officer in one of the last cavalry charges carried out by the British Army. When he got home from the battle he immediately wrote down the details while they were fresh in his mind so that no one could plunder the truth in the future for their own political ends. The full account of the battle was published just a year later, in 1899, in a book entitled *The River War: An Account of the Reconquest of the Sudan.* Kitchener hauled Churchill over the coals, but it didn't do his career much harm! Churchill even used to submit stories to *The Times*, despite Kitchener's orders to stop. He got around the ban by filing the reports in letters to his mother, who was American, and through contacts she got the stories published in the *Washington Post.*

I was proved right. Before I knew it, the history of the battle of Mirbat was being kicked around by the politicians and the Army's top brass as a political football. The death of Labalaba, one of the Regiment's greatest heroes, and one of my greatest friends, was used as a rebuke to the BNP after they were accused of hijacking British military history for racist ends. But Laba was a soldier, plain and simple, and one of the bravest men I ever knew – not someone who deserved to be dragged into the public arena. He was no card-carrying politician. In my book, to use history in this way is one step away from rewriting it.

It goes without saying that I would never do anything, such as revealing tactics or covert operations, that would put my colleagues' lives at risk. Why would I? Being in the SAS is all about respect and support from your comrades. That respect and support continues well after you retire. That is always my number one priority. There was no way I was going to put that support system in jeopardy. It was too important in helping me keep my head in the right place. Laymen, ordinary people, even close friends and family, cannot possibly begin to understand the life that SAS troopers lead, the experiences they've been through. It's not even worth trying to communicate it. My only measure of reality and sanity is with my own comrades. They know. They've been in my world. They were there too. They saw the unimaginable, did the unthinkable and felt the unspeakable.

It wasn't my best career move. I didn't think of the long-term consequences. SAS memoirs had already been published, but writing unsanctioned articles for a tabloid was pushing the boundaries too far. The articles duly appeared in the *Daily Mirror* over three days and they really ruffled the feathers of the Head Shed. It would have been fine to have a discreet article printed in *The Times*, but not to give the Regiment the mass-market treatment in a downmarket redtop like the *Mirror* – that was far too brash, far too in your face.

That's when the ban came. I was in shock. I hadn't expected this bolt out of the blue. I suddenly felt isolated and alone, cut off from the Regimental support system. Sure, I could meet up outside with my colleagues who'd also retired, but nothing can replace the feeling of pride and belonging when you go along to official Regimental functions. It's like being part of a family. That was my therapy. That was my counselling, my talking cure.

As if the ban wasn't bad enough, worse was to come. When it came to work, my phone suddenly stopped ringing. There was obviously an unofficial blacklist doing the rounds. I had it on good authority that the word went out from serving Ruperts to former colleagues who run all the firms in the private bodyguarding and security sectors. First banned, then blackballed! The final insult was when I heard on the grapevine that the Head Shed was looking for a way to take my Army pension off me. I was in serious financial difficulties. It felt like I'd just left the Regiment all over again. I was well and truly stressed. Was there a glimmer of light in this dark landscape? Well no, none at all.

26

A Living Hell

Worse was to come. Late one evening I was heading fast down a dual carriageway, eager to get home. The dual carriageway had been coned off to form a one-way system in both directions. Only the central set of cones separated you from oncoming traffic. As I was driving through this one-way system, a car approaching from the opposite direction suddenly swerved through the cones and came straight for me. I braced myself for the impact, locked my arms and turned the steering wheel hard left, just managing to avoid a head-on smash. There was an almighty 'bang' and a metal-on-metal screeching noise as he hit my offside door. The collision smashed in the doorframe which struck me on the head, nearly knocking me out.

The car rolled and came to rest on its roof in a ditch at the side of the road. I could feel the blood running down the side of my face as I released the seatbelt and crawled towards the passenger door. I couldn't believe it. This was a rerun of Bosnia. I was even using the same method to struggle out of the vehicle, but this time I could feel more pain. I didn't have the sleeping bags around me to cushion the impact. From my experience in Bosnia the fear of the vehicle bursting into flames returned, so I moved quickly to vacate the vehicle. As I collapsed into the ditch, blood pouring into my right eye, in my confused state I half-expected to see an ambulance with a Red Crescent on it.

I was rushed by ambulance to a local hospital. I was experiencing pain and swelling in both knees and both ankles and there was a stiffness in my wrists and elbows – the result of bracing myself for the impact. The skin on my right forearm and knee was ripped to shreds and hanging off in places. I also had a deep laceration on the right side of the forehead. I was not in good shape.

Back in Hereford two days later my worst fears were confirmed by the consultant orthopaedic surgeon – I had ruptured both the cartilage and ligaments of my knees. I'd be out of action for weeks.

I'd have plenty of time on my hands, but this was the last thing I wanted. Laid up and immobilized with nothing to do but twiddle my thumbs and stare into space. Time to brood, time to think back to my Army days. Time to think about all the good mates I'd lost. And was still losing. My car crash couldn't have happened at a more stressful moment. I had just heard on the Hereford grapevine that Nish, an old friend from B Squadron, had suffered a psychotic breakdown. He began to think his girlfriend was the devil and had stabbed her but thankfully hadn't killed her.

Sure, the stress hits you when you first leave the Regiment, when you walk through those camp gates for the last time. That's a huge change. Re-adjustment doesn't come any bigger than that. But here's a chilling statistic, this is the really devastating bit. The medics have studied squaddies who've committed suicide due to Post-Traumatic Stress Disorder. The average time between a man leaving the Army and topping himself is thirteen years. That's a helluva long time to feel bad. You'd think if they were going to end it all, they'd do it when they first retire from the Regiment, when they leave all their mates behind and at first their lives seem meaningless. You'd think the stress would fade with time. Everything else does – grief at losing a loved one, upset at a marriage breaking down. Time is the great healer, they say. Not true. If you've been in the Army, time is the great killer. The memories just fester over the years like ditchwater. They just get more and more stagnant, more and more stinking.

You're climbing Everest when you leave the Army. As the years go by it gets harder, not easier. You're toiling higher and higher up the mountain towards the danger area. Perhaps after thirteen years you reach the high-altitude death zone. At that point, for some, putting one foot in front of another becomes a huge effort. For them, the brain becomes more and more abnormal. Just like the climbers deprived of oxygen, their judgment becomes impaired, they become confused, they start to hallucinate. Their existence becomes a living hell. And just like the climbers, they don't care if they live or die. They are deprived of normality. They just want to lie down and give up. Like the Everest mountaineers, these men are fighting fit. They are highly trained, highly experienced professionals. But something gives way. Being hit by PTSD can be just as deadly as an enemy bullet.

Nish had fitted into the timeframe. He had already been on a cocktail of anti-psychotic drugs for some months. They made him drowsy and lethargic. He never went out. He thought the whole world was against him. He was a prisoner in his own front room. How could Nish, a man who'd won the Queen's Gallantry Medal, end up shuffling around with a vacant, spaced-out look on his face? Crack soldiers cracking up. That's bad.

If you go to the Regimental plot in St Martin's churchyard in Hereford you can see the headstones of Laba and all the others. At least they went out in a blaze of glory. Their deaths had a purpose, a meaning. For Nish it must have been like fighting the battle of Mirbat every single day of his life. Instead of hordes of Adoo charging at him, it was the demons of depression pouring across the plains towards him day after day after day. But the minute the battle's over and the war is won, our soldiers are discarded and rejected. The MoD acts as if they're somebody else's problem then. The physically and mentally wounded, they're a blot on society's conscience. They're kept hidden away, neglected and dismissed. They're only wheeled out once a year on Armistice Day at the Cenotaph.

Sometimes even your family can't help. I don't know what clocks up more damage to your marriage – joining the SAS or leaving it. When you go in, your family never know when you are going to be off at a moment's notice to some far-flung corner of the globe, how long you'll be gone or whether you'll ever come back. When you leave the SAS they have to cope with the aftermath of all that. When the guns fall silent, they can sound even noisier in your head. Your nearest and dearest have to cope with your mood swings, your drinking, your night sweats, the action-packed flashbacks playing on the big screen in your brain. You're still lumping into the enemy, still chopping them down as if it were yesterday.

I don't know about PTSD but PRAC (Post-Regimental Anti-Climax) can be just as big a problem. That's why I needed to keep active, to keep involved with projects and that's why being laid up on crutches was such a ballache. Too much time to think. Too much time for the guns to roar in my mind. I couldn't let it get to me, though. Self-discipline, that's what I needed. I drew on my military training to pull me through, those dark days in the Woolwich hospital and those first days out of the Army when I felt cut adrift from the world I knew and loved. I knew that I was alone. I had only myself to rely on to ensure that I didn't go the way of Nish and others like him. Andy McNab had the right idea. He'd seen his fair share of action and he states to this day, 'I only ever think about the next three hours. Today's today. If it works, it works. If it doesn't, it doesn't. You control what you can and the rest, fuck it!'

27

On the Ragged Edge

There was nothing to cling to apart from my deep-down stubbornness. *Nil Carborundum* – don't let the buggers grind you down. Somehow, I had to pull myself out of this dark pit I'd fallen into.

I compiled a hit-list of firms on the circuit and contacted them all. Zilch. Word had well and truly got round. There was nothing for it but to try to set up my own network of contacts. Being banned from the SAS, I could no longer get the mainstream jobs on the established circuit. I had to completely change my outlook, force myself to ring round for the fringe jobs that were often not only dubious to the point of being only borderline legal, but were considerably less well paid as well. When at last one of my calls was returned I was mightily relieved. A spark of daylight at last! Then my heart sank. I thought it was some kind of cruel wind-up.

'I've got a bit of work for you, Pete, if you're interested.'

'You bet.'

'A bit of BG work. This is the most intelligent principal you'll ever have looked after.'

'You've got me going now. What's the principal's name?'

'Flipper.'

'Flipper? Bit of an odd name that.'

'Not for a dolphin it isn't.'

'A dolphin? A bloody dolphin?'

'Very intelligent creatures, dolphins.'

'Yeah, but are you having a laugh? Bodyguard a dolphin?'

'Well, not bodyguard exactly…'

My caller went on to detail the task in hand. Windsor Safari Park had hit the rocks and gone into receivership. We heard all the staff were on the fiddle and were raking off a fortune because of the lax supervision. So some mates and I went down and kicked everyone out, including the gate and security staff.

The park had managed to rehome all its animals apart from one baby dolphin. The animal rights activists said it was cruel to keep it in captivity in a small pool, and that it was suffering. They threatened to break in and kill it, put it out of its misery. But in the event they took one look at us guys and decided against it, and eventually Winsor Safari Park managed to find a home for its dolphin. The park's still there, now called Legoland Windsor. So everyone lived happily ever after. Apart from me.

My career went downhill from there. My career was really bumping along the bottom. I had a string of similar jobs: safeguarding salmon from poachers on the River Dee in Scotland; protecting pheasants against gangs of thieves on the Lichfield Estate near Whitchurch in Hampshire; watching over beagles, rats and guinea pigs when animal rights activists planned to raid Ledbury Animal Testing Station; preventing elvers on the River Wye being stolen and spirited away in the dead of night to end up on the tables of rich Japanese businessmen. It was work, Jim, but not as we knew it. Champagne and diamonds this most definitely was not. But at least I was getting paid. That's always the bottom line.

* * *

Just when I thought it couldn't get any worse, it did. I was up against pond life of a different kind. Hippies! Every year at the summer solstice, druids flock to Stonehenge. The druids say that they can trace their roots back 4,000 years and claim it's their birthright to touch the stones. During the Seventies and through to the mid-Eighties they'd been allowed to have a free festival there every year at the solstice. In 1985, for some reason, the police and English Heritage decided to put an end to the festival gatherings.

Despite the ban, a large convoy of New Age travellers – calling themselves the Peace Convoy – headed for the stones. A four-mile exclusion zone was set up, the police tipping lorry-loads of gravel across the roads to prevent access. The police's infamous Special Patrol Group was deployed, and after a standoff lasting several tense hours the shit really hit the fan. The Special Patrol Group went in with all guns blazing, beating people with truncheons and smashing their vehicles with sledgehammers. It was ridiculously hard. There were women and children caught up in the battle, whole families arrested and separated, children locked up away from their parents. A court case later found the police guilty of wrongful arrest, assault and criminal damage. Ever since then at the solstice, the stones have been roped off and guarded.

At the solstice of 1995, the authorities were expecting trouble – Combat 18 types had taken to beating up the festival-goers at Stonehenge. That June was also the tenth anniversary of the Special Patrol Group's notorious deployment and the police didn't want to know. So the authorities hired us – all ex-SAS veterans, with combat experience stretching across three continents and two decades – to protect some stones from some hippies and some hippies from some thugs. My days guarding Flipper were starting to look like a career highlight.

The trouble all kicked off on the eve of the summer solstice. We had set up Hippie Control in the Stonehenge car park, which was nearly a quarter of a mile north of Stonehenge itself. Big Fred the Fijian, a good friend of Laba and Tak, was the team leader. The rest of us were ex-B and G Squadron. The most impressive guy there was John Barker (JB), ex-G Squadron. Tall, muscular, and dressed in a black karate suit, he could have quite easily starred in a remake of *The Terminator*. I looked at my watch. Nearly time to go on stag over at the stones. Suddenly something very colourful caught my eye. A double-decker London bus pulled into the car park and rolled to a halt. It was covered in psychedelic paintings that would have put John Lennon's Rolls-Royce to shame and the occupants looked like leftovers from Woodstock. 'Fucking amazing! I'm back in the Swinging Sixties,' I thought to myself as I left the car park.

I checked my radio was on and began my patrol round the stones. I stopped for a breather over to the south-east of the circle. I was stood marvelling at the construction and wondering how the fuck they managed to get those huge stones into position, when a glint of sun on glass caught my eye.

Looking south-east from Stonehenge, the ground dropped away towards the A303. Once across the road, the land formed a small hill with a wood on top. The horizon was about a thousand yards away. Through the mini-binocs I could see figures forming up out of the wood and making their way downhill. I knew instinctively this was the thugs' main assault group. I spoke into the radio, 'Contact, contact. The bus is a distraction. I repeat. The bus is a distraction. Deploy immediately to the south-east of the stones. Rent-a-crowd is coming in through the back door.'

'Roger that,' said Big Fred the Fijian. Within minutes the guys had arrived, Big Fred and JB leading. We did a quick appreciation of the situation and all came to the same conclusion. We shook out in extended line, Stonehenge behind us, and awaited the arrival of the opposition.

It was like being on the rifle range. Targets to your front. In your own time. Carry on. By now a handful of them had crossed the A303 and had realized that they had made a big mistake. It was a steepish climb up to the stones and we held the high ground. We had the tactical advantage, and they were going to have to fight uphill. We were now getting our first good look at the opposition. These were no longhaired hippies. Short hair, military-style jackets and Doc Marten boots, these were the hardliners, real Combat 18 thugs. They'd come here for a fight, not to hug the stones. But they'd made the most basic error in the book. Coming uphill, they were at a disadvantage. They couldn't get organized. They had no formation and began picking their way uphill in dribs and drabs.

The first of the opposition was now halfway up the hill. They were lead by a tall, well-built bruiser. 'See that fucker,' shouted Big Fred. 'I want him taken out.' JB, hard, fast and aggressive, moved forward. By the time Big Bruiser realized the danger it was too late. He tried hitting out, flailing his fists, but JB from his elevated position towered over the guy. One well-executed karate kick sent Big Bruiser staggering and reeling backwards. The thug lost his footing, hit the deck and rolled down the slope of the hill. A collective cheer went up from the lads.

At the sight of their leader being humiliated, the rest of the opposition began edging towards us aggressively. Their blood was up. They came straight for us, screaming obscenities, about a dozen of them charging en masse. As they closed in, you could see the hate in their eyes and hear the rasping of their breath as they laboured upwards. They didn't stand a chance. There was a flurry of tattooed fists flailing and Doc Martens swinging, but to no avail. They were literally fighting an uphill battle. They soon found themselves on their arses, rolling down the hill towards the A303. Things now became fragmented into individual punch-ups. A lot of the opposition had fallen back and only a few hardcore thugs were left. I swung at one shaven head and noticed a swastika tattooed behind his left ear. As he went flying, I thought 'David Stirling would be proud of me. The SAS still battling the scourge of the swastika!'

Out of nowhere, Big Bruiser had regrouped and was back, clambering up the hill. He was playing the big hero. He must have thought he would make one last stand to impress his mates. JB let out a roar and charged down the hill towards him. Big Bruiser took one look at the Terminator, turned on his arse and fled.

That was it. Job done. The last of the opposition could be seen fleeing up the hill on the opposite side of the A303. Time for a post-combat brew. We reorganized on the edge of the stone circle. We were just checking that none of our radios had been lost during the brawl when the hippies from the bus arrived. A rag-tag bunch of druids, bead-shakers and pendulum-swingers, it was like the fatigue party coming to clean up after the battle. 'Ah-ha, the *Stoned*henge Brigade,' I thought. Big Fred decided to use diplomacy. 'Who's your leader?' he asked, without a hint of aggression in his voice. A small, effeminate-looking guy wearing an Afghan jacket and beads stepped forward. 'What do you want?' said Big Fred quietly.

'Look man,' said the hippie. 'We don't want any trouble from you guys. All we want to do is touch the stones. This is the most magical place on the planet. When you touch the stones, you feel a vibration, just like hugging a tree, man. The warmth and energy goes right up your body. This is a temple. We just want to touch the stones, man.'

No problem. We organized them into a queue, took down part of the barrier, and one by one we allowed each hippie in to kiss and hug his favourite stone. Everyone was happy, and we saw in the solstice peacefully. Fuck soldiering, maybe I should have been in the Diplomatic Corps!

28

The Bodyguard

'If you're going to guard a body, it might as well be a beautiful one!' Pete Scholey was forever winding me up about my lack of good fortune work-wise compared to him. While I'd been scratching around guarding animals he'd been bodyguard to Miss World for six years. How lucky can you get? 'Tough job, but someone's got to do it,' he was always saying. Then he would add with a broad grin, 'Of course, I only do it to keep in touch with my feminine side.' If only! I was dreaming of doing some decent bodyguarding work. Then out of the blue my luck changed.

Over many years the SAS had developed special expertise in covert bodyguarding techniques – or close protection as we call it. Our reputation came before us, and we trained with the great and the good, politicians and royalty.

I was once Prince Charles' driver for a day of anti-ambush car drills. He swept in driving his vintage Aston Martin, which added a bit of James Bond glamour to the utilitarian training ground. Charles strode purposefully onto the driving range, fully kitted out for a mobile assault, and sat next to me in a car loaded to the gunwales with stun grenades, MP5s and reserve ammunition. I gave him a briefing, then we were off. I roared off at speed towards various pop-up targets on the range. As I executed a handbrake turn, our future king, window down, blasted away with the MP5 for all he was worth. He was really up for it, really getting into it. He was an excellent shot, and dropped all the targets. He'd grown up with guns and was as good a shot with an MP5 as he is with a Purdey, but he took even more delight in the flash-bangs – hurling them to cover our escape.

The Regiment was to be honoured by another visit from Prince Charles, this time accompanied by his wife, Princess Diana. We put on a fast roping demonstration for the royal couple, involving a helicopter hovering a hundred feet above a two-storey building with a flat roof. A thick hemp rope attached to the helicopter was then thrown out and left to dangle onto the roof. One by one, the members of the team grabbed the rope and abseiled a hundred feet down onto the flat roof, like sliding down a fireman's pole.

The demonstration went like clockwork, until the last assault trooper exited the chopper. He seemed to falter, lost his grip, and fell a hundred feet straight down onto the flat roof. As he hit the deck at a rate of knots, Prince Charles remained fairly cool, but Princess Di visibly stiffened. A shocked look came over her face and she turned white. Just before she looked about to pass out, her pale expression turned to disbelief as the fallen assaulter suddenly jumped up, dusted himself down and gave her a cheery wave.

It was a right royal stitch-up. The last abseiler to leave the helicopter had been a very realistic dummy, thrown out of the helicopter by one of the crew. The assaulter who came back from the dead had been lying flat on the roof from the start, lying concealed behind a three-foot-high wall that ran around the edge of the roof. There was relief all round and huge laughter from the Prince of Wales. Princess Di, however, still looked queasy. She really was in bits.

* * *

All this experience was to stand me in good stead. My next job came from one of the small, anonymous security firms on the circuit, the type of firm only ex-SAS would know about. The guy on the end of the line was Harry. He was the operational manager, and more importantly he was ex-B Squadron. I had worked with him on surveillance operations in Northern Ireland.

He started his pitch. 'I need a bodyguard. This one's high-risk, Pete. Nobody wants to touch it with a bargepole unless they go in mob-handed and that's not the client's style. You know the rule of thumb when dealing with a psychopath: it's three against one, three of the good guys against the headcase.'

I was beginning to feel a bit uneasy. I took a deep breath and said, 'I'm listening.'

He went on, 'The subject is an Australian criminal, basically, a gangster. He is mentally unstable and frequently carries a weapon. His name is Andrew Jefferson. He ran a small machine shop in Sydney which was a front for illegal activities such as reactivating deactivated weapons. There were some financial issues and the local police were hot on the case, so he decided to do a runner to England along with the equipment from his factory, which was crated up and shipped to Felixstowe docks. His last illegal activity before leaving for England was to visit his local Harley-Davidson dealer and ask if he could test drive one of their top-of-the-range bikes. He rode it straight down to the dockside where the ship for Felixstowe was being loaded, and hid the bike amongst the crated machinery for transportation to the UK. The whole shipment is being held in a bonded warehouse near the docks in Felixstowe. The Australian government has got involved and through the British courts managed to get a court order to seize the shipment before it was cleared by customs.

'Yesterday customs received a phone call from Jefferson. He said he was coming down to the bonded warehouse "to sort things out". With an edge of intimidation to his voice, he added that he hoped his shipment had cleared customs.

'Pete, this is where you come in. A solicitor from a London office and working on behalf of the Australian government will be standing in the warehouse reception waiting to serve Jefferson with a writ banning him from the warehouse. He needs protection. He will also issue the court order confiscating all his shipment. The firm of solicitors don't want a big team of heavies in reception in case Jefferson gets frightened off before the writ can be served. They want low profile, someone who can handle the situation on a one-on-one basis if things turn nasty. I thought with your experience dealing with Portuguese gangsters in Hong Kong you'd be up for it!'

The phone went silent. Now it was my turn. 'This begs one big question. Why hasn't he been arrested by the Brit police?'

'Because he hasn't done anything wrong in England and as of this moment in time there is no extradition order,' came Harry's reply.

'Let me just think about this one and I'll get back to you.' I put the phone down. Well, here was a criminal who lived by his own twisted set of rules. You can lie, you can cheat, you can steal, you can kill people, you can do any fucking thing you want and nobody does or says anything about it. He needed taking down.

I opened the bottom drawer of my desk and took out the black leather Zap gloves. They'd been given to me back in 1986 when I was still in the Regiment on the Counter-Revolutionary Warfare wing, by a visiting member of the FBI on what we called a tough guys' course – training the Feds in unarmed combat. I knew they'd come in useful one day. I slowly pulled the gloves on and examined the fit. In a hidden pocket on the back, just over the knuckles, was a solid lump of lead four inches long by two inches wide, the soft grey metal insert moulded nicely to the knuckles. A covert knuckle-duster! An equalizer! You could literally thump a stone wall with these and not come to any harm.

'Just like old times,' I thought. I called Harry and accepted the contract.

Two days later on a cold February morning I was standing in the reception of George Barker Ltd, customs clearance and customs brokers, with Chris the solicitor from the London office. This was a large facility with over 5,000 square metres of secure warehousing and twenty-four-hour CCTV, an alarm system connected to the local police station and a panic button in reception. I noted with some satisfaction that the CCTV cameras at the front covered the car park and reception.

The time was now 11am. The gangster should have been here by now. I removed the photo of Jefferson that Chris had given me from my inside pocket and began studying it. 'Do you think he's coming?' I didn't get time for an answer.

Out of the corner of my eye I caught sight of a black BMW entering the car park at speed. With a squeal of tyres the car skidded to a halt fifty yards from reception. A stocky, well-built figure dressed in a long, dark-blue Mafia-style overcoat emerged from the vehicle. It was Jefferson, a big man acting the part of an even bigger man. He headed straight towards reception with an air of clear and present danger. Maximum violence was written all over his face. I took one look at him and realized from past experience that there was no way I was going to reason with this guy. Make no mistake, this was going to be brutal.

My priority now was protecting Chris. I decided to carry out a pre-emptive strike, attack being the best form of defence. I grabbed the writ, stuffed it into my pocket, and then moved quickly through the door to reception, putting myself between Chris and Jefferson. By now I was in the car park pulling on my Zap gloves, making sure the soft lead inserts were moulded to my knuckles and the gloves were a snug fit. Jefferson, six feet of hulking Australian aggression, strode menacingly up to me. 'Keep your distance,' I barked. 'Step back and stay away.'

He gave me the hard-man stare. Pitiful.

I played his game and looked unflinchingly back, trying to out-stare him. 'Keep your distance,' I repeated.

'Get out of my face,' he growled.

I kept the icy stare zapping into his face.

'I said get out of my face!' and with that he produced an industrial-sized screwdriver from his inside pocket and brandished it like a knife. 'Get out of my face or I'll have your eyes, boy. I'll take your eyes out and eat them one by one in front of you like pickled onions on a cocktail stick.' He was now shaking with fury and making jabbing motions with the screwdriver.

I did step back and lower my stare but only to give myself time to think. 'I'm going to have to get one over on this fucker. I'm going to have to pull the old Queensberry Rules con,' I thought as I brought my gloved fists up and adopted a perfect boxing stance as though offering him a fair fight.

He took the bait. Looking cold and hard with a slight smirk on his face he said, 'OK, son, but without the gloves.'

I stepped back again, my eyes firmly fixed on the jabbing screwdriver. I removed the gloves and returned them to the pocket of my Barbour jacket. I could always get the right-hand glove on pretty quick in an emergency. I returned to my perfect boxing stance.

Jefferson threw the screwdriver to the ground and his fists came up into what could be classed as a reasonable boxing stance. Perhaps he had been a boxer in his youth like the Kray twins. The only bit he forgot about was his feet. Instead of standing side-on with his left leg leading, he stood with his legs apart, offering me as a target one of the most vulnerable parts of his body.

It was a kind invitation that I couldn't possibly refuse. I stepped in after him as though I was going to start boxing, then I brought my right boot up hard and fast into his groin. His eyes opened wide with shock and there was a deep intake of breath as though he was drawing his last. He staggered back several paces before falling to his knees, clutching his bollocks. As I moved in for the kill I noticed he was looking in the direction of his car. Suddenly he started scrabbling along the ground towards the BMW. For a big man he was quite agile. The adrenaline rush was probably blocking out the pain.

He was soon on his feet and within seconds he had the boot of his car open. Reaching in, he took out what looked like a heavy-duty crowbar that he must have got from the One-Stop Breaking & Entering Shop. He began flourishing the crowbar like a sword.

I reached quickly into my jacket pocket and retrieved the Zap gloves. I pulled them on and flexed my knuckles satisfyingly. At last, I get to use the gloves! I took off my Barbour jacket and was wrapping it around my left arm to use as a shield when – what a pity – out of the corner of my left eye I saw the blues and twos. A police car powered into the car park and screeched to a halt. Two members of the local plod jumped out and deployed their batons. As they locked him in handcuffs I stuffed the writ into his top pocket. 'Don't forget your paperwork,' I grinned as he was led away.

Shame I didn't get to use the gloves, though.

29

Mafia in Moscow

The incident with the Australian gangster proved a turning point. I started getting regular work providing security for top businesspeople at AGMs. I flexed my muscles at meetings for Manweb, British Airways, Shell, BAS and McAlpine. These all proved to be routine and run-of-the-mill, but nonetheless good experience. The Vickers AGM was a bit tastier. The great manufacturer of arms, tanks and warplanes, this was right up my street. But it's a contentious area of operations, and there was always going to be more potential for disruption by protesters, or infiltration by people spying on behalf of competitors in this fiercely competitive, multi-billion-pound global industry.

But what made this a stand-out meeting was the small matter of a motion to be discussed: that Vickers should sell off to either BMW or Volkswagen its most famous division – Rolls-Royce Motors. The prospect of this quintessentially British manufacturer falling into foreign hands exercised certain minds so strongly that death threats were sent to the chairman, Sir Colin Chandler. We beefed up our normal security arrangements and everyone was well and truly keyed-up. In the event, apart from angry exchanges from the floor, and one character playing the *Dambusters March* on a handheld ghetto blaster, the meeting passed off without incident and BMW won the rights to one of the most famous brands in the world.

Then came the big one. A principal of enormous wealth and influence, who was president and founder of a remarkable success story. In little over ten years since his company's formation in America, sales had rocketed to an eye-watering billion dollars a year. It's only a rare individual who can achieve that level of success. Sales were continuing to increase, products were expanding. The company was going from strength to strength. He'd well and truly cracked the American market. Now it was time to conquer the world. Starting in Moscow, then the assassination capital of the world. As soon as we arrived at the hotel, the atmosphere was heavy. 'We had a bit of a problem last week. You may have heard.' The concierge stared at us, weighing us up. 'A British businessman. He wasn't playing the game. He didn't understand the local rules. He was assassinated with a magazine full of AK-47 just outside the front door. Welcome to Moscow, gentlemen.'

This guy was going to take some serious bodyguarding.

The luxurious, five-star Moscow Marriott Grand was a stone's throw from Red Square, the Kremlin and the Bolshoi Theatre. As I gazed around the elegant reception hall I thought, 'If they openly kill people here, what do they do in the suburbs?' I glanced at my other team members, Rusty (the team leader) and John Mac (the mystery man on the balcony of the Iranian Embassy. John was the real deal, not a character from that famous volume of fairytales and tall stories entitled *One Thousand and One Walters*, or *The Iranian Knights* – written, of course, by unreliable narrators). I was reassured to be in good company. We were going to need plenty of top cover for this one.

With big opportunities come big dangers. Ask any prospector during a gold rush. After communism fell in the late Eighties and early Nineties, the former Soviet Union had collapsed into near economic and social anarchy. The transition from the old state-controlled economy to a free market model was a slow and painful one. Corruption, murders, contract killings and violent crime were now widespread and casual.

Bumbling Boris Yeltsin was head of government and the economy was in meltdown. With state spending grinding to a halt, hyper-inflation decimating savings, huge tax increases being imposed, unemployment rising to epic heights, whole swathes of industry gone to the wall, and any state enterprise which actually produced wealth having fallen into the hands of the privileged oligarchy, millions of ordinary people had been plunged into crisis. They were desperate to escape the rampant poverty.

This potent mixture of wealth and adulation presented a security challenge of the first order. This was our very first event in Russia. We were all going into the unknown, though I'd a pretty good idea it wasn't going to be a walk in the park. Back home, Pete McAleese – ex-D Squadron – had already painted a vivid picture of training Russia's Inland Revenue teams. No pen-pushers these. These tax inspectors were being trained in combat techniques for when they had to storm office buildings in full body armour. Not your normal tax inspectors.

We headed off to check out the venue for the big event – the sales convention the following day. The expected audience was 26,000. Not bad for your first event. The auditorium was massive, like an aeroplane hangar with seats. It looked just like the NEC with tiered rows all the way up to the roof, arranged in a 180-degree arc around the stage. I was reassured to know that we'd drafted in a load of conscripts from the Red Army as extra security. With an arena this big we'd need them. We checked and double-checked everything. No stone was left unturned. Nothing could be left to chance. I was standing with Rusty discussing the final plans when suddenly in saunters this guy who nonchalantly swaggers across the floor towards us. He was taller than me – and that's not something I say very often. A stocky Ronnie Kray lookalike, complete with slicked-back hair and double-breasted jacket. If he'd had the word 'Mafia' written across his forehead it couldn't have been more obvious. I whispered to Rusty, 'Hey, Russ. It's the local Gendarme. This guy's Mafia.'

Rusty nodded. 'Yep. Here we go.'

Big events inspire big curiosity. Full of cockiness, he strode up to us. 'Good afternoon, gentlemen.' He spoke remarkably good English. 'My name is Serge. I've been told you guys are in charge of security for tomorrow's event. Yes?'

'That's right, mate,' I said. 'You've got the right people.'

Without changing his impassive expression one iota he went, 'Great pity that. We are going to have to close you down.'

I played along. 'Whaaaat! What are you talking about?'

He went on, 'Your fire regulations are out of order.'

I couldn't believe it. He was pulling the oldest con in the book, the fire regulations. The Kray brothers used to play that one in London in the 1960s. Unbelievable! They were fifty years behind the racketeering times in Moscow. These guys didn't need finesse and they didn't bother.

I decided to wind our friend up a bit further. 'Fire regulations? That can't be right.' I looked nonplussed. 'We've had them all checked out. A fire officer from the Moscow Fire Department came round and gave us a certificate.'

'Ah, yes. But some new government regulations have just come in. Not everyone is up to date with them yet.'

I pushed him a bit further. 'Where exactly are you from?'

He didn't bat an eyelid. 'I'm from the authorities.'

I'd had enough of the pantomime. I said, 'Right, mate. Let's get in the back room and discuss it in private.' We had a little security office in the back of the building. We went in and locked the door so we could talk confidentially. The guy, still as cocky as ever, plonked himself in the only executive swivel chair as if he owned the place. Which effectively he did. As if to make his point, he casually unbuttoned his jacket and opened it to reveal his shoulder holster.

Rusty took control. 'OK, mate. What's the score?'

He persisted in the charade, really laying it on. 'It's your fire regulations. We've had an outside assessor check them out. They are out of order. A long time out of date. You are not qualified for an event of this size. Unfortunately we are going to have to close you down.'

This was not the time for the old school act, the stiff upper lip in the face of adversity, holding out for your own set of standards come what may. We had to play by their rules, simple as that. 'Let's cut to the chase,' said Rusty, 'How much will it cost to bring the venue up to date?'

He did a bit of chin rubbing. 'It is difficult to say…'

I could barely contain myself. I was pinching myself to stop myself bursting out laughing. He was like a cartoon gangster from the Sixties. Except this guy was for real. As was his gun.

He carried on doing his Marlon Brando impersonation. 'Well, let me see. These certificates don't come cheap, you know. A lot of work is involved.'

Rusty was getting impatient now. 'Look. Cards on the table. What do you want?'

'Let's say if you put in an envelope 300 tickets for the event tomorrow night, we can arrange all the details.'

So that was it. Sorted. Three hundred tickets for the black market. Touted at double the face value of $25 each, that's $15,000. A nice little earner for one night's work. I knew he would keep it sweet for us. We'd followed their rulebook. I knew he would put the word out to let the event go ahead without further interruption.

My heart sank when Serge turned up again three hours later with one of those looks on his face. Surely I hadn't got him so wrong? Was this the sting? Did he want another 300 tickets? He smiled. 'We do good business together. I like you and Rusty. To say thank you, my men will look after your event, make sure it goes smooth. You will find they are first class. They do a lot of this work in the bars and clubs around town.' It goes without saying that we accepted his kind offer.

The convention passed off without a hitch. Serge kept his bargain. His heavies did a good job and they had the advantage over us of speaking the language. Whilst the Red Army soldiers were stationed up and down all the aisles looking like ornate commissionaires, Serge's team were mixing it on the front barricades, keeping back the seething hordes of over-enthusiastic Muscovites, shouting and swearing at them in Russian.

Our principal jetted off back to the States early the next morning. We had a few hours to kill before our flight to London. Time for a bit of R & R, I thought. I had access to an S-class Mercedes that we'd used to ferry around the executives, so I thought I'd do a tour of the Moscow sights in it. I got hold of one of the Russian translators who'd been working with us and asked him to show me around. We got talking in the Merc and it turned out he was ex-KGB! Not only that, but he showed me his old ID card. There he was in his uniform with all his medals on. He had been a colonel! I asked, 'What are you doing as a translator?'

'Ah well. What can you do? When the Berlin Wall came down a lot of us KGB guys were kicked out. We were no longer needed. We've done what you guys have done. We've set up private security companies. Now I am a translator and bodyguard.'

So there I was being driven round Moscow by an ex-KGB colonel. I thought, 'My God! Times have changed. Fantastic!'

He insisted on taking me to the outskirts. 'You must see this,' he said. 'This is why the Russian Army is not going to win any more big wars. Look over there.' He was pointing to acres of allotments full of vegetables. Young men were tilling the soil. 'You see those men? They are conscripts in the Russian Army. They don't get paid properly or fed properly. They have to grow their own food. This is the Russian Army of today. Their morale is rock-bottom. They are only young kids, straight out of school some of them. And this is what they have to do.'

We headed back into town and suddenly he said, 'Watch out. Here we go.' In front of us there was a Portakabin and barriers, just like a

Northern Ireland checkpoint. 'Traffic police. It's the car,' he said. He pulled up into the side of the road just before the barriers. 'Do not worry. Do not worry. I will claim it on my expenses.' With that he got out his driving licence and a folded a hundred-dollar bill into the centre of it. 'Now watch this.'

We drove forward to the barrier. It was manned by this fierce-looking guy and he was dressed like the Gestapo. He knocked on the window. My driver wound the window down and they exchanged a few words in Russian. He handed the guard his licence. The guard made the hundred-dollar bill disappear into his inside pocket like Paul Daniels on speed. Up came the barrier and we were through without another word. As we drove off, the KGB guy said, 'If I hadn't done that, you see that Portakabin? They'd have whipped us in there and interrogated us for hours wanting to know who we were, where the car came from, where did we get our money, had we paid all the taxes. Standard procedure. You grease their palm and they wave you through. They see the car and they see dollar signs in their eyes.'

The trip came to a successful end. Serge had looked after us. They were clever people. Business is business, Russian style. As long as you greased the palms of the men who mattered, everything would be fine. They didn't want to kill the goose that laid the golden egg. They didn't want to double-cross people or make excessive demands which would deter companies from coming to Moscow altogether.

Suits you sir! I enjoyed this lifestyle, the world of big deals and bigger business. It was regular work and it was very well paid. The bonus with this job was that I really liked the principal. Being his bodyguard, I had to have many a restaurant meal with him. He wasn't at all the prima donna, the remote, ruthless boss. He was very friendly and approachable. That's why I was so devastated when he died at the tragically young age of forty-four.

After that, my work suddenly dried up. That was bad enough. But worse was to come. I was careering headlong towards the gutter.

Something happened which meant I was on the verge of losing my security operator's licence. If I lost that, I'd lost my whole livelihood.

How come my licence was under threat? I was up in court on a charge of assault and battery.

30

Revenge is Sweet

You can't beat a good punch-up. It's the best possible therapy, an instant stress-reliever. What is it the medics say to depressed people, 'Get more exercise'? Well a good punch-up is the finest stress-relieving workout in the world.

And I've had a few punch-ups in my time, probably more than my share. But was it all the result of the stress of combat? Was I going down with PTSD? Absolutely not. And I can prove it. Just like I got a piece of paper from Ward 11 to prove I was sane whilst I was still serving in the SAS, I can prove I'm not now suffering from PTSD. How can I do that? I'll tell you how. I can prove it because I beat up my next-door neighbour.

Trouble had been brewing for months. They were the original neighbours from hell, totally out of control. They'd have fearsome rows in the house with the windows wide open, and we'd hear the pair of them swearing at each other in the garden. The language was filthy. I was remarried by now, and my daughter couldn't even go in the garden at times, she was so upset. To make matters worse, he had a high-performance car with a loud exhaust. He'd often come back at one or two in the morning, deliberately revving it up on the drive, waking up the neighbourhood. I didn't storm in at the first provocation. I gave them bags of slack. I turned a blind eye, hoping it would go away. But it didn't.

It all came to a head in September. It was a lovely warm afternoon, and he'd recently purchased one of those mini-motorbikes, with a proper little engine and a proper tinny little noise. Really, really annoying. The pitch of the noise just cut right through you, and it was grating on my nerves. This particular day he'd started revving it in the middle of the afternoon and he went on revving it for at least an hour and a half. I'm all for a bit of give and take, a bit of live and let live. But at the end of the day, I'm not Mother Teresa. I thought, 'Right! Enough's enough. I must have words.'

I went out and looked over the fence. There he was, sitting on his little bike, completely oblivious to the rest of the world, mindlessly revving it. I said, 'Excuse me, mate. Is there any need to keep revving that bike?' He didn't say anything. He simply glanced up. Straightaway I could see the look of insolence on his face. So I said 'Look, I'm an ex-engineer. Revving it like that will damage the cylinder and the piston.' He still didn't say anything, but his expression hardened into one of total contempt. I gave him one last chance. 'Are you going to stop making that racket? You're upsetting my daughter.' Silence. Another screaming rev of the engine. 'I'm asking you for the last time,' I said. 'Are you going to pack it in?'

He glanced up with disdain. 'You can fuck off.'

By this time his missus had come out to see what all the commotion was about. A real mouthy one she was. She sneered at me and said, 'You heard what my husband said. You can fuck off.'

That's when I snapped. I raced down our drive and round towards their house. His missus was standing at the gate, an iron bar in her hand. She must have kept it just inside the house in case of emergencies. I thought, 'I'd best not go near her. Scrapping with a woman won't look too good.' So I vaulted over the fence to go straight down the side of their house where her husband was and bypass her. I was still very much in control of my anger. I was still willing to talk to this guy. I walked quietly up to him. I had yet to utter a single swear word. But as he saw me coming, he leapt off the bike, and held it up by the handlebars as if it was a shield. I closed in on him, still willing to talk. He suddenly reared up the bike and tried to ram it into my groin. I jumped back to avoid the impact. I thought, 'Fuck this for a game of soldiers. That's it.'

Whack! I punched him straight into the side of his jaw. Not hard enough to really hurt him, just enough for him to get the message. Trouble is, he didn't. He staggered backwards a couple of steps, then recoiled back towards me like a ship's cannon. He grabbed a piece of trellis fence from the ground and tried to ram it into me. I seized hold of the thing and we started wrestling with it. He was quite handily built and his rage had made him even stronger. He was like a bear on steroids and he was pushing me backwards. This was awkward. His garden was a tip and I was in danger of tripping up over the discarded rubbish. I dug my feet in, summoned up all my strength and held him steady. 'You can't do this,' I said. 'You aren't in the club.'

For a split second he looked puzzled. 'What club, you wanker?'

I reached round the side of the trellis and measured my fist against his nose with a real piledriver of a punch. Smack!

'Welcome to the Hellfire Club!' I roared, as he collapsed backwards.

The red mist started to come down. I wanted to teach the scrote a lesson in neighbourly respect he'd never forget. I wanted to practice my tap dancing skills on his head. But then I suddenly had a flashback to Hong Kong. That's what held me back. Oh, no, no, no. I can't do that. I'll be in deep trouble. That would be actual bodily harm.

I had to restrain myself. Reasonable force only. That's when I knew I wasn't suffering from PTSD. It would have been so easy for me to lose it and beat the man to a pulp. If I'd been suffering from PTSD that's what would have happened. There's no way I'd have had the self-control.

He was in a complete daze, the trellis fence still on top of him. He raised his head a fraction, trying to focus on me. He pointed a shaky finger at me and spat the words out, 'You've had it now. You've had it now.'

'Best get away from here,' I thought. 'I've proved my point.' So I strode away. His wife took a step back and dropped the iron bar as if it was red-hot. Was she scared of me? Nah. I'd caught her eyes. That's when I knew I was in trouble. There was no look of concern for her husband's welfare, no look of fear that she was about to be assaulted by this next-door Neanderthal. Just lots and lots of pound signs. Oh, no! Here we go. The 'C' word. Compensation! Next thing I know, her mobile was out. She was phoning the police, getting the first shout in.

I went back to my house, made a brew, sat down and waited for the coppers to arrive. I looked at the clock and thought, 'Let's see how long they take to respond.' It didn't take them very long at all. I heard the screech of brakes – they'd obviously been watching too many cops and robbers programmes on TV. Next thing, I hear the bang-bang-bang on the door. These two coppers came in. 'We've had a report you've attacked your next-door neighbour.'

I said, 'I'm the victim here. Why don't you go and arrest him? He attacked me. I used self-defence.'

The copper goes, 'Your neighbour's got blood all over his face. I don't see any blood on your face, Mr Winner.'

A modern-day Sherlock Holmes, obviously. I said, 'Have you not seen the mini-motorbike? He attacked me with that.'

'We've got no evidence of that. We have a report from his wife that you attacked him. We're going to have to charge you with common assault and take you down the station.'

I said, 'Aren't you going to arrest him too?'

'We can't. We've no evidence. They made the complaint. That's the procedure. We have to arrest you. We won't handcuff you if you come quietly.'

I was really hacked off. I was taken to the local nick and locked away in a cell like a common criminal, with only a hard wooden bench to sit on. They wouldn't give me anything to eat, only a cup of tea. They charged me officially with common assault and I pleaded not guilty. In due course I was processed in the normal manner – mugshot, fingerprints, DNA sample for the database, and finally a statement with the duty solicitor. I didn't get back till eleven at night.

Then the witness statements came through. I knew it! I absolutely knew it! At the top of the witness sheet there's a space for 'Occupation'. And what high-flying careers did these two fine, upstanding citizens pursue? What contribution were this well-adjusted couple making to the greater good of society? What noble, selfless task filled their days? Unemployed! Both of them. Now there's a shock. I was up against the Charge of the Benefits Brigade.

This is how we get treated in Civvy Street. Our society turned on its head where the layabouts get the benefit of the doubt, the cushy treatment over veterans like me who've fought for Queen and country for years and put our lives on the line so many times. So much of a welcome home for the conquering heroes. So much for gratitude at having done my duty and kept the country safe. A topsy-turvy world. The coppers didn't want to know my story. They just didn't want to know. They took the line of least resistance. No thought put into it. No intelligence. The quicker they can tick the boxes and complete the paperwork the better.

It hurt to see the card the neighbours played, a really cynical one, a real blow below the belt. In their statement it wasn't, 'Mr Winner did this. Then Mr Winner did that.' It was, 'The ex-SAS man did this. The ex-SAS man did that.' When did the world change exactly? Being in the SAS was no longer a matter of pride and honour. It now counted against you. It now meant you were an object of suspicion. The chances were you were some out-of-control, homicidal hatchet man. A wild man from the mountains.

The wheels of justice turned very slowly. I had over six months of anxiety and stress before my case came up. The big fear was that I would be found guilty. I was in serious danger of getting a criminal record for assault. Once I was on the CRB database, I'd lose my Security Industry Authority licence and that would be me well and truly stuffed for future work. No pressure, then.

I got a good solicitor on my case. It cost me an arm and a leg, but it turned out she was worth her weight in gold. It was only just before the hearing that I was told a new witness had come forward. What I didn't know was that my solicitor had sent her assistant round the neighbourhood, knocking on all the doors to ask for witnesses. 'Mrs Cheshire. She's the old lady who lives right opposite, right across the road from you. She sits in the window a lot. She saw everything. She can confirm that you were attacked first. She also saw the wife brandishing the iron bar. What's more, she's willing to testify in court.' Thank God for that. The cavalry was coming to the rescue – the cavalry in a cardigan.

Before we went into court my solicitor said to me, 'Look. Do you want to make a deal with your neighbours?'

I was aghast. 'What kind of deal?'

'Do you want to plead guilty to breach of the peace? If you do that, you don't get a criminal record. All you get is a slapped wrist, a hefty fine and that's the last you'll hear of it.'

I was very tempted. Even though we had a witness, I felt the case could still have gone either way. I didn't trust the courts one little bit. I didn't want a record. I didn't want to lose my SIA licence. So I said to my solicitor, 'Are you sure I won't get a criminal record with breach of the peace?'

'Yes. It's a much lesser charge than common assault. It's hardly worth mentioning. It's just a paperwork exercise. The other advantage is that they can't pursue you for compensation.'

That's what did it. That's what made me swallow my pride. It would have been bad enough being found guilty of something I didn't do. But to have to pay good money out of my own pocket to those two wastes of space would have really hurt. So I said, 'Have a word with the scrotes. See what they say.'

She disappeared to speak to the prosecution and came back a few minutes later. 'They don't want to deal. They want you in the box for common assault.'

That was it. They wanted compensation.

The hearing lasted all afternoon, nearly five hours. The prosecution was making a real meal of it, but I did have a bit of top cover. Pete Scholey came along to give me a character reference, but somehow they never called him. The magistrates retired for half an hour to discuss the verdict.

Innocent! It turned out the chief magistrate was very fair and the neighbour didn't have a leg to stand on. The magistrate said, 'You are a very credible witness, Mrs Cheshire. You stated that this man attacked Mr Winner first. Mr Winner was acting in self-defence.' She also confirmed that the wife had brandished an iron bar in an aggressive manner. Case dismissed.

It was a huge relief. An amazing stroke of luck to have such a witness. Luck has been with me so many times. I've had plenty of knockbacks but I've had some huge lucky breaks too. The air support arriving just in time at Mirbat, the Red Crescent ambulance appearing in the middle of the night in Bosnia, just happening to be back in B Squadron when the Iranian Embassy kicked off. And so it goes on.

I soon found out that I didn't need to beat the neighbour and his like to a pulp, anyway. I was about to find a different and much better way of getting my own back on benefits layabouts. One weekend, as I flicked through the pages of the *Sunday Times* in the local supermarket, a headline jumped out. 'SAS versus the Benefit Cheats'. It was a report on a team of ex-SAS soldiers working undercover tracking down and convicting benefits fraudsters. Was that up my street or what? I was so excited I even bought the newspaper.

My luck was back! The security company's spokesman and director was none other than Alistair Mackenzie –my old B Squadron troop officer from twenty-five years ago. He was a good man, Alistair, a seasoned soldier, a very experienced jungle warfare officer. A New Zealander, he'd seen action in Vietnam. Being a Kiwi, he was very down to earth, a breath of fresh air. He hadn't been through the brainwashing of the Eton Rifles. He was approachable, friendly, no airs and graces.

I dashed to my office, scrambled about in the bottom drawer of my desk and bingo! dug out his card. He'd given it to me when I'd bumped into him at the SAS Golden Jubilee celebrations in 1991. I never throw any contact away, no matter how old. You can't afford to in this game. Amazingly, his number hadn't changed and I got through right away. It was just like the old days. When you've done surveillance work together in South Armagh like we had, you're friends for life. After the mini-Regimental reunion over the phone, we got down to business. He described the work his firm was doing and asked if I was interested.

Do I want to do help in a covert operation to crack down on benefit fraudsters? Is the Pope Catholic? Now it was time to take my revenge.

* * *

It seemed at first like just another routine day at work. My job was to train specialist anti-fraud investigation officers of the Benefit Agency in foot and mobile surveillance, so they could track down and prosecute all the bad-back merchants that we find grafting on building sites and pumping iron in gyms. I was standing in an anonymous-looking room in a nondescript building in a suburb of Birmingham. This was the crew room and sat before me was a team of surveillance operators. There was a blonde in the front row. Laura, she was called. Baby-faced, very pretty, she seemed way too young to be doing this kind of work.

I did a last-minute check of my training aids and began my briefing. 'Exercise *Fiddlers on the Hoof*. Foot surveillance. Area: Bearwood.'

I placed a magnetic counter on the sketch map indicating the main area of the exercise. 'Situation and background: members of the Fiddler gang have been visiting post offices and financial institutions in the area.

'Subject: Pete Fiddler.

'Age: 45 to 50.

'Build: stocky, athletic.

'Clothing: red T-shirt, blue jeans, Nike trainers.

'Distinguishing marks: broken nose.

'Height: five foot ten to six foot.

'Hair: medium brown.'

There were a couple of smirks at the realization that I was describing myself.

'Execution of task as follows:

'Team: same as yesterday – eyeball, backup, tail-end Charlie.

'Timings: on plot for 1300hrs – HSBC Bank, 526 Bearwood Road.

'Route: as per sketch map.'

I traced the route to the exercise area with my laser spot marker.

'Emergency rendezvous point: back here in the crew room. Any questions?' I looked around the room. 'No questions. I am impressed. You must be good. Remember, you're only as good as the information you get.'

'Give me fifteen minutes' start.' With that I was out the door, heading for the centre of town to lead them a merry dance up and down the high street.

Twenty minutes later my earpiece crackled into life. 'Standby–standby–standby. The subject is heading in the general direction of the exit of the bank. Wait. Wait. The subject is out–out–out into the main. Can anyone take?'

'Roger that. Laura has the eyeball. Subject has gone left–left–left and is walking up Bearwood Road towards the junction with Sandon Road.'

I stopped outside a large shop, using the window as a mirror to see what Laura was up to across the other side of the road. Not good. She was the eyeball, she should have been behind me – not across the road. How could she check what I was up to from that distance? If I was drawing cash from a cash machine how could she shoulder-surf me from thirty metres away? That meant her backup was out of position too. He should have been behind her, on my side of the street too. Only the tail-end Charlie should have been on the other side, so the team could get two angles on the subject. Laura would learn. It was just her lack of experience.

Suddenly I saw in the reflection of the window this huge Mike Tyson lookalike approach Laura. I could see his lips moving. He was talking to her. That's odd. Maybe they know each other. Nothing to worry about. She's obviously bumped into a friend. Next minute, the finger was going. He'd started to poke her in the chest. I could see him looking agitated. Oh, no. Either a lovers' tiff – or something more sinister.

It was at this point that she cracked. This was no friend. Forgetting to deliver her cover story, she panicked. No matter how much you drill people in the training room, tell them to always have a reason for being out there, tell them not to do anything that makes them stand out, live the cover, act naturally, think ahead – no matter how much you train them, it can all come crashing to pieces in an instant.

She ran across the street to me, her eyes wide with fear. 'Pete! Pete! That guy. He's onto us. He thinks we're the drugs squad. We're compromised. What are we going to do?' She was in shock.

Suddenly a simulated exercise had turned into a real exercise. I pressed the Pressel switch on the radio concealed in the pocket of my jacket. 'Compromise. Compromise. Bomb burst. Bomb burst. Back to the crew room at your own speed.'

The rest of the team were OK. He hadn't spotted them. But Laura and I were committed. He'd seen her run across the road to me and knew I was involved too. I said, 'Right Laura. Nice and easy. We'll walk up the street at a leisurely pace, turn left at the top and make our way back to base. Don't worry. We'll be fine.'

No such luck. Out of the corner of my eye, I could see a man. He walked down a side street and jumped into a really flashy, top-of-the-range BMW. 'You don't get one of those selling the *Big Issue*,' I thought as he pulled out into the high street. I knew straightaway he was the main man. He drew alongside us and started crawling along at walking pace, shadowing us, trying to intimidate us. I thought, 'I'm not having this. He could be leading us into a trap. He could have been on his mobile calling for half a dozen of his mates to meet us up at the top of the street. And before you know, we're in the deep brown stuff. The whole thing's escalated.'

Time to take control. I stepped into the road in front of him and flagged him down. I went round to the driver's side and tapped on his window. The window wound down and before I could say anything he jumped in, 'You're drugs squad, aren't you? What are you doing round here? What are you doing in my area? You and that girl. What are you up to?'

Talk about brazen! You'd think he owned the place. But like the Russian mafioso, that's probably pretty much what he did.

I pulled out one of my cover stories and dusted it off. 'We're not drugs squad. We're property developers.' That threw him. You could see the mental cogs turning, slowly. Then he said, 'What do you mean? What are you talking about?'

I used the broken-record technique. I said, 'We're not the drugs squad. We're property developers. We're looking for run-down properties to do up. We're in the buy-to-let business. See that place over there, above that shop. That's the type of thing. That looks like it could be bought nice and cheap and done up.' I pinched myself to stop laughing and added with a straight face, 'Do you know any more like that in the area?'

'Whaaat? I saw you talking. You were speaking into a radio.'

I pulled out a digital voice recorder. 'Taking notes, mate. I give it to the girl to type up back in the office.'

'So, you guys are property developers, are you?'

'Yeah. You obviously live around here. You don't know any other run-down properties you can put us onto?'

'Errr…' He was completely bewildered. He didn't know what to make of us. In the end, he bought the pitch and drove off.

Laura was well and truly shaken up, very subdued. It was good experience for her.

* * *

A day in the life of a dole-buster. It can be hard graft, but then again, we all have to work hard. We've got a huge army to support – an army of people on benefits.

Six million on state handouts at the last count, and rising.

Postscript

'Civilian life, it's a rat race.' Tak once said to me. 'That's why you have to be the biggest rat to survive!' I replied. And somehow, survive I have – at least, my first twenty years of civilian life! Hopefully there'll be at least another twenty to follow.

I'm still tracking down and trapping the fraudsters. It's a good sector to be involved with, a growth industry. These days, there are only three things that are certain in life: death, taxes, and benefit cheats. So, it's nice, steady work. The other advantage is that it's mainstream, working for the Civil Service. After being on the fringe, on the ragged edge so often, it's now back to respectability. Let's hope I can stay there this time. Let's hope there are no more ups and downs in my roller-coaster career. I could do with a bit of steadiness and stability for a change.

I'm not only back to the mainstream, but I've now become a pillar of the Establishment! I was recently asked to work on a TV series, *Special Forces Heroes*, with Lord Ashcroft, deputy chairman of the Conservative Party. You can't get more Establishment than that!

I'm still banned from the Regiment. But you can't dwell on that. You have to move on in life. Even the SAS have moved on. In 1999, they transferred from their former base at Stirling Lines in Hereford to bigger facilities at RAF Credenhill, twelve miles away. Where the original camp stood, there's now an estate of smart, modern houses. So many memories tarmacked over, the Killing House reduced to someone's back garden.

Looking back over my career, do I have any regrets? What about the fight in Hong Kong and the whipping that followed? Not at all. That was self-defence. I wouldn't be here now if I hadn't looked after myself. What about Big Zil and the Stingers? Sounds like a Sixties pop group, doesn't it? Sure, if things had worked out, if I'd had a few Stingers tucked away in the back of my vehicle, I would probably be a millionaire by now. But then you win some, you lose some.

Same with KAS Enterprises, the firm that gave me my first job after leaving the SAS. I was in on the ground floor. With David Stirling as chairman, Crookie as MD, and my old comrade Tak as a director, I was really well positioned. I might have been on the board by now, with Tak running the show. It's just a pity the firm got embroiled in an industrial espionage scandal and went out of business! That's life…

Do I regret being RTU'd from the Regiment? No. I managed to get back in, that's the main thing, and just in time for the Embassy siege. What about being banned from the SAS for publishing articles in the *Daily Mirror*? Do I regret that? No, not really. It's just part of the rough and tumble. It's part of the person I am. What about beating up Carl at the OC's wedding? He bullied Malcolm. Bullies deserve all they get.

No, I have just one regret. And it's a big one. The only thing that bothers me now is that the Regiment is about to unveil by the Clock Tower at their new base in Credenhill a life-size statue of my friend, colleague and brother-in-arms – Labalaba, hero of Mirbat, one of the most important battles ever fought by the British Army.

And, being banned, I won't be there to see it.

Glossary

.303	Lee Enfield bolt-action rifle
66 LAW	Light Anti-tank Weapon System, a disposable 66mm anti-tank rocket
9-milly	nickname for the 9mm Browning thirteen-shot pistol; can also refer to 9mm ammunition
ABR	advanced battle reaction
Adoo	Dhofaris who espoused the Communist cause; (general) enemy
Armalite	alternative name for the M16 assault rifle
Askar	armed tribesman
basha	waterproof shelter made from a poncho; can also mean barrack room, house, bed etc.
BATT	British Army Training Team, the SAS unit training the Sultan's loyal forces in Oman
Batt House	BATT headquarters
BET	behavioural exposure therapy
BHM	British Military Hospital
Bradbury Lines	SAS barracks until 1999, in Redhill, Hereford. Later renamed Stirling Lines
buckshee	free; a freebie
bukit	hill, mountain (from the Malay)
Carl Gustav	84mm anti-armour recoilless rifle

casevac	casualty evacuation, removal of injured to aid post or hospital
CBF	Commander British Forces
CES	complete equipment schedule
CO	Commanding Officer
Cobra	Whitehall's domestic emergency situation room
CPO	command-post orderly
crap-hat	failure; member of the regular Army
cross-grain	march over hills direct from summit to summit
CRW	counter-revolutionary warfare
CT	Communist terrorist
cyalume stick	light-stick attached to clothing or lifejacket, activated by squeezing; visible from up to a mile away
D11	Metropolitan Police elite firearms team
DF	direction-found
DG	Dhofar Gendarmerie
dickers	in Northern Ireland, youths who note security forces' movements
DPM	Disruptive-Pattern Material camouflage
dragon light	hand-held searchlight
DZ	dropping zone
EU	Emergency Unit
Figure 11	man-shaped target on firing range
Firqat, FKW	Firqat Khalid bin Waalid, company of Dhofaris loyal to the Sultan
frag	fire at (from fragmentation granade)
FST	field surgical theatre
full battle order	fully armed

Gemini	large rubber dinghy
GOC	General Officer Commanding
GPMG	General-Purpose Machine Gun, belt-fed 7.62mm machine gun
green slime	nickname for Intelligence Corps (from their distinctive green berets)
Guryunov	Soviet 7.62mm medium machine gun
hangi	Fijian feast
Head Shed	nickname for senior officers
hexamine stove	lightweight stove burning blocks of solid fuel
ISFE	instantaneous safety fuse electric
Jenson's Violet	purple-coloured medication
Kremlin	nickname for intelligence section at Regimental headquarters
L42	sniper rifle, based on the Lee Enfield. The standard British Army sniper rifle until the 1990s
LFT	liver-function test
LMG	light machine gun
LSL	landing ship logistics
LZ	landing zone
M202	66mm multi-shot portable flame weapon, firing incendiary rockets
M79	grenade launcher
mag	magnetic north
majnoon	'mad one' (from the Arabic)
maroon machine	nickname for the Parachute Regiment (from their maroon berets)
MFC	mortar fire controller
mixed-fruit pudding	mortar fire pattern, two HE shells to one white phosphorous

MO	medical officer
mod plod	MoD policeman
MT	motor transport
OC	officer commanding
O group	orders group
OGs	olive-green Army clothing
pig	an RUC armoured car
PIRA	Provisional IRA
POST	Post-Operational Stress Trauma
PTSD	Pos-Traumatic Stress Disorder
QM	Quartermaster
QRF	quick-reaction force
RAOC	Royal Army Ordnance Corps
RCL	75mm recoilless anti-armour weapon
RE	Royal Engineers
re-entrant	valley running into side of a hill
REME	Royal Electrical and Mechanical Engineers
REMFs	rear-echelon motherfuckers
RF	Reconnaissance Force
Rigid Raider	fast assault boat
RPD	Soviet 7.62mm light machine gun
RSM	Regimental Sergeant Major
RTU	Returned to Unit (of origin)
Rupert	officer
Sabre Squadron	SAS combat squadron. There are four, A, B, D and G
SAF	Sultan's Armed Forces (of Oman)
sangar	protective wall built of stone or sandbags

sarbe	small radio used for ground-to-air communication
scran	food
SF (general)	sustained fire
SF (Ireland)	security forces
shake-out	preparation for combat
shamag	cloth worn on head as protection from sun
sit rep	situation report
SLR	7.62mm self-loading rifle
souk	Middle Eastern market
SP	superintendent
spider	sleeping quarters, so called because it has eight 'legs' – dormitory areas – off one central section
Sports and Social	SAS barracks
SSM	Squadron Sergeant Major
stag	period of watch
Startrek	air strike
sustained-fire (SF) kit	heavier-barrelled GPMG, mounted on a tripod and equipped with a dial sight, enabling it to fire at night on preset targets
tout	informer
trig point	summit of hill
vet rep	vertical replenishment (by helicopter)
wads	sandwiches
Wali	governor of province (Oman)
wet rep	weather report
XM203	M16 assault rifle equipped with underslung 40mm grenade-launcher